Lecture Notes in Computer Science 2326
Edited by G. Goos, J. Hartmanis, and J. van Leeuwen

Springer

Berlin
Heidelberg
New York
Barcelona
Hong Kong
London
Milan
Paris
Tokyo

Dan Grigoras Alex Nicolau
Bernard Toursel Bertil Folliot (Eds.)

Advanced Environments, Tools, and Applications for Cluster Computing

NATO Advanced Research Workshop, IWCC 2001
Mangalia, Romania, September 1-6, 2001
Revised Papers

 Springer

Series Editors

Gerhard Goos, Karlsruhe University, Germany
Juris Hartmanis, Cornell University, NY, USA
Jan van Leeuwen, Utrecht University, The Netherlands

Volume Editors

Dan Grigoras
University College Cork, Computer Science Department
College Road, Cork, Ireland
E-mail: d.grigoras@cs.ucc.ie

Alex Nicolau
University of California, Information and Computer Science Department
444 Computer Science Building, Irvine, CA 92697-3425, USA
E-mail:nicolau@ics.uci.edu

Bernard Toursel
University Lille 1, Laboratoire d'Informatique Fondamentale de Lille (LIFL)
59655 Villeneuve d'Ascq, France
E-mail: bernard.toursel@lifl.fr

Bertil Folliot
University Paris 6, LIP, 8, rue du Capitaine Scott, 75015 Paris, France
E-mail: bertil.folliot@lip6.fr

Cataloging-in-Publication Data applied for

Die Deutsche Bibliothek - CIP-Einheitsaufnahme

Advanced environments, tools, and applications for cluster computing : NATO
advanced research workshop ; revised papers / IWCC 2001, Mangalia, Romania,
September 1 - 6, 2001. Dan Grigoras ... (ed.). - Berlin ; Heidelberg ; New York ;
Barcelona ; Hong Kong ; London ; Milan ; Paris ; Tokyo : Springer, 2002
  (Lecture notes in computer science ; Vol. 2326)
  ISBN 3-540-43672-3
CR Subject Classification (1998): C.2, D.1.3, D.4, F.1.2, K.4.4, C.1, D.2

ISSN 0302-9743
ISBN 3-540-43672-3 Springer-Verlag Berlin Heidelberg New York

Springer-Verlag Berlin Heidelberg New York
a member of BertelsmannSpringer Science+Business Media GmbH

http://www.springer.de

© Springer-Verlag Berlin Heidelberg 2002

Typesetting: Camera-ready by author, data conversion by PTP-Berlin, Stefan Sossna e. K.
Printed on acid-free paper   SPIN 10846725   06/3142   5 4 3 2 1 0

Preface

Started by small group of well-known scientists with the aim of sharing knowledge, experiences, and results on all aspects of cluster computing, the initiative of a workshop on cluster computing received more attention after IFIP WG 10.3 and IEEE Romania Section accepted our request for sponsorship. Moreover, the application for a NATO ARW grant was successful, leading to a greater interest in the workshop. In this respect, we have to say that we chose Romania in order to attract scientists from Central and Eastern European countries and improve the cooperation in the region, in the field of cluster computing.

We had an extremely short time to organize the event, but many people joined us and enthusiastically contributed to the process. The success of the workshop is wholly due to the hard work of the organizing committee, members of the program committee, key speakers, speakers from industry, and authors of accepted papers. The workshop consisted of invited and regular paper presentations, followed by discussions, on many important current and emerging topics ranging from sheduling and load balancing to grids. The key speakers devoted their time and efforts to presenting the most interesting results of their research groups, and we all thank them for this . All papers were peer reviewed by two or three reviewers.

The proceedings published by Springer-Verlag include 8 invited papers and 24 regular papers, in that benefited from discussions during the workshop. We once again thank the authors for their efforts in preparing high-quality papers.

The workshop was generously sponsored by NATO Scientific Affairs Division, and co-sponsored by the IFIP Working Group 10.3, and IEEE Romania Sections. The "Gh. Asachi" Technical University, "Al. I. Cuza" University, and Black Sea University Foundation greatly contributed to the organization of the event. We also received generous support from the Romanian Ministry of Education and Research, Microsoft Romania, BRD-GSG, and Romaqua Group.

We would like to thank Mitica Craus for his help in processing this volume, and Delia Mitrea, Cristian Butincu, and Cristian Amarandei for their assistance with local organization matters.

March 2002

Dan Grigoras
Alex Nicolau
Bernard Toursel
Bertil Folliot

Chairs

Alex NICOLAU, University of California at Irvine, USA
Bernard TOURSEL, Université des Sciences et Technologies de Lille, France
Bertil FOLLIOT, Université Pierre et Marie Curie, Paris, France
Dan GRIGORAS, Technical University of Iasi (on leave), Romania

Organizing Committee

Bertil FOLLIOT, Université Pierre et Marie Curie, Paris, France
Dan GRIGORAS, Technical University of Iasi, Romania
Alex NICOLAU, University of California at Irvine, USA
Isaac SCHERSON, University of California at Irvine, USA
Bernard TOURSEL, Université des Sciences et Technologies de Lille, France
Wolfgang GENTZSCH, SUN Microsystems, Grid Middleware, Palo Alto, USA

Program Committee

Florian Mircea BOIAN, University "Babes-Bolyai", Cluj-Napoca, Romania
Valentin CRISTEA, "Politehnica" University Bucharest, Romania
Michel COSNARD, INRIA Lorraine, France
Bertil FOLLIOT, Université Pierre et Marie Curie, Paris, France
Guang GAO, University of Delaware, USA
Wolfgang GENTZSCH, SUN Microsystems, Grid Middleware, Palo Alto, USA
Claude GIRAULT, Université Pierre et Marie Curie, Paris, France
Lucio GRANDINETTI, University of Calabria, Italy
Dan GRIGORAS, Technical University Iasi, Romania
Toader JUCAN, University "Al. I. Cuza" Iasi, Romania
Alex NICOLAU, University of California at Irvine, USA
Can OZTURAN, Bogazici University, Turkey
K. PINGALI, Cornell University, USA
L. RAUSCHWERGER, Texas A&M University, USA
Isaac SCHERSON, University of California at Irvine, USA
Bernard TOURSEL, Université des Sciences et Technologies de Lille, France
Marek TUDRUJ, Institute of Computer Science, Polish Academy of Sciences, Poland
Andrew WENDELBORN, University of Adelaide, Australia

Key Speakers

Alex NICOLAU, University of California at Irvine, USA
Bernard TOURSEL, Université des Sciences et Technologies de Lille, France
Isaac SCHERSON, University of California at Irvine, USA
Bertil FOLLIOT, Université Pierre et Marie Curie, Paris, France
Ionut LOPATAN, Microsoft Romania
Can OZTURAN, Bogazici University, Turkey
Marek TUDRUJ, Institute of Computer Science, Polish Academy of Sciences, Poland
Hai JIN, Huazhong University of Science and Technology, China
Lothar LIPPERT, GENIAS Software GmbH, Germany
Valentin CRISTEA, "Politehnica" University Bucharest, Romania
Dan GRIGORAS, Technical University Iasi, Romania

Sponsors and/or Supporting Organizations

North Atlantic Treaty Organization (NATO)

International Federation for Information Processing (IFIP) W.G. 10.3

IEEE Romanian Section

Technical University of Iasi

"Al.I.Cuza" University

Black Sea University Foundation

Microsoft Romania

Banca Romana pentru Dezvoltare (BRD) – GSG

Romaqua Group

Table of Contents

Grid Computing: A New Technology for the Advanced Web

Wolfgang Gentzsch

Sun Microsystems, Inc., Palo Alto, USA

Wolfgang.Gentzsch@Sun.COM

Abstract. The aim of our Grid Computing team at Sun is to take Cluster and Grid computing onto the next level of widest acceptance. For this purpose, we present a three-tier Grid architecture which relates to an intuitive model, including Cluster, Campus and Global Grids, which allows users to embrace Grid Computing starting with their current compute clusters, and moving to the next level of Grid implementation in an evolutionary way. In addition, we present a complete Grid software stack for all three Grid stages, which contains modules developed at Sun and by our partners.

1 Grid Components: Networks, Computers, Software

Mankind is right in the middle of another evolutionary technological transition which once more will change the way we do things. And, you guessed right, it has to do with the Internet. It's called "The Grid", which means the infrastructure for the Advanced Web, for computing, collaboration and communication.

The Internet itself has dramatically changed over the last three decades. While, in the late Sixties, it was built mainly to provide scientists with an infrastructure for faster communication via electronic mail, it has rapidly grown and improved since then, mainly because of three driving elements: networks, computers, and software.

In the mid Nineties, George Gilder predicted the "Network Abundance". Every nine months, total network bandwidth doubles. For many years, every day, thousands of miles of fiberoptic cables are laid down, ready for deployment in private and business applications. While many of us still suffer from 56 bps (Bits/sec) telephone modem speed, researchers and enterprises have already access to networks with a bandwidth of 10 million bps, and some even up to one billion bps. Soon, we will see 100 billion bps and more. Thus, network bandwidth will grow by a factor of 5000 over the next 10 years. Just this July, the US National Science Foundation approved the $53 million DTF Distributed TeraScale Facility project, a network with 40 billion bps, connecting research centers in San Diego (SDSC), Pasadena (Caltech), Urbana-Champaign (NCSA), and Chicago (ARNL). It seems that there is no limit.

Another building block of the Internet are the computers. Today, for example, there are over one hundred million PCs in homes and at work, plus some 10 million powerful compute servers, from midrange to high-end, used at ISP Internet Service Providers, or for high-performance scientific, engineering and commercial appli-

D. Grigoras et al. (Eds.): IWCC 2001, LNCS 2326, pp. 1-15, 2002.

cations. Their performance doubles every 18 months, which was observed and predicted by former Intel Chairman Gordon Moore in 1965. Thus, computer performance will grow by a factor of 100 over the next 10 years, then breaking the Petaflops Performance Barrier. This will make today's handheld electronic devices soon very powerful nodes in the Internet.

The third and most complex Internet building block is software, either for running the networks and the computers and their intercommunication - then called the *middleware*, or for solving our day-to-day problems and running our business, called *application* software. The ever increasing benefit, resulting in the combination of the networked computers, the software to run them, and the people who use them, is called Metcalfe's Law, after Bob Metcalfe, who developed Ethernet at Xerox Parc, in 1973: "The usefulness of a network equals the square of the number of users."

These three laws of Gilder, Moore, and Metcalfe, respectively, and the technological evolution they describe, are currently converging into and enabling the Advanced Web, on top of the Internet infrastructure. Past Internet and World Wide Web mainly enabled information provision, retrieval and exchange, and some e-commerce.

The new Advanced Web adds a wide variety of opportunities, based on computing, collaboration and communication, for individuals, groups, research and engineering teams, and for the whole community. It will provide great services in our private, community, and business environments. Universal connectivity gives users immediate and easy access to any kind of information and service they want, helps them in solving problems and in making personal and business decisions, and allows them to easily offer their own services to anybody. The new Advanced Web changes the way we live and work.

Enter *The Grid*. The term has been derived from the "Power Grid" infrastructure which provides electricity to every wall socket. In our context, The Grid describes the technology infrastructure for the Advanced Web, for computing, collaboration and communication.

2 Distributed Computing and the Grid

In the early Nineties, research groups started exploiting distributed computing resources over the Internet: scientists collected and utilized hundreds of workstations for parallel applications like molecular design and computer graphics rendering. Other research teams glued large supercomputers together into one virtual metacomputer, distributing subsets of a meta-application to specific vector, parallel and graphics computers, over wide-area networks, e.g. the computer simulation of multi-physics applications like the interaction of a fluid with a rotating propeller blade. Additionally the scope of many of these research projects was to understand and demonstrate the actual potential of the networking, computing and software infrastructure and to develop it further.

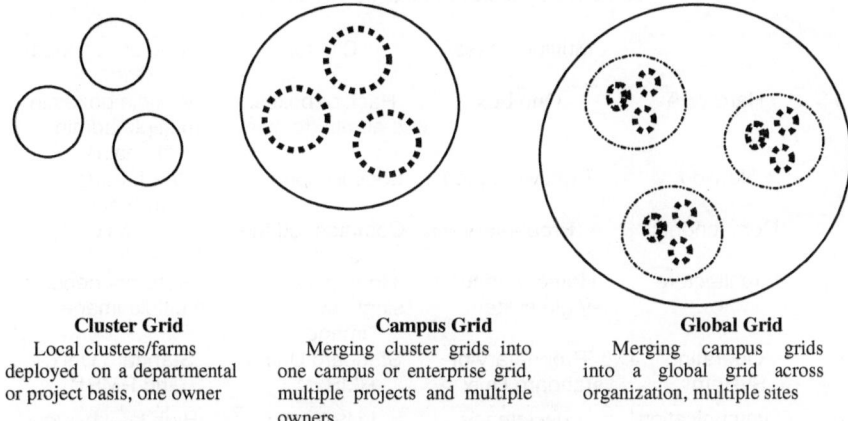

Cluster Grid	**Campus Grid**	**Global Grid**
Local clusters/farms deployed on a departmental or project basis, one owner	Merging cluster grids into one campus or enterprise grid, multiple projects and multiple owners	Merging campus grids into a global grid across organization, multiple sites

Fig. 1. Evolution of the Grid

Multiprocessor Systems (MPs), Clusters, Grids are examples of distributed computing architectures. In MPs, processors are tightly coupled, through shared memory or high-speed interconnect (e.g. crossbar switch). Examples are PVPs (parallel vector processors). They are most suitable in HPC High Performance Computing, for parallel applications which rely on fast message passing communication among their parallel processes.

Clusters, on the other hand, are loosely coupled single or multiprocessor computers, interconnected through networks which are one or two orders of magnitude slower than MP interconnects. Examples are Beowulf clusters made of commercial off-the-shelf hardware and running Linux; or the Sun Technical Compute Farm (TCF), running Solaris/TM Operating System. They are mostly used for heavy throughput computing, distributing many (usually non-parallel) compute jobs onto the processors, collecting individual results back into one global result (space). Examples are in the film industry, rendering of thousands of frames to produce a movie, or the design and test simulations to build the next generation VLSI chip in EDA Electronic Design Automation. Or in bioinformatics, scanning hundreds of thousands of sequences in genomics and proteomics.

While MPs and Clusters are single systems, usually in one single administrative domain, Computational Grids consist of clusters of networked MPs and/or Clusters, located in multiple different administrative domains, scattered over departments, enterprises, or distributed globally even over the Internet. Naturally, therefore, these grids involve a much higher degree of complexity, especially at the middleware layer, to run, administer, manage, and use these distributed computing resources, and on the application layer, to design, develop and run the appropriate software which efficiently deploys such grids.

Table 1. Distributed Computing Taxonomy

		Multiprocessor	Cluster	Campus & Global Grid*
1	Hardware	One box	Rack or boxes, one admin domain	Multiple boxes in multiple admin domains
2	Network	Tightly coupled	Loosely coupled	Via Intranet or Internet
3	Components	Proprietary	Common, off the shelf	Mix
4	Architecture	Homogeneous, single system	Homogeneous, single system image	Heterogeneous, multiple images
5	Operating System	Proprietary or standard Unix	Standard Unix + RMS **	Standard Unix + Grid RMS**
6	Communication	Low latency, high bandwidth	... In between ...	High latency, low bandwidth
7	RMS Resource Management	E.g. Solaris Resource Manager	Sun Grid Engine, PBS	GRD (Campus), Globus, Legion (Global)
8	Cost/price	Expensive buy	Inexpensive buy	"Rent" CPU cycles
9	Computing paradigm	Parallel and supercomputing	Throughput computing	Both; metacomputing, collaborative computing
10	Users	One/more groups	One group/owner	Groups, Communites
11	Examples	NEC SX5, Sun Starfire/tm	Beowulf, Sun TCF	Campus, Enterprise,...

*) Current state-of-the-art   **) Resource Management Software

In short, The Grid is a distributed computing architecture for delivering computing and data resources as a service, over the Internet, in much the same way that electricity is delivered over the power grid.   It is the next logical step in the technology infrastructure, which connects distributed computers, storage devices, mobile devices, instruments, sensors, data bases, and software applications, and provides uniform access to the user community for computing, collaboration and communication. Examples of current grids are the NASA Information Power Grid (IPG); the DoD Distance Computing and Distributed Computing Grid (DisCom 2); the NSF NCSA National Technology Grid; NetSolve for accessing and sharing mathematical software; Nimrod for campus-wide resource sharing; SETI@Home for searching for extraterrestrial intelligence; the CERN DataGrid, processing Petabytes of particle data per year from its Large Hadron Collider experiment; or the APGrid connecting many computer centers in Asia and the Pacific Rim, in the near future.

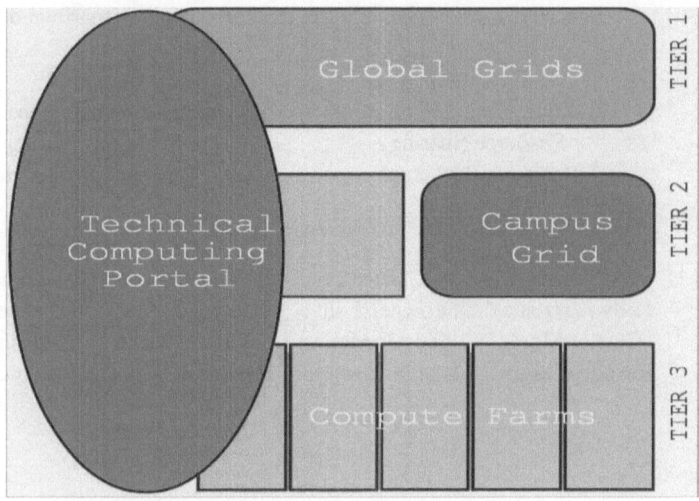

Fig. 2. Three Grid Layers: The Global, Campus and Cluster Layer

3 Evolution of Cluster, Campus, and Global Grids

Grids can be represented in one general 3-tier grid architecture, including Cluster Grids, Campus and Enterprise Grids, and Global Grids. The complexity of these grids depends on many facts, but most importantly on the number of grid resource owners, and on the number of different grid sites.

A computational grid is a hardware and software infrastructure that provides dependable, consistent, pervasive, and inexpensive access to computational capabilities. In the near future, These grids will be used by computational engineers and scientists, experimental scientists, associations, corporations, environmental, training and education organisations, states, consumers, etc. They will be dedicated to on-demand computing, high-throughput computing, data-intensive computing, collaborative computing, and supercomputing, potentially on an economic consumer/supplier basis. Grid communities, among others, are national grids (like ASCI), virtual grids (e.g. for research teams), private grids (e.g. for a car manufacturer's CrashNet and its suppliers, for collaborative crash simulations), and public grids (e.g. Consumer networks).

These grids enable users to combine nearly any set of distributed resources into one integrated metacomputing workbench to allow users to measure nature (e.g. with microscope or telescope), process the data according to some fundamental mathematical equation (e.g. the Navier-Stokes equations), and provide computer simulations and animations to study and understand these complex phenomena.

Tier 1	Global Grid (multiple owners / multiple sites) Security, Authentication, Grid Resource Mgmt, Distributed Data			
Tier 2	Campus 1 (multiple owners / one site) Resource Sharing Resource Brokerage		Campus 2 (multiple owners / one site) Resource Sharing Resource Brokerage	
Tier 3	Cluster 1 (1 owner/1 site) Cluster Mgmt Resource Mgmt	Cluster 2 (1 owner/1 site) Cluster Mgmt Resource Mgmt	Cluster 3 (1 owner/1 site) Cluster Mgmt Resource Mgmt	Cluster 4 (1 owner/1 site) Cluster Mgmt Resource Mgmt

Today, we see the first efforts to more systematically exploit these grid computing resources over the Internet. So called peer-to-peer computing projects, like SETI@home, Distributed.Net, and Folderol, let Internet users download scientific data, run it on their own computers using spare processing cycles, and send the results back to a central database. Recently, an academic project called Compute Power Market, has been initiated to develop software technologies that enable creating grids where anyone can sell idle CPU cycles, or those in need can buy compute power much like electricity or telephony today.

4 Grid Computing Challenges

Most of the underlying sophisticated technologies for grids are currently under development. Prototype grid environments exist like public-domain projects Globus and Legion. Research in resource management is underway in projects like EcoGrid, and the basic building block for a commercial grid resource manager exists with Sun Grid Engine software.

There are a number of public-domain Global Grid environments, such as Globus and Avaki (former Legion). The GGF (Global Grid Forum), founded in 1998, unites hundreds of computer scientists in working groups to discuss the one common grid architecture. Some of the challenges they are addressing are:

- development of application software for the grids that identify and access suitable computing resources in a distributed environment
- definition of standard interfaces to enable communication among the different grid building blocks, and

- facilitation of application development guaranteeing authenticated access and secure data transfer
- service tools for monitoring, accounting, billing and reporting
- design of network protocols for message formats and exchange.

Security in grids is a particularly difficult problem. Resources being used may be extremely valuable and are often located in distinct administrative domains. The applications and data using these resources may be extremely sensitive, and often represent a company's crown jewels. Therefore, the users need to have a "key" to the resources and the data, with uniform authentication and authorization. But there should be only one single sign-on, even in case of using hundreds of distributed resources to solve one complex problem. Existing software security standards like SSL and X.509 are being enhanced to achieve this. Current grid software environments like Globus and Legion already contain such a grid security infrastructure.

Another hard problem in Computational Grid environments is distributed resource management (DRM). Starting with networked workstations and with client/server environments, in the early Nineties, the objective then was to use these networked computers more efficiently, from an average of some 20% in unmanaged environments, up to 98% average usage in environments today controlled by DRM software like Sun Grid Engine, Condor, LSF, and PBS.

5 Sun and Grid Computing

Sun Microsystems is strongly committed to Grid Computing, expressed in its visions about "The Network is the Computer", or "Sun ONE Open Network Environment", or in Sun's contribution to open technologies like Java, Jini, and Jxta. The objective of Sun's cross-company wide Grid Computing organization is to establish Sun as the category leader in Grid Computing, by helping to build the Grid Community that will foster innovation, engagement, investment and awareness at all levels, and by delivering the products and services required by Sun's Grid Computing partners and customers.

Over the past few years, Sun has developed the Sun Grid Computing Software Stack, consisting of software building blocks for the general 3-tier grid architecture, including Cluster Grids, Campus or Enterprise Grids, and Global Grids. At the Cluster Grid level, Sun provides Sun Grid Engine, Solaris Resource Manager, HPC ClusterTools, Sun MC Management Center, and Jxta, and basic cluster management tools. At the Campus or Enterprise level, in addition, there is the Sun Grid Engine Broker, which eventually interfaces into the Global Grid level with technologies like Globus and Avaki. In addition, Sun's Technical Computing Portal serves as an entry portal for the Cluster, Campus, and Global Grids.

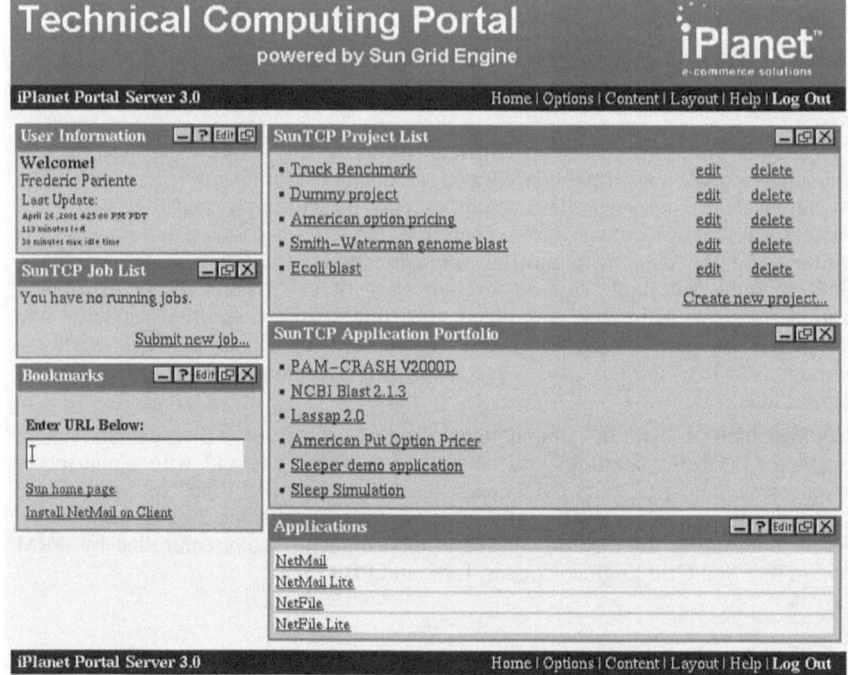

Fig. 3. Every Grid Needs an Easy-to-Use Grid Access Portal

6 Sun Grid Computing Building Blocks

SUN GRID ENGINE (SGE) is a distribute resource manager that transparently matches incoming job requests optimally to available compute cluster resources like cpu, memory, I/O, and software licenses. SGE provides system administrators with the job accounting and statistics information needed to monitor resource utilization and to determine how to improve resource allocation.

The interface allows to define and control user access to computer resources, so that each user's rights and priorities lead to the increased utilization of the cluster grid. The interface enables to specify job options for priority, hardware and license requirements, dependencies, and time windows. An easy-to-use command line and a GUI-based interface is available to help users submit and control jobs. SGE allows managing batch, interactive, checkpointing, and parallel jobs. Users are in control of their local machine, thereby virtually eliminating the possibility that they will not have access to their own machine when they need it.
http://www.sun.com/gridware

Sun TCP Technical Computing Portal			

	Global Grid Sun TCP, SGE Broker, Globus, Avaki, Cactus, Punch, ...			
Tier 1				

	Campus 1 Sun TCP, SGE Broker		Campus 2 Sun TCP, SGE Broker	
Tier 2				

	Cluster 1	Cluster 2	Cluster 1	Cluster 2
Tier 3	Sun TCP, Sun Grid Engine	Sun TCP, Sun Grid Engine	Sun TCP, Sun Grid Engine	Sun TCP, Sun Grid Engine
	ClusterTools	ClusterTools	ClusterTools	ClusterTools
	SRM/SunMC/J xta	SRM/SunMC/J xta	SRM/SunMC/J xta	SRM/SunMC/J xta
	IRO,QFS,SAM ,FS	IRO,QFS,SAM ,FS	IRO,QFS,SAM ,FS	IRO,QFS,SAM ,FS
	Cluster Mgmt	Cluster Mgmt	Cluster Mgmt	Cluster Mgmt

SUN GRID ENGINE BROKER (formerly the Global Resource Director), provides workload management by fine-grained policy management and dynamic scheduling. Enterprise goals such as on-time completion of critical work or fair resource sharing are expressed as policies that determine how computing resources are used and shared. SGE Broker allocates resources among jobs when a job is dispatched, and throughout its lifetime. This insures that the most important work at any instant receives its deserved system share by allowing newly-arrived, more important work to take resources away from less important executing jobs. Important features are multiple policies (functional priority, share-based, urgency-based, override system), automated policy enforcement, and an interface for accounting and monitoring resource utilization. SGE Broker helps site managers to gain overview on the resource utilization profile of an enterprise, to distribute resources fairly, and to implement level-of-service agreements.The Sun Grid Engine Broker is available from the Grid Engine Open Source web site.
http://www.sun.com/software/gridware/gridengine_project.html/

SOLARIS RESOURCE MANAGER (SRM) enables increased resource availability for users, groups, and applications. It complements Sun Grid Engine by providing the ability to allocate and control major system resources, such as CPU, virtual memory, and number of processes, WITHIN a multi-processor system.

After a resource policy is set, the system administrator can walk away, confident that mission-critical applications will get the resources they demand. Additionally, users and applications will receive a more consistent level of service. SRM redefines the traditional model of hosting an individual application on a single system. Now, server resources utilizing the Solaris Operating Environment can be controlled using methods similar to mainframe-class systems.

Multiple applications and groups receive a consistent level of service on a single server. In fact, resources can be allocated to the individual user. Resource utilization may actually increase because unused capacity is dynamically allocated to active users and applications. This results in significant cost savings and greater administrative flexibility. SRM provides a means for proactively controlling system resources. Other tools only allow a system administrator to see when valuable resources (processes, CPU, or memory) are about to be exhausted. At that time, the system administrator must react quickly to prevent mission-critical applications from failing.

SRM not only provides resource usage reports, it reduces the likelihood of resource exhaustion because it guarantees resources to key applications and users. The benefit of this is this makes the performance of an application more predictable, and ensures that system response times are not adversely affected by other tasks on the system.
http://www.sun.com/software/resourcemgr/overview/

SUN MANAGEMENT CENTER (SunMC) helps increase service levels and decrease administrative costs in enterprise computing environments. SunMC enhances application availability, optimizes performance and scalability, and simplifies management of Sun hardware, Solaris Operating Environment and applications. It is based on an agent-based architecture that provides a powerful single point of management for the enterprise, making better use of administrative resources and yielding better efficiency per dollar spent on system management.

SunMC is designed to improve customers' ability to do predictive fault analysis, gain anywhere access to systems management tools, and offer higher end-user availability. A Java GUI offers a common look and feel for all applications and can be accessed from anywhere on the network, greatly increasing administrator efficiency. A web-based interface makes management information available from Web browsers, for anytime, anywhere access.

Grouping of objects provides an easy way to define and invoke complex tasks on a set of managed objects. For example, a user can set up properties or change thresholds and alarm actions and then apply this complex assignment to a collection of managed objects. The ability to schedule and automate tasks that previously were done manually is a significant time-saver.

Proactive event/alarm management and predictive failure analysis help increase system availability. This feature includes a new interactive knowledge base for events and alarm resolution that grows with customer experience. Filtering capabilities help pinpoint problems quickly, even in systems with thousands of objects or nodes. Data view capability allows users to create their own display configurations to show data in ways that are most convenient or meaningful to them.

And, the Sun Management Center 3.0 Developer Environment allows to create and modify Sun Management Center modules through a new intuitive and powerful GUI module builder.
http://www.sun.com/software/solaris/sunmanagementcenter/

JXTA PEER-TO-PEER TECHNOLOGY: The Internet has evolved into an "expanded Web" with multi-dimensional layers that reach deep into the Web and wide across the network to the edge. As more resources migrate to the Internet and as more users access this expanded Web, the problem of simply finding, getting, and using information and resources becomes more complex and time consuming.

With the help of the developer community, Project JXTA technology aims to allow quicker, easier, more natural access to critical information and resources. JXTA-based applications will attempt to take the complexity out of the users' online experience. Outlining a unified approach by working with open interfaces will assure future additions to the Internet (i.e., Web services, device access) have the ability to work together and provide users with more timely, meaningful content.

The goal of JXTA is to make it easier to use the Internet, harnessing the value of the network across multiple platforms. The value of more efficiently accessing useful information drives more users to the network centric computing model for which Sun provides the infrastructure. JXTA is a piece of this infrastructure and will make it easy for developers to create innovative applications.

JXTA enables new, intelligent applications for users to naturally find the information they are really looking for without the return of irrelevant results, to easily connect with any peer or node on the network to get instantaccess to resources, and to effectively use that information in a meaningful way - Find it, Get it, Use it. For example, JXTA will enable new applications that allow critical information to follow users across different network access points (PDA, laptop, cell phone, etc.) so the information is easily accessible and remains at users' fingertips.
http://www.sun.com/software/jxta/ or http://www.jxta.org

SUN TECHNICAL COMPUTING PORTAL (TCP), utilizing iPlanet Portal Server and Sun Grid Engine resource manager, provides a simple, net-centric interface to High Performance Technical Computing (HPTC) Services. Now extremely powerful, CPU- and storage-intensive applications for Technical Computing - Genomics, Financial Modeling, Crash Test Analysis, for example - can be provided over the Web as simply as traditional services such as Mail and Calendering. This advance is made possible by the synergy between iPlanet Portal Server, Sun's Grid Engine resource manager and other Sun High Performance Computing technologies.

Sun's Technical Computing Portal (TCP) provides high performance and technical computing (HPTC) users a secure Web-based single point of delivery to access services, content, and complex applications. Users have the freedom to access technical applications remotely through an Internet/ Intranet browser anytime, anywhere using simple point-and-click interfaces. No UNIX skills required. Through TCP, users can: Upload input files with the click of a button. Submit jobs remotely. Manage job submission via forms (instead of command line arguments). Dynamically check the status of jobs. Receive email notification when jobs are complete. Download/visualize output files.

SUN HPC CLUSTERTOOLS offers parallel development and system management tools, bringing Sun's network computing vision to high-end technical markets. It is a complete integrated environment that provides middleware to manage a workload of highly resource-intensive applications and delivers an end-to-end software development environment for parallel distributed applications. Sun HPC ClusterTools offers a comprehensive set of capabilities for: Parallel Program Development, Resource Management, System Administration, and Cluster Administration.

Sun HPC ClusterTools brings high-performance computing software development and production environment management capabilities to the entire range of Sun computing platforms running Solaris Operating Environment from desktop systems and workgroup servers to Sun high-end servers. Users of Sun HPC ClusterTools software experience the advantages of the unique integrated design environment in all stages of their work from parallel application software development and production runs to post-processing while making the most efficient use of most appropriate compute resources. Sun HPC ClusterTools supports standard programming paradigms, like MPI message passing.
http://www.sun.com/software/hpc/

JIRO MANAGEMENT FOR STORAGE NETWORKS makes it possible to deliver intelligent management services for networked devices through a platform-independent, industry-defined development environment. Using the principles of Java[tm] technology, Jiro technology provides an innovative architecture for connecting and managing complex distributed environments such as storage networks. With its network-centric model for development and deployment, Jiro technology brings higher levels of interoperability, adaptability, and manageability to today's enterprise networks.

Jiro technology introduces the concept of a standard management domain that includes base management services such as events, logging, lookup, scheduling, security, and transactions. It provides a standard interface for locating and communicating with these services as FederatedBeans[tm] components. In addition, Jiro technology provides a dynamic services model to support the deployment, updating, and recall of complete distributed management applications composed ofFederatedBeans components. By handling communication, persistence, security, and other difficult aspects of distributed applications, Jiro technology eases the creation of automated and policy based management applications that solve the problems of configuring, monitoring, diagnosing and troubleshooting network devices, software, systems, and storage in an intelligent and automated fashion.
http://staging-draft.central/jiro/index.html

SUN QFS AND SAM-FS provide a hierarchical data-sharing file system and storage system software designed to enable Sun's customers to intelligently share, place, backup and archive data with automation and ease, resulting in efficient use of their storage resources. The flagship products, Storage and Archive Manager-File System (SAM-FS) and Quick File System (QFS), are advanced storage management solutions designed to deliver high performance and automated file and media management to data intensive applications.

SUN QFS is a standard file system for Solaris environments that can be shared and is designed to solve file system performance bottlenecks by maximizing file system performance in conjunction with the underlying disk technology and storage hardware.

SUN SAM-FS is a high performance, 64 bit Solaris file system and volume manager with fully integrated storage and archive management features that manages and protects large volumes of data and a virtually unlimited number of files. SAM-FS is also designed to provide continuous automatic and unobtrusive backup of work-in progress, effective long-term data storage, and GUI-based management tools for flexible control of high performance storage systems.
http://www.sun.com/storage/software/

7 Grid Users, Markets, Business

Grids are especially suitable in science and engineering. Biochemists, for example, can exploit thousands of computers to screen hundreds of thousands of compounds in an hour. Hundreds of physicists worldwide pool computing resources to analyze petabytes (10^15 bytes) of data from CERN's Large Hadron Collider experiment. Climate Scientists visualize, annotate, and analyze terabytes of computer simulation datasets. An emergency response team couples real-time data, the actual weather model, and population data. Engineers in the automotive industry combine their multidisciplinary results with analysis data from their suppliers. A community group pools members' PCs to analyze alternative designs for a local road. And many more.

"The Grid" itself is not a piece of software, not a product which one can sell into specific technical or commercial markets. It is very much like the Web - we cannot sell the Web. The Grid is simply the evolving next generation of the Advanced Web. And like the Web, The Grid will be ubiquitous. It will simply become the basic IT infrastructure for all markets, where it makes sense. What hardware/software companies can and will provide is the appropriate hardware and software stack - the gridware - which helps organizations meet their IT requirements on top of these grids.

We are ready to build such grids today. But there is no commonly agreed standard, there is no common architecture yet. Currently, there is still a lot of manual work involved to set up and run a prototype grid for computing, collaboration, and communication.

Since the Grid is still a highly technology-driven software infrastructure, there are mainly three user groups: the early adopters, the early majority, and then everybody else. Currently, we are in the early-adopter phase: Users are highly technology oriented, like in research and education and in some large engineering companies. Currently, grids are being built together with these users.

To have a closer look at what kind of grid activities some companies already provide, let's take Sun Microsystems as an example.

Sun's origins are in distributed computing. Originally Sun stood for "Stanford University Network,". Scott McNealy's vision was "the network is the computer." Today, one might say that the grid is the computer. Since its beginning, Sun contributed to network computing and grid technologies, for example with Java/tm, Jini/tm, Jxta/tm, and with Sun Grid Engine and Sun HPC ClusterTools/tm technology, which both have become open source projects recently. In addition, there is the iPlanet/tm Grid Access Portal, the Solaris Resource and Bandwidth Manager, the Sun Management Center, and the LSC Distributed Storage Manager. Sun Grid Engine is integrated with the major grid technologies currently developed and deployed in the Grid community, such as Globus, Legion, Punch and Cactus. Sun is currently forming these building blocks into one integratable stack.

Sun is actively involved in building a large number of grids, Departmental Grids, Campus Grids, Research Grids, and Enterprise Grids, mainly within a customer program called "The Sun Center of Excellence". One example is the Edinburgh Parallel Computing Center (EPCC), a Sun Center of Excellence in Grid Computing. It is the location of the UK National eScience Center (along with eight regional centers). Basically, the eScience program is to build a UK-wide Grid which interconnects all these distributed computing centers to aid scientists in their research. Edinburgh will evaluate software building blocks like Sun Grid Engine, the iPlanet/tm Portal Server, Sun Management Center, Sun HPC ClusterTools, and Forte/tm Workshop to build the next generation Grid infrastructure. Through this infrastructure, EPCC will deliver compute power to and exchange expertise with its partners in research and industry all over the UK.

Another example is the Ohio Supercomputer Center (OSC), which became a Sun Center of Excellence for High Performance Computing, earlier this year. Together with Sun, OSC is building the grid infrastructure which enables distributed computing, collaboration, and communication with other partners, e.g. Ohio State University, Universities of Akron and Cincinnati, Nationwide Insurance, and Exodus.

One more example is the Technical University of Aachen, Germany, which is a Sun Center of Excellence for Computational Fluid Dynamics. Among other objectives, the Center will be providing remote access to its large Sun system (which will grow to over 2 Teraflops) for researchers on the university campus, much like an ASP Application Service Provider. Therefore, one of their grid contributions is the enhancement of open source Grid Engine toward a Grid Broker, using the software code available in the Grid Engine open source project.

8 Beyond the Web

Soon, grids will break out into commercial and industrial computing. Grid computing is already implemented in many industrial settings, on a departmental or enterprise level. Up to now it has gone by many different names, such as compute farms, cluster computing, etc.. For example, Caprion Pharmaceuticals has recently worked with Sun engineers to implement Sun Grid Engine for proteomics, on a large server farm. Grids are also coming into the commercial setting through third parties, since many ASPs and ISPs are implementing grid-enabled access to applications. So in the end, Grid Technology will become the glue which will unite both technical and commercial computing. Just as we have "The Web" today, we then will have "The Grid".

The Grid forces us to reinvent the network itself: the data centers, the clients, the applications, and the services. Everything is changing. Everything will be seen in the context of grids - Campus Grids, Enterprise Grids, Research Grids, Entertainment Grids, Community Grids, and many, many more. The network will be service driven, the clients will be light-weight appliances with Internet or wireless access to any kind of resources. Data centers will be extremely safe, reliable, virtually always available, from anywhere. Applications will be part of a wide spectrum of services delivered over the network, such as compute cycles, tools for data processing, accounting and monitoring, with customized consulting, with additional information and communication tools, and with software which allow you to sell or trade your results.

The good news is that there will be no disruptive change in the technology or in the way we use it. For many good reasons: We currently have so many new technologies on the table that we will be busy enough to efficiently implement them. This takes time. Then, after we have interconnected all kind of computing devices through grid infrastructures, the next step will be to embed and hide these devices into any kind of thing that serves our daily business and private needs, in our houses, cars, airplanes, clothes, the environment, maybe some even in our body.

References

1. http://www.csse.monash.edu.au/~rajkumar/papers/TheGrid.pdf
2. http://www.globus.org
3. http://www.legion.virginia.edu
4. http://www.mpk.com/grids
5. http://setiathome.ssl.berkeley.edu
6. http://www.distributed.net
7. http://www.ComputePower.com
8. http://www.popularpower.com
9. http://216.120.55.131/
10. http://www.parabon.com
11. http://www.hpcportal.de
12. http://www.csse.monash.edu.au/~rajkumar/ecogrid/
13. http://www.sun.com/Gridware/

Beyond Flexibility and Reflection: The Virtual Virtual Machine Approach

B. Folliot[2], I. Piumarta[2], L. Seinturier[2], C. Baillarguet[1], C. Khoury[2], A. Leger[2], and F. Ogel[1]

[1] INRIA Rocquencourt, Domaine de Voluceau
78153 Le Chesnay, France
[2] Laboratoire d'Informatique Paris VI, Université Pierre et Marie Curie,
4, place Jussieu, 75252 Paris Cedex 05, France
firstname.name@inria.fr,
http://www-sor.inria.fr/projects/vvm

Abstract. With todays wide acceptance of distributed computing, a rapidly growing number of application domains are emerging, leading to a growing number of ad-hoc solutions, rigid and poorly interoperable. Our response to this challenge is a platform for building flexible and interoperable execution environments (including language and system aspects) called the Virtual Virtual Machine. This paper presents our approach, the first two realisations and their applications to active networks and flexible web caching.

1 Introduction

As distributed computing becomes widely spread, new application domains are emerging rapidly, introducing more and more heterogeneity into distributed environments: firstly, because of the rapid hardware evolution (especially with embedded devices) and secondly because each new application domain comes with it's own semantic, constraints and therefore set of dedicated abstractions.

To face those heterogeneity issues, current approaches lead to the design of complete, new, dedicated programming/execution environment, including language and operating systems aspects. As a result, programming and execution environments, while being well adapted to some given application domains and/or hardware, remains static, rigid and poorly interoperable..

Our response to this problem is a new, systematic approach for software adaptation and reconfiguration based on a language and hardware independent execution platform, called the Virtual Virtual Machine (*VVM*)[6].

The *VVM* provides both a programming and an exection environment, whose objectives are (i) to allow the adaptation of language and system aspects according to a specific application domain, such as smart cards, satellites or clusters; (ii) to achieve dynamic extensibility, by changing "on the fly" the execution environment (adding protocols, hardware support, algorithms or even "bug correction"); (iii) to provide a common language substrate on wich to achieve interoperability between different languages/application domains.

D. Grigoras et al. (Eds.): IWCC 2001, LNCS 2326, pp. 16–25, 2002.

The remainder of this paper starts by presenting the *VVM* approach and architecture in Section 2. The first two prototypes and their applications are described in Section 3 and 4 respectively. Section 5 describes an example of application in the domain of flexible web caching. Related works appear in Section 6, followed by conclusions and perspectives in Section 7.

2   Virtual Virtual Machine Project

Most modern distributed applications or environments are composed of complex and heterogeneous interacting components. Dealing with this heterogeneity raises severe obstacles to interoperability.

The virtual machine approach is a step in the right direction, allowing intersystems interoperability, portability and promoting mobility/distribution with a compact code's representation and security mechanisms. But there are still dedicated to specific application domains. Let's consider SUN's Java Virtual Machine: it corresponds to an application domain where there is high amount of available memory, limited acces to the underlying system and no quality of service.

The apparition of new application domains, with different characteristics, implies new virtual machines to match new requirements (for a given architecture, as JavaCard for smartcards or KVM for mobile phones, or some software needs like real time (RT Java) or fault tolerance). This proliferation of "ad-hoc" virtual machines breaks the interoperability capabilities of the approach.

If virtual machines are a good step but are still far too rigid, why not to "virtualize" them. Hence, instead of developping a new virtual machine for each new application domain, a specification is dynamically loaded into the *VVM*. This specification describes a virtual machine adapted to this application domain.

The main goal of this architecture, is to bring adaptation, flexibility, dynamicity and interoperability to applications, without sacrifying the performances.

Figure 1 gives a simplified vision of this architecture. The *VVM* runs on top of an existing OS or on bare hardware. The lower layer (called μVM) represents the OS and hardware dependent part. On top of it is the core of the *VVM*:(i) the *Virtual Processor*, wich provide a low-level execution engine based on a language-neutral internal representation and elementary instructions; (ii) an *object memory* (and the associated pure object model), with garbage collection;(iii) some *input methods* that allow dynamic loading of execution environment specification.

Such a specification is called a *VMLet*. It is a high level description of the language and/or the system aspects of a programming/execution environment dedicated to a given application domain. Because of having a single execution mechanism for all the *VMLets*, it promotes interoperability (and reuse of code) between applications but also between application domains (and their respective environments). This interoperability can range from simple data exchange to mobile computations. It allows the sharing of physical and/or logical ressources and permits aggressive optimizations.

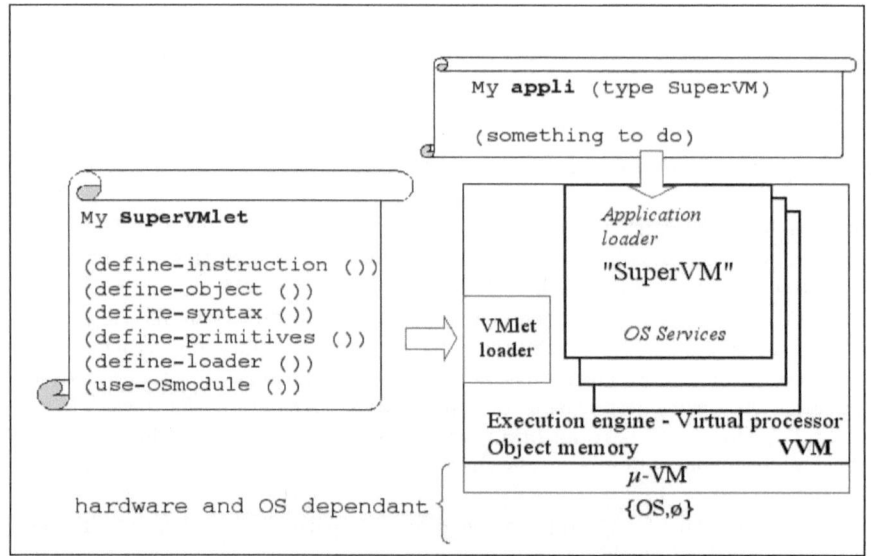

Fig. 1. The *VVM* architecture.

Once the *VVM* has loaded a *VMLet*, it adapts/extends itself so that it contains the semantic and functionnalities of the described virtual machine. Hence there's only one meta-level: the *VVM becomes* the VM described in the *VMLet*, thus the performances should be equivalent to the similar "hand-coded" virtual machine. Then, applications written for this environment can be loaded and executed as if they were running on a dedicated VM.

Dynamic extensibility comes from the ability to add and/or redefine "on the fly" everything in the environment, in response to requirements or execution conditions change. Interoperability can be achieved by having a single execution engine, and thus a common language substrate that can be used to exchange data and code between applications and/or *VMLets*.

3   The Reflexive Virtual Machine

The first step toward the *VVM* was the Reflexive Virtual Machine (*RVM*). It is a scheme-like interactive virtual machine that is able to modify dynamically its own primitives and instructions sets.

This dynamic flexibility provides the *RVM* with the ability to adapt/extend itself at runtime and thus turns itself into a virtual machine dedicated to a given application domain, without loosing its flexibility.

Not only can the language of the virtual machine be extended at runtime by adding instructions or primitives, but it can also be adapted to some domain-specific semantics, by adding user-level extension from classes and inheritance (which do not exist in traditional lisp-like languages) to semaphores or lightweight processes.

Although quite limited, the *RVM* has been used to experiment *VMLets* programming, and especially in the context of active networks. Active networks represent an emerging application domain that is therefore, as we mentioned, addressed via lots of differents and dedicated solutions, without any interoperability between.

From the dozens of existing protocols, we quoted two: *PLAN* [9] and *ANTS* [21]. When *PLAN* rely on packets containing both data and code, *ANTS* uses a *deployment* phase. During this phase, the protocols are sent to the routers with a *protocol id*, after what only data and the id of the protocol to be used needs to be sent. Each of those protocols represents an extreme on the full range of possible active network protocols.

So we defined two *VMLets* (one for each protocol), including language/operating system aspects and an API. We keep the front-end lisp-like language of the *RVM* and reuse the socket's services of the underlying UNIX OS (select, send, receive,...). Concerning the APIs, we mimic *PLAN* and *ANTS* 'ones. Thus, by loading such a *VMLets*, the *RVM* transforms itself to an active router (that understand *PLAN* and/or *ANTS*, depending on what is loaded).

As a first result, each *VMLet* is two order of magnitude smaller than the corresponding original implementation[1]. By simply loading the two *VMLets*, we obtain an active router that is able to proceed both *PLAN* and *ANTS* 's packets.

The next logical step is to define a generalisation of the active network application domain, called Active Active Networks, that will allow (i) to select the most appropriate protocol, according to some requirements, at any time; (ii) a dynamic deployment of any active network protocols, giving us an opportunity to explore the different possible strategies between *PLAN* and *ANTS*.

4   YNVM Is Not a VM

The current prototype, called the *YNVM*, is a dynamic code generator that provides both a complete, reflexive language, and an execution environment. The role of the *YNVM*, from the *VVM* project point of view, is to allow the dynamic generation of domain-specific virtual machines.

To achieve that, the *YNVM* provides four "basic" services:

Code generation: a fast, platform and language independent dynamic compiler producing efficient native code that adheres (by default) to the local platform's *C* ABI[2];

---

[1] counted in bytes of source code.
[2] Application Binary Interface

Meta-data: are kept from the compilation, thus allowing higher-level software to reason about its implementation or the environment's one, and dynamically modify them;

introspection: on dynamically compiled code, the application and the environment itself;

Input methods: giving access to the compilation/configuration process at all levels.

The objective is to maximise the amount of reflective access and intercession, at the lowest possible software level, while preserving simplicity and efficiency. The execution model is similar to *C*, thus providing total compatibility with native applications and systems libraries. In addition to this *C*-like execution model, the use of a dynamic code generator allows performances similar to statically compiled *C* pograms.

Thanks to this compatibility any application can be build with a mix of *C/C++* and *YNVM*'s code, according to the semantics of each part of the program.

What's more is that even if it still uses a scheme-like front-end language, the introspection's facilities and the implementation's reification, allow you to change language features for ease of development. For example, by simply dynamically changing the parser, it is possible to switch from a functionnal paradigm to an imperative and infix *C* syntax style, letting the programmer choose, for each component of its application, the most appropriate paradigm to write it.

5   Flexible Web Caching

To illustrate the advantages of putting the flexibility, reflection and the dynamicity at the lowest possible software level (in the execution environment itself), we have developped a flexible web cache (called *C/NN*[3]) on top of the *YNVM*.

Flexibility in web caches comes from the ability to configure a large number of parameters[4] that influence the behaviour of the cache (protocols, cache size, and so on). What's more, some of these parameters, such as user behaviour, change of protocol or the "hot-spots-of-the-week" [17], cannot be determined before deploying the cache.

However, reconfiguring current web caches involves halting the cache to install the new policy and then restarting it, therefore providing only "cold" flexibility.

WebCal [13] and CacheL [2] are examples of web caches that bring flexibility through the use of domain-specific languages (DSLs). Being dedicated to a particular domain, a DSL offers a powerful and concise medium in wich to express the constraints associated with the behaviour of the cache. However, in spite of being well-adapted to the specification of new cache behaviour and even to

---

[3] The *Cache with No Name*

[4] See the configuration file for Squid...

formal proofs of its correctness, a DSL-based approach does not support "warm" reconfiguration.

Other work [1] proposed a dynamic cache architecture, in which new policies are dynamically loaded in the form of components, using the "strategy" design pattern [8]. While increasing flexibility, it is still limited: it is only possible to change those aspects of the caches behavior that were designed to be adaptable in the original architecture. This is the problem of using rigid programming languages/environments to build dynamically reconfigurable applications: limited reification and dynamicity lead to limited reconfigurability.

Because of it's being build directly over the *YNVM*, *C/NN* inherits its high degree of reflexity, dynamicity and flexibility and so provides "warm" replacement of policies, on-line tuning of the cache and the ability to add arbitrary new functionality (observation protocols, performance evaluation, protocol tracing, debugging, and so on) at any time, and to remove them when they are no longer needed.

In particular, as the reconfiguration strategy is a policy too, an administrator could dynamically define new or reconfigure existing adminstration/reconfiguration rules, performance metrics and associated monitors. Here are some examples of such reconfigurations:

1. when the request rate becomes high, the cache can start to manage a "black list" of servers with low response time and stop caching their documents (direct forward of the requests).
2. if the "byterate" is going down to a threshold, the cache can automatically switch to another policy[5], that saves more bandwidth (even with a worse hitrate or mean response time).

The *VVM* approach lets us instantiate an execution environment dedicated to web caching so that writing a new replacement strategy (from a paper) takes a tens of minutes (for someone familiar with *YNVM*) and the results is about a few lines of code, see figure 2 for an example. Because everything can be changed "on the fly" in the *YNVM*, it was possible to mix different paradigms in *C/NN*'s code (the functional scheme-like front-end and some statically compiled *C*), making code writing even more easy, quick and natural. Figure 2 shows an example of reconfiguration script, written in an infix style, including a reconfiguration function (*switch-to*), a new replacement policy (*filter-policy*, based on one found in [3]) and the reconfiguration command.

Solutions to software dynamic reconfiguration usually implie some "meta level" and degraded performances. Hence our main goal: to bring dynamic flexibility, reflexion and performances together.

Because of the quality of the code generator, the performances of an *YNVM*'s application are almost equivalent to *C* programs (and even sometimes better due to very aggressive optimization and partial evaluation techniques). We have compared *C/NN* to the widely used *Squid* cache version 2.3 on the basis of

---

[5] the choice can be based on meta-data associated with strategies and multi-criterion decision algorithms.

```
// cache reconfiguration function
defun switch-to(new-policy, num-to-re-evaluate){
  let head = get-worst(repository, num-to-re-evaluate);
  current-policy = new-policy;
  while(head){
    http-repository.update(repository, cell.data(head));
    head = next-cell(head);
  }
};
// a new replacement policy
defun filter-policy(doc) {
  if (system.strncmp("text",http.mimeType(doc),4))
    size-cost(doc);
  else
    gds-cost(doc);
};

// reconfiguration command (re-evaluate 20% of the cache)
switch-to(filter-policy,
          http-repository.size(repository)/5);
```

Fig. 2. A complete reconfiguration script.

their average response time (that is the performance criteria the user actually see): based on different traces collected at INRIA (from 100K to 600K requests). *Squid*'s response time is a few more than 1 sec, *C/NN*'s was about 0.83 sec. Handling a hit takes about 130 μs and about 300 μs for a miss. So having a dynamically reconfigurable web cache doesn't seem to imply having a less performant one.

Probably the most important issue is the cost of a reconfiguration. Switching from a policy to another pre-defined one, takes less than 50 μs. Because adding some new functionality implies compiling new codes, the amount of time needed to proceed a reconfiguration depends on the complexity of the extension that is being added, but defining a new replacement strategy takes about 400 μs, and can be compared to handling one request.

6 Related Work

The Virtual Virtual Machine project can be compared to different approaches.

Some work is being done around specialisable virtual machines, that is the generation of new, dedicated virtual machines for a given application domain and environment (operating system, hardware,...), as for example *JavaCard* [11] or *PLAN* [9]. The main difference with these approach is that (i) it does not provide the common language substrate and thus results in isolated virtual machines, without any hope of interoperability; (ii) the specialised virtual machines, once generated, are still static and not flexible.

Flexible operating systems, such as *SPIN* [18] or *Exokernel* [4], and meta object protocol projects are also comparable to our project, however they focuse only on system's aspects and do not provide language flexibility. The security policy, needed to control the extensibility, although it is still a policy, and therefore should be extensible, is a static design choice that can not be changed. We argue that different application domains will probably have different security requirements and semantic, hence it is the responsability of (i) the administrator to customize inter-*VMLets* security rules; (ii) the *VMLets* to define security rules for a given application domain.

To address emerging application domains work is being done on embedded operating systems, as *MultOS* [14], *μClinux* [20] or SUN's *KVM* [12]. Each of those environments, while being well dedicated to emerging computing, are still rigid, closed and poorly interoperable.

Another research domain our work can be compared to is language interoperability. The objective is to support multiple language, and to allow them to interoperate, in a single execution environment. The *Universal Virtual Machine* [10] project from IBM aims at executing both *Java*, *Smalltalk* and *Visual Basic* applications. Nevertheless, it still only a rigid extension to an existing (*Smalltalk*) virtual machine (that understand three language instead of one): while allowing the support for three different language, it is neither reflexive nor extensible.

Microsoft *.Net* [15] is another project from this research domain. Microsoft framework aims at responding to the need of every possible user/application. Thus, it applies a "one-size-fit-all" approach which is known to (i) poorly face the evolution of applications requirements and/or semantics; (ii) penalize performances; (iii) be closed, and thus to impose artificial constraints to developpers. At the opposite, we want to give any user/application the ability to adapt the execution environment to its requirements and/or semantics, which result in a (i) better match with applications needs; (ii) more evolutive solution, as each emerging application domains will not implie an update of the framework; (iii) more performant execution environment, as an application will never suffer from a "one-size-feet-all" services like in traditionnal operating systems.

7 Conclusions and Perspectives

This paper presented our approach to dynamic flexibility and interoperability, based on a meta execution environment. The *RVM* and the *YNVM* have shown to be efficient for writting execution environment (few hundreds of line each) in two different contexts: active networks and flexible web caching. The resulting *VMLets* are small compared to traditionnal implementations. The *YNVM* have demonstrated that we can come close to having the best of several worlds: flexibility, dynamicity, simplicity and performances. It demonstrates that reconfigurability can be simple, dynamic and have good performances.

With the *VVM* projects we continue to investigate a systematic approach for building flexible, adaptable and interoperable execution environments, to free applications from the artificial limitations on reconfiguration imposed by programming environments.

The *YNVM* has been ported on bare hardware (PowerPC) and thus provides an environment for building dynamically dedicated and flexible operating systems. This gives applications an opportunity of executing "standalone", avoiding the need for a traditionnal operating system and its associated overheads and/or predefined abstractions.

Concerning active networks, work is being done on a generalisation of existing protocols, to achieve *Active Active Networks*. In *AAN*, the active protocols and the deployment protocols are dynamically instantiated on the machines.

The *Virtual Virtual Machine* may look as an ambitious project, but it seems to be highly relevant to address many current and upcoming topics like set-top-boxes, active networks, mobile telephony and embedded systems, to name but a few.

References

1. O. Aubert, A. Beugnard, *Towards a Fine-Grained Adaptivity in Web Caches*, in Proceedings of the 4th International Web Caching Workshop, April 1999.
   `http://www.ircache.net/Cache/Workshop99/Papers/aubert-0.ps.gz`
2. J. Fritz Barnes and R. Pandey *CacheL: Language Support for Customizable Caching Policies*, in Proceedings of the 4th International Web Caching Workshop, April 1999.
   `http://www.ircache.net/Cache/Workshop99/Papers/barnes-final.ps.gz`
3. E. Casalicchio and M. Colajanni *Scalable Web Cluster with Static and Dynamic Contents*, in Proceedings of IEEE International Conference on Cluster Computing (CLUSTER 2000), Chemnitz, Germany, December 2000.
4. M.F. Kaashoek, D.R. Engler, J. O'Toole, *Exokernel: an operating system architecture for application-level ressource management* Proceedings of the 15th ACM Symposium on Operating System Principles, Copper Mountain, Colorado, December 1995.
5. B. Folliot, *The Virtual Virtual Machine Project*, Proccedings of IFIP Symposium on Computer Architecture and High Performance Computing, Sao Paulo, Brasil,October 2000.
6. B. Folliot, I. Piumarta and F. Ricardi, *A Dynamically Configurable, Multi-Language Execution Platform* SIGOPS European Workshop 1998.
7. B. Folliot, I. Piumarta, L. Seinturier, C. Baillarguet and C. Khoury, *Highly Configurable Operating Systems: The VVM Approach*, in ECOOP'2000 Workshop on Object Orientation and Operating Systems, Cannes, France, June 2000.
8. E. Gamma and al. *Design Patterns: Elements of Reusable Object-Oriented Software*, Addison-Wesley, 1994.
9. M. Hicks and al. *PLAN: A Packet Language for Active Networks*, in Proceedings of the International Conference on Functional Programming, 1998.
10. IBM plans cross-platform competitor to Java, InfoWorld Electronic, April 1997.
11. `http://www.javacard.org`
12. `http://www.java.sun.com/products/cldc/wp/`

13. G.Muller, L.Porto Barreto, S.Gulwani, A.Trachandani, D.Gupta, D.Sanghi, *WebCaL: A Domain Specific Language for Web Caching*, in 5th International Web Caching and Content Delivery Workshop, 1999.
14. http://www.multos.com
15. http://www.microsoft.com/net/
16. S. Patarin and M. Makpangou, *Pandora: a Flexible Network Monitoring Platform* Proceedings of the USENIX 2000 Annual Technical Conference, San Diego, June 2000.
17. M. Seltzer, *The World Wide Web: Issues and Challenges* , Presented at IBM Almaden, July 1996.
18. B. Bershad, S. Savage, P. Pardyack, E. Gun Sirer, D. Becker, M. Fiuczynski, C. Chambers and S. Eggers, *Extensibility, Safety and Performance in the SPIN Operating System* Proceedings of the 15th ACM Symposium on Operating System Principles, Copper Mountain, Colorado, December 1995.
19. http://www.squid-cache.org/
20. http://www.uclinux.org/
21. D.Wetherall, J. Guttag, D. Tennenhouse. *ANTS: A Toolkit for Building and Dynamically Deploying Network Protocol*, in Proceedings of IEEE OPENARCH'98, San Fransisco, USA, April 1998.
22. S. Michel, K. Nguyen, A. Rosenstein, L. Zhang, S. Floyd and V. Jacobson, *Adaptive Web Caching: towards a new global caching architecture*, Computer Networks and ISDN Systems, 30(22-23):2169-2177, November 1998.

Programming Models for Cluster Computing

Dan Grigoraş

Computer Science Department
University College Cork
Cork, Ireland
d.grigoras@cs.ucc.ie

Abstract. This paper reviews the current programming models for clusters. While client-server continues to be by far the dominant model, parallel and peer-to-peer computing are gaining importance. Parallel cluster computing offers the means of achieving high performance at a low cost. Peer-to-peer is an expression of the changing features of cluster/grids, mobility and heterogeneity being among the most important. All models have merits but none can cover all aspects of interest, making the topic of cluster computing model an open issue.

1   Introduction

Cluster computing is a very promising trend in computer science and technology, as it is based on existing hardware that can deliver better performance. Taking notice of the low use of networks' PCs and workstations across all organizations, and of the large aggregate quantities of computing resources, any investment in a parallel system becomes questionable. The cost/performance ratio of networks of computers is very competitive to supercomputers, making them very attractive, and any upgrade of the network components transforms in an upgrade of the system as an ensemble, postponing the replacement decisions [1-3]. This is in contrast to parallel systems characterized by a short life time. By running components of a cluster management software (CMS), any networked computers can be used as a cluster and execute demanding parallel jobs. Moreover, Internet allows us now to consider the possibility of theoretical infinite resource computer – the global grid [4].

While the academic community is investigating more the potential of networks for parallel computing, companies are more interested in features like availability and fault tolerance. However, recently, many companies showed interest in cluster/grid high performance computing that increases their competitiveness, and major software providers are working towards meeting their demands [5-9].

The merge of networking and parallel technologies raises the natural question of the computing model appropriate for cluster computing. There is not a simple answer so far, as several models coexist, in different flavors, and none proves to be the right one, in all respects.

The current dominant computing model for the networks is client-server [10]. Basically, this corresponds to sequential execution. There is only one running thread of the application at a time, irrespective of the placement of the client and server on

D. Grigoras et al. (Eds.): IWCC 2001, LNCS 2326, pp. 26–35, 2002.

separate machines. Even if the server is multi-threaded and the host is a multi-processor computer, the client still waits the server's results. The client and the server have different roles and their relationship is not symmetric.

The use of multiple computers as a single resource offers, in a natural way, opportunities for parallel execution. While, at the beginning, the message-passing paradigm was undisputable, the extended acquisition of multiple-processors servers (SMP) re-ignited the dispute among message passing and shared-memory adepts.

Peer-to-peer computing is a different approach as all computers are peers, and if there exist a server, its function is just to manage directories and redirect initial messages among peers. All the partners play the same roles, and any host in the net can create dynamically a cluster to solve one demanding problem. There are many advantages, like a higher tolerance to faults, and a more effective answer to network traffic or computers overload problems.

In section 2, we will consider the main features of clusters and grids that have to be considered by programmers. Section 3 is a review of the current cluster computing models, followed by a comparative analysis in section 4. The paper ends with conclusions.

2 Features of the Cluster Architecture

Clusters and grids are networked computers managed as a single resource. In this respect, they can be considered as a multi-computer parallel architecture that operates under specific circumstances. Any networked computer that runs components of the CMS on top of its operating system is a true or potential member of one or several cluster(s). It is visible in the cluster, it offers resources and services, and it can ask for resources or services. It runs local and remote tasks, and it is supposed to provide not only resources and services, but performance too. This is an important aspect, as the availability does not transform automatically in performance.

2.1 Cluster Concepts

There are in use several terms for the same architecture, like networks of workstations (NOW), clusters, and grids. We are speaking of cluster, if the system is of relative low size, which however may consist of up to thousands of CPUs, and the grid, when huge trans-continental or even inter-continental computing resources are working together. The concept of grid, similar to power grids, involves also people and supplementary technical or documentary resources.

CMS has a hierarchical structure, of the client-server type, where the manager plays the top role. It registers and monitors all resources, and receives jobs for execution. When a new job is received, the manager tries to match its requirements, assign resources and start execution. When the execution is finished, the computing resources are released. The same computers can belong to different clusters or grids, simultaneously, and multiple jobs can run within each cluster.

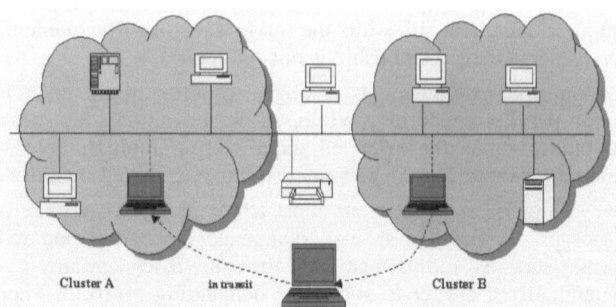

Fig. 1. Two clusters, A and B are created on a local network. Notice the heterogeneity of the network and the possibility to connect mobile devices.

Clusters can be classified according to different parameters that take into account the components source (commodity or not), the target applications, level of security, sharing policies, and the geographic distribution. Currently, more important aspects are concerned with homogeneity/heterogeneity, and mobility.

Regarding the hardware resources, the node computer can be single CPU or multiple CPUs. In both cases, each CPU is running multiple tasks, either local or remote.

At the system level, there are new features with a high impact on both administration of resources and user access and use. The most important are the heterogeneity, the mobility and the dynamic change of the configuration. Users are mobile and they need to be provided with access to resources and services wherever they log in, and a uniform view of their working environment. Devices are mobile too and need to connect to points of presence. The support for mobility requires an advanced infrastructure that integrates suitable protocols, mechanisms and tools.

2.2 Supporting Services

Cluster and grid technologies build most of their capabilities on existing network protocols and services [11].

2.2.1 Discovery and Addressing Resources and Services

Any individual entity of a distributed system is granted a name that uniquely identifies it. Examples of such entities are users, computers and services. Naming services associate names with entities, allowing them to be found on that base. There are many naming services, such as DNS (Domain Name System). This is the Internet's naming service that converts names to IP (Internet Protocol) addresses, using a predefined hierarchical naming scheme. The DNS names' syntax reflects the administrative boundaries. COS Naming (Common Object Services) is the naming service for CORBA applications, that allows applications to store and access references to CORBA objects.

The naming and discovery services have to keep pace with the rapid changes of networking. From simple schemes, where scalability and flexibility were of no concern, they evolved towards associative and mobile agents solutions. There are logically centralized solutions, where global directories store addressing information for existing resources, and de-centralized ones, where interrogating local managers identifies resources [12].

2.2.2 Communication and Coordination among Entities

Communication plays a major role in distributed computing. It should be reliable and fast. Most systems use Internet TCP/IP or UDP/IP protocols, although faster protocols like VIA (Virtual Interface Architecture), Active Messages or Fast Messages are available.

Coordination models have been extensively studied in the context of distributed systems [13-14].

In the frame of mobility, the coordination strategy can be one of the following: client-server, meeting oriented, blackboard, and Linda-like [15]. The client-server coordination is effective for sharing information in a local execution environment. The meeting coordination introduces the concept of meeting points, where mobile components can interact. However, a meeting point requires a strict temporal coupling that cannot be guaranteed in all cases. Blackboards eliminate the temporal condition, by defining repositories for resources and services information and a place to store messages. Associative blackboards implement a coordination model similar to Linda. Information is stored in the form of tuples and retrieved in an associative way through a pattern-matching mechanism.

For example, there will be an effective protocol for detection of termination. If one component of the distributed application runs infinitely, or it does not respond, it compromises the whole execution. Obviously, there should be a mechanism to prevent such situations or to take appropriate measures of fault detection and recovery.

2.2.3 Security

Free and open access to computing resources and services is rarely acceptable. Distributed systems are successful in the measure in which they provide a reasonable level of protection to undesirable intruders.

3 Programming Models

Networks were designed on the assumption that communication is reliable and secure, making possible the share of resources and services. Clients address servers, running on powerful or unique computing resources. Although this model is by far the dominant distributed computing model, different patterns of execution or users' new goals suggest other approaches.

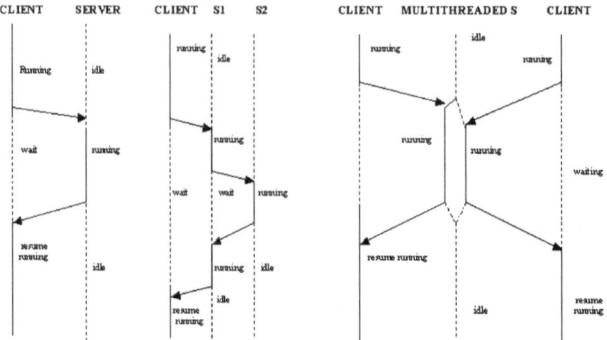

Fig. 2. A client addresses the server and waits the result. The server can become a client for another server. Multithreaded servers process multiple calls simultaneously.

3.1 The Client-Server Paradigm

The client-server paradigm is easy to understand and use, as it complies to the von Neumann sequential style of instruction execution. The application is composed of clients and servers. Whenever a client needs a service, it addresses the server that can provide that service. In most cases it waits results from server, or at least a confirmation that the service was executed successfully. The server itself can be a client for another server, and a concurrent server may process multiple requests simultaneously [16].

This model has several advantages, besides its simplicity, most important being the natural way of application structuring and the possibility to reuse common services.

At the beginning, client-server programming with sockets was difficult and error-prone. To avoid lower level programming issues, the remote procedure call (RPC) abstraction was introduced [17]. The client addresses now the server service as a call to the (remote) procedure.

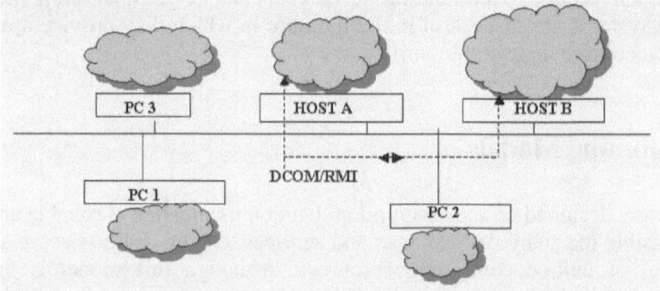

Fig. 3. The component object model increases the flexibility and reusability of client-server applications.

Due to its merits of well structuring the application and reusability, the component object model was ported to networks. Technologies like Microsoft COM/DCOM and Sun Java RMI, and Java Beans allow network-based components to interact in a client-server manner. For interoperability, the Object Management Group's common object request broker architecture (CORBA) was introduced as a middleware standard. Studies like [18] analyze the performance of CORBA-based client-server architectures, showing the role of distributed application workload.

3.2 Parallel Computing Models

Parallel programming, in the form it is ported from parallel computers, has to accommodate possible different co-existing parallel architectures. It does not take into account the main features of clusters, like heterogeneity, unpredictable communication latencies and the interference among local and remote jobs. Parallel computing assumes a homogeneous configuration, a dedicated network defined by predictable communication latencies and a single operating system that manages the resources, users and tasks. On the contrary, non-dedicated clusters are usually heterogeneous, use non-dedicated networks with unpredictable latencies and each node runs its operating system. There is a danger in transferring the difficulties of parallel computers programming to clusters and grids. For users, portability and scalability issues are of major concern.

In the message-passing programming model, a job consists of one or more processes that communicate by calling library routines to send and receive messages to other processes. Communication is one-to-one or collective. In most PVM [19] and MPI [20] implementations, a fixed set of processes is created at program initialization, and one process is assigned per processor. As these processes may execute different programs, the parallel computing model is sometimes referred to as multiple program multiple data (MPMD) to distinguish it from the SPMD model in which every processor   executes the same sequence of instructions.

The shared memory paradigm can be used with SMP servers, or single CPU networked computers. In the former case, the outer/coarser level of parallelism is implemented by message passing, in the latter a global virtual address space is defined on top of distributed nodes, giving the illusion of a global shared memory. There is a third cluster architecture, where some powerful servers have SMP architecture, but most nodes are single CPU computers, making even more difficult programming parallel applications. In this case, some nodes will execute shared-memory code, OpenMP being the library of choice, while others will execute message-passing code [21]. OpenMP API implements the fork-join model of parallel execution that can be associated with C/C++ and Fortran programming languages [22]. An OpenMP program begins execution as a single thread called the master thread. It implements synchronization mechanisms like barrier and lock. OpenMP is usually used to parallelize loops, respecting the SPMD model.

If the cluster has a star topology, where each node is a SMP, domain decomposition is the strategy for assigning work to each node. Within each sub-domain, fine grain parallelism is exploited, as several processors share a global memory space.

A user friendlier development consists of a graphic user interface and tools to automate the process of application design, execution and debug. All those components are considered to form the basis of visual parallel languages [23]. Three programming techniques are investigated, the skeleton or template, the dataflow, and process based. The skeleton approach offers the user a set of most common code components that can be glued together [24]. However, it is impossible to have a full set for all applications, and therefore the designer will still be forced to write code that should integrate with existing one. A distributed application can be modeled as a coarse-grain graph, where nodes can be from as simple as single instructions to other (condensed) graphs [25]. The computation paradigm is based in this case on the dataflow concept. The process based model uses graphs too, but now the nodes are processes. Within the code of each process, there exist communications with other processes, defined as either calls to message passing libraries, or other communication structures.

3.3 Peer-to-Peer Computing

Peer-to-peer computing (P2P) is a new approach [26]. Computers share resources as computing cycles, storage or files, via networks. For example, SETI@home uses idle Internet connected computers to run an application that analyze radio-telescope data as part of the SETI (Search for Extraterrestrial Intelligence) project of California University. Peers communicate with one another to distribute tasks and return results. It is very appealing as there is no hierarchy and all participants have the same functionality. Many applications can benefit on these properties, like Napster did. Some of them use a central server for storing and managing directories, others use direct communication. For example, Gnutella has no server.

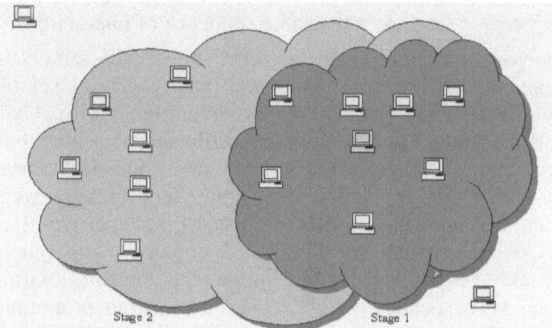

Fig. 4. When the peer-to-peer model is chosen, a computer (initiator) can create dynamically a cluster for executing the distributed application.

A user registers to a Gnutella host, which then spreads the user's address and content to other machines, that continue the process [27]. This information spreading can be modeled as a wave that affects the neighborhood of the initiator.

Peer-to-peer systems offer the possibilities for exploiting space locality, and to avoid single points of failure [28]. However, the core operation is efficient location of data and services. The JXTA project [29] aims at creating software and system primitives commonly used by all peer-to-peer systems (interoperability), offer platform independence and ubiquity.

4 Comparative Analyses of Existing Models

In order to achieve the aims of cost-effectiveness in respect to both performance and easy of use, clusters have to be as simple to use as personal computers [30]. In other words, seamless access to cluster resources is a key issue.

First of all, we have to define the set of parameters that take into account both ease of use and performance. In our list, three parameters deal with the former, and four with the latter.

The complexity of programming according to one of the three cluster computing models is a matter that directly affects the number of users. The fact that client-server has such a huge dominancy can be explained by its simplicity, especially in the RPC flavor. Programming parallel applications was difficult even in the case of homogeneous parallel systems. Unless users are provided with supporting tools that increase the level of abstraction, the same resistance will be encountered as in traditional parallel computing. Peer-to-peer is simpler as it has a dynamic evolution: resources and services are collected when they are needed and from the vicinity of the requestor.

Concerning the supporting services, client-server is most advanced, parallel and peer-to-peer on clusters being in the research phase. On the contrary, the highest performance and scalability can be achieved by parallel and peer-to-peer computing.

Mobility associated with heterogeneity is a complex issue. Users and devices will be more and more mobile, and will request connection everywhere.

Network faults occur permanently, and there is no way of eliminating them. However, designers can provide means for reducing faults frequency and a fast recovery. Parallel and peer-to-peer seem to offer better chances of fault tolerance as multiple resources are involved and new configurations can be created easily.

Table 1. A set of parameters to discern among cluster computing models.

Parameter	Client-server	Parallel	Peer-to-peer
Complexity	Low	High	Low
Support services	Exist	Scarce	No
Potential for high performance	Low	High	High
Scalability	Low	High	High
Mobility	No	High	High
Fault tolerance	Low	High	High
Security	High	High	Low

When network resources and services are made available outside the organization, unlawful intruders can be expected. There is an important on-going research effort towards increasing the security, but full security is not a feasible goal. However, due to its stability and established techniques, the client-server model offers more security than parallel and peer-to-peer computing.

Table 1 presents the set of parameters we chose and the corresponding values for existing cluster computing models.

5 Conclusions

Currently, several computing models coexist on clusters and grids, everyone having advantages and disadvantages. Although, the client-server model is the most popular and will continue to dominate, it will lose competition in the field of high performance computing, where parallel computing models are the appropriate solution. However, designing correct parallel applications is not easy, and current networks induce new degrees of complexity because of communication unpredictability, devices heterogeneity and mobility. A simpler approach that conserves the parallel execution potential is the peer-to-peer model.

It is unlikely to witness very soon the emergence of a specific cluster computing model, but many features of existing models will join in creating effective cluster computing environments.

References

1. Buyya, R. (Ed.): High Performance Cluster Computing: Architectures and Systems, Volume 1, Prentice Hall, 1999.
2. Buyya, R. (Ed.): High Performance Cluster Computing: Programming and Applications, Volume 2, Prentice Hall, 1999.
3. Buyya, R., Baker, M. (Eds.): Grid Computing, Springer Verlag, 2000.
4. Foster, I., Kesselman, C.: The Grid: Blueprint for a New Computing Infrastructure, Morgan Kaufmann Publishers, 1999.
5. http://www.sun.com/grid
6. http://www.veritas.com
7. http://www.platform.com
8. http://www.ibm.com
9. http://www.rainfinity.com
10. Coulouris, G., Dollimore, J., Kindberg, T.: Distributed Systems. Concepts and Design, Addison-Wesley, 2000.
11. Cluster Computing White Paper, http://www.dcs.port.ac.uk/~mab/tfcc/WhitePaper/final-paper.pdf, 2000.
12. Grigoras, D.: Discovery of Resources for Distributed Application Execution in Dynamic Clusters, UCC TR-02-02, February 2002.
13. Adler, R.M.: Distributed Coordination Models for Client-Server Computing, IEEE Computer, vol. 29, no.4, April 1995, p.14-22.
14. Gelernter, D., Carriero, N.: Coordination Languages and their Significance, Comm. ACM, vol.35, no.2, February 1992, p.96-107.

15. Cabri, G., Leonardi, L., Zambonelli, F.: MARS: A Programmable Coordination Architecture for Mobile Agents, IEEE Internet Computing, July-August 2000, p.26-35.
16. Brown, C: Unix Distributed Programming, Prentice Hall, 1994.
17. Bloomer, J.: Power Programming with RPC, O'Reilly and Associates, Inc.
18. Abdul-Ftah, I., Majumdar, S.: Performance of CORBA-Based Client-Server Architectures, IEEE Transactions on Parallel and Distributed Systems, vol.13, no.2, February 2002, p. 111–127.
19. http://www.epm.ornl.gov/pvm/
20. http://www-unix.mcs.anl.gov/mpi/
21. Giraud, L: Combining Shared and Distributed Memory Programming Models on Cluster of Symmetric Multiprocessors: Some Basic Promising Experiments, CERFACS Tech. Rep WN/PA/01/19.
22. http://www.openmp.org
23. Cunha, J.C., Kacsuk, P., Winter, S.C. (Eds): Parallel Program Development for Cluster Computing. Methodology, Tools and Integrated Environments, Nova Science Publishers Inc., 2001.
24. Schaeffer, J., Szafron, D., Lobe, G., Parsons, I.: The Enterprise Model for Developing Distributed Applications, IEEE Parallel and Distributed Technology, vol.1, no.3, 1993, p.85-96.
25. Morrison, J.P.: Condensed Graphs: Unifying Availability-Driven, Coercion-Driven and Control-Driven Computing, T.U. Eindhoven, 1996.
26. Clark, D.: Face-to-Face with Peer-to-Peer Networking, IEEE Computer, January 2001, p. 18 – 21.
27. Ripeanu, M., Iamnitchi, A., Foster, I.: Mapping the Gnutella Network, IEEE Internet Computing, January-February 2002, p. 50-57.
28. Morisson, J.P., Power, K.: Compeer: Peer-to-Peer Applications on a Peer-to-Peer DCOM Architecture.
29. Gong, L.: JXTA: A Network Programming Environment, IEEE Internet Computing, May-June 2001, p. 88-95.
30. Savage, J.E.: Models of Computation. Exploring the Power of Computing, Addison-Wesley, 1998.
31. Fan, C.C., Bruck, J.: The Raincore API for Clusters of Networking Elements, IEEE Computer, September-October 2001, p.70–76.

About Design and Efficiency of Distributed Programming: Some Algorithmic Aspects

Bernard Toursel

University of Sciences and Technologies of Lille
Ecole Universitaire d'Ingénieurs de Lille
Laboratoire d'Informatique Fondamentale de Lille
(L.I.F.L.) ESA CNRS 8022
59655 Villeneuve d'Ascq cedex France
toursel@lifl.fr

Abstract. This paper summarizes a talk at the NATO ARW on distributed computing. It deals with some algorithmic aspects when programming with this paradigm, related to the lack of methodologies and tools useful to design distributed programs efficient, independent of the environment and able to automatically adapt to the evolutions of the program execution and of the platform characteristics.

1 Introduction

This talk deals with some algorithmic aspects related to the design and the efficiency of distributed programming. It is not an exhaustive analysis but only some reflections about problems met by programmers when designing distributed programs and researching an efficient execution. These observations are made in the following context:

- we focus on a cluster computing environment with costly communications in a peer to peer approach and not in a SMP or CC-NUMA parallel paradigm,
- we are not considering regular problems allowing some partial or total automatic parallelisation,
- we are interested by the distributed execution of dynamic and irregular problems, i.e. programs the execution of which are unpredictable.

With these paradigms, we comment some algorithmic aspects related to both the design of distributed programs (DPs) and their efficient execution. The first question is what is a good distributed algorithm ? Following, we present some considerations about the independence of the execution platform and then about data distribution and sharing. The next section deals with synchronous versus asynchronous DPs and the last two are concerned with the choice of the parallelism degree and the possibilities offered by speculative works and hybridation in DPs.

D. Grigoras et al. (Eds.): IWCC 2001, LNCS 2326, pp. 36-46, 2002.

2   Sequential /Distributed Programs

A sequential algorithm execution may be viewed as a repetition of steps. In an efficient sequential algorithm, the next step uses the maximum of the information elaborated by the previous one. The more it can use the previous and existing information, the less work it has to run and the more efficient it is.

We wonder now how this property of a maximal use of data can be preserved when we try to parallelise the sequential algorithm.

2.1   Information, Synchronization, and Communications

When transforming a sequential algorithm into a distributed one, we try to preserve the property of a maximal use of data from step to step. The first attempt is to transform a sequential algorithm into a parallel one by changing each step into a parallel step (it is sometimes impossible when neither data nor work can be split into distinct parts). If we wish that the next step uses the maximum of information issued from the previous one, we need to build a global information gathering the partial result of each parallel part of the previous step (see fig. 1- a and b). This implies a synchronization phase between each step and a lot of communications for both global information calculus and broadcasting the global information. In an ideal distributed algorithm, each parallel branch would be independent: locally the successive steps might run with only local information. In this case, there is no need of communications for global information building and broadcasting. However it appears that at one step less information is available for each branch and this leads to a loss of efficiency of the algorithm. Usually, it is necessary to inform each parallel branch with other information issued from previous branches, which needs some communications and synchronization tools (see fig. 1 - c).

2.2   An Example: A Genetic Algorithm

In order to illustrate this point, let us consider an example, the transformation of a sequential genetic algorithm into a distributed one. The principle of a classical genetic algorithm is to transform a population P whose elements are possible solutions of the problem to obtain a good (best) solution ; the transformation of the population uses two different operations: the cross over operation (which transforms 2 parents into 2 children) and the mutation operation (to enlarge the fields of solutions). At each step, the quality of the best found solution is appreciated.

In a naive parallelisation, the population is fragmented and distributed: the cross over and mutation operations operate with individuals of the population which are not necessary in the same location. This induces first, communications and waiting delays during each step execution and   secondly, a global phase for the exchanges of best solutions found in each parallel branch.

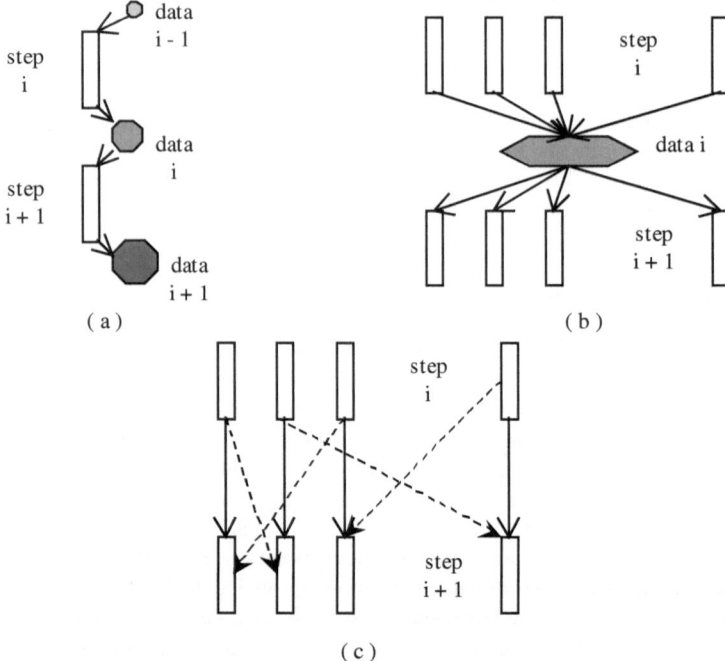

Fig. 1. Sequential algorithm (a), synchronous parallel algorithms (b) and distributed algorithm (c)

In a less naive approach, we can restraint the operations between individuals located in the same processor. The global phase for exchanging the best found solutions is still necessary and may be implemented in a synchronous or asynchronous way. A common solution is the island model of the distributed genetic algorithm: Each site holds a sub-population on which are repeated local transformations and from time to time, the sub-populations exchange their best found solution. By this way, the sub-population can evolve with a minimum of communications, but each local work is poorer and less efficient since the sub-population is smaller and there is no global information between the successive steps. This remark is general when each local work uses a poorer information ; in a general way, when the sequential algorithm is known to converge to a convenient solution, it is not a priori assured that the parallel form, which is often a new algorithm, has a similar property (in the present example this is assured).

2.3 About the Parallelisation of Sequential Algorithms

From the previous considerations, we can make the following first remark:

Remark 1.
- the parallelisation of a sequential program often leads to inefficient distributed programs. A parallel design is required which needs some conceptual efforts by the programmer and particular parameters sometimes difficult to define,
- it is not assured that the parallel adaptation of a sequential algorithm maintains the convergence to the solution as the sequential program (in many situations, it is truly a new algorithm and the comparison with the sequential program is not easy).

3 Independence from the Execution Platform

An ideal distributed program (DP) might be designed in a total independence of the execution platform used. This independence is related to different aspects: the available network, the system and middleware used, the programming environment.

We can distinguish three levels of networks for meta-computing :

- High performance clusters: these clusters are dedicated clusters with fast networks (SCI, Myrinet...) and SSI (Single System Image) features.
- Standard clusters: connecting some tens of PC and workstations with conventional Ethernet connection,
- Large scale network: internet based network of local clusters with very heterogeneous systems and geographical dispersion.

It is difficult to design efficient DP independently of these cluster levels which present distinct performances which affects programming (granularity and degree of parallelism, cost of synchronization, programming style...).

The programmer as to know the possibilities offered at the software level too: it is quite different to be in a Java/RMI environment, in a message passing approach using MPI tools or using Corba component for example. The middleware features are also very important (Distributed Shared memory -DSM- context, consistency control of duplicated shared data, fault tolerance mechanism, load balancing including task migration, cluster administration...). If some facilities are not included in the available environment, the programmer has to consider them while designing his program.

Remark 2. In spite of the desire to design general DP, independent from the execution platform, we have to admit that the DP design, the programmer effort for DP, the DP efficiency are yet constrained by the limits of the environment used, both the hardware environment, the software environment and the programming environment.

4   Data Distribution and Sharing

The use of cluster computing is the result of two evolutions: the availability of a cheap installed platform and the necessity of computing big programs. These big programs associate now both intensive calculus and big amount of data. Relating to programs running big amount of data, we can distinguish two kinds of programs:
- programs such as the amount of work is depending on the size of *initial* data (depending on the size of problem or the size of external data bases),
- programs such as the amount of work is *unpredictable*, i.e. internal data are generated by the program execution

In the both situations two main problems appear:
- fragmentation and distribution of the data (both initially and dynamically),
- data sharing, which is a conventional problem in an execution context without shared memory.

4.1   Fragmentation and Distribution of Data

In a common situation the amount of work grows with the size of data and the problem of the fragmentation and distribution of data is a major question for an efficient execution.

In the first context of work function of the initial data size (as in centralized or distributed database), we are in the classical case of data parallelism where three questions are to be asked in order to generate an efficient execution:
- how to split the data structures into fragments: by the programmer (following what methodology) or automatically (with what tools and constraints? using some programmer's annotations ?)
- how to distribute the data fragments: usually by the programmer at the beginning or more and more automatically now, using some information about the load of processors,
- is the data distribution definitive or is a re-distribution needed for each step of calculus? Generally such a re-distribution is costly in terms of synchronization and communications.

In the second situation, the amount of work to run is unpredictable because either we are in the case of a slow convergence to the result, generally without need of data re-distribution, or internal data are generated by the program execution. This last case appears when the domain to explore to elaborate the solution is growing (for example in optimization problems) ; it is generally a hard problem because we have to make dynamically a re-distribution of the data set (partially or totally) for each step.

In both cases, we note a lack of methods and methodology to help the programmer for data fragmentation and for the problem of the transparent distribution of fragments, a lot of researches with different paradigms and with various and contrasted results.

4.2 Data Sharing

The question of data sharing is a conventional problem in systems without shared memory. Two approaches are mainly followed: without data duplication or with data duplication. Without data duplication, it is generally an easy solution but with costly communications and with some problems of bottleneck to access shared data. Data duplication leads to the well known data consistency problem with the choice between strong (five levels) or weak (some levels) consistency models and the definitions of thresholds and update frequencies to maintain data consistency.

4.3 About Data Distribution and Sharing

Concerning the problems related to data fragmentation, distribution and sharing, we have the following remark:

Remark 3. The whole execution of a distributed program is strongly dependent of the fragmentation, distribution and sharing mode. However we can note:
- a lack of methodologies to help the programmer to DP design, particularly of methods useful for dynamic data fragmentation,
- many researches lead now to various results for data or objects distribution, taking into account the power and load of processors or the dynamic relations between objects, depending on the execution platform used,
- a major problem is the need and the frequency of dynamic data re-distribution. An important effort has to be done when designing a DP to minimize this fact and to optimize the communications and synchronization.

5   Synchronous /Asynchronous DP

5.1 Introducing Asynchronism

The use of asynchronism is one of the more efficient tool to exhibit parallelism: it allows to overlap the communication time by calculus and avoids staying idle waiting for some synchronization or remote result. The resort to asynchronism leads to some questions: is this asynchronism possible in any case, where may be the difficulties for asynchronism use?

Usually, a programmer proceeds in two phases to design a DP: he first designs his DP with synchronous steps ; then, he tries to asynchronize the synchronous steps. The transformation of a program composed of successive synchronous steps into a program with asynchronous steps is illustrated in figure 2.

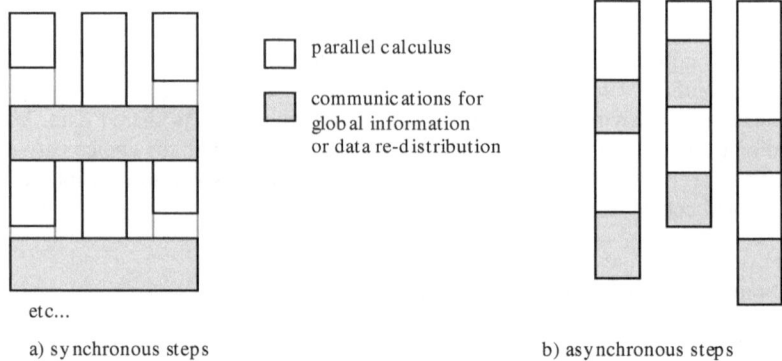

etc...

a) synchronous steps   b) asynchronous steps

Fig. 2. Synchronous and asynchronous DPs

5.2 An Example: Asynchronous Data Distribution

The following example shows how a synchronous approach for a DP may be transformed into first an asynchronous form and secondly into a multi-threaded pipe-lined program. We consider in this example the treatment of data provided by a single source (the example may be extended to more complex situations with multiple distributed sources).

The first design is shown in fig 3. The initial data base is read from a disk, fragmented depending on a particular criteria and stored on the disk. In a second phase, knowing the size of each fragment, a best distribution can be calculated and the fragments are distributed for treatment.

A first amelioration is to try to distribute the fragmentation phase (fig. 4). In such an approach, each part of the data base may be locally fragmented in a parallel way, but a distribution phase is then necessary, preceded by a synchronization phase needed to calculate the global information (i.e. size of fragments) useful to elaborate the optimal fragment distribution.

In the previous approach, the global program is slowed down both by the initial distribution of the data base and the synchronization phase needed for the distribution. We can overcome these points by introducing more asynchronism by using a multi-threaded pipe-lined approach (fig. 5). The fragmentation-distribution phase is transformed into a pipe-line phase using three threads : the first one (*block read thread*) reads successive data blocks from the disk ; each block is then fragmented (by a *block fragmentation thread*) and as soon as a fragment block is full, it is sent to a processor (*block distribution thread*). This allows to begin earlier the parallel calculus on the

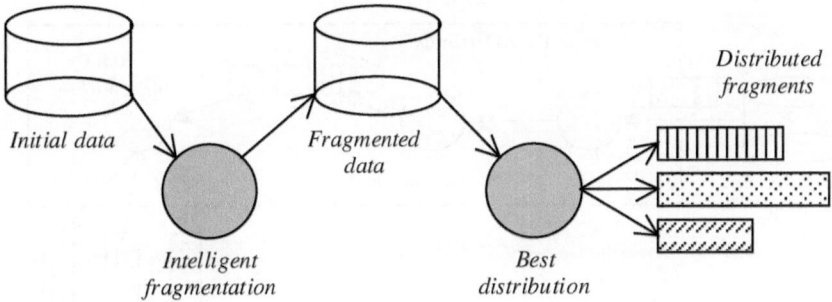

Fig. 3. A synchronous data distribution

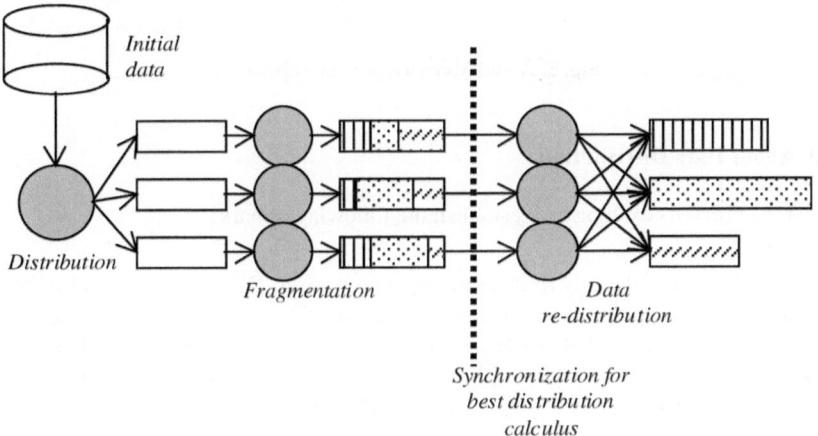

Fig. 4. Parallel fragmentation and distribution

blocks of the different fragments (no idle waiting time) but a good distribution of fragments is not assured as we don't know the fragment sizes when the distribution begins.

This example illustrates the two conflicting aims: in one hand, to obtain the best distribution of fragments allowing a good load distribution but introducing idle time for synchronization and collecting global information ; on the other hand, to begin the treatments without waiting time, as soon as a piece of data is available, but with no assurance for the quality of the distribution.

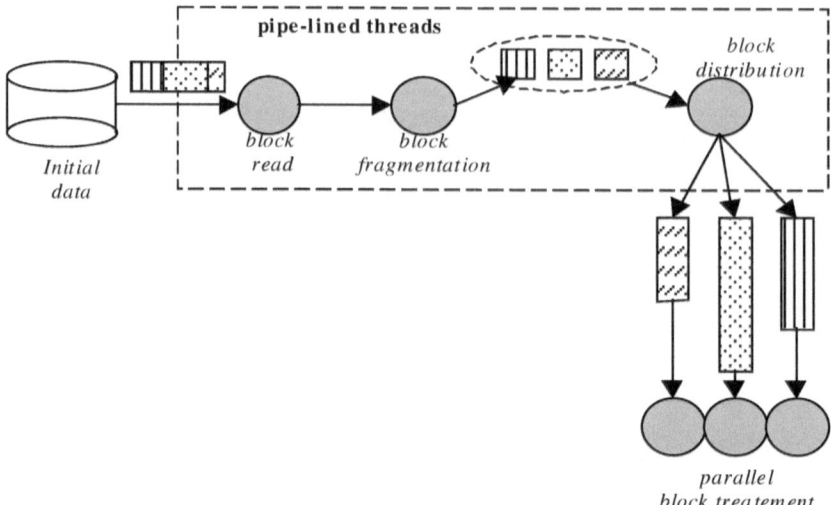

Fig. 5. A multithreaded pipe-line approach

5.3 About Data Distribution

From the previous example, we establish the following remark:

Remark 4. To introduce or to increase asynchronism in DP leads to a more efficient execution (overlapping communications by calculus, no waiting time idle for synchronization barrier) but is less optimal in terms of distribution and load balancing since decisions are taken without global knowledge. Once again, we verify a lack of guide, methodology or tool to help the programmer in designing DP.

6   Degree and Granularity of Parallelism

When designing a DP, the programmer tries to be as general as possible, i.e. the more independent of the execution platform (particularly the number of processors) and the more independent of the initial data set. Such an independence raises two questions: how to design the degree of parallelism and how can this degree be dynamic (determined at the beginning of the execution or modified during the execution). It is well known that too much parallelism is inefficient (too small granularity and too much communications). When the program is very dependent of the data size, it is possible to define parameters at the beginning of the execution in order to adapt the degree of parallelism to the size of data. This adaptation is more difficult during the execution, for example when the data size is growing at run time: to modify the degree of parallelism during the execution may have hard consequences on the calculus of global information and on synchronization operation. When the parallel tasks are independent, this adaptation is easier in some model where a non fixed number of processors can take a piece of data in a general (centralized or distributed) data set.

In a general case, it appears difficult to adapt and modify dynamically the degree of parallelism depending on the size of data and its evolution. The programmer has to foresee the possibilities of expansion, by using adaptive thresholds and some parameters for the degree of parallelism, to calculate global information and run synchronization operations.

Remark 5. As a new remark we can emphasize the absence of general/automatic tools allowing the program to spread automatically by a self adapting of its degree of parallelism.

7   Others Aspects: Speculative Work and Hybridization

Distributed programming allows some techniques which are impossible or not easy to implement in sequential programming:
-   to run *speculative* works, exploiting idle processors,
-   to run simultaneously different cooperative algorithms: *method hybridization.*

Speculative works allows to anticipate some works by using idle processors, for example when the number of processors is greater than the degree of parallelism required by the program. If this work is not useful it is forsook else the result is available in advance.

We focus on hybridization techniques. Hybridization of methods consists in running simultaneously different cooperative methods. To solve a problem, different methods may present distinct advantages and drawbacks depending on the evolution of the program execution. It may be very advantageous to use simultaneously different methods by allocating them distinct CPU time in processors and to implement cooperation between these methods by exchange of partial results. Such an approach implies to be able to appreciate the contribution of each method to the solution progression and to regulate dynamically the part of each algorithm. For example, in an optimization problem, we can hybridize a genetic algorithm (allowing breadth search) with a taboo algorithm (allowing depth search) and to implement a variable and dynamic repartition of each method depending on the moment of the execution (program beginning or not), the contribution of each method and the cluster load and availability.

Remark 6. The use of dynamic hybridization of several methods and the possibility to develop speculative work on idle processor are very promising approaches to improve the resolution of complex problem in distributed programming.

8 Conclusion

This presentation has dealt with the following points:
1. The validity of a parallel algorithm issued from a sequential one,
2. The difficulty to be independent of the execution platform (hardware and software),
3. The lack of tools for an easy and dynamic program fragmentation and the limited tools for the automatic distribution of work,
4. The function and the limits of asynchronism use,
5. The difficulty to manage the degree of parallelism of a program, in a general and dynamic way,
6. The possibilities offered by distributed programming in terms of speculative work and hybridization of methods.

From all the previous remarks, we can emphasize some directions for research work:
-   the design of tools and methodologies to help the programmer to design distributed programs,
-   the development of tools allowing dynamic, adaptive and automatic design of the degree of parallelism required,
-   the necessity to improve and generalize available tools for dynamic and adaptive distribution of work.

A Collaborative Environment for High Performance Computing

Valentin Cristea

Computer Science Department
POLITEHNICA University of Bucharest
valentin@cs.pub.ro

Abstract. The paper presents the main features of **CoLaborator**, a Romanian multi-user collaborative environment for education and research in the field of High Performance Computing (HPC). Its main goals are: to offer wide access to an important research infrastructure (a HPC server) usually very expensive, by the integration of this infrastructure into a collaborative environment and by its efficient shared use; to provide additional services, such as the support for documentation and training in HPC, consultancy, and high qualified specialised services; and to support concurrent learning and research activities by using collaborative techniques. It is a good vehicle for students to learn from the experience of other researchers.

1. Introduction

The recent progress in Information and Communications Technologies (ICT) provide effective support to implement virtual organisations. As Internet and intranets extended over the primitive services (access to distant nodes, e-mail and file transfer), they play an active role in the design, implementation, and management of virtual organisations, having a huge influence on the quality of business processes. In a virtual organisation complementary resources of cooperating entities are integrated to support a particular group endeavour, regardless of the geographically locations of people or resources [1]. Virtual organisations include virtual enterprises, virtual laboratories, virtual environments for design and virtual manufacturing companies, virtual classrooms and virtual universities.

Obviously, ICT had influenced the scientific research, which was based, in a natural way, on the collaboration among people and research teams working together on the same project, in virtual laboratories. These are virtual environments that provide access to information or knowledge repositories (facilitating knowledge sharing, group authoring, etc.) or to remote instruments (coordinating their use). Collaboratories allow people to form joint research teams for the life of a project and then disperse [2].

Several types of collaboratories exist. In data-driven collaboratories, the researchers are able to access common information (or knowledge) repositories, and to concurrently modify them. Examples include the Worm Community System, which has capabilities ranging from sharing data up to an electronic forum, and TeleMed [3],

D. Grigoras et al. (Eds.): IWCC 2001, LNCS 2326, pp. 47–59, 2002.

in which the virtual patient record forms the basis for a collaborative environment with multiple users browsing and editing a patient record simultaneously.

Collaboratories can provide remote access to scientific instruments or to expensive resources. More recent, advances in collaboration oriented and distributed computing systems based on Web technologies led to the development of the Collaborative Web Computing Environment (CWCE) [4] as a new sub-discipline of Computer Supported Cooperative Work (CSCW). Examples include the Tango system [5] based on a Java collabortive environment, PageSpace [6], which supports interactions among distributed software components and active processing, and DAMMP [7], which collects massively computer power by shipping aplets to the clients.

In this paper, we present **CoLaborator**, which is a Web-based collaboration-oriented virtual environment for education and research in HPC. The structure of the paper is as follows. Section 2 shortly presents the history of distributed computing education and research in Romania highlighting the premises for the development of CoLaborator. Section 2 defines the architecture of the environment, which forms the framework of the development of its compex functionality, includes a more detailed description of the services offered by CoLaborator, and gives some information about their design and implementation. In the rest of the paper further development plans and projects are presented.

2. History

The parallel and distributed computing was one of the major subjects for the Computer Science and Engineering Department of "Politehnica" University of Bucharest and other Computer Science and Engineering departments from the main Romanian universities. The improvements to the curricula after '89 added new courses to the domain of parallel and distributed computing (e.g., Parallel architectures, Parallel algorithms, Languages for distributed programming) and new chapters dedicated to this domain in many courses (e.g., Operating systems, Data base, Graphics, Artificial intelligence, and so on). The modifications were carried out according to the recommendations of some highly recognized international professional organizations, such as ACM.

The Computer Science and Engineering Department of "Politehnica" University of Bucharest is one of the most active factors in establishing a national "technical and scientific culture" on the subjects related to parallel and distributed computing. For example the international summer school PARADIS on parallel and distributed systems has been organized each year starting from 1992. Also, the TEMPUS project DISCO (DIStributed COmputing) was developed with the participation of nine universities from Romania and nine universities from Western Europe. As a result of this project, the curricula for short time education related to Parallel and Distributed computing was established and many course support materials have been produced. At the same time, research collaboration with teams from Amsterdam, Torino, Grenoble, Marseilles, Bochum universities was started. The project set up Education Centers on Distributed Processing in Bucharest, Cluj-Napoca, Craiova, Iasi and Timisoara.

Table 1. Specific subjects studied in DISCO

Distributed and High Performance Computing	HPC, HPCC, Internet computing, cluster, grid, metacomputing
Communications and protocols	TCI/IP, Internet, ATM, Fast Ethernet, Giga Ethernet, etc.
Programming models	Shared variables, message passing (MPI), OO computing, client-server, proxy computing, mobile agents
Middleware	Sockets, RPC, RMI, CORBA, DCOM Distributed transaction processing, distributed data access Web applications Security

In 1995, the Numerical Methods Laboratory team of Politehnica University of Bucharest launched the HPC National Initiative in the frame of Romanian Open Systems Event - ROSE '95. Also in 1995, the team did the first feasability study regarding the establishment of first HPC Center in Romania, financed by Romanian Ministry of Research. In 1996, the laboratory installed the first test Ethernet LAN (Beowoolf cathegory distributed system with 16 nodes) running PVM, MPI and latter PETSc.

During 1996-1998, research of parallel and distributed algorithms for electromagnetic devices analysis, design and optimisation (based on distributed simulated annealing and genetic algorithms) were carried on, financed by MCT and MEN. The results were presented at the most important international conferences: IEEE CEFC, Compumag, IGTE etc. and published in IEEE Transaction on Magnetics.

Despite the important results obtained in the domain of parallel and distributed computing by Romanian research and education, very few steps were realised to develop the necessary infrastructure to support these activities. The education on parallel and distributed computing cannot be realized using only simulated environments. There are subjects for which "real" hardware solutions are absolutely necessary.

In 1997, the National Commission for Academic Scientific Research - CNCSU had the initiative to use World Bank funds in order to finance some multi-user research bases (BCUM). The aim of this initiative was to enhance the support for advanced reasearch in key research areas for the future development of Romania and the implication of MSc and PhD students in this research. Therefore, CNCSU open a competition for BCUM project proposals.

The financing organizations established a set of selection criteria for choosing the winning grants: subjects with wide long-term impact, large accessibility to acquired resources, optimal organization of the research teams.

After a rigorous selection, CNCSU approved the financing of the pilot phase of the project **CoLaborator**. The project is realised by a consortium from the Computer Science and Engineering Department of "Politehnica" University of Bucharest, the Numerical Methods Laboratory of "Politehnica" University of Bucharest, the Medicine and Pharmacy University of Cluj-Napoca, University of Galati, and the Technical University of Iasi. The funding of the project devoted to setting up the **CoLaborator** was provided by the Romanian Ministry of Education and Research, and the World Bank.

3. General Presentation of CoLaborator

CoLaborator is a multi-purpose virtual laboratory that supports the education and research in the area of High Performance Computing (HPC).

CoLaborator develops **a new paradigm for intimate collaboration** among computer scientists, computational scientists and researchers from a diversity of domains. For them, CoLaborator provides a coherent system of material, informational, and methodological resources and knowledge that will facilitate the enhancement of scientific research. This will accelerate the research and dissemination of basic knowledge, and will minimize the time between scientific discovery and its application. Promoting advanced and interdisciplinary research will have an impact on Romanian industry and society ("national challenge problems"), by the activity of the Romanian research teams and/or by international cooperation.

Another main goal is to provide **wide shared access**, for the Romanian academic community, to a HPC server, usually very expensive, by its integration into a collaborative network and by its efficient shared use. This will provide the Romanian academic community with a powerful resource, able to support the solving of a variety of research problems that require intensive computation.

CoLaborator aims to attract and **train young researchers** in the field of high-performance computing and of Computational Science and Engineering, by creating the premises for research programs development in the framework of M.Sc. and PhD education. The "culture" specific to this top domain will be promoted, with strategic implications in the Romanian Information Society.

Supporting the **transfer of technology** in the field of high-performance computing will be a major benefit for Romanian industry, for national research institutes, as well as for research, design and development centres. An important side effect will be the increase of the national industry competitiveness.

3.1 CoLaborator's Architecture

CoLaborator has a complex functionality, which is built as a composition of simpler functions forming the hierarchical architecture presented in Figure 1.

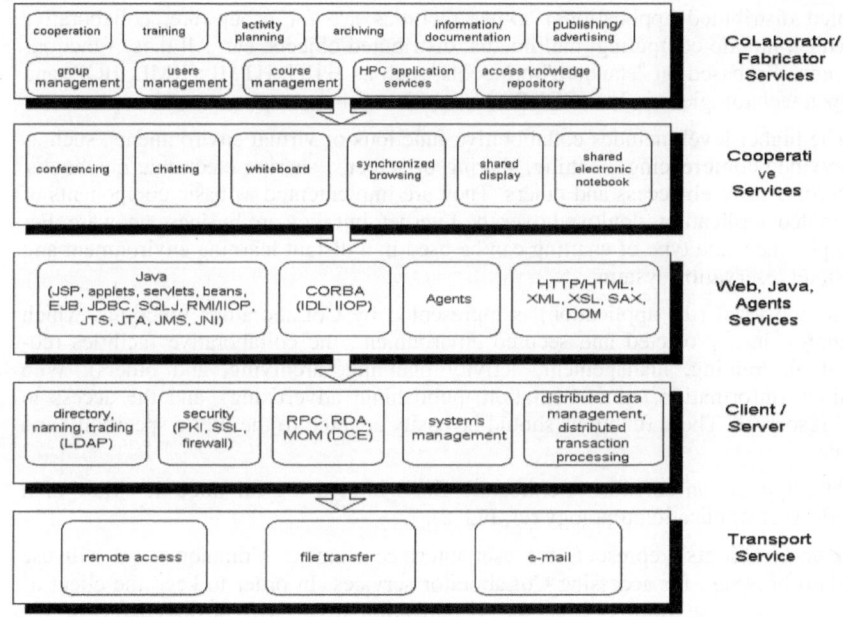

Fig. 1. CoLaborator architectural layers

The base of the hierarchy (TCP/IP) includes "standard" information exchange functions, such as remote access, e-mail, and file transfer. They are the "ground" of any Internet/intranet environment. All the other services are built on the assumption that the basic TCP/IP functionality is provided. Obviously, the technology used to build the environment infrastructure determines the performance (response time, efficiency, availability, fault tolerance, etc.) of overall services offered to users, and the design of the environment should cope with possible scarce performance.

Basic Client/Server functions refer to remote procedure calls, accessing remote data, and message passing. Management and support functions that are needed to administrate clients and servers across the network must be considered in this category. Thus, directory, naming and trading functions permit the clients to locate the servers. Security provides the authentication, privacy, authorization and non-repudiation. Other functions are included to provide synchronization, concurrency, deadlock avoidance or recovery. Facilities for measuring the communication traffic and sites workload, and for improving the overall performance are also included here.

The next level is represented by advanced middleware functions needed for different classes of distributed applications. Distributed data management and transaction management permit access and update of distributed and replicated data. The Web supports not only the access to organized collections of information, but also the deployment of distributed applications over the Internet and intranets (Web-enabled distributed applications). Other facilities are for groupware, collaborative activities, mobile computing, multimedia, distributed objects, etc. All these functions are generally based on "standard" protocols, such as HTTP/HTML, XML, IIOP, and on open technologies, such as CORBA, Java, and agents.

The higher level includes collaborative functions of virtual environments, such as audio/video conferencing, chatting, sharing of screens, sharing electronic notebooks, synchronizing Web access and others. They are implemented as basic components of distributed applications deployed over the Internet, but they are business unaware. For example, the same type of chatting can be used in a distant learning environment and in a hotel reservation system.

The top level (the application) is represented by CoLaborator's functions, which integrates, in a protected and secured environment, the collaborative facilities (co-operation, training, management, activity planning, archiving, and others), Web facilities (information / documentation, publishing, advertising), and the access to HPC resources. These functions should be easily adapted to the user's specificity and profile.

The application software architecture fits within a logical three-tier view of a generic Web application topology (cf. Fig. 2).

Tier-1 (Clients) represents the user interface element. Common users will use standard browsers for accessing CoLaborator services. In order to keep the client as simple as possible (thin client), the visualization tasks will be in charge of the application server. This applies equally to users from Internet and to internal application clients, which will have to interact with the Web server for using the application. Obviously, communication with Internet users will use some trusted TCP/IP network, i.e., they will be Extranet users. Nevertheless, some clients (such as the HPC software administrators, which have a privileged remote access to administration tools) may communicate directly with the application server over some standard communication protocol. The internal network provides greater bandwidth and thus the application clients might be able to support a richer set of graphical controls and elements. One of the most common of the open communication protocols used for application clients is the Internet Inter-ORB Protocol (IIOP).

Provision is made for further extensions of client types (such as users of pervasive computing devices or clients). In their case, some gateway service will be required to support a communication protocol that is recognized by the client device, for example, a Wireless Application Protocol (WAP) Gateway for mobile computing.

Tier-2 (Web Application Server) is responsible for handling incoming requests from Tier-1 Internet users and dispatching these requests to the application server. Additionally it may be responsible for user authentication requesting user credential information such as user ID and password (using encryption protocols and Secure-HTTP or HTTP over Netscape's Secure Sockets Layer (SSL)). In addition to visualization functions mentioned before, the application includes CoLaborator services and, of course, the application control logic.

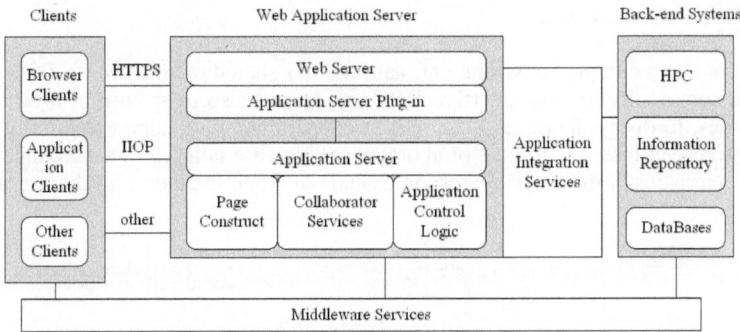

Fig. 2. CoLaborator three tiers logical topology

The Application Integration Services will provide the connectivity to the Tier-3 services at the back-end. It includes connectors (to link the application server environment to the external-services), application messaging (that provides message-based communication between applications in a heterogeneous environment, with assured delivery of messages), and component integration (that "wraps" existing procedural-based applications and transforms them in object-components).

Tier-3 (External Services) is hosting the vital parts of CoLaborator, namely the HPC Server and the Information Repository Server. It is also the tier that hosts the various resource managers that the Web application server will have to coordinate with in order to access CoLaborator information.

In the sequel, we give a more detailed description of the functionality provided by the CoLaborator environment, and of the solutions adopted so far for satisfying the requirements imposed by the infrastructure which supports it. More specific:
CoLaborator has to support cooperative work in cross-organizational teams, mediated through network computers. All CoLaborator activities are goal oriented. Teams are dynamically formed to achieve the goal, and then new associations can be made.

The collaboration is possible across media and equipment with different characteristics (from LANs to WANs and dial-up connections of low performance), having different OS support (from Windows to different versions of UNIX), and with different software tools and applications.

People need to collaborate synchronously or asynchronously. The collaboration sessions must be persistent, despite the existence of non-continuous connectivity.

Produced information should be immediately broadcasted to interested people. This claims for new technologies such as push media. Also, information and mechanisms, which help people to find each other and to discover the potential services, are needed.

Information and services offered by CoLaborator environment should cross boundaries with other similar environments, for a controlled cooperation.

3.2 CoLaborator Services

CoLaborator is a complex environment that provides shared remote access, for a large research community, to an expensive HPC server, but also to scientific information repositories, to distant learning tools, and to cooperative work supporting tools (Fig. 3). The foreseen features of the CoLaborator services are tailored in accordance with the characteristics of the available resources and with their evolution on short term.

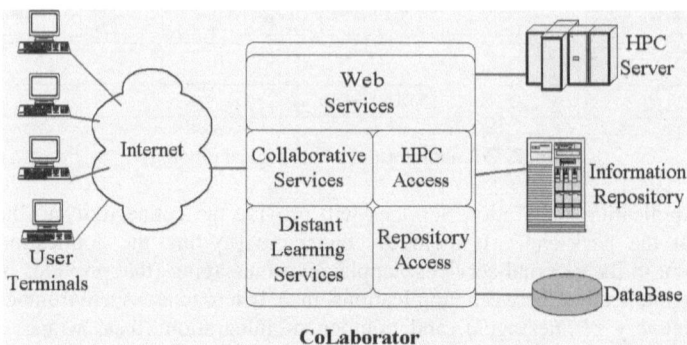

Fig. 3. CoLaborator Services

HPC Server Access

A very important service offered by CoLaborator is the easy access to the HPC server. Its integration in the RoEduNet network makes the resource available to a large number of users, geographically distributed all over the country. From their local desktop facilities, all users can submit jobs to be run on the HPC server and all can get back the results.

Table 2. Sun enterprise E10000 HPC server configuration

Hardware	32 ULTRA SPARC II - 400 MHz processors, 16 GB RAM, 527 GB HDD with 432 GB RAID, Backup tape system.
Software	Solaris operating system, Oracle 8i database management system. Software development tools (C, C++, F77, F90 compilers, MPI, NAG SMP, sun performance library, Sun open GL library)
Application software	MATLAB, ANSYS

Among other things, the HPC access service should cope with the following aspects:
- providing the resource and network quality-of-service claimed by the users
- preventing unauthorized access to resources and

- preserving the integrity of the HPC server, as well as the integrity, confidentiality, and secrecy of the legitimate users data.

A completely automated access policy is provided to accommodate the requests with the availability of the HPC resources and with the administration policy. It has to be based on a robust mechanism and to monitor multiple requests, keeping trace of their status, arbitrating between users and accounting for resource use.

HPC Information Repositories Access

Although the Web contains a vast amount of scientific and technical information related to HPC, researchers are often frustrated by the difficulties in finding relevant information quickly. This is due, primarily, to the limited capacity of the RoEduNet external links, but also to the week performance of the general search systems (like Alta Vista, Lycos, Yahoo and others) which are not filtering the information they index, and use word-based, not content-based index methods.

Improving the efficiency of documentary activities can be achieved by creating information repositories in CoLaborator, and by adding search tools and index databases focused on HPC. As a side effect, a decrease of the load on international lines is foreseen.

Collaborative Tools

Computing tools for sustaining the scientific cooperation are at the hart of a collaborative environment. Some of them are already in wide use, such as electronic mail and the World Wide Web but new tools have recently been developed. CSCW is now a powerful technology to support collaborative design and project development in which multiple individuals, geographically distributed, act as a bounded whole in order to develop a scientific product. As part of the academic world, CoLaborator will include on-line and distance learning training tools. Collaborative tools are used for: Project management, Team management, Class management, Course management, and Web access to HPC applications.

CoLaborator is an agent-based environment, in which the agents are an active part of the cooperative processes, give participants intelligent support for their activities, and lead to a collaborative human-machine problem solving paradigm.

Information agents represent one important contribution of intelligent agent technology to CSCW. Information agents are intelligent program modules that are able to travel in Internet and access multiple information sources for seeking relevant data. In contrast to traditional Web search engines, an information agent is capable of a semantic interpretation of the retrieved information, of filtering this information according to user's preferences and criteria, and of an heuristic classification of data based on the user's profile. The agent learns the user's preferences and profile while working for her. It may also be able to collaborate with other similar agents to discover new sources of information and to cooperatively filter what was found.

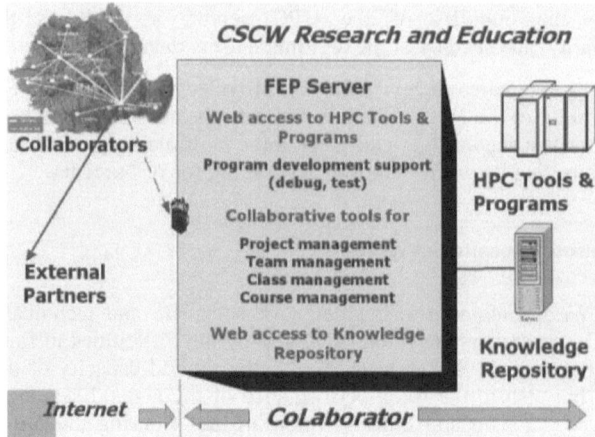

Fig. 4. Collaborative services

A learner in the environment is endowed with his own digital personal agent (Figure 5). A dedicated window can be activated when the user wants to interact with his personal agent but the personal agent may react and make the learner aware of its presence when relevant information has to be communicated. The personal agent is responsible for monitoring the user's actions, for creating the learner's history and preference profile, and for entering in dialogue with personal agents of other learners.

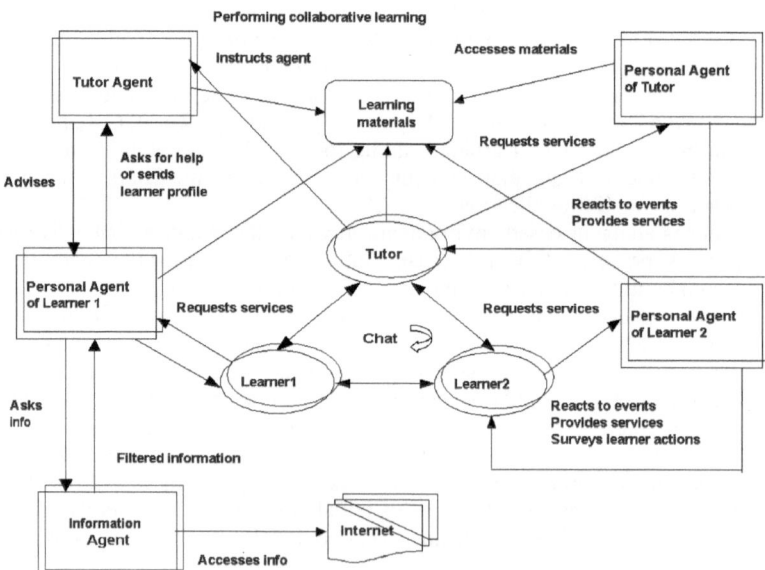

Fig. 5. Agent based cooperation in CoLaborator

The learning system has an information agent, which is responsible for retrieving and filtering information from specified sources that can range from the on-line course materials to the entire Web.

We have identified two roles in the learning system: the *learner* and the *expert* or the *tutor* (Figure 5). Both have their own personal agents, may access the information agent, but have different positions towards a third special agent in the system, namely the *Tutor Agent*. This one has to learn from expert's decisions and may be used by the learners to obtain advice on specific problem instances.

Another way in which intelligent agents may support the collaboration is developing a learner's model and using this model to custom problem solving so that it suits the student level of knowledge and achievement. In working collaboratively, student models have to be correlated so that a common problem solving level is achieved.

4. Further Development

CoLaborator is part of the Romanian National Center for Information Technology, which includes several other centers and laboratories :

Academic Center for Distributed Informatics

> Database Laboratory
> e-Business Academy Laboratory
> Network Management Laboratory
> Computer Networks Laboratory
> Distributed Applications Laboratory.

Some of these laboratories are sustained by important IT companies, such as Sun, Oracle, Compaq, IBM, Microsoft, ICL, HP, Motorola, and others. Their aim is to improve research efficiency, technology transfer, and external visibility of the Center. Important projects under development are related to the upgrade of the Politehnica LAN communication infrastructure, and to the improvement of the resource use and management through building a Campus GRID.

The Center is involved in National projects for the Information Society development in Romania, such as new applications for e-Education and e-Research, information services for citizens, which are based on open standards and technologies. Also, the Center develops collaboration with foreign partners, such as: Free University of Amsterdam, Technical University Delft, Institut National Polytechnique de Grenoble, Politecnico di Torino, University of Marseille, INRIA France, Fokus Germany, HPCC Edinburgh, Maryland University, and George Mason University.

5. Conclusion

The paper presented the CoLaborator virtual environment, which is under development in the framework of a project financed by the Romanian Ministry of

Education and Research and by the World Bank. Its main goal is to build a Web-based collaborative environment for HPC by using standard commercial or public domain software, which will be evaluated and extended where necessary. The main features of the collaborative environment, which were presented in this paper, have also been established. Additionally, we developed several tools for supporting collaborative activities and we started their extension and integration in the system.

References

1. Kouzes, R.T., et al.: Collaboratories: Doing Science on the Internet, IEEE Computer, Vol. 29, No. 8, August (1996).
2. Cutcosky, M.R., et al.: Madefast: Collaborative Engineering on the Internet,Comm. of the ACM, Vol. 39, No. 9, September (1996).
3. Kilman, D.G., Forslund, D.W.: An International Collaboratory Based on Virtual Patient Records, Comm. of the ACM, Vol. 40, No. 8, August (1997).
4. Lee, C. et al.: Collaborative Web Computing Environment: An Infrastructure for Scientific Computation, IEEE Internet Computing, No. 2, March-April (2000) p.27-35.
5. Beca, L. et al.: Web Technologies for Collaborative Visualization and Simulation, T.R. SCCS-786, Northeast Parallel Architectures Center, Jan (1997).
6. Ciancarini, P. et al.: Coordinating Multiagent Applications on the WWW: A Reference Architecture, IEEE Trans on Software Eng. Vol. 24, No. 5, May (1998) p. 362-375.
7. Vanhelsuw, L.: Create Your Own Supercomputer with Java http://www.javaworld/jv-01-1997/jv-01-dammp.html (1997).
8. Agarwal, D. et al.: The Reality of Collaboratories, Ernest Orlando Lawrence Berkeley National Laboratory (1998).
9. Agarwal, D., et al.: Tools for Building Virtual Laboratories, Ernest Orlando Lawrence Berkeley National Laboratory(1998).
10. Atkins, S.E., et al.: Toward Inquiry-Based Education Through Interacting Software Agents, IEEE Computer Vol. 29, No. 5, May (1996).
11. Cristea, V.: CoLaborator - a Multi-user Research Environment. In Preprints of the "First International Symposium on Concurrent Enterprising, ISoCE'98", Sinaia (1998)a p. 159-167.
12. Cristea, V.: CoLaborator and the Actual Trends in HPC. "Scientific Journal of UP Timisoara", Vol. 43(57), No.3 (1998)b p. 39-48.
13. Detmer, W.M., Shortliffe, E.H.: Using the Internet to Improve Knowledge Diffusion in Medicine, Comm. of the ACM, Vol. 40, No. 8, August (1997).
14. Evans, E., Rogers, D.: Using Java Applets and CORBA for Multi-User DistributedApplications, IEEE Internet Computing, Vol. 1, No. 3, May-June (1997)
15. Florea, A., Moldovan, Al.: An Intelligent E-mail Agent. In Proceedings of ROSE'96, the 4th Romanian Conference on Open Systems, 30 October -2 November, Bucuresti (1996) p. 91-99.
16. Fox, G.C., Furmanski, W.: Petaops and Exaops: Supercomputing on the Web IEEE Internet Computing, Vol. 1, No. 2, March-April (1997).
17. Geist, Al: DOE2000 Electronic Notebook Proposal http://www-itg.lbl.gov/~ssachs/doe2000 (1998)
18. Grunday, M., Heeks, R.: Romania's Hardware and Software Industry Institute for Development Policy and Management, April (1998).
19. Larsen, C., Johnston, W.: Security Architecture for Large-Scale Remote Environments, Ernest Orlando Lawrence Berkeley National Laboratory (1997).

20. O'Leary, D.E.: The Internet, Intranets, and the AI Renaissance IEEE Computer Vol. 30, No. 1, January (1997).
21. Lesser, V.R. Multiagent Systems: An Emerging Subdiscipline of AI, ACM Computing Surveys, Vol. 27, No. 3, September (1995).
22. Maly, K.: Interactive Distance Learning over Intranets, IEEE Internet Computing, Vol. 1, No. 1, January-February (1997).
23. McGrew, T.: Collaborative Intelligence, IEEE Internet Computing, Vol. 1, No. 3, May - June (1997).
24. Mowshowitz: Virtual Organization, Comm. of the ACM, Vol. 40, No. 9, September (1997)
25. Mowbray, T.J., Ruh, W.A.: Inside CORBA Distributed Object Standards and Applications Addison Wesley (1997).
26. National Coordination Office for CIC Technology for the 21st Century National Science and Technology Council (1998).
27. Orfali, R., Harkey, D.: Client/Server Programming with Java and CORBA, John Wiley & Sons, Inc., New York (1997).

Layer 4 Fault Tolerance: Reliability Techniques for Cluster System in Internet Services

Guang Tan, Hai Jin, and Liping Pang

Internet and Cluster Computing Center
Huazhong University of Science and Technology, Wuhan, 430074, China
hjin@hust.edu.cn

Abstract. Cluster systems have been showing their great advantages in today's Internet services for their high scalability and high availability. Linux Virtual Server (LVS), one of the popular technologies in building Internet services based on cluster, with its layer 4 scheduling strategy, is gaining increasing interests by ISPs as well as researchers. This paper proposes three new methods to achieve a connection-level (layer 4) fault tolerance for Load Balancer, one of which is called incremental backup and the other two are state mirroring. With these methods, the connections maintained in the primary machine can be safely restored in the backup machine in case of the primary's failure without any loss on unfinished work, thus ensuring high availability for the Load Balancer. Compared with previous work, our schemes are more efficient and flexible. Although they are based on LVS, these methods can also be applied to other architectures with layer 4 switching.

1 Introduction

With the explosive growth of the Internet and its increasingly important role in our lives, the traffic on the Internet is increasing dramatically. Servers can be easily overloaded in a very short time. This situation is especially severe for a popular web server. Cluster system, with its high scalability and high availability, provides a good solution for this problem. In such a system, a machine named Load Balancer accepts all clients' requests and redirects them to real servers by a certain scheduling algorithm. The real servers reply to the users directly or via Load Balancer.

There are various schemes to implement Load Balancer [1][2][3][4][5][8][12]. Linux Virtual Server (LVS)[8][12] is a typical one. In LVS, the scheduling is implemented at IP-level by extending the TCP/IP stack of Linux kernel to support three IP load-balancing techniques: NAT (*Network Address Translation*), IP Tunneling and Direct Routing. Single IP image is achieved. LVS is adopted by many large web sites such as UK National JANET Cache, linux.com [8].

However, there still exist some problems for LVS in real applications. One major issue is its fault tolerance. Being a single point of failure, Load Balance should have some precaution to guarantee its normal running in the event of failure. Fault tolerance of Load Balance can be implemented on different levels: host-level or connection-level (layer 4). The host-level scheme only ensures there is a backup machine to come into work when the Load Balancer fails, but the connections of user

D. Grigoras et al. (Eds.): IWCC 2001, LNCS 2326, pp. 60–68, 2002.
© Springer-Verlag Berlin Heidelberg 2002

requests maintained in the Load Balance will be lost. This will result in failure of the transaction between clients and server. Clients are required to reissue their requests and get the service once again. For a long running time service, such as Video-on-Demand, this is a serious problem on QoS. Therefore, a fault tolerance mechanism concerned with the connections is needed.

This paper proposes three new schemes to achieve fault tolerance. One is called incremental backup, and the other two are called state mirroring. These schemes enable the backup machine to take over Load Balancer smoothly without loss of established connections when errors occur. The failover is transparent to the clients.

The rest of this paper is organized as follows: Section 2 describes the implementation principle of LVS and discusses its characteristics with regard to fault tolerance. Section 3 and section 4 describe and compare the schemes proposed in this paper. Section 5 briefly discusses some related works, and section 6 ends with conclusions.

2   LVS Implementation and Its Fault Tolerance Features

LVS (version 0.9.14) is implemented based on IP masquerading. Masquerading [8] is originally designed for firewall, hiding many hosts behind one IP address, and re-labeling all packets from behind the firewall so that they appear like coming from firewall itself. However, traditional masquerading does not support operations of distributing incoming packets to multiple servers, which is required in a scalable server. With LVS extension, the front-end machine, called Load Balancer, can evenly distribute the traffic among the real servers by using a designated algorithm.

Being a bridge between outside and internal network, Load Balance takes care of address mapping between external and internal network. The key data structure in the implementation of Load Balance is *ip_masq*, which records the IP addresses and ports of the client, real server and Load Balance. All *ip_masq*s are organized in a hash table. When a client issues a connection request to the cluster server, Load Balancer selects a real server and allocates an entry in the hash table for this connection. Load Balancer will then redirect the packets of the client requests to the proper real server according to this entry. Figure 1 illustrates the workflow of LVS with IP Tunneling or Direct Routing.

In LVS, Load Balancer locates between the clients and the real servers. If Load Balancer fails, all the client request connections are broken. Therefore, in order to restore all the connections kept by Load Balancer in case of failure, the backup node needs an identical *ip_masq* hash table with Load Balancer to establish the same working environment as the one before failure occurs. In this paper, we propose two approaches to achieve this:

- Incremental Backup: Extract the information of *ip_masq*s and transfer it to the backup machine periodically. When handling failover, reconstruct the *ip_masq* table in the kernel according to the backup information.
- State Mirroring: Like Load Balancer, the backup machine also accepts IP packets from clients, and establishes a synchronous mirror image in the kernel using the scheduling mechanism of LVS.

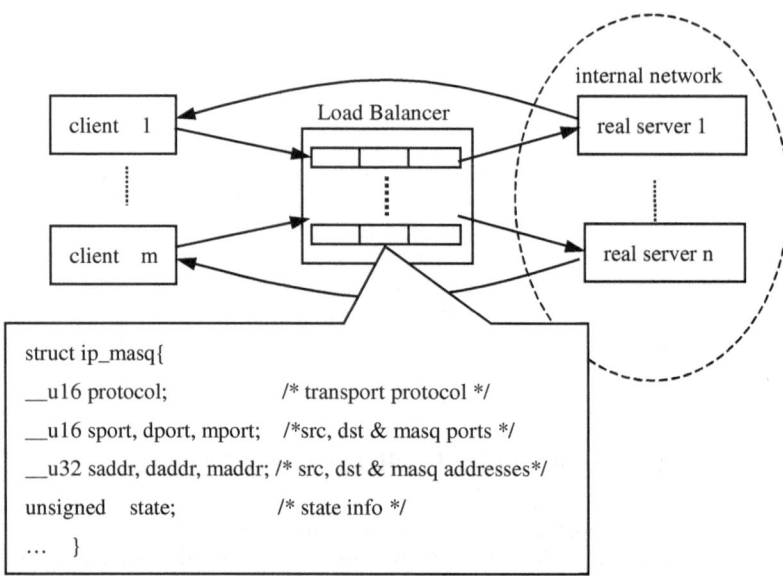

Fig. 1. LVS with IP Tunneling or Direct Routing

3   Incremental Backup Approach

Since each *ip_masq* holds a connection, it is necessary to backup all or most of the information of *ip_masq*s periodically. However, in a heavy traffic network environment like a popular web site, there may be millions of connections clustered in Load Balancer. The size of one *ip_masq* is 128 bytes, so it will be an extremely heavy burden for Load Balancer to collect and transfer all its *ip_masq*s. To avoid this problem, the key information must be carefully extracted from the *ip_masq*s and a highly efficient transferring method should be studied.

Our policy is to backup *ip_masq*s incrementally, that is, backup only the changes of *ip_masq*s' states. However, *ip_masq* has 10 states and the state changing is so frequent that it is very arduous to trace all the changes and record them. We classify the state changes into two kinds: from NON-ESTABLISHED to ESTABLISHED and from ESTABLISHED to NON-ESTABLISHED, which correspond to the establishment and withdraw of a connection respectively. What we choose as backup objects are those marked as "ESTABLISHED" *ip_masq*s (whose states are IP_MASQ_S_ESTABLISHED). Therefore, it can ensure that the established connections will not be stopped after failover.

As for the *ip_masq*s, we collect the key information including the IP addresses and port numbers of the clients, Load Balancer and the real server, and store them in a data structure *ip_masq_backup*. The size of *ip_masq_backup* is only 36 bytes. The rest of the *ip_masq* will be set according to the local environment when reconstructing the whole *ip_masq* during failover.

3.1 Algorithm Design

A pointer array *ip_vs_newcomer* and a link table *ip_vs_leaver* are used to record the information related to the changes of connection states. The pointers of newly activated *ip_masq*s (from NON-ESTABLISHED state to ESTABLISHED state) are added to *ip_vs_newcomer*. For newly deactivated *ip_masq*s (from ESTABLISHED state to NON-ESTABLISHED state), their corresponding *ip_masq_backup*s are inserted into *ip_vs_leaver*. Figure 2 gives out the algorithm in detail.

```
Global variables description
    int newcomer_count: number of newly established connections in
         the latest backup interval

    int established_count: number of established connections in the
         system
Function
ip_vs_changes_record(struct ip_masq *ms, int new_state)
{
   old_state = ms->state;
   if (new_state != old_state) {
     if (masq_active == FALSE &&
         new_state == ESTABLISHED){

       /*add the pointer of ip_masq to ip_vs_newcomer */
       addnewcomer(ip_vs_newcomer, ms);
       newcomer_count ++;
       established_count ++;

       /* if the number of newly established connections reaches a
          certain rate of the total number of current connections,
          then activate backing up process */
       if (newcomer_count >= established_count *
                           (1 - backup_rate)){
            start_backup_transfer();
            ip_vs_newcomer_flush();
            ip_vs_leaver_flush();
            newcomer_count = 0;
       }
     }else if (masq_active == TRUE &&
               new_state != ESTABLISHED) {
         /* if the connections to be deleted is established in
         the same backup interval, just remove it in
         ip_vs_newcomer */
         if (find(ip_vs_newcomer, ms) == TRUE){
             delete(ip_vs_newcomer, ms);
             newcomer_count --;
             established_count --;
         }else
             addleaver(ip_vs_leaver, ms);
     }
   }
}
```

Fig. 2. Incremental Backup Algorithm

In this algorithm, the variable *backup_rate* indicates the ratio of connections that can be successfully restored after failover to the whole number of connections in current system. Figure 3 shows the relationship between *backup_rate* and the checkpoints.

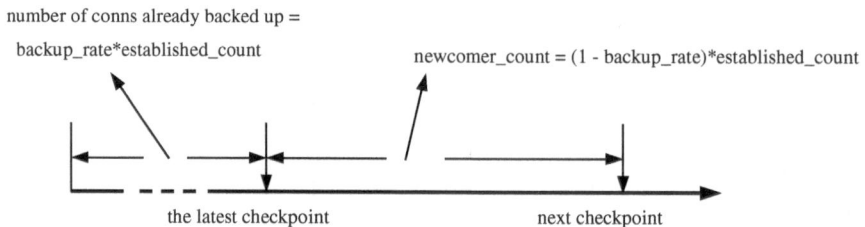

Fig. 3. Relationship between *backup_rate* and Checkpoints

From the algorithm we find that the closer the variable *backup_rate* to 1, the more frequent the backup information will be transferred and the higher the overhead will be. This variable can be set by users from a specific system call. It provides a flexible tradeoff approach for users between the quality of backup and system performance.

We implement the above algorithm in a Linux kernel function ***ip_vs_set_state*** (ipvs-0.9.14-2.2.16). The original function of this call is to increase or decrease the counts of active and inactive connections of the real servers.

3.2   Backup Data Transferring and *ip_masq* Table Reconstruction

The backup information is generated from the kernel. If we transfer it by using socket from user space, the extra overhead will be great. Our policy is to transfer the information in the kernel directly by extending the socket interface ***send*** and make it send the designated data from the kernel.

We add one additional option *MSG_KERNEL* to the option parameters of ***send*** system call, indicating a transfer of data directly from the kernel space. Meanwhile we use the existing parameters, such as buffer parameters, to pass the control information, such as *backup_rate* variable to the kernel. The system call sets a socket pointer variable in the kernel, with which the function ***start_backup_transfer*** can transfer data to the backup machine.

For the backup machine, the data is stored in a user buffer and collated according to its tag. When reconstructing the *ip_masq* table, the data is written to the kernel through a system call. Then the backup machine takes over the IP of the Load Balancer by using spoofing gratuitous ARP technique [6].

3.3   Performance Analysis

The algorithm performs a set of operations on hash table *ip_vs_newcomer*. The algorithm overhead will increase with the expansion of the table. However, this overhead could be very low if we shorten the period of backing up data. In this case we record only very few items in the hash table before we transfer the data. On the other hand, the long recording duration will cause the backup data lost in case of failure and a great number of connections would be broken, making the backup process meaningless. Therefore we ignore the operation cost on hash table in the following discussion.

When the *backup_rate* is 100%, the algorithm overhead reaches its maximum. Assuming during a certain time unit, the number of newly established connections is C_{come} and the number of newly withdrawn connections C_{leave}, the size of data to be transfer is:

$$TotalBackupData = (C_{come} + C_{leave}) * sizeof(ip\_masq\_backup) . \tag{1}$$

Some access statistics for some busiest web sites are given in [7]. According to the statistics, the busiest web site can accept at most 5000 connections in a second. Supposing no connection request is refused and the number of newly withdrawn connections equals to the number of newly established ones, that is

$$C_{come} = C_{leave} = 5000 . \tag{2}$$

then we have

$$TotalBackupData = (5000 + 5000) * 36 = 360K (bytes) . \tag{3}$$

This overhead is acceptable. For the backup machine, the main task is to accept and collate the data, so the overhead is quite low. Backup machine can also be a real server if needed.

4   State Mirroring Approach

For state mirroring approach, the backup machine accepts the incoming requests synchronously with Load Balancer and creates a mirror image of *ip_masq*s using LVS's scheduling mechanism. When handling failover, the backup machine simply takeovers Load Balancer's IP and continues the work.

We propose two approaches for the state mirroring:

- **Parallel state mirroring**: Forward a replication of a packet to the backup machine each time Load Balancer forwards the packet to the real server.

- **Serial state mirroring**: The incoming packets first go into Load Balancer. Then they are all forwarded to the backup machine. After being scheduled by the backup machine, they are forwarded to the real servers.

The principles of these two methods are shown in Figure 4 and Figure 5, respectively.

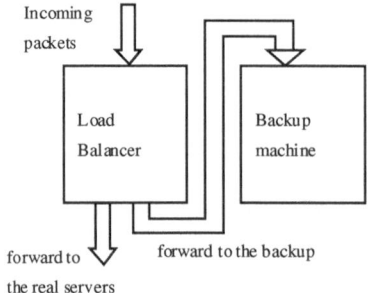

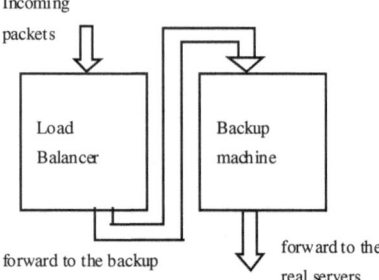

Fig. 4. Parallel State Mirroring   **Fig. 5.** Serial State Mirroring

For parallel state mirroring, packets are forwarded to both the real servers and the backup machine simultaneously, without extra overhead to the CPU. However, a half of its internal network bandwidth is sacrificed for the backup processing. For some densely accessed Internet service such as WWW, this method might decrease the throughput of the system. Parallel state mirroring can be used in some data-intensive services like Video-on-Demand or FTP, in which a system often needs to support at most several thousand concurrent sessions. This imposes a very light load on the Load Balancer. When the Load Balancer is down, the Back Machine takes over the packet streams and continues the scheduling. Whether the Load Balancer really fails will not affect the normal scheduling because it will not accept and forward any packets once its IP address is took over.

For serial state mirroring, all packets will be scheduled twice, which increases the response delay of the service. In a high-speed network environment like 100Mbps Fast Ethernet, however, this extra hop would add no more than 1 ms to the network delay. Compared to the medium round-trip 187 ms in the Internet [7], this delay can be ignored. Note that this estimation is based on the assumption that the scheduling time of the CPU is negligible in general condition. In fact, lots of experiments on the performance of LVS prove this [8]. Therefore, this mirroring approach can be adopted by services that are not sensitive to respond time. The failover procedure is similar as that for Parallel Mirroring: when the IP address of LVS is taken over by the Backup Machine, the incoming packets will automatically change their directions and go into the Backup Machine.

The implementations of these two schemes are relatively simple. The key issue is to control the forwarding of packets. New system call can be added to set whether the packets would be forwarded after the scheduling and the destination of forwarding. Note, these two schemes only consider the IP Tunneling and Direct Routing techniques of LVS, in which all the response packets go to the clients directly without passing through Load Balancer.

5   Related Works

A host-level fault tolerance scheme for Load Balancer was proposed in [8]. The "fake" software [6] is used for the backup node to takeover the IP addresses from Load Balancer when it fails.

Berkeley's MagicRouter [1] proposed a load balancing strategy using a user-level process on the front end to interpose the packets stream. A fault tolerance scheme based on logs of state changes is put forward. In this scheme, every change of the states of connections on the Load Balancer is announced by a broadcast in the private network, and the backup machines update their states accordingly. However, in a busy network environment with frequent changing of TCP states, the backup process might be rather costly.

IBM's TCP router [5] uses TCP routing technology to balance the load across the real servers. Each TCP router (Load Balancer) has a buddy server, which will take over its IP in case of failures. The failover only considers the host-level fault tolerance.

In [11], an overall backup scheme is discussed in detail, including the issues of extracting the information of connections and reconstructing the *ip_masq* table. The whole *ip_masq* table is backed up by getting data from the kernel. The backup information is set to the kernel of backup machine through the same system call with different parameters.

6   Conclusions and Future Work

This paper presents three layer 4 fault tolerance schemes for cluster-based Internet services using Linux Virtual Server. The incremental backup scheme provides a parameter for the user to tune his backup quality, and it requires a relatively low overhead on the network and the CPU. However, this algorithm is tied to the implementation details of LVS, making it difficult to be ported to other platform without significant modification. Compared with this algorithm, the state mirroring methods appear to be more general. Although they are discussed based on LVS, the idea of these schemes can be easily implemented on other architectures. But they will sacrifice some network bandwidth or increase the response delay of the service.

We implemented the incremental backup algorithm based on IPVS-0.9.14-2.2.16 in our cluster server, called WanLan-1. To verify the fault tolerant feature of our scheme, we carried out some experiments for two typical Internet applications: Video-on-Demand and FTP. The experiment environment includes a cluster system with a Load Balancer and two real servers. All these experiments show great benefit using fault tolerant features of LVS to satisfy the QoS for applications.

Layer 4 switching, though highly efficient and flexible, is now often combined with other higher level scheduling technology, such as content-aware scheduling, to achieve a more powerful ability of load-balancing. This brings new challenge for our fault tolerance algorithm. The extra information of connections must be taken into account in the incremental backup process. Therefore, keeping pace with the development of switching technology is one major task in our future work. We will also further study the performance of these scheduling algorithms, which will be an important guidance for users in choosing the proper method to improve the availability of their Internet services.

References

1. E. Anderson, D. Patterson, and E. Brewer, "The Magicrouter: An Application of Fast Packet Interposing", *Proceedings of Second Symposium on Operating Systems Design and Implementation*, May, 1996.
2. D. Andresen, T. Yang, and O. H. Ibarra, "Towards a Scalable Distributed WWW Server on Workstation Clusters", *Journal of Parallel and Distributed Computing*, Vol.42, pp.91-100, 1997.
3. Cisco Local Director, Cisco Systems, Inc., http://www.cisco.com/univercd/cc/td /doc/pcat/ld.htm
4. P. Damani, P. E. Chung, Y. Huang, C. Kintala, and Y. Wang, "ONE-IP: Techniques for Hosting a Service on a Cluster of Machines", *Proceedings of 6th International World Wide Web Conference*, April 1997.
5. D. Dias, W. Kish, R. Mukherjee, and R. Tewari, "A Scalable and Highly Available Server", *Proceedings of COMPCON'96*, pp.85-92, 1996.
6. S. Horman, "Creating Redundant Linux Servers", *Proceedings of the 4th Annual Linux Expo*, 1998.
7. P. Killelea, *Web Performance Tuning: Speeding Up the Web*, O'Reilly & Associates, 1998.
8. Linux Virtual Server Project, http://www.LinuxVirtualServer.org/.
9. High-availability Linux Project, http://www.linux-ha.org/.
10. W. R. Stevens, *TCP/IP Illustrated, Volume 3: TCP for Transactions, HTTP, NNTP, and the UNIX(TM) Domain Protocols*, Addison-Wesley Pub Co., 1996.
11. J. Xiao, *Linux Virtual Server Based Cluster System and its IP Fault Tolerance Technology*, Master Thesis, Huazhong Univ. of Sci. & Tech., China, 2001.
12. W. Zhang, S. Jin, and Q. Wu, "Scaling Internet Services by Linux Director", *Proc. of 4th Intl. Conf. on High Performance Computing in Asia-Pacific Region*, May, 2000, pp.176-183.

Computational Issues in E-commerce Trading Exchanges

Can Özturan

Dept. of Computer Eng., Boğaziçi University, Istanbul, Turkey,
ozturaca@boun.edu.tr,
http://www.cmpe.boun.edu.tr/~ozturan

Abstract. The classical meaning of trading involves establishment of a pairwise matching, (i.e. formation of directed cycles of length two between buyers and sellers). In this paper, we look at computational issues that arise in trading by bartering. Bartering enables us to have richer trading patterns. In bartering, we can form arbitrary length directed cycles/hypercycles among barterers of items and hence establish more complex trading arrangements. We review some earlier results and also present some new results on parallel generation of hypercycles in the single instance multi-item bartering problem. We report computational results obtained on our Linux cluster.

1 Introduction

In the most common form of trading, money and the item purchased are exchanged in a cyclic pattern. Several advantages of this kind of trading can be enumerated - the most important being that the value of the sold item can be stored as a certain amount of money that can later divided and spent on other trades. If the money that is stored retains its value robustly, then this kind of trading is quite advantageous. However, if the value of money held depreciates rapidly, for example, due to inflation or devaluation, then alternative means of trading such as bartering become more attractive [6]. The buy/sell transaction that is carried out using money can be thought as a bartering transaction: Money is bartered for a commodity by the establishment of a cycle of length two involving the buyer and the seller. In the most general form of bartering, however, we can have trading arrangements that may involve transactions among barterers arranged in cycles of arbitrary lengths. Figure 1(a) shows a directed graph with nodes representing items available for bartering and edges representing bartering requests. The edge(s) coming out of an item indicates that the item can be bartered for any one of the requested items. A cycle in this directed graph indicates a possible trading arrangement. We may want to trade as many items as possible. In this case, our problem becomes that of finding a set of vertex disjoint cycles with maximum cardinality.

On the Internet, we can find several e-commerce sites that offer bartering services. However, these sites are mostly using barter units and not offering fully

D. Grigoras et al. (Eds.): IWCC 2001, LNCS 2326, pp. 69–76, 2002.

automated *direct* bartering services. The aim of this paper is to analyze and experiment with difficult computational problems that should be solved by a fully automated electronic barter exchange.

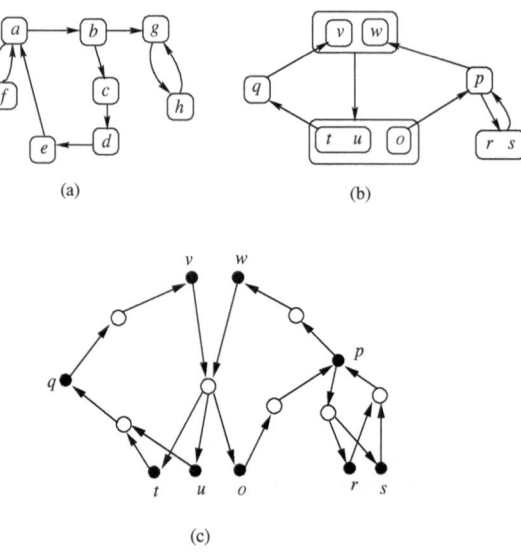

(a)   (b)

(c)

Fig. 1. Single instance, single item bartering example (a). Single instance multiple item bartering example (b) and its AND/OR graph representation (c).

In a bartering problem, it is possible to have multiple (distinct) items as sources and targets of request edges. It is also possible to have multiple instances of the same item. Hence, we can classify the bartering problems into the following categories:

1. Single instance, single item bartering,
2. Multiple instance, single item bartering,
3. Single instance, multiple item bartering,
4. Multiple instance, multiple item bartering.

Figure 1(a) is exemplifies type (1) problem. Figure 1(b) illustrates type (3) problem. If an item have multiple copies, then we get the multiple instance versions of the bartering problem.

An algorithm for problem (1) is available in the literature not in the context of bartering but rather in the context of cycle factors of graphs. The algorithm by Gutin [5] (or see [2, p. 146]) solves with $O(n^3)$ complexity the maximum cardinality cycle subdigraph problem by transforming it to an assignment problem. This is exactly the same problem as (1). Minimum cost flow algorithms for problems (1) and (2) have been presented in [8]. Problem (3) is NP-complete and is described in [7]. In this paper, we will focus only on problem (3). Since (3) is NP-complete, massive computational power is required to solve even small instances of this problem. *Hypercycles* (defined in the next section) give possible multiple item bartering arrangements in problem (3). Unfortunately, as was proved in [7], even the problem of finding a single hypercycle is NP-complete. After presenting definitions and formal problem statement in the next section, we will outline our exhaustive depth first based search strategy that is used to generate hypercycles in Section 3. We will also look at parallelization and load balancing issues of hypercycle generation problem in Section 4. Finally, we present some computational results obtained on our local Linux cluster.

2 Definitions and Problem Statement

We review the definitions presented in [7]. A *directed hypergraph* $H(V, E)$ consists of two sets V and E where V is a set of vertices and E is a set of *hyperarcs*. Each hyperarc $e = <V_t, V_h>$ is an ordered pair of non-empty subsets V_t and V_h of V. In the directed hypergraphs we consider, V_t and V_h will be disjoint. Here, V_t (V_h) is the set of vertices that appear in the tail (head) of the hyperarc e. The in-degree of a vertex, $id(v)$, is defined to be the number of times vertex v appears in the heads of hyperarcs. Similarly, the out-degree of a vertex, $od(v)$, is the number of times vertex v appears in the tails of hyperarcs. The set of vertices that appear in the tail or head of a hyperarc is called a *hypernode*. A *directed subhypergraph* $H'(V', E')$ of $H(V, E)$ is defined as a directed hypergraph with:

$$E' \subseteq E \qquad and \qquad (\bigcup_{e \in E'} head(e)) \bigcup (\bigcup_{e \in E'} tail(e)) \subseteq V' \subseteq V.$$

A *cycle* in a directed graph is a connected subgraph in which for all vertices v in the subgraph, we have $id(v) = od(v) = 1$. Various definitions of hypercycle exists in the literature [1,3,12]. In this paper, we will simply extend the definition of cycle in directed graphs to directed hypergraphs: Hence a hypercycle will be defined as a connected subhypergraph of the directed hypergraph in which for all vertices v in the subhypergraph, we have $id(v) = od(v) = 1$.

The single instance multiple item bartering problem represented by the directed hypergraph H is defined as the problem of finding a set $\{C_1, \ldots, C_k\}$ of vertex disjoint hypercycles in H such that $\sum_{i=1}^{k} |C_i|$ is maximized.

In directed graphs that represent the single instance single item bartering problem, cycles are located in strongly connected components. Similarly, in directed hypergraphs, hypercycles are located in hyper-strongly connected components. A hyper-strongly connected component of a hypergraph $H(V, E)$ is a maximal subset V' of vertices of V such that its induced subhypergraph $H'(V', E')$ is *hyper-strongly connected*. A directed hypergraph is hyper-strongly connected if for every pair of vertices u and v (with u and v belonging to different hypernodes), there is a path from u to v and from v to u. In directed graphs, existence of strongly connected components implies existence of cycles. This, however, is *not* the case for directed hypergraphs (refer to [7] for an example). We also note that whereas the problem of finding a hypercycle is NP-complete, the problem of finding hyper-strongly connected components is in P.

Directed hypergraphs have also been known as AND/OR graphs [10, p. 21]. Figure 1(c) shows the AND/OR graph representation of the directed hypergraph shown in Figure 1(b). Here, the black nodes are the OR nodes that represent the items and the white nodes are the AND nodes that represent the hyperedges. In the rest of our paper, we will use the AND/OR graph representation and terminology.

3   Parallel Hypercycle Generation for Single Instance Multi-item Bartering

One way to solve the single instance multiple item bartering problem is as follows: (i) Generate the hypercycles, (ii) form the weighted undirected intersection graph with each vertex in this graph representing a hypercycle C_i with weight $|C_i|$ and edges representing non-empty intersections with vertices representing other hypercycles, (iii) solve the weighted maximum independent set problem on this graph. A lot of research has been performed for solving the maximum independent set problem. But not much work has been done on hypercycle generation. We, therefore, just refer to the literature on maximum independent set problem [4] and concentrate only on the hypercycle generation in the rest of the paper.

To generate the hypercycles, we first find the hyper-strongly connected components. Then on each hyper-strongly connected component, we employ an exhaustive depth-first based search strategy. Our exhaustive search strategy is similar in idea to that of Tiernan's [11] that was performed on directed graphs. While traversing the directed graph, a chain graph basically resides on the stack and if the last vertex on the stack connects to the first (start) vertex on the stack then it is reported as a cycle. On the directed hypergraphs, however, the situation is more complicated. Starting with an AND node, and proceeding in depth first fashion, AND nodes are also pushed on an explicit stack. The OR nodes reside on the implicit recursive procedure call stack. If the AND nodes and the OR nodes that currently reside on the stacks form a hypercycle, then they are reported as such. The check for whether the set of AND nodes and OR nodes on the stacks form a hypercycle is done by keeping track of counters which are updated throughout the traversal:

- INOR: number of items appearing on the heads of outgoing arcs from AND nodes,
- OUTOR: number of items appearing on the tails of incoming arcs into an AND nodes,
- INDEGAND: total in-degrees of AND nodes,
- OUTDEGAND: total out-degrees of AND nodes.

A hypercycle is formed when all these counters are equal. Figure 2(a) and (b) show two snapshots of a traversal (indicated by bold lines) and the values of the corresponding counters.

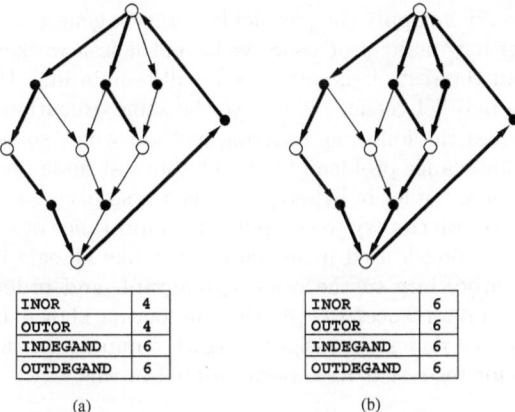

INOR	4
OUTOR	4
INDEGAND	6
OUTDEGAND	6

INOR	6
OUTOR	6
INDEGAND	6
OUTDEGAND	6

(a)   (b)

Fig. 2. Contents of counters during traversal: (a) is not a hypercycle yet and (b) is a hypercycle.

Let $\{a_1, \ldots, a_n\}$ be the set of AND nodes in our directed hypergraph. Similar to Tiernan's [11] strategy for the enumeration of cycles in directed graphs, we first generate all hypercycles (if there is any) that start with AND node a_1 and that may include some or all of the rest of the AND nodes $\{a_2, \ldots, a_n\}$. Then we generate all hypercycles that start with AND node a_2 and and that may include some or all of the AND nodes $\{a_3, \ldots, a_n\}$. This is repeated for the rest of nodes in a similar fashion. We, therefore, define our task, T_i as the process of enumerating all cycles (if there is any) that include the vertex a_i and some or all of the vertices from the set $\{a_{i+1}, \ldots, a_n\}$.

In order to parallelize hypercycle generation, we keep a master processor which distributes each of these tasks to worker processors that ask for tasks when they are free. As part of task T_i, first the hyper-strongly connected algorithm is run on the subhypergraph that includes only the AND nodes $\{a_i, \ldots, a_n\}$. If a hyper-strongly component is found that includes the AND node a_i, then the exhaustive hypercycle search procedure is invoked on this component. If there is no component or if there are components that do not include the AND node a_i, then the processor returns and asks for the next task from the master processor.

4   Load Balancing Problem

Severe load imbalance problem may arise in the above parallelization strategy. Since a task is defined as finding all the hypercycles including node a_i and some or all of $\{a_{i+1}, \ldots, a_n\}$, then the order i assigned to a node should be chosen carefully. Consider the example given in Figure 3(a). The topmost node numbered as 1 is included in all the cycles. Hence, if it chosen as the first task, then all the hypercycles will be generated by the first task. The other tasks i.e. identified by starting vertices $2, \ldots, 18$ will generate no hyper-strongly connected components. Hence, if we apply the parallel hypercycle generation to this ordering, then no matter how many processors we have, the first worker processor will do all the work and the rest of the processors will remain idle. Hence, both the sequential and the parallel versions will have the same execution time.

We have employed the following ordering method which sometimes helps to decrease the load imbalance problem: Since the topmost node (i.e. labelled as 1) in Figure 3(a) appears in a lot of hypercycles, then it so because of its *popularity* or *importance*. Hence, we can try to compute the importance of a node by using, for example, the techniques used in search engines like Google [9]. If we apply the page ranking procedure to the same hypergraph and order the nodes in ascending order of importance, we get the numbering shown in Figure 3(b). Here the most popular nodes are assigned higher numbers. In the next section, we report timings for tests that have been ordered in this way.

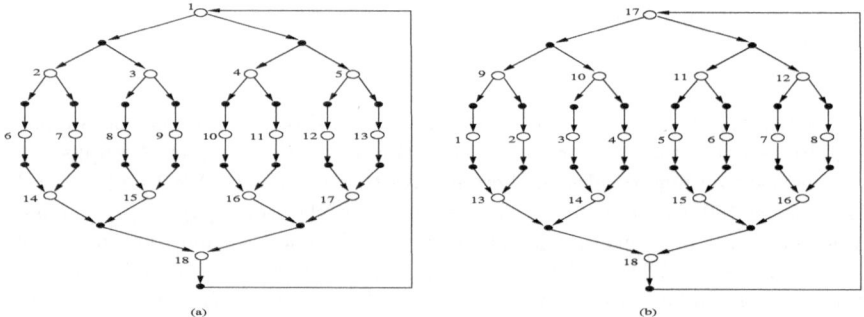

Fig. 3. An example with vertex ordering that leads to heavy imbalance (a), vertex ordering that leads to better load balance (b).

5   Computational Results on a Cluster

We carry out the following tests on a Linux cluster with nodes having Pentium II 400Mhz CPU and 128 MB memory.

– Test 1: A larger version of directed hypergraph in Figure 3 with ordering done as in (a). In this version, there are 298 AND nodes and 341 OR nodes.
– Test 2: Same directed hypergraph as in Test 1, but this time vertices ordered by ranking as in Figure 3(b).
– Test 3: A randomly generated example with 25 OR nodes and 54 AND nodes having in and out degrees in the range 1..3. The whole hypergraph formed is hyper-strongly connected.
– Test 4: Same directed hypergraph in Test 4, but this time vertex ordered by ranking.

The timing results obtained are shown in Table 1. In the column labelled as number of processors, 1 indicates the master and the other number indicates the number of worker processors.

Table 1. *Tests and timings in seconds*

No. of Processors	Test 1	Test 2	Test 3	Test 4
1+1	0.70	0.68	285.7	409.8
1+2	0.52	0.34	143.6	204.9
1+4	0.52	0.18	141.5	115.5
1+8	0.52	0.11	141.5	88.5
1+16	0.52	0.07	141.5	88.8

The results in the table show that ordering the nodes by ranking in tests 1 and 2 did reduce the imbalance among the tasks. In tests 1 and 2, there are actually 8 tasks which have hyper-strongly components. The rest of the tasks do not have hyper-strongly connected components. This explains why having more than 8 worker processors will not decrease the execution time. The results for tests 3 and 4 show that ordering by ranking does not always work. This is because, whereas ordering by ranking may help to reduce load imbalances among tasks, it also changes the way the directed hypergraph is traversed. Hence, the hypercycle search activity is also affected by this change. The change in order may cause the search routine to take longer while finding hypercycles.

The above tests were meant to illustrate load balancing issues that arise in hypercycle generation. The execution times for these tests were in seconds range. However, we have also run other tests which took hours. It is not the number of nodes in the whole hypergraph, but the size of each strongly-connected component that dictates the execution time. Also, in general when the in-degrees and out-degrees of AND nodes increase, the execution times increase drastically. In our tests, when we move to hyper-strongly connected components with 55 or more AND nodes, the execution times start to explode.

6   Discussion and Future Work

In this paper, we have generalized the classical notion of trading by allowing bartering in arbitrary sized cycles and hypercycles. In the context of multiple item bartering, we have looked at the issue of hypercycle generation. Since finding a hypercycle is an NP-complete problem, we have explored some techniques of parallelizing it. We developed proof-of-concept code that generated hypercycles in parallel on our cluster.

We believe that we have just touched the tip of the iceberg in this paper and that a lot more needs to be done. We have also seen massive research being done in the area of complementary auction problems but almost no mention of bartering problems. We believe that bartering problems have much more applicability than the auction problems. In the future, we will concentrate our efforts on reducing the hypercycle search space by employing hyper-strongly connected components algorithm on partitioned subsets of AND nodes.

Acknowledgement. The computations carried out in this paper were run on the ASMA cluster built as part of Turkish Science and Research Council (TÜBITAK) project under grant EEEAG-199E009.

References

1. G. Ausiello, R. Giaccio, G. F. Italiano, and U. Nanni. Optimal traversal of directed hypergraphs. Technical Report TR-92-073, The International Computer Science Institute, Berkeley California, 1992.
2. J. Bang-Jensen and G. Gutin. *Digraphs: Theory, Algorithms and Applications.* Springer-Verlag, 2000.
3. C. Berge. *Hypergraphs: Combinatorics of Finite Sets.* Elsevier, North Holland, 1989.
4. I. M. Bomze, M. Budinich, P. M. Pardalos, and M. Pelillo. The maximum clique problem. In *Handbook of Combinatorial Optimization*, volume 4. Kluwer, 1999.
5. G. Gutin. Finding a longest path in a complete multipartite digraph. *SIAM J. Discrete Math.*, (6):270–273, 1993.
6. C. Krauss. To weather recession, argentines revert to barter. *The New York Times*, May 6, 2001.
7. C. Ozturan. Directed hypergraph model for barter exchanges. Technical Report FBE-CMPE-01/2001-8, Dept. of Computer Engineering, Bogazici University, Istanbul, June 2001. (Available: http://www.cmpe.boun.edu.tr/ ozturan/cmpe2001-9.ps).
8. C. Ozturan. Network flow models for electronic barter exchanges. Technical Report FBE-CMPE-01/2001-9, Dept. of Computer Engineering, Bogazici University, Istanbul, June 2001. (Available: http://www.cmpe.boun.edu.tr/ ozturan/cmpe2001-9.ps).
9. L. Page, S. Brin, R. Motwani, and T. Winograd. The page rank citation ranking: Bringing order to the web. Technical report, Standford Digital Libraries, Working Paper, 1998.
10. J. Pearl. *Heuristics*. Addison Wesley, 1984.
11. J. C. Tiernan. An efficient search algorithm to find elementary circuits of a graph. *Communications of the ACM*, 13(12):722–726, 1970.
12. A. V. Zeigarnik. On hypercycles and hypercircuits in hypergraphs. In *Discrete Mathematical Chemistry (DIMACS Series in Discrete Mathematics and Theoretical Computer Science)*, volume 51, pages 377–383. American Mathematical Society, 2000.

Embedded Cluster Computing through Dynamic Reconfigurability of Inter-processor Connections

Marek Tudruj

Institute of Computer Science, Polish Academy of Sciences
ul. Ordona 21, 01–237 Warsaw, Poland
tudruj@ipipan.waw.pl

Abstract. Architectural solutions and program execution methods for multi–processor systems based on dynamically reconfigurable distributed memory processor clusters are discussed in the paper. First, general assumptions for embedded dynamic cluster computing in distributed memory systems are presented. Then, embedded cluster computing based on the dynamic on–request inter–processor connection reconfiguration is described. Next, embedded cluster computing based on the look–ahead reconfiguration of inter–processor connections is discussed. It includes system architectures with centralized and decentralized connection reconfiguration control. Implementation of the proposed architectural solutions based on some market available processors is also discussed.

1 Introduction

Multi–cluster parallel systems enable cost–effective mapping of parallel program tasks into computing hardware. It results primarily from distribution of computing power of a system to parallel programs decomposed into groups of co–operating tasks. The efficiency results also from distribution of inter–process communication to different hardware means depending on their communication latencies. The distribution of tasks among clusters improves efficiency of a system due to processor load balancing and better control of the use of communication resources. All this makes that cluster computing have recently become a domain of intensive research supported by many practical implementations [1,2,3,4,5,6, 7]. In commercially available multi–cluster systems, a cluster constitutes a set of processors that communicate in most cases through shared memory. Mutual communication among clusters is done by an additional communication network. The standard feature is that internal and external cluster communication is implemented using different hardware means that have different latencies. The internal latency is generally much lower than that of external communication. However, another common feature is that the internal cluster communication latency is very sensitive to the cluster size. This is especially visible when communication is based on shared memory where the impeding elements can be the memory bus or single access memory modules. Using different hardware means for internal and external communication makes that the size of clusters is fixed.

D. Grigoras et al. (Eds.): IWCC 2001, LNCS 2326, pp. 77–91, 2002.

The cost of hardware implementation of interconnected fixed size clusters additionally pushes the cluster designs towards small sizes. These tendencies result quite often in incompatibility between the desired size of clusters implied by the application programs and the physical system structure.

This paper is directed towards architectural solutions for multi–cluster systems where the size and the composition of processor clusters are dynamic during program execution. The communication model assumed for this paper is message passing. System solutions based on shared memory clusters are proposed in [8,9]. Cluster composition is determined accordingly to program needs on the basis of the program graph analysis. The structures of clusters are organized and modified in program run time. Therefore, they can match optimal execution of the given sets of programs where the communication has a predictable behavior. In this sense, such cluster computing is embedded i.e. dedicated to given application programs. Application programs include usually also communication of unpredictable character. For these parts of programs, additional communication means (networks) are assumed in the proposed architecture, such as packet switching networks based on the wormhole routing. The paper is concerned with systems based on circuit (link connection) switching. Such systems assume point–to–point connections between processors and enable non–packetized data formats, efficient for time critical applications. In this respect, the proposed solutions support fine grain parallelism. Communication based on link connection switching is usually affected by connection setting (reconfiguration) latency and a blocking effect of point–to–point connections existing between processors. The paper presents solutions that eliminate these defects for parallel programs that have deterministic control. The solutions are based on the look–ahead dynamic connection reconfiguration approach [10,11] applied at the level of system architecture and program execution paradigm.

Multi–processor systems with link connection switching were built several years ago with the use of transputers [12,13,14,15] that acted as data processing and communication processors. Although transputer's speed has not been developed, its communication models have contributed to the development of communication techniques. In current implementations, some very efficient multi–link DSP processors that have appeared in recent years on the market, can be used as communication processors.

The paper consists of five parts. In the first part, the proposed embedded cluster computing paradigm is explained. The second part presents the implementation of this paradigm through dynamic on–request reconfiguration of inter–processor connections. In next two parts of the paper, embedded cluster computing based on the dynamic look–ahead connection reconfiguration is discussed, assuming the centralized and decentralized control. The last part of the paper discusses viability of the proposed solutions on the basis of some market–available components.

2   Embedded Cluster Computing Paradigm

Common and successful use of cluster computing depends on its flexibility i.e. applicability for efficient execution of both coarse and fine grain parallel programs. Coarse grain parallelism imposes no major problems, however, great design challenges are faced at the level of fine grain parallelism. Two fundamental architectural features in multi–processor systems have to be considered for efficient implementation of fine–grain parallelism: system decomposition method into processor clusters and control of communication topology inside and outside clusters. Communication latency in fixed connection structure is usually much lower than with dynamic connections created for each communication. This feature is especially advantageous for multi–processor systems based on circuit (link connection) switching and can be exploited to design efficient multi–cluster systems. Systems based on link connection switching assume direct point–to–point connections between processors, so that message transmissions through intermediate processor nodes are eliminated. The circuit switching paradigm can also better meet hard communication efficiency requirements since it enables exchange of non–packetized messages. The overall efficiency of this paradigm depends very strongly on the way the control of inter–processor connections is organized during program execution. Direct inter–processor connections in such systems should dynamically map inter–process communication locality existing in application programs. Two kinds of communication locality in programs can be identified:
– spatial communication locality where a limited number of processes residing in some processors communicate in a time interval of program execution,
– temporal communication locality where communication in a time interval is performed many times between the same processes residing in some processors.

Identification of these localities in programs, enables optimized mapping of program execution into dynamic processor clusters. The spatial locality results in aggregation of inter–processor connections in decomposed system hardware resources (processor clusters). The temporal locality results in the reuse of inter–processor connections (temporarily fixed connections in clusters). Such approach assumes creation of system configurations based on dynamic processor clusters dedicated to execution of a given set of application programs. We call this kind of cluster computing the embedded cluster computing. It provides an efficient way for execution of parallel programs with fine grain parallelism.

Processor clusters can have fully or partially connected internal connection structure. However, the fully connected structure is impractical when the cluster size becomes large. A more useful is a reconfigurable temporal partially connected structure that enables flexible adjustment of cluster structure to program needs. The communication locality can be identified by an analysis of the program graph at compile time. It can be also determined during program execution if the programming environments have included the respective efficient functional mechanisms. In this paper we will discuss program execution paradigms based on dynamically organized processor clusters that correspond to dynamic embedded cluster computing model based on compile–time program analysis. In

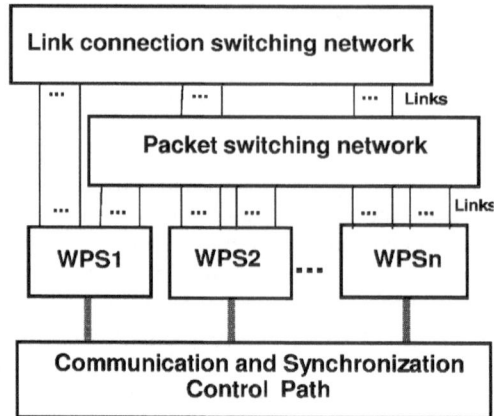

Fig. 1. General system structure for embedded cluster computing

program parts that show weak space and time localities, communication is close to the "all–to–all" type among a large number of processors and/or the communication is of unitary character and there is no iterative use of connections in any proximity of time. In these cases there is no possibility or advantage in creating clusters with any fixed internal connections and communication should be performed using connections that are created on request and disappear after use. Such pattern corresponds to the commonly known packet switching model.

The above discussion implies that realistic parallel systems should enable inter–processor connections that have two basic types of behavior: volatile and temporarily permanent. They should be based on two communication models: packet switching and link connection switching used in parallel during pro-

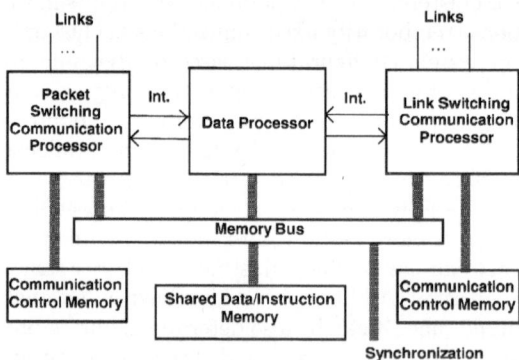

Fig. 2. The structure of a worker processor subunit

gram execution. Additionally, the communication system should enable both synchronous and asynchronous communication. The general structure of a system that can fulfil these requirements is shown in Fig. 1. It is based on two kinds of communication networks used in parallel in the system as opposed to networks with adaptable control of communication paradigm, proposed in [17]. WPSi is a worker processor subsystem that performs parallel processes in a program. Its general structure is shown in Fig. 2. The system based on such multi–mode and multi–behavioural communication infrastructure provides the valuable effects such as adjusting system structure to program needs, efficiency of communication, strong reduction of communication start–up time, efficiency in the use of hardware resources, simpler message structures and smaller control software overheads.

In multi–processor systems reconfigurable through inter–processor connection switching, programs can be executed with the following strategies for the control of connection setting: static reconfigurability, semi–dynamic reconfigurability, dynamic reconfigurability on request, look–ahead dynamic reconfigurability. Program execution control paradigms based on these methods are shown in Fig. 3. Out of these paradigms, the last three can be used to organize dynamic processor clusters that correspond to embedded dynamic cluster computing.

3   Embedded Cluster Computing by the On–Request Dynamic Connection Reconfiguration

Dynamic embedded processor clusters can be created by establishing, on asynchronous requests, permanent connections inside groups of processors. This paradigm will be explained considering only this part of the total communication system shown in Fig. 1, which uses the link connection switch. Its general structure in a centralized control version is shown in Fig. 4. In this structure, the global control subsystem (GCS) controls connection setting in the link connection switch. The connections can be set on request as a result of reconfiguration instructions that precede communication instructions in an application program. The data transfer itself is included into a control message dialog (configuration request, connection acknowledge, link release) that takes place (by the Reconfiguration Control Path) between communication processors of worker processor subsystems (WPSi) and the link connection controller (CGS).

Dynamic embedded cluster computing can be also achieved by a new strategy for the control of dynamic inter–processor connections that is called the "connection by communication" paradigm [16]. It assumes that dynamic inter–processor connections with different types of behavior are created on–line and co–existing during program execution. The controlled connection behavior concerns time characteristics and the communication model in which a connection is used: synchronous or asynchronous. The inter–processor connections are established by data communication instructions without execution of additional connection configuration directives. A connection can be set on–line or the type of an existing one can be transformed for the defined communication model. The

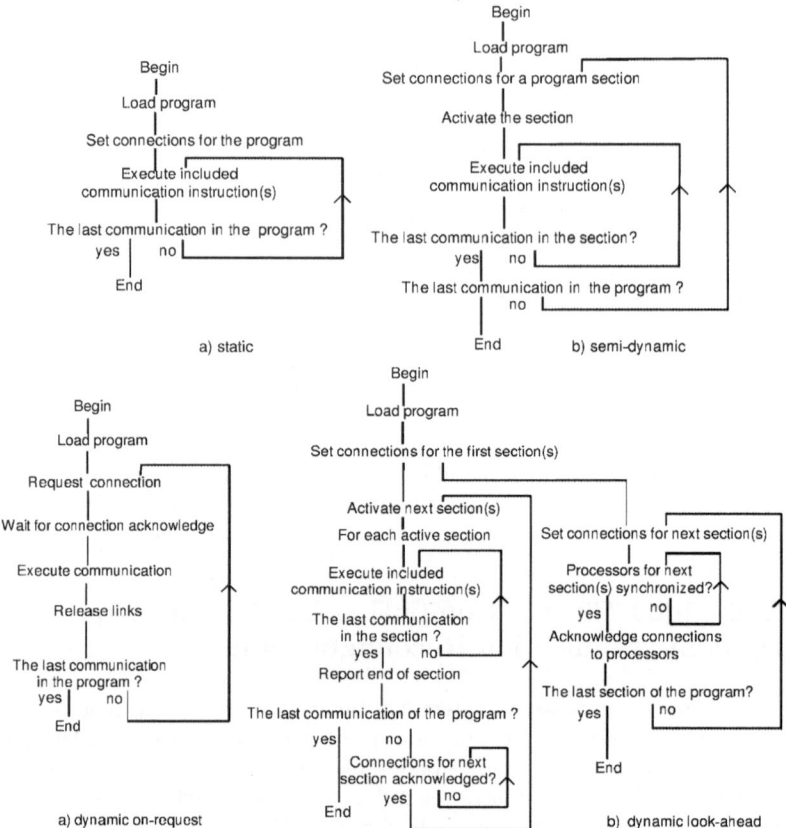

Fig. 3. Program execution control with connection reconfiguration

connections last application program dependent time. In this way data communication instructions have residual effect on inter–processor connections.

Four communication models are supported by the system communication hardware: volatile connection asynchronous communication, volatile connection synchronous communication, permanent connections asynchronous communication and permanent connections synchronous communication. Out of them, the three last models are provided by the link connection switch. Volatile asynchronous communication is implemented in the packet switching network. The communication model is defined by the type of channel used in a communication instruction. There are 4 pools of channel identifiers.

A volatile connection can be destroyed when the involved processor links are required to create another connection and when all communication directed to these links has been completed. A permanent connection can be disrupted only

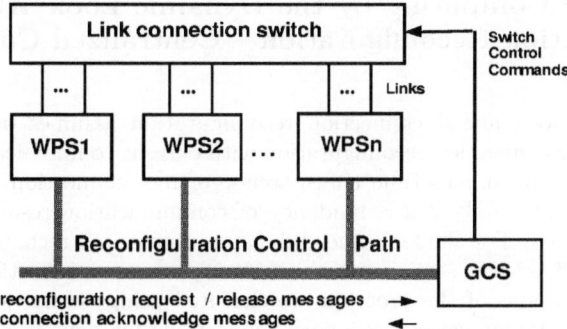

Fig. 4. Basic structure of the on–request reconfigurable system

by a special communication instruction bound with the creative instruction, also if all communication directed to this connection has been completed.

A synchronous volatile connection remains in the switch after a communication in the respective channel but it can be destroyed if the links are required for a new connection. Each connection is created after synchronization ("rendez–vous") of connection requests coming from all communicating processors. The GCS can use an existing connection or it can create a new one, if there are available free links of involved processors. The GCS processor sends connection acknowledges to all communicating processes. After communication, a link release is sent to the GCS. For each existing connection, it maintains a counter of the issued acknowledges and received link releases. A volatile connection can be cancelled if the counter status shows zero.

A permanent synchronous connection is created for communication done according to the synchronous (CSP–like) model. First, connection requests are sent to the GCS for synchronization for a given channel. The synchronized link connection can be created if there are free links of processors. If the requested connection already exists as volatile, it can be transformed into a permanent one. Permanent synchronous connections can be used for communication specified in the volatile connection channels and synchronous permanent channels. A permanent synchronous connection can be disrupted by the synchronized connection requests coming from the same processors, in the same permanent synchronous channel that was used for the connection creation. The disruption is done if the counter of acknowledges and done by the connection shows zero.

Permanent asynchronous connections are created for communication in which sender and receiver(s) are not synchronized. The pool of asynchronous permanent channels is subdivided into three parts: creative, standard and disconnecting. Connection requests in a creative channel first have to get synchronized. All involved processors are acknowledged after a connection is set. Communication using the connection is done in standard asynchronous channels. For the asynchronous transmissions, buffers are provided at the receiver processors.

4   Cluster Computing by the Dynamic Look–Ahead Connection Reconfiguration – Centralized Control

The dynamic look–ahead connection reconfiguration assumes overlapping of inter–processor connection reconfiguration with current communication through processor links. It enables time transparency of link connection setting. Such a solution is viable only if a redundancy of communication resources is available in the system. For the look–ahead dynamic connection reconfiguration, the program is divided into sections in which inter–processor connections are fixed. While some sections of the program are executed using connections organized in one set of communication resources, connections for next program sections are organized in redundant resources. When the execution of previous sections is completed, program execution is switched to new sections that will use new look–ahead organized connections in spare communication resources.

Program sections for execution with the look–ahead connection reconfiguration are determined by an analysis of the program graph at compile–time. Program sections define embedded dynamic clusters of processors. The program graph is built of communication and control nodes connected by activation and communication edges, Fig. 5. The nodes and communication edges in the graph are assigned to processors and processors links. Section subgraphs are mutually disjoint in respect to communication edges connecting processes allocated to different processors. Section subgraph composition is so chosen, as to have all the connections needed by a section, prepared in advance in the spare communication resources with no communication delay of involved communication.

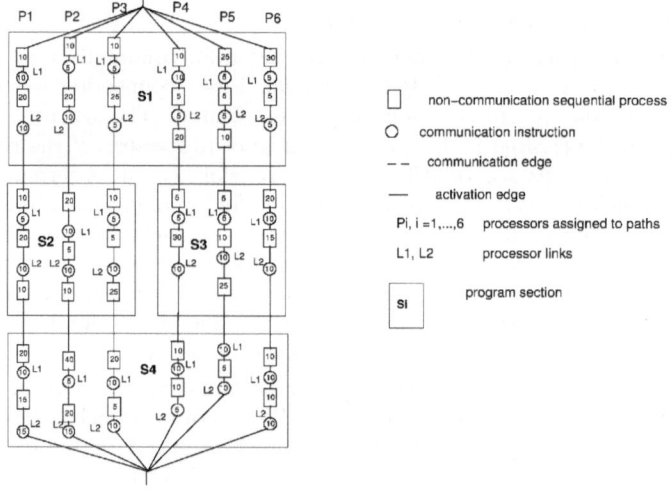

Fig. 5. A program graph partition for the look–ahead connection reconfiguration

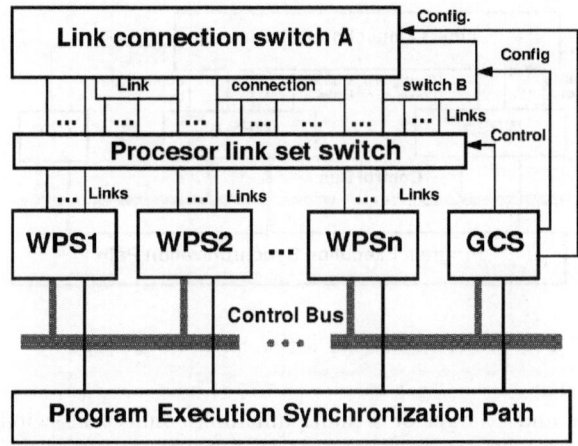

Fig. 6. Dual link connection switch architecture principle

The granularity of program execution control with the look–ahead connection reconfiguration defines different compositions of dynamic processor clusters that correspond to identified program sections and different program execution strategies. The globally synchronous strategy defines clusters that contain all processors in the system. The asynchronous processor–restraint strategy defines clusters that contain subsets of all processors. With the asynchronous link–restraint strategy, clusters are composed of one sender and one or several receiver processors. If the second strategy is applied, all the three kinds of processor clusters can be organized during execution of a program. The real execution of the program divided into sections (clusters) will be time consistent with the estimated program graph execution schedule if the control structure of the program is fully deterministic. In other cases, execution time of program threads can vary, which can be a reason of some control execution delays.

The communication resource redundancy provided in the system can concern link connection switches, processors or processor links. The general structure of a look–ahead link connection reconfiguration system with two connection switches is shown in Fig. 6. The Control Bus is used for the exchange of reconfiguration control messages (connection requests, acknowledges and link releases). The Program Execution Synchronization Path is used to synchronize end of section reports coming from worker subsystems. The synchronization, when implemented in hardware, enables a very efficient look–ahead reconfiguration control close to time transparency. Instead of using multiple processor sets, links of each worker processor subsystem can be divided into two subsets: one used for the execution of a current program section and the other used for the configuration. This enables to have one link connection switch in the system, Fig. 7. This solution is the cheapest in terms of hardware, however, it requires processors with a larger

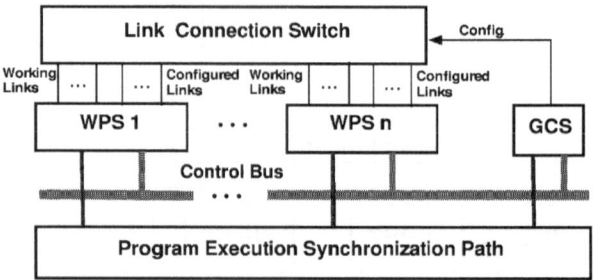

Fig. 7. Partitioned link set architecture principle

number of links and a larger or a multi–unit link connection switch. With the current technology both requirements can be fulfilled.

A genetic algorithm was designed which defines program graph partitions into sections in the way to minimize partitioned program execution time in the embedded cluster system based on the look–ahead dynamic reconfiguration [18,19]. The partitioning algorithm takes into account time parameters of the application program and time parameters of the look–ahead reconfiguration control. The reconfiguration control is modeled as subgraphs inserted automatically between the boundaries of sections. The homogeneous representation of the program and the reconfiguration control hardware/software enables an easy evaluation of partitioned program execution time which includes time overheads introduced by reconfiguration control. These evaluations are used as the fitness function of the genetic algorithm while searching for the best program graph partitions. Experiments performed with the use of the partitioning algorithm for different program and reconfiguration control parameters show that the look–ahead dynamic connection reconfiguration is especially suitable for programs with fine grained parallelism and systems with large reconfiguration control latencies.

5   Cluster Computing Based on the Dynamic Look–Ahead Connection Reconfiguration – Distributed Control

The architecture based on the multi–bus inter–processor connection switch with the double link connection system, Fig. 8, enables an efficient implementation of embedded cluster computing through the look–ahead dynamic reconfiguration based on distributed control [20,21].

For each data link, outgoing from a communication processor, there are two intermediate lines which can be directly connected to the data busses. When one line is connected to an executive bus, the connection of the other line to a configured bus can be created according to a request sent from the communication processor through by the control line.

The data link can be switched between these lines for execution of consecutive program sections. The sections (dynamic processor clusters) are defined

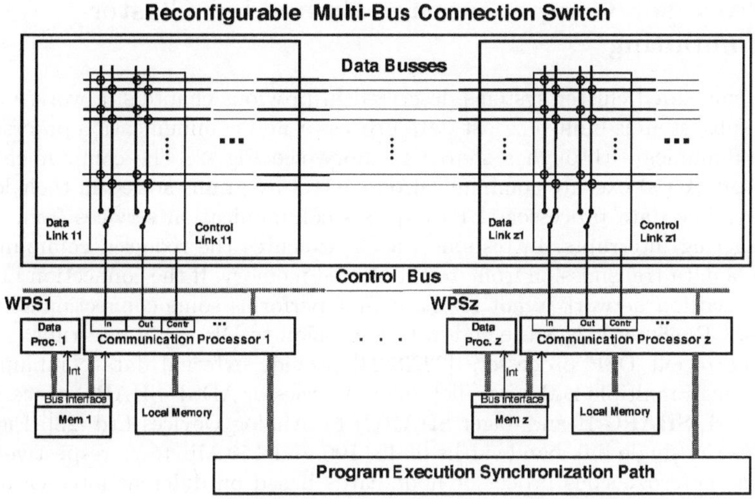

Reconfigurable Multi-Bus Connection Switch

Fig. 8. Multi–bus system architecture principle

at compile time in the result of the program graph analysis. A program section determines the time interval where connections between a number of worker subsystems WPSi are fixed. For each next section, there are provided free busses for configuration of necessary connections. A communication processor can create its connections for next section when the involved bus becomes free. Each sender processor acquires the token of the bus which is to be used for its connection, creates its new connection of the alternative data line, sends the connection synchronization request to all its receivers, waits for the section receiver synchronization signal, switches its data lines to alternative data lines when the data lines are free, then starts using the data bus. Each receiver processor waits for the receiver synchronization request, creates its new connections of the alternative data lines, switches its data line to the newly created connection when the data lines are free, sends a receiver synchronization signal, starts using the data bus to perform receive instructions. Program sections should be composed so as not to delay execution of communication (due to reconfiguration control) or to delay as little as possible. A cluster can contain a single or multiple sender processors depending on the time and spatial communication locality in the program. Synchronization for reconfiguration control is done at the level of all receiver processors in the cluster by a hardware synchronization circuit. The strategy for program partitioning into sections depends on the number of available hardware circuits for synchronization of reconfiguration states in processors.

6 Processor Components for Embedded Cluster Computing

In the embedded cluster systems described in previous chapters, a worker processor subsystem is built of a fast data processor and communication processors that communicate through a shared memory, see Fig. 2. The communication processors (CPs) execute communication control programs stored in their local memory. The data processor (DP) requests communication services from CPs by triggering interrupts. In response, a CP executes the required communication by a data transmission from/to the shared memory. If the connection in the communication network is not ready, it first performs some connection setting actions. CP acknowledges the end of transmission to DP by an interrupt.

Some recent DSP processors [22,23,24] provide external data communication through multiple DMA parallel links. A series of ADSP SHARC processors (SHARC I, SHARC II and Tiger SHARC) by Analog Devices Ltd [23], Fig. 9, provides the single link bandwidths of 40, 100 and 150 Mbytes/s respectively.

Some heterogeneous processor node cards based on different inter–card interfaces are commercially available from several vendors [25,26,27,28]. Such a card generally includes a powerful data processor with RAM memory and one to three PCI Mezzanine Card (PMC) slots in which communication processors with a RAM memory can be inserted. A PMC card communicates with the data processor via the PCI interface.

Some of the cards and their producers are enlisted below:

PCI: DECAlpha + 2 x PMC slots (Alpha Data)
PowerPC + 1 (2) PMC slots (Transtech DSP)
ISA: DECAlpha + 2 PMC slots (Alpha Data)
VME: 3 x PMC slots (Alpha Data)
PowerPC + 2 PMC slots (Transtech)

The PMC cards are populated with different multi link processors, FPGA units and memory units in configurations shown below:

(SHARC I or SHARC II or TIGER–SHARC) + memory
DECAlpha + memory
PowerPC + memory
Texas C4x + memory
FPGA + memory
TIGER–SHARC + FPGA + memory
T9000 + memory

The PMC cards are produced among others by Transtech DSP, Alpha Data and Sundance. Some fast crossbar switches [29] enable dynamic connections of links of communication processors. No multi–bus inter–processor connection switches are yet commercially available.

7 Conclusions

System architectures and program execution paradigms for embedded cluster computing based on dynamically organized processor clusters were presented

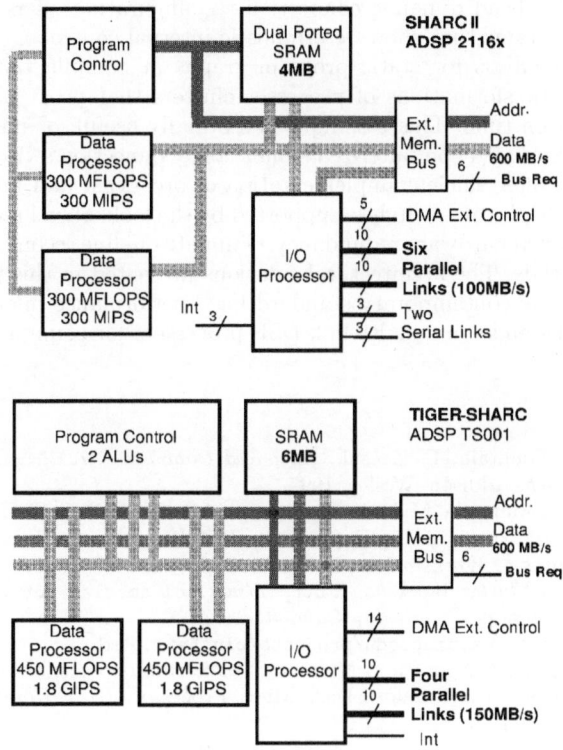

Fig. 9. General structures of some SHARC ADSP processors

in the paper. Co–existence of four types of inter–processor connection behavior during execution of parallel programs is assumed. It implies a new architecture of the interconnection network in the system – based on circuit and packet switched communication. The control paradigm for the on–request inter–connection setting in the message passing parallel systems can be based on a residual effect of data communications. The paradigm can reduce execution time of programs which show space and temporal locality of communication.

The on–request reconfiguration control introduces time overheads that can reduce advantages of the co–operative work of dynamically created processor clusters. The look–ahead dynamic connection reconfiguration enables overlapping of communication, computations and reconfiguration of inter–processor connections during program execution, however at the cost of introduction of hardware communication resource redundancy. The look–ahead dynamic connection reconfiguration enables time transparency of reconfiguration control for on–line created processor clusters and adjusting system structure to program needs. The look–ahead dynamic connection reconfiguration offers the best advantages for programs that show deterministic internal control.

Automatic analysis for static program graphs at compile time can determine dynamic transformations of processor clusters that provide the minimal program execution time. This technique is especially useful for numerical computations and extended computerized simulation. Connection switches based on multiple–busses offer efficient implementation of broadcast and multicast communication. Multiple–bus switches, supported by the look–ahead reconfiguration control and internal hardware redundancy, eliminate on–line reconfiguration control time overheads. The architectural solutions presented in this paper can be implemented using contemporary standard high–performance micro–processors for computations and some multi–link DSP processors for communication.

References

1. D. Sima, T. Fountain, P. Kacsuk: *Advanced Computer Architectures; A Design Space Approach*, Addison–Wesley, 1997.
2. Y. Kanaka, M. Matsuda, M.Ando, K. Kazuto, M.Sato: "COMPaS": A Pentium Pro PC–based SMP Cluster and its Experience, *IPPS Workshop on Personal Computer Based Networks of Workstations*, LNCS 1388, pp. 486–497. 1998.
3. *"Pentium Pro Cluster Workshop"*, http://www.scl.ameslab.gov/workshops/
4. *"Scalable Clusters of Commodity Computers"*,
   http://www.csag.cs.uiuc.edu/projects/clusters.html
5. Encore Computer Corporation, *Multimax Technical Summary*, March 1987.
6. D. Lenoski et al.: The Stanford Dash Multi–Processor, *IEEE Computer*, Vol. 25, N. 3, 1992, pp. 63–79.
7. Convex Press, *Convex Exemplar Architecture*, 1994, pp. 239.
8. M. Tudruj, L. Masko: An Architecture and Task Scheduling Algorithm for Systems Based on Dynamically Reconfigurable Shared Memory Clusters, *Proceedings of NATO Advanced Research Workshop on Advanced Environments, Tools and Applications for Cluster Computing, Mangalia, Sept. 2001* also *LNCS (this volume)* Springer Verlag.
9. M. Tudruj, L. Masko: A Parallel System Architecture Based on Dynamically Configurable Shared Memory Clusters, *Proceedings of Parallel Processing and Applied Mathematics Conference PPAM'2001*, Naleczow, Poland, 4–6 Sept. 2001, LNCS, Springer Verlag.
10. M. Tudruj: Multi–transputer architectures with the look–ahead dynamic link connection reconfiguration, *World Transputer Congress'95*, Harrogate, U.K., September 1995.
11. M. Tudruj: Look–Ahead Dynamic Reconfiguration of Link Connections in Multi–Processor Architectures, *Parallel Computing'95*, Gent, Sept. 1995, pp. 539–546.
12. T. Muntean: SUPERNODE, Architecture Parallele, Dynamiquement Reconfigurable de Transputers, *11–emes Journees sur l'Informatique*, Nancy, January. 1989.
13. P. Jones, A. Murta: The Implementation of a Run–Time Link–Switching Environment for Multi–Transputer Machines, *Proc. of the NATUG 2 Meeting*, Durham, Oct. 1989.
14. A. Bauch, R. Braam, E. Maehle: DAMP – A Dynamic Reconfigurable Multiprocessor System With a Distributed Switching Network, *2–nd European Conf. on Distributed Memory Computing*, Munich, 22–24 April, 1991, pp. 495–504,

15. M. Tudruj: Dynamically Reconfigurable Multi–Transputer Systems with Serial Bus Control, EUROMICRO'92 Short Notes, *Microprogramming and Microprocessing.*, V. 37, 1993, pp. 149–152.
16. M. Tudruj: "Connection by Communication" Paradigm for Dynamically Reconfigurable Multi–Processor Systems, *Proc. of the Int. Conf. on Parallel Computing in Electrical Engineering, PARELEC'2000*, Trois–Rivieres, Canada, Aug. 2000, pp. 74–78.
17. J. Duato et al.: A High Performance Router Architecture for Interconnection Networks, *Proceedings of the International Conference on Parallel Processing*, 1996, Vol. 1, pp. 61–68.
18. E. Laskowski, M. Tudruj: Program Graph Partitioning for Execution by Processor Clusters with the Look–Ahead Connection Reconfiguration, *Proc. of the Int. Conf. on Parallel Computing in Electrical Engineering, PARELEC'98*, 2–5 Sept. 1998, Bialystok, Poland, pp. 94–99.
19. E. Laskowski, M. Tudruj: A Testbed for Parallel Program Execution with Dynamic Look–Ahead Inter–Processor Connections, *Proc. of the Int. Conf. on Parallel Processing and Applied Mathematics Conference, PPAM'99*, 14–17 Sept. 1999, Kazimierz Dolny, Poland, pp. 427–436.
20. M. Tudruj, B. Toursel, R. Briki: Look–Ahead Dynamic Inter–processor Connection Reconfiguration Based on Multi–Bus Connection Switches, *Proc. of the Itl. Conf. on Parallel Computing in Electrical Engineering, PARELEC'98*, Bialystok, Sept. 1998, pp. 86–93.
21. M. Tudruj, B. Toursel, R. Briki: Multiple–Bus Inter–Processor Communication with the Look–Ahead Connection Setting, *Proc. of the 3-rd Int. Conf. Parallel Processing and Applied Mathematics Conference, PPAM'99*, Kazimierz Dolny, Sept. 1999, pp. 228–237.
22. Texas Instruments, *TMS320C4x User's Guide*, 1992.
23. Analog Devices Ltd, *Digital Signal Processing*, http://www.analog.com/technology/dsp/index.html
24. Berkeley Design Technology Inc., *Buyer's Guide to DSP Processors*, 1995.
25. Transtech Parallel Systems Ltd., http://www.transtech.co.uk
26. Transtech–DSP Ltd, *Analog Devices DSP Cards*, http://www.transtech-dsp.com/sharcdsp/index.html
27. Apha Data Parallel Systems Ltd, http://www.alphadata.co.uk/hardhome.html
28. Sundance Multiprocessor Technology Ltd., *Boards and Modules*, http://www.sundance.com/index.html
29. Applied Micro Circuits Corporation, *Network Interface Products, Data Book*, 1999.

Parallelisation of Wave Propagation Algorithms for Odour Propagation in Multi-agent Systems

Eugen Dedu[1], Stéphane Vialle[1], and Claude Timsit[2]

[1] Supélec, 2 rue Édouard Belin, 57070 Metz, France
dedu@ese-metz.fr, Stephane.Vialle@supelec.fr
[2] University of Versailles, 45 avenue des États-Unis, 78035 Versailles Cedex, France
Claude.Timsit@prism.uvsq.fr

Abstract. Multi-agent systems are a model of distributed computing. Agents perceve their environment and a classical agent percept is a kind of odour sensing. The odour is spread in the environment by resources, and is simulated by a value which increases as the agent approaches the resource. A useful model of odour propagation is the wave propagation model. This article discusses some sequential and parallel methods to implement it. The mixing between these sequential and parallel methods is also shown, and the performance of some of them on two shared-memory parallel architectures is introduced.

1 Introduction

There are large and distributed systems where an efficient or an optimum solution has to be found. A promising way to cope with such systems is the distributed computing. Currently, an appropriate model to simulate such systems is the multi-agent model. An agent is defined as an entity with a proper behaviour, found in an environment, which senses it by its percepts and acts upon it through its effectors [3]. One of the goals of the simulation of populations of agents is to study emergence mechanisms: individual behaviours of agents which give efficient global behaviours, for example the trail-following in foraging ant populations [1].

Agent behaviour uses agent percepts. One of the percepts used in multi-agent systems is the "odour", simulated by a value in each square which is greater as it is nearer to the resource [9]. As such, these values, called potentials in the following, allow agents to find the way to resources in environment. Potentials are spread through the environment by resources. A square may be influenced by several resources. For our model we have taken a simple but sufficient hypothesis: if a square is influenced by several resources, it receives the value of the *strongest* potential (another hypothesis is taken in [9], where overlapping potentials add). As the potential propagation represents in some cases a great part of the execution time of the simulator [9], we have studied their parallelisation.

This article is divided as follows. Firstly, we describe the wave propagation model, used to propagate the potential of resources. Secondly, some sequential

D. Grigoras et al. (Eds.): IWCC 2001, LNCS 2326, pp. 92–102, 2002.

methods to implement it are presented. General parallelisation methods and their mixing with sequential ones are presented afterwards. Finally, the performance of two parallel implementations, based on one sequential method, is introduced.

2   Wave Propagation Model

The potential propagation consists of spreading decreasing potentials from a resource. It allows agents to find the way to resources by following increasing potential. We have made the assumption in our model that the potential in each square is equal to the potential of the resource minus the distance to it: $p(d) = p_R - d$. We use a 4-connectivity of squares. In an environment without obstacles, the distance between two squares is simply $|dy| + |dx|$. However, in the presence of obstacles, this formula is no longer appropriate. The wave propagation model allows to surpass obstacles (Fig. 1).

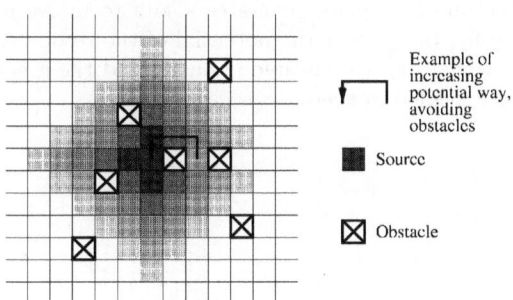

Fig. 1. Illustration of the potential spread by a resource.

3   Sequential Methods

3.1   Recursive Potential Computing

These methods create the potential fields by propagating successively the potential of each resource. The propagation of each resource is done recursively.

Recursive with depth-first propagation. In this method, the propagation starts from each resource and is recursively spread on the environment through a depth-first mechanism while decreasing the value of the current potential ($P(S)$ is the potential in square S):

    clear (set to 0) the potential of all the squares
    for all square S containing a resource **do**
      prop-square $(S, P(S))$

procedure prop-square (square S, potential p)
if $P(S) < p$ **then** $\{S$ needs to be processed$\}$
    $P(S) \leftarrow p$
    if $p > 1$ **then**
       for all neighbour N of S **do**
          if S is not an obstacle **then**
             prop-square $(N, p-1)$

The key point of this method is that the call to recursive function `prop-square` gives a *depth-first* propagation. The depth-first recursion is simple to implement, since it is automatically provided by modern programming languages. However, this is a case where the depth-first search is not efficient. The reason is that the potential of some squares is successively updated. Figure 2 presents such an example, where the neighbours are taken in N, E, S, W order (potential of resource is 4). The potential of the square at right of the resource receives two values: It is firstly set to 1, then to its correct value 3. Moreover, an update of the potential of a square generates also a recursive update of all its neighbours[1]. Generally, the greater the potential of the resource, the bigger the number of squares which receive multiple updates, and the greater the number of updates which are needed in average for each square.

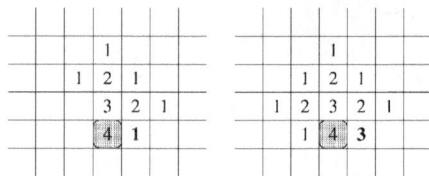

Fig. 2. Two steps during the depth-first propagation of a resource. The square at the right of the resource updates its potential twice.

Recursive with breadth-first propagation. We have implemented a similar method, which avoids the successive unuseful updates (as given by the previous method) by doing a *breadth-first* propagation. The breadth-first search mechanism and the recursion were simulated with a (FIFO) queue that stores the elements used in recursion.

Because this method uses the breadth-first search, each square is modified only once. As such, the number of updates of squares is equal to the number of squares in the potential field.

---

[1] For the sake of precision, the number of times each square (except the squares in N direction) is updated is $\left\lfloor \frac{k+1}{2} \right\rfloor$, where k is the final potential of the square.

3.2   Iterative Potential Computing

These methods sweep several times the whole environment, updating each square when necessary.

Iterative with fixed potential. This method, presented by Bouton [2], starts by putting the potential of each resource in its square. Then, during the first iteration, all the environment is swept in order to find all the squares containing the greatest potential p. Each time a square with potential p is found, all its neighbours having potential less than $p-1$ are given a potential of $p-1$. During the second iteration, all the squares with potential $p-1$ are found and their neighbours with a lower potential are given potential $p-2$. The iterations continue until the potential 1 is reached. At this step, the propagation is completely finished on all the environment.

This method has the advantage to be simple, so it does not add execution overheads. Nevertheless, the high disadvantage of this method is that during each step all the environment is swept, which leads to a lot of unnecessary processed squares.

Iterative with variable potential. This is similar to the previous method. The difference between them is that, during each step, instead of processing only squares with a given potential p, this method compares each square with its neighbours, updating it if one of them has a higher potential.

3.3   Distance-Storing Methods

In these methods each square stores not potentials, but *distances* to resources. This is possible because the place of resources is fixed during the simulation.

Distance-storing of all influent resources. In this method, each square stores the identifier (a unique number) of every resource which can influence its potential during the simulation, and the distance to it. When the potential of a square needs to be known, the influence of each resource on it can be simply calculated by using the distances it stores and the actual potential of each concerned resource. Then the strongest potential can be chosen.

This method has the advantage that the potential can be computed on demand (only for the needed squares), which can be very fast. As an example, if agents are found on 1% of the squares, then the potential of a maximum of 5% of the squares is calculated (the square itself and its four neighbours). Another advantage of this method is that the computations for each square are independent, so no special parallelisation method (to avoid parallelisation conflicts) is needed. Nevertheless, its drawback is that it has a high memory requirement, because it stores in each square information about every resource which can influence it.

Distance-storing of the most influent resource. This method looks like the previous one. However, instead of storing in each square the identifier of *all* the resources which can influence it, it stores the identifier of only the most influent one. The most influent resource is the resource which gives the potential of the square, i.e. it gives the maximum potential in the case of overlapping fields.

This method is more difficult to implement than the previous one. However, since only one resource is stored in each square, it needs less memory space. In conclusion, it seems to be a very good trade-off between memory requirements and execution time. Nevertheless, it seems to be very difficult to find an algorithm which updates the resource frontiers when resource potentials evolve.

4   Parallelisation Methods

This section deals with parallelisation methods which can be applied to the sequential algorithms described above. Some of the combinations between the parallelisation methods and the sequential algorithms are possible without any modification, others are inefficient, while others are not possible. Their mixing is presented in Table 1 and will be detailed below.

Table 1. Mixing between the parallelisation methods and the sequential ones.

Parallelisation\Sequential method	Recursive	Iterative	Distance-all	Distance-most
Fixed domain partitioning	ok	ok	first stage only	ok
Changing domain partitioning	ok	ok	first stage only	ok
Processor-private environments	ok	inefficient	inefficient	ok
Mutex-based	ok	ok	no	ok

4.1   Fixed Domain Decomposition

This is the classical domain decomposition parallelisation [5]. The basic principle is that each processor is affected to a different domain. The number of domains is equal to the number of processors, and each processor is bound to a distinct domain in our environment. We have used a horizontal decomposition, where each domain has the same number of lines[2] of environment.

The complete propagation is done in three stages (Fig. 3). The first stage propagates the potential of all the resources in each domain *separately*, setting the correct potential on each square of its domain. This can be done with any of the sequential methods, according to Table 1. This stage of propagation is sufficient when the sequential method based on storing all the influent resources is used.

The second stage copies the frontiers to a memory accessed by other processors, called *buffer* in the following. No synchronisation point is needed, since

---

[2] Or differing by 1 line if the number of lines is not divisible by the number of domains.

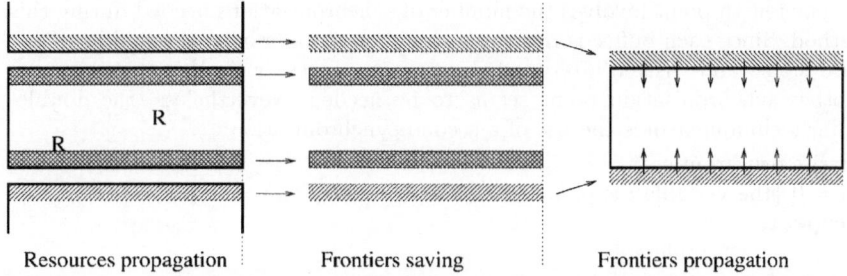

| Resources propagation | Frontiers saving | Frontiers propagation |

Fig. 3. For each processor, the propagation is completely done in three stages: resources propagation, frontiers saving (only 2 frontiers in this figure), and frontiers repropagation, the last two stages being repeated several times.

there is no sharing conflict: each processor reads and writes its own data (domain and buffers).

The third stage repropagates in each domain separately the potentials of all the frontiers. Four points need to be discussed in this stage, presented in the following. Firstly, a synchronisation point is mandatory to cope with the sharing of the buffers.

The second point involves the main part of this stage: the repropagation of the frontiers. This is similar to the first stage (propagation), except that the propagation starts from all the points of the domain frontiers (and not from resources, as some of the propagation methods).

Thirdly, the second and the third stages are repeatedly executed until no change of potential is done on frontiers during the third stage. At this moment, the propagation is entirely done in all the environment.

Figure 4 (left case) presents an example where two repropagations are necessary. During propagation, the obstacles prevent the square X to receive the potential from resource R. A first repropagation allows intermediate squares to receive correct potential values, and only the second repropagation can put the right potential into square X. The other two examples in Fig. 4 present cases when a domain is interposed between resource R and square X.

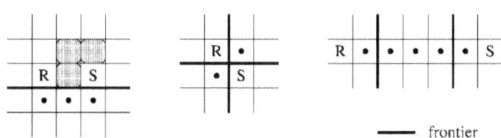

Fig. 4. Examples where two repropagations are needed for square X to receive the correct potential value from resource R (suppose the only resource influencing X is R).

The fourth point involves the number of synchronisations needed during this method. Since each buffer is read by a neighbour processor at the middle of the third stage, and written afterwards by its own processor (in the second stage), another synchronisation point seems to be needed. Nevertheless, the double-buffer technique avoids the use of a second synchronisation:

write own frontiers
i = 0 {the variable i is private to each processor}
repeat
    write own buffers[i]
    synchronisation point
    read neighbours' buffers[i]
    i = 1 - i {choose the other set of buffers}
    write own frontiers
until no change of potential on any square of the frontiers

4.2   Changing Domain Decomposition

The fixed domain decomposition method needs several repropagations to complete the potential spreading in the environment. The purpose of the changing domain decomposition is to reduce the number of repropagations.

The distinctive feature of this method is that the domain decomposition changes when the frontiers are repropagated. Figure 5 presents such a case, with 4 processors used by the propagation and 3 processors used during the repropagation. The new frontiers are now located at some distance from the old ones. If the distance between the old and the new frontiers is larger than the potential field length of any resource, the potentials of the new domain frontiers do not change, thus no synchronisation point is necessary.

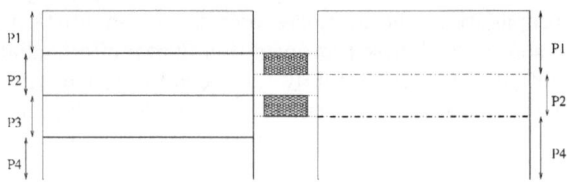

Fig. 5. The repropagation changes the decomposition in order to move off the frontiers.

A disadvantage of this method is that the cache is not well exploited. Since a lot of squares are processed by different processors during propagation and repropagation, cache conflicts appear [6], degrading the performance.

4.3   Processor-Private Environments

As a first step (Fig. 6), each processor processes a part of the resources, and updates its potential field on a *whole* processor-private copy of the environment. After that, as the second step, the environment is updated using the processor-private copies of the environment: each square of the environment receives a potential equal to the maximum potential of the corresponding squares of the processor-private environments. This solution has higher memory requirements (for the private environments) and leads to a lot of cache misses for the second step, since each processor reads private environments.

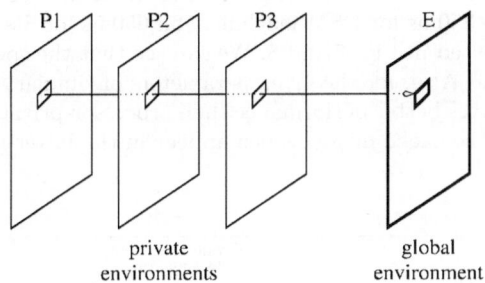

Fig. 6. Example of data decomposition for the wave propagation algorithm (3 processors).

4.4   Mutex-Based Parallelisation

In this method, each processor propagates the potential of a part of the resources (data decomposition). To solve the concurrent access to squares influenced by several resources, a mutex (variable used to ensure a *mut*ual *ex*clusion region) per square or per group of squares is used. This leads to numerous and expensive mutex operations.

5   Performance

We have implemented two parallelisation methods: fixed domain partitioning, and processor-private environments. Four sequential implementations were taken into account: recursive with depth-first and breadth-first propagation, and iterative with fixed and variable potential. As shown in Table 1, it is inefficient to use processor-private environment with iterative methods. Therefore, we chose to use the recursive breadth-first method for the two parallelisation methods above.

The programming language used was the C language. The SMP machine was a Workgroup 450 Sun server[3] with 4 processors running Linux, the compiler used was gcc (GNU Compiler Collection), and the parallel library was Posix threads [7], linux threads[4] implementation. The DSM [8] machine was an Origin 2000 [4] with 64 processors running Irix, the compiler used was its native one, MIPSPro, with Irix native multi-threading library.

For these tests, an environment with 512x512 squares was used, containing 10% obstacles. The number of resources was 1% of the squares, and their potential was 16.

For each test, four executions were done, and the execution time of the slowest processor in each execution was kept. The average time among these was taken into account for experimentation results. The execution time of the propagation part in sequential is 350ms for DSM machine, and 650ms for SMP machine. The speed-ups are presented in Fig. 7 and 8. We can see that the speed-ups on both machines are similar. Also, for the given parameters of simulation, the fixed domain partitioning gives better performance than processor-private environments. The reason can be the cache misses which appear in the latter method.

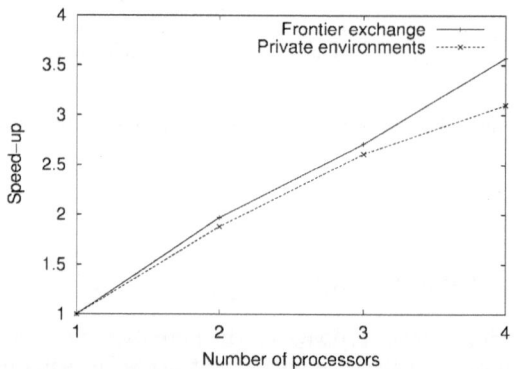

Fig. 7. The speed-up on an SMP machine.

6   Conclusions

This article has introduced four parallelisation and six sequential algorithms of the wave propagation model. We have experimented two parallelisation algorithms, using an efficient and compatible sequential algorithm for the processing of their sequential part. We have obtained good speed-ups up to four processors

---

[3] http://www.sun.com/servers/workgroup/450.
[4] http://pauillac.inria.fr/~xleroy/linuxthreads.

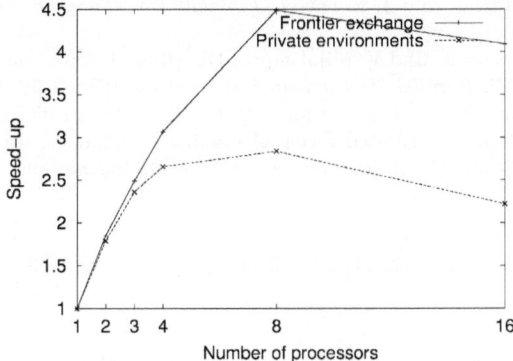

Fig. 8. The speed-up on a DSM machine.

on both SMP and DSM architectures: speed-up greater than 3 on 4 processors. But performance decreases using more processors. Therefore, our future work will be guided to the following directions:

- Optimising the implementations, such as reducing useless cache misses.
- Implementing and evaluating algorithms with higher memory requirements, such as the method based on distance-storing of all influent resources.
- Implementing and evaluating other parallelisation methods.

Finally, an original and promising direction seems to be the tolerance of minor errors in the potential propagation, which would decrease the execution times without affecting agent performance.

Acknowledgements. Support for this research is provided in part by a grant from *Région Lorraine* (France), and access and support to Origin 2000 super-computer are provided by *Charles Hermite Centre* (France).

References

1. C. Adami. *Introduction to Artificial Life.* Springer-Verlag, 1998.
2. L. Bouton. ParMASS : un simulateur de systèmes multi-agents parallèle. Master's thesis, Université de Nancy-I, Supélec, LORIA, June 1998.
3. J. Ferber. *Les systèmes multi-agents. Vers une intelligence collective.* InterEditions, 1995.
4. J. Fier. Performance tuning optimization for Origin2000 and Onyx. Available at `http://techpubs.sgi.com/library/manuals/3000/ 007-3511-001/html/ O2000Tuning.0.html`.
5. I. Foster. *Designing and Building Parallel Programs.* Addison-Wesley Publishing Company, 1995.
6. M. D. Hill and J. R. Larus. Cache considerations for multiprocessor programers. *Communications of the ACM*, 33(8):97–102, Aug. 1990.

7. B. Nichols, D. Buttlar, and J. P. Farrel. *Pthreads Programming.* O'Reilly & Associates, Sept. 1996.
8. J. Protić, M. Tomašević, and V. Milutinović. Distributed shared memory: Concepts and systems. *IEEE Parallel & Distributed Technology*, 4(2):63–79, Summer 1996.
9. G. M. Werner and M. G. Dyer. BioLand: A massively parallel simulation environment for evolving distributed forms of intelligent behavior. In H. Kitano and J. A. Hendler, editors, *Massively Parallel Artificial Intelligence*, pages 316–349. MIT Press, 1994.

Parallel and Distributed Solutions for the Optimal Binary Search Tree Problem

Mitică Craus

"Gh.Asachi" Technical University of Iasi
Computer Engineering Department
6600 Iaşi, Romania
craus@cs.tuiasi.ro

Abstract. A parallel and a distributed implementation for a very important problem in the searching theory, the optimal binary search tree (BST) problem, is presented and analyzed. Implemented as a VLSI array, the algorithm for building the optimal BST uses $O(n^2)$ processors and has the parallel time complexity $O(n)$. A search is solved in $O(\log n)$ time. On a cluster of computers, the binary search tree is organized on two levels: the first level corresponds to the BST of searching intervals and the second level is the level of the BST for effective searching within an interval. A hybrid solution is also considered. The best variant depends on the hypothesis of the searching problem.

1 Distributed Searching Structures and Algorithms

Usually, a wide area distributed database has not a single index of all information. That is the case of a national or regional network of electronic libraries or a distributed internet searching engine.

Which is the most adequate data structure for a distributed index? There are a lot of searching data structure (optimal binary search trees, AVL trees, 2-3 trees, 2-3-4 trees, B-trees, red-black trees, splay trees, digital search trees, tries [1,5,6]) but are they enough for a distributed index? The answer seems to be negative.

The internal relationships of an index usually have the topology of a digraph and this data structure is not adequate for efficient search algorithms. Building spanning tree [3] in a dynamically manner on the digraph representing the key relations in the index may be a way to use the search algorithms for trees. On the other hand, a distributed index imposes the distribution of the digraph over the network.

Also, the search algorithms for distributed search data structures differ from that for locally search data structures.

In a distributed search engine, a single user query starts in one place and the result should be returned to that one place. Centralized control of the searching process will direct where to search next and determine when the search is completed. With a fully distributed search, there is no central control.

D. Grigoras et al. (Eds.): IWCC 2001, LNCS 2326, pp. 103–117, 2002.

Both searching with centralized control and with no central control have advantages and disadvantages.

The main advantage of a centralized search is the control of the searching process but a centralized controller managing the entire process can become a bottleneck.

The advantages of a distributed search is that it offers greater processing power with each remote server performing part of the search, and avoids the bottleneck of a centralized controller managing the entire process. One problem with no central control is that often the same area is searched multiple times. Another problem of distributed searching is uniformity of evaluation. With several search engines each performing their searches using their own criterion for ranking the results, the synthesis of the various results is a difficult problem.

Which is the best solution for searching in a distributed index: centralized or distributed search? This is a problem. The answer seems to be the distributed search but the centralized search has its advantages that cannot be neglected.

Our paper is concerning with the problem of building a distributed search structure adequate to very fast centralized searches. This structure is a distributed binary search tree. It may be used for indexing a wide area distributed database. There are some researches in the indexing information retrieval area [4] but we have no information to be one referring to a distributed index based on binary search tree, organized in such a manner that the keys with the high probability of searching are reached faster then the others.

2   Optimal Binary Search Tree Problem

Let us consider $A = (a_1, a_2, ..., a_n)$ a sequence of data items increasing sorted on their keys $(k_1, k_2, \ldots, k_n)$. With these items it follows to be built a binary search tree [1].

Each item a_i is searched with the probability $p_i, i = 1, 2, \ldots, n$. Let us denote by q_i the probability to search the item x with the property that $a_i < x < a_{i+1}, i = 0, \ldots, n$, where $a_0 = -\infty, a_{n+1} = +\infty$. In these conditions $\sum_{i=1}^{n} p_i$ is the probability of success, $\sum_{i=0}^{n} q_i$ is the fail probability and $\sum_{i=1}^{n} p_i + \sum_{i=0}^{n} q_i = 1$.

Given $P = (p_1, p_2, \ldots, p_n)$ and $Q = (q_0, q_1, q_2, \ldots, q_n)$,the optimal BST is that for which the medium time to solve the search operations has the minim value. In the perspective of medium time computing, the BST is inflated with a set of pseudo-vertices corresponding to the failure intervals. The pseudo-vertices become the new leaves of the BST. A pseudo-vertex e_i will correspond to the search operations for values that belong to the interval (a_i, a_{i+1}) (see Fig. 1).

The time cost for a such tree is the medium time for solving a searching operation i.e:

$$\text{cost}(T) = \sum_{i=1}^{n} p_i * \text{level}(a_i) + \sum_{i=0}^{n} q_i * (\text{level}(e_i) - 1)$$

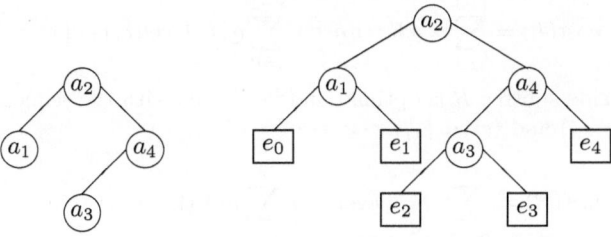

Fig. 1. Inflating a BST with pseudo-vertices e_i

where $\mathtt{level}(a_i)$ represents the number of comparisons that are executed when it is searched the item a_i.

The expression $p_i * \mathtt{level}(a_i)$ represents the cost of the searching for the item a_i and $q_i * (\mathtt{level}(e_i) - 1)$ is the cost for a searching in the interval (a_i, a_{i+1}). From $\mathtt{level}(e_i)$ the value 1 is subtracted, because the decision that the searched value belong to an interval (a_i, a_{i+1}) is not produced at the level of the pseudo-vertex but at the level of its parent.

For the sequence A, a set of binary search trees can be built. One of them is optimal. Let us denote this tree by T.

From the dynamic programming point of view, the tree T is the result of a sequence of decisions referring the vertex that becomes root of the optimal BST corresponding to a sequence $(a_{i+1}, a_{i+2}, ..., a_j), i \in \{0, 1, ..., n-1\}, j \in \{1, 2, ..., n\}, i < j$.

Let use denote by $c_{i,j}$ the cost of an optimal BST that has the vertices from the sequence $(a_{i+1}, a_{i+2}, ..., a_j)$ and the pseudo-vertices from the sequence $(e_i, e_{i+1}, ...e_j)$.

Lemma 1. The matrix $C = (c_{i,j})_{i,j=0,...,n}$ can be computed by the following recurrence:

$$c_{i,j} = \min_{i+1 \leq k \leq j} \{c_{i,k-1} + c_{k,j} + w_{i,j}\} \tag{1}$$

where $w_{i,j} = q_i + \sum_{l=i+1}^{j} (p_l + q_l)$

Proof. Let us consider the sequence $(a_1, a_2, ..., a_r, ..., a_n)$ increased sorted and let us suppose that during the first step the item a_r is selected to become root.

According to the optimality principle, it follows :

The left side subtree L is optimal and it is built with the sequences $(a_1, a_2, ..., a_{r-1})$ and $(e_0, e_1, ..., e_{r-1})$:

1

$$\text{cost}(L) = \sum_{i=1}^{r-1} p_i * \text{level}(a_i) + \sum_{i=0}^{r-1} q_i * (\text{level}(e_i) - 1)$$

The right side subtree R is optimal and it is built with the sequences $(a_{r+1}, a_{r+2}, ..., a_n)$ and $(e_r, e_{r+1}, ..., e_n)$:

$$\text{cost}(R) = \sum_{i=r+1}^{n} p_i * \text{level}(_i) + \sum_{i=r}^{n} q_i * (\text{level}(e_i) - 1)$$

Obs. The values `level()` are considered in the subtrees L, R.
The cost associated to the tree T becomes:

$$\text{cost}(T) = p_r + \text{cost}(L) + \text{cost}(R) + \sum_{i=1}^{r-1} p_i + \sum_{i=0}^{r-1} q_i + \sum_{i=r+1}^{n} p_i + \sum_{i=r}^{n} q_i.$$

The sums $\sum_{i=1}^{r-1} p_i + \sum_{i=0}^{r-1} q_i + \sum_{i=r+1}^{n} p_i + \sum_{i=r}^{n} q_i$ represent the additional values that appear because the tree T introduces a new level.

$$\text{cost}(T) = p_r + \text{cost}(L) + \text{cost}(R) + q_0 + \sum_{i=1}^{r-1}(p_i + q_i) + q_r + \sum_{i=r+1}^{n}(p_i + q_i)$$

Using the notation $w_{i,j} = q_i + \sum_{l=i+1}^{j} (p_l + q_l)$, it results:

$$\text{cost}(T) = p_r + \text{cost}(L) + \text{cost}(R) + w_{0,r-1} + w_{r,n} = \text{cost}(L) + \text{cost}(R) + w_{0,n}$$

Following the definition of $c_{i,j}$ we have:

$$\text{cost}(T) = c_{0,n}, \ \text{cost}(L) = c_{0,r-1} \ \text{and} \ \text{cost}(R) = c_{r,n}$$

The above relation becomes

$$c_{0,n} = c_{0,r-1} + c_{r,n} + w_{0,n} = \min_{1 \le k \le n} \{c_{0,k-1} + c_{k,n} + w_{0,n}\}$$

Generalizing, it results the recurrence (1).
Obs. $c_{i,i} = 0$.

As the Lemma 1 states, the recurrence (1) is used to compute the matrix of the values of optimums that, at its turn, will be the base for building the optimal BST.

Theorem 1. The binary search tree built following the relation (1) is optimal.

Proof. The relation (1) assures that $c_{0,n}$ is minimum over all costs of the binary search trees built from the sequence $(a_1, a_2, ..., a_n)$. Thus, the binary search tree built following the relation (1) has minim cost, consequently it is optimal.

After a BST is built other two important problems are the following: searching for a value and updating the tree.

The searching algorithms depend of the BST implementation. The implementation on a single sequential computer involves searching algorithms different of that corresponding to the implementations on VLSI arrays or clusters of computers.

Also, the updating problem is different for sequential computers, VLSI arrays, and cluster of computers. Often, it is necessary to rebuild the entire tree. This is an important reason for designing efficient algorithms for the building of optimal BST's. The parallel or distributed algorithms should be an alternative.

A distributed implementation of a BST is justified when the necessary space for storing the tree exceeds the memory resources of the host. This situation may appear in database of astronomical dimension (library, search engine).

3   VLSI Implementation of the Optimal Binary Search Tree Problem

3.1   A Technique to Implement Uniform Recurrences into VLSI Arrays

For an uniform recurrence there exists some techniques to implement it into a VLSI architecture. One of them is given by C. Guerra in [2] and can be resumed as it follows:

Let us consider an uniform recurrence given by the following relation:

$$c(\bar{i}) = f(c(\bar{i} - \bar{d}_1), ..., c(\bar{i} - \bar{d}_s)) \tag{2}$$

where: f is a given function, $\bar{i}$ is a vector from a index set I^n and $\bar{d}_1, ..., \bar{d}_s$ are constant vectors that belong to the set I^n and define the data dependence $([\bar{d}_1, ..., \bar{d}_s] = D)$.

We consider now a VLSI architecture [7] defined as follows: each module is assigned to a label $l \in L^{n-1} \subset \mathbf{Z}^{n-1}$; the communication model is described by the matrix $\Delta = [\delta_1, ..., \delta_s]$, where δ_i is the vectorial label difference of the adjacent modules.

A linear time-space transformation is defined by the pair

$$\Pi = \begin{bmatrix} T \\ S \end{bmatrix} \tag{3}$$

where: $T : I^n \to \mathbf{Z}$, is the *timing* function and $S : I^n \to L^{n-1}$ is the *space* function.

The associated transformation matrices are also denoted by T and S.

To have a correct execution order of the operations, T has to satisfy the following conditions:

$$T(\bar{d}_i) > 0, \forall \bar{d}_i \in D \tag{4}$$

The system (4) may have k solutions ($k \geq 0$). If $k \geq 2$ than it is selected the solution that minimizes the global execution time.

The function S has to satisfy the conditions (5):

$$S(\bar{i}) = S(\bar{j}) \Rightarrow T(\bar{i}) \neq T(\bar{j}), \forall \bar{i}, \bar{j} \in I^n \tag{5}$$

This means that different computations cannot be executed at the same time in the same place (module).

3.2   The Conversion of the Optimal BST Non-uniform Recurrence into a System of Two Uniform Recurrences

The recurrence (1) is not uniform. This handicap may be surpassed. Using again Guerra's methodology, the recurrence (1) can be converted into a system of two uniform recurrence. We will follow step by step the technique used by Guerra for a recurrence of type $c_{i,j} = \min_{i<k<j}\{f(c_{i,k}, c_{k,j})\}$ and we will adapt it to the recurrence (1).

The relation (1) defines an index set $I^3 = \{(i, j, k); 0 \leq i < j \leq n, i < k \leq j\}$ corresponding to the minimization operation and an index set $I^2 = \{(i, j); 0 \leq i < j \leq n\}$ of index pairs associated to the variable c. This variable appearing on both sides of the relation (1) introduces non-constant data dependencies. A dependence matrix is defined as the difference of the index vectors of the variable c on the left and right side of any assign statement.

So, the dependence matrix

$$D_{ij} = \left[\begin{bmatrix} i \\ j \end{bmatrix} - \begin{bmatrix} i \\ k-1 \end{bmatrix}, \ k = i+1, \ldots, j \quad \begin{bmatrix} i \\ j \end{bmatrix} - \begin{bmatrix} k \\ j \end{bmatrix}, \ k = i+1, \ldots, j \right]$$

looks as follows:

$$D_{ij} = \begin{bmatrix} 0 & \ldots & 0 & 0 & -1 & -2 & \ldots & i-j \\ j-i & \ldots & 2 & 1 & 0 & 0 & \ldots & 0 \end{bmatrix}$$

The first step of the process of converting the non-uniform recurrence (1) in a uniform one consists of adding the absent indices to variables on the left or right side of the relation (1). For adding the index k to the variable c_{ij} on the left side of (1) it is necessary to specify an appropriate ordering for the computations corresponding to the vector (i, j, k) in order to introduce as much parallelism as possible. Guerra's strategy is to identify among the computations indexed by the set I^3 chains of linearly dependent computations, i.e. computations that have to be performed in a certain order. To do this, from (1) is extracted a subset C of assignments corresponding to constant dependencies. A linear time function T is derived only for such subset. If τ is the actual timing function for the set I^2, than it has to satisfy the conditions $\tau(i, j) \geq T(i, j), \forall (i, j) \in I^2$. The set C is characterized by the matrix D resulted from the intersection of the matrices $D_{ij}, \forall (i, j) \in I^2$:

$$D = \begin{bmatrix} 0 & -1 \\ 1 & 0 \end{bmatrix}$$

The linear time transformation $T : I^2 \rightarrow \mathbf{Z}$ has to satisfy the condition (4). That is:

$$TD = [T_1 \quad T_2] \begin{bmatrix} 0 & -1 \\ 1 & 0 \end{bmatrix} > [0 \quad 0]$$

It results $T_2 > 0$ and $T_1 \leq -1$.

The optimal values that satisfy the above equations are $T_2 = 1$ și $T_1 = -1$. Thus the function T is defined by:

$$T(i,j) = j - i$$

The function T will be uses to find a schedule of the computations indexed by I^3 according with the availability of the variable $c_{i,k-1}$ and $c_{k,j}$ on the right side of (1). The function τ has to satisfy $\tau(i,j) > \tau(i',j')$ if $T(i,j) > T(i',j')$). Thus, a partial ordering $">_T"$ on I^3 can be defined as follows:

$$(i,j,k') >_T (i,j,k'') \Leftrightarrow \max\{T(i,k'-1), T(k',j)\} > \max\{T(i,k''-1), T(k'',j)\}$$

The minimal elements with respect to $">_T"$ are:

$$\begin{cases} (i,j,(i+j+1)/2), & \text{if } i+j \text{ is odd} \\ (i,j,(i+j)/2) \text{ and } (i,j,(i+j)/2+1), & \text{if } i+j \text{ is even} \end{cases}$$

The partial ordering $"<_T"$ produces decompositions of the I^3 into chains that correspond to linearly ordered computations. Among all the possible decompositions, that for which the chains are sorted according to the index k is of interest. It results a decomposition in two such chains as it follows:

$$\begin{cases} (i,j,(i+j+1)/2), (i,j,(i+j+1)/2-1), ..., (i,j,i+1) \\ (i,j,(i+j+1)/2), (i,j,(i+j+1)/2+1), ..., (i,j,j) \end{cases} \text{ if } i+j \text{ is odd}$$

and

$$\begin{cases} ((i,j,(i+j)/2), (i,j,(i+j)/2-1), ..., (i,j,i+1) \\ (i,j,(i+j)/2+1), (i,j,(i+j)/2+2), ..., (i,j,j) \end{cases} \text{ if } i+j \text{ is even}$$

Now, the recurrence (1) can be restructured into a system of two uniform recurrences, each corresponding to a chain. The order of the computations in each uniform recurrence is given by the ordering defined on the chain. These computations are described by the following algorithm:

for $i = 0$ **to** n **do**
   $c_{i,i} \leftarrow 0$; $w_{i,i} \leftarrow q_i$;
end for
for $i = 0$ **to** n **do**
   $a"_{i,i,i} \leftarrow c_{i,i}$; $c_{i,i,i} \leftarrow c_{i,i}$;
end for

```
for l = 1 to n do
  for i = 0 to n − l do
    j ← i + l;
    /* INIT LOOP-1 and LOOP-2 */
    if (i + j) = odd then
      k ← (i + j + 1)/2;
      /*A1*/
      a'_{i,j,k−1} ← a"_{i,j−1,k−1};
      if k = i + 1 then
        /*A2*/
        b'_{i,j,k} ← c_{i+1,j,j}
      else
        b'_{i,j,k} ← b'_{i+1,j,k};
      end if
      c'_{i,j,k−1} ← a'_{i,j,k−1} + b'_{i,j,k}; c"_{i,j,k} ← c'_{i,j,k−1};
    else
      k ← (i + j)/2;
      a'_{i,j,k−1} ← a'_{i,j−1,k−1};
      if k = i + 1 then
        b'_{i,j,k} ← c_{i+1,j,j}
      else
        b'_{i,j,k} ← b'_{i+1,j,k};
      end if
      c'_{i,j,k−1} ← a'_{i,j,k−1} +' b_{i,j,k};
      k ← (i + j)/2 + 1;
      if k = j then
        /*A3*/
        a"_{i,j,k−1} ← c_{i,j−1,j−1}
      else
        a"_{i,j,k−1} ← a"_{i,j−1,k−1};
      end if
      /*A4*/
      b"_{i,j,k} ← b'_{i+1,j,k};
      c"_{i,j,k} ← a"_{i,j,k−1} + b"_{i,j,k};
    end if
    /*LOOP-1*/
    for k = round((i + j)/2) − 1 downto i + 1 do
      a'_{i,j,k−1} ← a'_{i,j−1,k−1};
      if k = i + 1 then
        b'_{i,j,i+1} ← c_{i+1,j,j}
      else
        b'_{i,j,k} ← b'_{i+1,j,k};
      end if
      c'_{i,j,k−1} ← min(c'_{i,j,k}, a'_{i,j,k−1} + b'_{i,j,k});
    end for
```

```
/*LOOP-2*/
for k = trunc((i + j)/2) + 2 to j do
   if k = j then
      a"_{i,j,k-1} ← c_{i,j-1,j-1}
   else
      a"_{i,j,k-1} ← a"_{i,j-1,k-1};
   end if
   b"_{i,j,k} ← b"_{i+1,j,k};
   c"_{i,j,k} ← min(c"_{i,j,k-1}, a"_{i,j,k-1} + b"_{i,j,k});
end for
w_{i,j} ← w_{i,j-1} + p_j + q_j;
/*A5*/
c_{i,j,j} ← min(c'_{i,j,i}, c"_{i,j,j}) + w_{i,j};
c_{i,j} ← c_{i,j,j};
   end for
end for
```

3.3 Mapping the Optimal BST Uniform Recurrences into a VLSI Array

After the transformation of the recurrence (1) in two uniform recurrences, we can apply Guerra's technique to map it into hardware.

Timing Function: Using the above new specification of the recurrence (1), from LOOP-1 and LOOP2 it will be extracted the matrices of constant data dependencies D_1 and D_2, respectively:

$$
\begin{array}{ccc} c' & a' & b' \end{array} \qquad\qquad \begin{array}{ccc} c'' & a'' & b'' \end{array}
$$

$$
D_1 = \begin{bmatrix} 0 & 0 & -1 \\ 0 & 1 & 0 \\ -1 & 0 & 0 \end{bmatrix} \qquad D_2 = \begin{bmatrix} 0 & 0 & -1 \\ 0 & 1 & 0 \\ 1 & 0 & 0 \end{bmatrix}
$$

The dependencies between variables in LOOP-1 and LOOP-2 (global dependencies) are defined be the assignments A1 - A5 .

The goal is to find a linear time transformation for each set of local data dependencies so that they satisfy the global dependencies. Let be $\lambda = [\lambda_1 \quad \lambda_2 \quad \lambda_3]$, $\sigma = [\sigma_1 \quad \sigma_2 \quad \sigma_3]$ and $\tau = [\tau_1 \quad \tau_2 \quad \tau_3]$ the transformation vectors corresponding to the LOOP-1 , LOOP-2 and the assignment A5, respectively.

From (4) it results:

$$
\lambda \bar{d} > 0 \text{ pentru } \bar{d} \in D_1; \quad \sigma \bar{d} > 0 \text{ for } \bar{d} \in D_2
$$

This means:

$$
\lambda_1 \leq -1 \quad \lambda_2 \geq 1 \quad \lambda_3 \leq -1
$$

$$\sigma_1 \leq -1 \quad \sigma_2 \geq 1 \quad \sigma_3 \geq 1$$

The global dependencies A1-A5 add the following

$$\lambda[i \quad j \quad (i+j+1)/2-1]^t > \sigma[i \quad j-1 \quad (i+j+1)/2-1]^t$$

$$\lambda[i \quad j \quad i+1]^t > \tau[i+1 \quad j \quad j]^t$$

$$\sigma[i \quad j \quad j-1]^t > \tau[i \quad j-1 \quad j-1]^t$$

$$\sigma[i \quad j \quad (i+j)/2+1]^t > \lambda[i+1 \quad j \quad (i+j)/2+1]^t$$

$$\tau[i \quad j \quad j]^t \geq \max\{\lambda[i \quad j \quad i]^t, \sigma[i \quad j \quad j)]\}$$

It results for the timing function the following transformation matrix:

$$\begin{bmatrix} \lambda \\ \sigma \\ \tau \end{bmatrix} = \begin{bmatrix} \lambda_1 & \lambda_2 & \lambda_3 \\ \sigma_1 & \sigma_2 & \sigma_3 \\ \tau_1 & \tau_2 & \tau_3 \end{bmatrix} = \begin{bmatrix} -1 & 2 & -1 \\ -2 & 1 & 1 \\ -2 & 1 & 1 \end{bmatrix}$$

Thus,

$$\lambda[i \quad j \quad k]^t = -i+2j-k, \ \sigma[i \quad j \quad k]^t = -2i+j+k \text{ and } \tau[i \quad j \quad j]^t = -2i+2j.$$

Space Function: Let us consider an architecture Mesh-Connected (Fig.2) given by the pair $[L^2, \Delta]$, where L^2 is the set of labels (x, y) assigned to the computing modules (the processors) and Δ is a matrix that defines the array interconnections:

$$\Delta = \begin{bmatrix} 0 & 1 & 0 \\ 0 & 0 & -1 \end{bmatrix}$$

Let us denote by S', S'' and S the space functions corresponding to the computations from the LOOP-1, LOOP-2 and the assignment A5, respectively. The associated transformation matrices will be:

$$S' = \begin{bmatrix} S'_{11} & S'_{12} & S'_{13} \\ S'_{21} & S'_{22} & S'_{23} \end{bmatrix} \text{ for the LOOP} - 1$$

$$S'' = \begin{bmatrix} S''_{11} & S''_{12} & S''_{13} \\ S''_{21} & S''_{22} & S''_{23} \end{bmatrix} \text{ for the LOOP} - 2$$

$$S = \begin{bmatrix} S_{11} & S_{12} & S_{13} \\ S_{21} & S_{22} & S_{23} \end{bmatrix} \text{ for the assignment A5}$$

The coefficients of the matrices S', S'' and S have to respect the condition (5) and the restrictions imposed by the global dependencies. This means the following: if two variables belonging to different modules are processed at the moment t and respectively t' with $t - t' = d$, then the distance between this two modules cannot be greater than d. By the distance it is understood the number of wires that link the two modules.

Thus, from $A1$ is results:

$$S'[i \quad j \quad (i+j+1)/2-1]^t = S''[i \quad j-1 \quad (i+j+1)2-1]^t + \bar{d}_1; \qquad \bar{d}_1 \in \Delta$$

This because $\lambda[i \quad j \quad (i+j)/2]^t - \sigma[i \quad j-1 \quad (i+j)2]^t = 1$ imply execution of the two computations $S'[i \quad j \quad (i+j)/2]^t$ and $S''[i \quad j-1 \quad (i+j)2]^t + \bar{d}_1)$, in the same processor or in adjacent processor (connected by a directed link).

Similarly, from $A2 - A4$ it is obtained:

$$S'[i \quad j \quad i+1]^t = S[i+1 \quad j \quad j]^t + \bar{d}_2; \quad \bar{d}_2 \in \Delta$$
$$S''[i \quad j \quad j-1]^t = S[i \quad j-1 \quad j-1]^t + \bar{d}_3; \quad \bar{d}_3 \in \Delta$$
$$S''[i \quad j \quad (i+j)/2+1]^t = S'[i+1 \quad j \quad (i+j)2+1]^t + \bar{d}_4;$$
$$\bar{d}_4 = \delta_i + \delta_j \quad \delta_i, \delta_j \in \Delta$$
$$S[i \quad j \quad j]^t = S[i \quad j \quad i]^t + \bar{d}_5; \quad \bar{d}_5 \in \Delta$$

A solution for the system of equations resulted from the application of the restrictions imposed by global dependencies, is the following:

$$S' = \begin{bmatrix} S'_{11} & S'_{12} & S'_{13} \\ S'_{21} & S'_{22} & S'_{23} \end{bmatrix} = \begin{bmatrix} 0 & 1 & 0 \\ 1 & 0 & 0 \end{bmatrix}$$

$$S'' = \begin{bmatrix} S''_{11} & S''_{12} & S''_{13} \\ S''_{21} & S''_{22} & S''_{23} \end{bmatrix} = \begin{bmatrix} 0 & 1 & 0 \\ 1 & 0 & 0 \end{bmatrix}$$

$$S = \begin{bmatrix} S_{11} & S_{12} & S_{13} \\ S_{21} & S_{22} & S_{23} \end{bmatrix} = \begin{bmatrix} 0 & 1 & 0 \\ 1 & 0 & 0 \end{bmatrix}$$

It results:

$$S'[i \quad j \quad k]^t = S''[i \quad j \quad k]^t = S[i \quad j \quad j]^t = [j \quad i]^t$$

This means that all the computations for a variable $c_{i,j}$ in the recurrence (1) are located in the processor labelled $(x,y) = (j,i)$

From

$$S'D_1 = \begin{bmatrix} 0 & 1 & 0 \\ 1 & 0 & 0 \end{bmatrix} \overset{\begin{matrix} c' & a' & b' \end{matrix}}{\begin{bmatrix} 0 & 0 & -1 \\ 0 & 1 & 0 \\ -1 & 0 & 0 \end{bmatrix}} = \begin{bmatrix} 0 & 1 & 0 \\ 0 & 0 & -1 \end{bmatrix} .$$

it is derived that $c'_{i,j,k}$ do not move along the array , $a'_{i,j,k-1}$ move to the right ($\rightarrow$) and $b'_{i,j,k}$ move up ($\uparrow$).

Analogously,

$$S''D_2 = \begin{bmatrix} 0 & 1 & 0 \\ 1 & 0 & 0 \end{bmatrix} \overset{\begin{matrix} c'' & a'' & b'' \end{matrix}}{\begin{bmatrix} 0 & 0 & -1 \\ 0 & 1 & 0 \\ 1 & 0 & 0 \end{bmatrix}} = \begin{bmatrix} 0 & 1 & 0 \\ 0 & 0 & -1 \end{bmatrix}$$

implies that $c''_{i,j,k}$ do not move along the array , $a''_{i,j,k-1}$ move to the right ($\rightarrow$) and $b''_{i,j,k}$ move up ($\uparrow$).

In the figure 2, the VLSI array that implements the optimal BST problem is depicted.

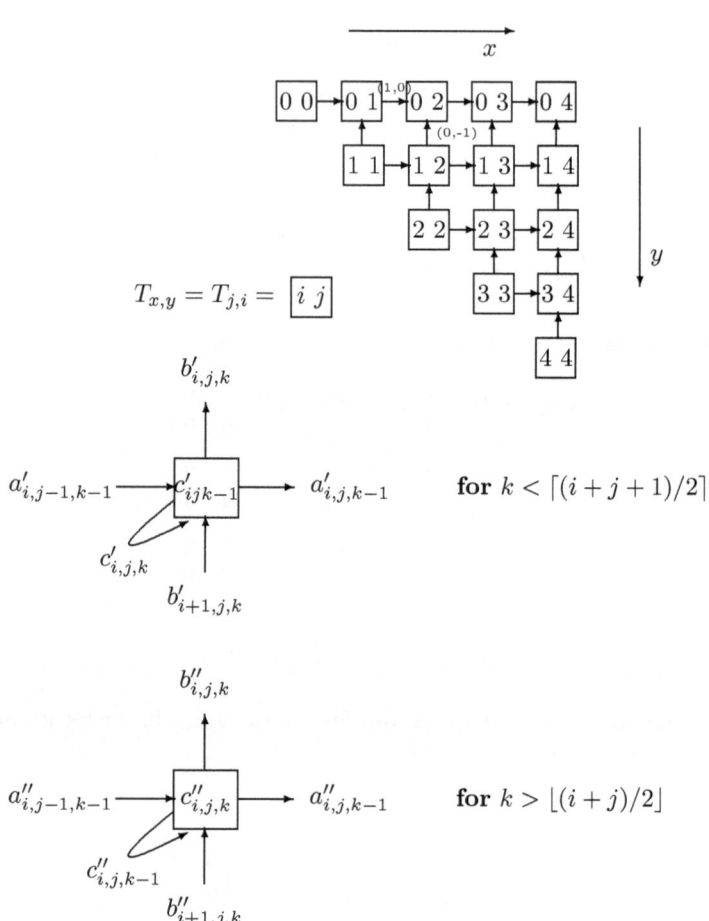

Fig. 2. The VLSI array for the optimal BST problem

4 Distributed Implementation of a BST on a Cluster of Computers

The main idea for a distributed implementation of a BST corresponding to n searching keys on a cluster of m computers is the following:

1. An optimal BST corresponding to a set of m intervals is built; each interval contains approximately the same number of searching keys;

2. For each interval, a computer in the cluster is assigned and the corresponding optimal BST is built.

4.1 The Optimal BST Corresponding to a Set of m Intervals

This step implies the creation of a partition $\mathcal{P}$ of the real numbers set $\mathbb{R}$. The member intervals are unions of subsets of keys (vertices) and key-intervals (pseudo-vertices) that contain approximately the same number of searching keys. Let us consider $\mathcal{P} = (I_1, I_2, ..., I_m)$

An interval $I_i \neq I_m$ is defined as follows:

$$I_i = e_l \cup \{a_{l+1}\} \cup e_{l+1} \cup \{a_{l+2}\} \ldots \cup e_{h-1} \cup \{a_h\}$$

$$l \in \{0, 1, \ldots, n-1\}, h \in \{1, 2, \ldots, n\}, l < h, \quad i \in \{1, \ldots, m-1\}$$

The probability of searching for a value from I_i is

$$P(I_i) = q_l + p_{l+1} + q_{l+1} + p_{l+2} \ldots + q_{h-1} + p_h$$

The last interval of the partition will be I_m

$$I_m = e_l \cup \{a_{l+1}\} \cup e_{l+1} \cup \{a_{l+2}\} \ldots \cup e_{n-1} \cup \{a_n\} \cup e_n, \quad l \in \{0, 1, \ldots, n-1\}$$

Its associated probability will be:

$$P(I_m) = q_l + p_{l+1} + q_{l+1} + p_{l+2} \ldots + q_{n-1} + p_n + q_n$$

Obs. The pseudo-vertex e_i was used in the above relations instead of the interval (a_i, a_{i+1}).

The relation $I_i \preceq I_j \Leftrightarrow i \leq j, \quad i, j \in \{1, \ldots, m\}$ is an order on $\mathcal{P}$.

With the items $I_1, I_2, ..., I_m$, a binary search tree $T_\mathcal{P}$ will be built. Each item I_i is searched with the probability $P(I_i)$. Unsuccessful searches are not possible.

The time cost for a such tree is the medium time for solving a searching operation. The searching for the value x means to find the interval I_i that contains x.

$$\text{cost}(T_{\mathcal{P}}) = \sum_{i=1}^{m} P(I_i) * \text{level}(I_i)$$

Let use denote by $C_{i,j}$ the cost of an optimal BST that has the vertices from the sequence $(I_i, I_{i+1}, ..., I_j)$.

Using a similar technique as the one used for obtain the recurrence (1), it results:

$$C_{i,j} = \min_{i<k<j} \{C_{i,k-1} + C_{k+1,j} + W_{i,j}\} \tag{6}$$

where $W_{i,j} = \sum_{l=i}^{j} P(I_l)$.

Theorem 2. The binary search tree built from the relation (6) is optimal.

Proof. The relation (6) states that $C_{1,n}$ is minim over all costs of the binary search trees built from the sequence $(I_1, I_2, ..., I_m)$. Thus, the binary search tree built according to the relation (6) has minim cost. This proves its optimality.

It results that the problem of building the tree $T_{\mathcal{P}}$ does not differ in essence from the ordinal problem: the building of an optimal BST for a sequence $A = (a_1, a_2, ..., a_n)$ of data items increasing sorted on their keys $(k_1, k_2, \ldots, k_n)$.

4.2   The Optimal BST Corresponding to an Interval of Keys

For each interval I, it will be build an optimal BST. Let it be T_I. The corresponding algorithm will use the same strategy as in the case of the building the tree T for the sequence $A = (a_1, a_2, ..., a_n)$. In a pre-processing step, the probabilities will be inflated to have their sum equal to 1.

4.3   The Distribution of the Trees to the Cluster Members

The computer that will compute and store $T_{\mathcal{P}}$ depends of the cluster topology. In a cluster organized as a ring of computers may be useful to have the tree $T_{\mathcal{P}}$ inside of every cluster member. In the case of a star topology it is enough to store the tree $T_{\mathcal{P}}$ in the central computer.

4.4   The Searching for a Value x

A search for value x will be executed as follows:

First, the interval I that contains x will be identified . This means a search inside of the interval-tree $T_{\mathcal{P}}$.

In the next step, the value x will be searched in the key-tree T_I corresponding to the interval I.

5 Hybrid Implementation

In a cluster of computers that can hosts VLSI arrays, the distributed and VLSI implementation can be combined in order to obtain a better performance for the problem of building and rebuilding of a wide binary search tree. This means that the VLSI implementation of the optimal BST problem may be used at the level of the cluster members.

6 Conclusion

The Optimal Binary Search Tree problem has a lot of solutions and a lot of open problems. One of them is the optimal distributed implementation.

The VLSI array implementation is optimal but for large number of keys it appears the problem of the hardware excessive cost. A solution may be to use processes instead of processors and to use the same processor to solve bigger tasks than "min" operations.

Our solution for the distributed BST implementation is not optimal but it is acceptable efficient. Clusters are difficult because of the cost of communications. The balancing of the cost of the communications inside the cluster with the cost of the local searching in the cluster members may be a way to solve the problem of the optimal distributed implementation for a BST. This is an open problem.

For an astronomical index, a cluster implementation seems to be better than external memory storage. Obvious, the internal memory search is faster that the searching on an external memory but sometime the cost of the communication between the cluster members reduces this advantage. Our solution of finding relatively fast, by means of the interval tree, the cluster member which contains the part of the tree that can answer to the search query, reduces enough the cost of the communications to make attractive the solution of distributing the BST into a cluster of computers.

References

1. Horowitz, E., Sahni, S., Anderson-Freed, S.: Fundamentals of Data Structures in C, Computer Science Press, New York (1993)
2. Guerra, C.: A Unifying Framework for Systolic Design, LNCS 227, Springer-Verlag, Berlin Heidelberg New York (1986) 46–56
3. H. Attiya, Welch, H.J.: Distributed Computing: Fundamentals, Simulations and Advanced Topics, McGraw-Hill, London (1998)
4. Rogers, W., Candela, G., Harman, D.: Space an Time Improvements for Indexing in Information Retrieval, National Institute of Standards & Technology, Gaithesburg (2001)
5. Baase, S., Van Gelder A.: Computer Algorithms: Introduction to Design & Analysis, Addison Wesley Longman (2000)
6. Heileman, G.: Data Structures, Algorithms and Object-Oriented programming, McGraw-Hill, New York (1996)
7. Leighton, F.T.: Introduction to Parallel Algorithms and Architectures: Arrays, Trees, Hypercubes, Morgan Kauffman (1992)

A Framework for Efficient Sparse LU Factorization in a Cluster Based Platform

Laura Grigori

INRIA Lorraine - Université Henri Poincaré
Nancy, France
Laura.Grigori@loria.fr

Abstract. In this paper we address necessary issues in developing an efficient parallel sparse LU factorization without pivoting in a cluster technology. The algorithm we propose reduces the communications between processors by using an adequate mapping algorithm. The volume of communications during parallel symbolic factorization is decreased by using the notion of symmetric pruning of the directed graph of L.

1 Introduction

Transforming a matrix into its LU form is an important basic operation included in the direct methods of solving an unsymmetric linear system of equations $Ax = b$. This is even more relevant in the sparse case where intelligent algorithms and efficient implementations can lead to lesser memory requirements and to the exploitation of more available parallelism.

Today's approach states that, to solve a sparse linear system by a direct method, four operations are involved. First find a matrix permutation P that preserves the sparsity of A. Next, determine the fill by symbolically factoring A and set up the structures of L and U. Finally, numerically factor A and solve two triangular systems to find the solution vector x.

The direct method for an unsymmetric sparse matrix is materialized by two classes of algorithms. They are differentiated by the solutions presented to the problem of maintaining the numerical stability when the matrix is not diagonally dominant. In earlier solutions, the partial pivoting was used during the LU factorization. More recently, another approach (proposed in [1]) avoids the variations in the structures of L and U introduced by the partial pivoting; it develops techniques that replace the partial pivoting while still maintaining the numerical stability. As of today, at least one scalable and very efficient distributed algorithm was developed for the LU factorization without pivoting [1].

Concerning the parallel implementation of the sparse LU factorization without pivoting, cluster computing environments [2,3] have several specific traits that differentiate them from distributed memory machines.

Communication. The most distinctive trait of a cluster is probably the communication technology used among processing elements. This is usually the same technology used for LAN access: Ethernet (some clusters are built around a more dedicated mesh like

D. Grigoras et al. (Eds.): IWCC 2001, LNCS 2326, pp. 118–125, 2002.

Myrinet, but those are particular cases). The bandwidths and latencies associated with the various Ethernet technologies are usually inadequate for fast transfers between the processing elements. This is why, more than what is required in a common parallel case, it is important to design parallel algorithms that require very little interaction between processing elements of a cluster.

Processing Elements. The number of processing elements in a cluster is much smaller than what is available in distributed memory parallel machines. Typical clusters have from 2 to 32 processing elements while for example an entry level Origin2000 DSM has 32 processors. Dedicated Origin2000's have been built that contain 2048 processors. The processing units in a cluster are usually chipsets from the Intel Pentium class while processors in distributed memory machines tend to be dedicated architectures (see for example IBM Blue Gene). Due to different market models, processors in clusters tend to be much faster than processors in a multiprocessor machine. This is due to the simplicity of building a cluster. In the time one multiprocessor machine is architected and built, two or three generations of general purpose Intel chipsets are taken to the market, each time at faster speeds. For example, building a cluster today might use Pentiums at 1.5Ghz while the fastest supercomputer is now the IBM SP Power3 with RS/6000 "ASCI White" at 375Mhz[1].

Memory. Memory sizes, hierarchies and architectures are very different in the case of clusters. The memory size of a PC is usually larger than the size associated to a PE in a multiprocessor. The total size is still balanced, in the sense that roughly the same memory space is available in a multiprocessor machine as in a cluster (each PE has less memory than a PC but there are more PE's).

Hard Disk. Hard disk space per processing element is usually larger in a cluster than in a multiprocessor, for the same economic reasons presented in a previous paragraph. However, the transfer rates tend to be smaller in clusters' disks than in a multiprocessor.

This paper's outline is as follows: in section 2 we briefly review notions related to the LU factorization as well as algorithms that implement it. Section 3 presents a mapping algorithm proposed by Pothen and Sun in [4] which reduces the communications between processors. In section 4 we present different techniques to improve the efficiency of the sparse LU factorization in a cluster environment, and in section 5 we conclude the paper.

2   Review of Sparse LU Factorization

2.1   Symbolic Factorization

Let A be a sparse unsymmetric $n \times n$ matrix with m nonzero elements that can be decomposed without pivoting into $L \times U$, where L is lower triangular with unit diagonal and U is upper triangular. We define $F = L + U - I$ to be the filled matrix containing both L and U. In what follows, $G(A)$ denotes the directed graph associated with matrix A, a_{ij} represents the element of row i and column j of matrix A, while $A(:, i : j)$ represents all the subscripts of the columns from i to j of A.

---

[1] See the Top 500 list of most powerful computer sites at http://www.top500.org.

The aim of the symbolic factorization is to compute the structure of F, containing all the nonzero elements of the matrix A and the elements becoming nonzero during the numerical factorization. Consider a column j of U for which u_{ij} is nonzero. The column j will be updated during the numerical factorization by the column i. During the symbolic factorization, we need to include the elements of column i of F in the column j of F.

In figure 1 we present an example matrix A (left), its directed graph (middle) and the filled matrix F (right) obtained after the symbolic factorization.

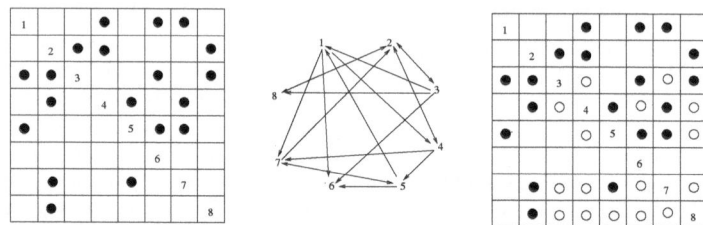

Fig. 1. Example matrix A, its directed graph and its filled matrix F.

Gilbert and Peierls proposed in [5] a symbolic factorization algorithm starting from the following idea: when we arrive at the computation of column j, the nonzero structures of the first $j-1$ columns of L and U are known, together with the graph $G(L(:,1:j-1))$. These columns are used to compute column j as follows: for each element of $A(:,j)$, we traverse the graph of $L(:,1:j-1)^T$. All the nodes reached during this traversal belong to the structure of column j of F.

A consequence of this is that when determining the structure of $U(:,j)$ the traversal of $G(L(:,j-1))$ is done in a topological ordering, this generates the nonzeros of the column j in a topological order. Then during the numerical factorization this order can be used as a valid order to update the column j and this idea is used by several solvers. In figure 2 we illustrate the symbolic factorization of the column 7 of the example matrix A from figure 1.

Several optimizations were done on the Gilbert Peierls symbolic factorization algorithm. The first optimization, called symmetric reduction, tries to reduce some redundant edges of $G(L)$ and it was introduced in [6] by Eisenstat and Liu. The second optimization, proposed in [7], is to use supernodes (columns of L with an identical structure) during the symbolic factorization.

Pruning the symbolic structure. The symmetric reduction was introduced in [6] by Eisenstat and Liu to reduce some redundant edges in the graph of L by using the symmetry of the filled matrix F. The symmetric reduction of $L(:,1:j)$ is obtained by removing all nonzeros l_{ki} for which $l_{ji}u_{ij} \neq 0$ for some $k > j$.

In the Gilbert Peierls symbolic factorization algorithm, the symmetric pruning can be computed by an efficient method [6], and this significantly reduces the total factorization

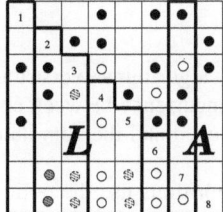

Fig. 2. The symbolic factorization of the column 7 for the example matrix A from figure 1.

time. A supplementary array $fsnz$ stores the first symmetric nonzero found for each column i. All the columns $j > fsnz[i]$ being updated by i will access those entries in the structure of $L(:, i)$ that are less than or equal to $fsnz[i]$.

In the example matrix in figure 2, the elements l_{42} and u_{24} are nonzero, and the symmetric pruning applies. Thus, the elements l_{72} and l_{82} don't need to be considered during the depth first traversal from node 2.

Unsymmetric supernodes. Using the supernode concept, we try to group together successive columns with the same nonzero structure, so they can be treated as a dense matrix. This leads to a speed-up of the symbolic factorization and this scheme was used in the SuperLU solver [7].

At the end of each symbolic factorization step, we decide whether the new column j belongs to the same supernode as column $j - 1$. Furthermore, to compute the column j we use the previous supernodes instead of using the columns $1, \ldots, j - 1$. The columns 4 and 5 of L in the example matrix in figure 2 has the same structure, and thus they are grouped in a same supernode.

The optimizations introduced in the Gilbert Peierls symbolic factorization algorithm lead to important practical gains in efficiency. The experimental results in [6] show that the symmetric reduction significantly reduces the symbolic time. In [7] the impact of supernodes is measured and the savings in symbolic factorization are outlined.

2.2 Numeric Factorization

In this section we present the numeric factorization step of the LU factorization, with a brief overview of its implementation in the today's published literature. The goal of this step is to numerically compute the factors L and U exploiting efficiently the memory hierarchy and the parallelism introduced by the sparsity.

The first goal is attained by the usage of the supernodes, notion that we already presented in the previous subsection in the context of the symbolic factorization. This leads to a better usage of the BLAS3 routines during the computations.

The advances in the second goal are less satisfactory. For example in the distributed version of the SuperLU solver [1], a 2D distribution of the matrix on a 2D grid of processors is used, and then the algorithm iterates over the supernodes and each processor computes its blocks, using blocking receives and sends MPI operations.

3 Mapping Algorithm

In this section, we are interested in algorithms to distribute the columns among processors by taking advantage of the concurrency between columns such that the communication between processors are reduced and the communications and computations are overlapped.

Many of the sparse matrix algorithms use the notion of elimination tree to model the parallel factorization. They were first used in the symmetric case, and a detailed description of the role and use of elimination trees can be found in [8]. In the case of an unsymmetric matrix, the elimination tree of $A + A^T$ gives all the dependencies which can appear during the symbolic factorization. An important property says that columns belonging to disjoint subtrees of the elimination tree can be computed in parallel with no overlap in data access. This property should be used to map subtrees to processors, thus keeping dependent columns on the same processor.

The elimination tree of $A + A^T$ is usually used to reorder the rows of the matrix A in order to reduce the fill-in. At the beginning of the symbolic factorization this tree being known, its use does not introduce any overhead in the symbolic or the numeric factorization algorithm.

Several mapping algorithms were proposed in the literature, in the context of the Cholesky factorization. One of these is the proportional mapping algorithm proposed by Pothen and Sun in [4]. This algorithm tries to achieve low communications and takes into account the workload distribution of the tree. It starts by assigning all processors to the root. The columns of the root are assigned in a wrap-map manner to these processors. Then it considers the subtrees of the root in descending workload order. It assigns to each such subtree a number of processors proportional with the workload of the subtree. The method continues until only one processor remains assigned to each subtree. Due to rounding to integral number of processors, some details in implementing the algorithm are important in obtaining an effective mapping, and these details are explained in [4]. The advantage of this algorithm is that the communications in a subtree are bounded to only between the processors assigned to this subtree, thus ensuring a low communication cost.

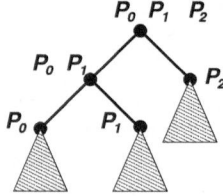

Fig. 3. Example matrix A, its directed graph and its filled matrix F.

Due to its low communication cost, the proportional mapping algorithm is an appropriate choice to use to map the columns to processors in a parallel solver. In figure 3 we illustrate the execution of the algorithm, where we dispose of 3 processors, namely P_0, P_1, P_2. In this example, the left subtree has a two times larger workload compared to the right subtree, and thus it receives processors P_0, P_1. The algorithm continues on the left subtree until each subtree has assigned only one processor.

Remark that in each subtree the computations are independent, and when such a subtree is assigned to only one processor, there is no communication between processors. The communications appear in the upper part of the tree, where a node has assigned more than one processor. In fact in this case, we have to assign the node to only one processor, and different strategies can be used. We will discuss this strategies later in this paper, in each particular case of the usage of this proportional mapping algorithm.

4 Parallel Sparse LU Factorization

In the previous sections, we presented a state of the art of the sparse LU factorization, and a known algorithm to map the columns to processors during sparse factorizations. In this section we will concentrate on the parallelization of the sparse LU factorization in a cluster environment. In particular on the use of the proportional mapping algorithm in the context of the symbolic as well as numeric factorization. We will highlight its advantages for a cluster computing environment and we will show how we can reduce the volume of the communications.

Symbolic factorization. To implement an efficient parallel symbolic factorization using the Gilbert Peierls algorithm, we have to group dependent columns on a same processor, while balancing the load between processors. We propose the use of the proportional mapping algorithm on the elimination tree of $A + A^T$, as following. At each step of the algorithm, if a root receives more than one processor, then we assign the root to the least loaded processor. The algorithm continues recursively to assign processors to each subtree proportionally to its workload, until each subtree receives only one processor.

A new problem arises here. The proportional mapping algorithm needs to know the load associated to each column. This is done by using again the elimination tree of $A + A^T$. In fact, as the factors of $A + A^T$ are an upper bound of the factors L and U of A, we can evaluate an upper bound for the load of each column by using the column counts of the factors of $A + A^T$. Efficient algorithms exist to compute the row and column counts of the factor L of a symmetric matrix, without computing the factor itself.

We consider the symbolic factorization of each column as a task. The workload associated with each task is given by the upper bound of the number of operations performed to compute the symbolic factorization of this column. Each node of the tree has as workload the sum of the workloads of its descendents plus the workload corresponding to that column of L and U.

This approach was already used in the context of a parallel out-of-core symbolic factorization [9], were we have proved experimentally that the proportional mapping algorithm is effective on a small number of processors, that is it effectively reduces communications between processors, while balancing the load.

Recall that the columns factored in the upper part of the tree will induce communications between processors. To further reduce the volume of these communications, we use the following observation: to compute a column j, the Gilbert Peierls algorithm will use only the pruned parts of the previously computed columns. As the pruned part of a column has often a size much smaller than the column itself, we can reduce the volume of communications by sending only the pruned part of each column.

To implement this idea, we use a supplementary send buffer, where before each send, we copy in a contiguous memory area the pruned parts of the first column of each supernode. A send operation is done after the computation of several columns, when one of the following criteria is satisfied: the size of the send buffer is reduced by pruning compared to the sizes of the columns to be sent by a certain proportion p; the number of the columns to send is bigger then a certain threshold t. The proportion p and the threshold t are tuned parameters set up experimentally.

Numeric factorization. The proportional mapping algorithm can be used also in the context of the numerical factorization to distribute the blocks between processors. This time, the mapping algorithm is applied on the elimination tree of $\bar{A} + \bar{A}^T$, where $\bar{A}$ is the matrix obtained after the partitioning of A in supernodes.

Several techniques can be employed to map a supernode which has more than one processor in its associated set. These techniques use classic list scheduling algorithms to map the blocks of a supernode on its associated processors.

To enable complete overlap between communication and computation, we implement a fully asynchronous algorithm. To receive columns from the other processors, an asynchronous nonblocking MPI_Irecv is pending. As long as raw memory is available, we try to receive necessary columns from the other processors by checking the status of the pending receive. As soon as a column is received, we post a new pending receive and try to receive new columns.

5   Conclusions and Future Work

In this paper we discuss necessary issues in developing an efficient parallel sparse LU factorization without pivoting in a cluster technology. The algorithm we propose reduces the communications between processors by using an adequate mapping algorithm. The volume of communications during parallel symbolic factorization is decreased by using the notion of symmetric pruning of the directed graph of L. Our future work includes the experimentation of these techniques in a cluster environment.

References

1. Li, X.S., Demmel, J.W.: A Scalable Sparse Direct Solver Using Static Pivoting. 9th SIAM Conference on Parallel Processing and Scientific Computing (1999)
2. Pfister, G.: In Search of Clusters. second edn. Prentice Hall (1998)
3. Sterling, T., Becker, D.J., Dorband, J.E., Savarese, D., Ranawake, U.A., Packer, C.V.: Beowulf: A Parallel Workstation for Scientific Computation. International Conference on Parallel Processing (1995)
4. Pothen, A., Sun, C.: A Mapping Algorithm for Parallel Sparse Cholesky Factorization. SIAM Journal on Scientific Computing (1993) 1253–1257
5. Gilbert, J.R., Peierls, T.: Sparse partial pivoting in time proportional to arithmetic operations. SIAM Journal on Scientific and Statistical Computing 9 (1988) 862–874
6. Eisenstat, S.C., Liu, J.W.H.: Exploiting Structural Symmetry in Unsymmetric Sparse Symbolic Factorization. SIAM Journal on Matrix Analysis and Applications 13 (1992) 202–211

7. Demmel, J.W., Eisenstat, S.C., Gilbert, J.R., Li, X.S., Liu, J.W.H.: A Supernodal Approach to Sparse Partial Pivoting. SIAM Journal on Matrix Analysis and Applications **20** (1999) 720–755
8. Liu, J.W.H.: The Role of Elimination Trees in Sparse Factorization. SIAM Journal on Matrix Analysis and Applications **11** (1990) 134–172
9. Cosnard, M., Grigori, L.: A Parallel Algorithm for Sparse Symbolic LU Factorization without Pivoting on Out of Core Matrices. ACM International Conference on Supercomputing (2000)

Task Allocation Using Processor Load Prediction on Multiprocessors Cluster

Thierry Monteil and Patricia Pascal

LAAS-CNRS, 7 avenue du Colonel Roche 31077 Toulouse, France,
monteil@laas.fr, ppascal@laas.fr

Abstract. This paper describes a tool called Network-Analyser that increases the efficiency of clusters for parallel computing. Two important features are provided by this tool. First, it is organized in three hierarchical levels to collect information on workstations state. Secondly it provides several task allocation policies. In this paper a new policy that uses both instantaneous and average workstations loads to estimate tasks expected execution times, is developed. The multiprocessors workstation model used is based on round robin queuing system. A differential equation is established to describe transient state of the queuing system. Then an integral equation allows to estimate the expected execution time of regular parallel applications by mixing the deterministic processes of the parallel application with the stochastic load of the workstation.

1 Introduction

A cluster is a distributed memory machine in which independent processors are connected to a network. This kind of architecture is in fact similar to these of current parallel machines like Cray T3x or IBM SPx. Despite this similarity, using a cluster for parallel computing is quite difficult. Machines heterogeneity and independence, multi-users operating system are a few of these difficulties.

Distribution of processors on several machines and use of several networks make communications between tasks of a parallel application more difficult than on a real parallel machine. Many studies and tools have been done to hide heterogeneity and distribution of machines network. New operating systems (MOSIX [1], V system [2]) or softwares on current operating system (PVM [3], LANDA [4], MPICH [5]) have been developed. Machines are shared between several users to handle their different activities. This induces one of the main problem for the performance of parallel applications on these architectures. The important fact is that the execution times of tasks depend on the varying load conditions prevailing on each selected processor. Actually, several parallel applications with different numbers of tasks and different grains might be sharing the same processors at the same time. Optimal sharing of these resources is a complex problem, and many approaches have been developed.

D. Grigoras et al. (Eds.): IWCC 2001, LNCS 2326, pp. 126–135, 2002.

The first work on this problem was done by proposing a new algorithm to predict execution time of parallel applications on a set of independent uniprocessor machines [6]. After this first step, the model will be extended by introducing communications between tasks. Simple network as bus have been modeled [7]. The use of multiprocessors machines on cluster has forced to extend the model of prediction. This paper proposes a new algorithm for dynamic load balancing on multiprocessors cluster. First the tool called Network Analyser is described and then the mapping algorithm.

2   Observation and Mapping Tool: Network-Analyser

The Network-Analyser system provides six main services. It collects information on workstations states (CPU load, processes states, input/output, ...). It makes statistics on processes and users, for instance CPU or memory consuming. It saves some information on the last 24 hours. With this service, a user can see the workstation load during the execution of a parallel application at any time (present or past). It provides a library which can be used by all systems (LANDA [4] communication kernel, PVM [3], MPICH [5]) to get all information collected by the Network-Analyser. Moreover, this library proposes several algorithms for task allocation. It visualizes all data in a graphical environment (real time and post-mortem visualization). It predicts workstations load. It observes global traffic and point to point communications between workstations.

The Network-Analyser is structured in a three level hierarchical architecture (figure 1). Each workstation has a daemon which collects information (load daemon). Workstations are organized into cluster with one master per cluster (cluster daemon). Only one workstation has a global view of the machines and centralizes aggregated data (supervisor daemon). This architecture is the result of a study that was undertaken on several possible organizations. A performance evaluation has been done to ensure that this solution will minimize response time and traffic for networks of hundreds of workstations. The same UNIX process is able to handle any of the three daemon functions (load, cluster, supervisor). The supervisor daemon is in charge of global decisions regarding task allocation. It is supplied with fault tolerant algorithm : security communications are periodically exchanged between daemons of the different levels. An election algorithm is run when the supervisor or a cluster daemon fails. At each level (supervisor daemon, cluster daemon) a set of substitute machines is always active and takes place in the election algorithm.

3   The Proposed Mapping Algorithm

The central problem for a good load balancing is to take into account the loads and various parameters of workstations to estimate precisely the expected time to run a parallel application. Dynamic mapping policies are most of the time based on minimization or maximization of some cost function. This last one

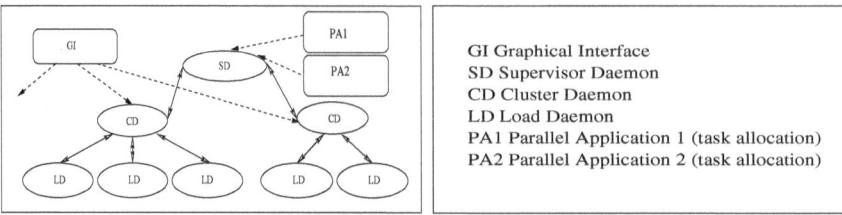

| | GI Graphical Interface |
| SD Supervisor Daemon |
| CD Cluster Daemon |
| LD Load Daemon |
| PA1 Parallel Application 1 (task allocation) |
| PA2 Parallel Application 2 (task allocation) |

Fig. 1. Architecture of the Network-Analyser

is often derived from queuing models. Performance measures of these models relevant to task mapping are the number of processes in the queues [8], the system response time [9][10], the time to complete all mapped processes [9] or the inactivity time of processors [11]. Another criterion can also be to maximize the system throughput [9]. All of these task allocation policies only take into account the instantaneous machines states. They do not take into account the dynamical behavior of the system.

The approach developed here is based on a stochastic modeling of the system. For that purpose, a dynamic model of the workstation load (load differential equation) is developed. The parameters of this model are predicted on the basis of past measures. Information on the instantaneous and average state is used in the estimation model. The differential equation gives the evolution of the number of processes in the run queue. With this prediction and the processor time needed by a process, the expected execution time of a process is then calculated. Processes mapping is then done by minimizing the expected execution time of the parallel application using a minimum longest processing time approach.

3.1   Studies of Different Multiprocessors Schedulers

Linux. The study of Linux 2.4.2 scheduler is based on the kernel's files : kernel/sched.c and include/linux/sched.h. The job of a scheduler is to arbitrate access to current CPU between multiple processes. There are three scheduling policies : SCHED_OTHER for a traditional UNIX process, SCHED_FIFO for real-time processes (FIFO policy), SCHED_RR for real-time processes (round-robin policy).

The SCHED_OTHER policy will be explained. When a process need a processor it is added to the run queue. In the run queue there are processes which are running on a processor and processes waiting for a CPU. The run queue is examined periodically by the scheduler : it compares the goodness (a sort of dynamic priority) of each process waiting for a CPU and chooses the best one. The goodness is calculated with the field counter of the task structure (number of ticks left to run in this scheduling slice), with the process nice (static priority given by user) and with the affinity the process has for the CPU: if the process ran on this CPU it is given an advantage.

Solaris. Solaris 7 is an Operating Environment developed by SUN. There are different structures in Solaris : user thread, lightweight process and kernel thread. The kernel thread is the entity that is actually put on a dispatch queue and scheduled. It is the kernel thread, not the process, that is assigned to a scheduling class and priority. The scheduling class defines the policy and algorithm applied to processes or threads. It is based on values established in a table called dispatch table. The scheduler code uses this table with information based on waiting time and how recently the thread had execution time on a processor for selecting a thread to run on a processor. The different scheduling classes are : Timesharing (TS: threads have priorities and a time slice is given to them), Systems (SYS: there is no time-slicing and no modification of the priority), Real time (RT : threads run at a fixed priority) and Interactive (IA). The kernel dispatch queue model is essentially a series of arrays of linked lists of threads, where each linked list is composed of threads at the same priority level. The dispatcher queue model in Solaris involves not only per-processor dispatch queues, but also a global queue of threads that run at a priority level high enough to cause kernel preemption. The dispatcher performs three basic functions : it finds the best priority runnable thread, places it on a processor for execution and manages the insertion and removal of threads on the dispatch queues. The dispatcher looks for work at regular intervals on the queues. The preemption queue is searched first for high-priority threads, followed by the per-CPU dispatch queues. Each CPU searches its own dispatch queues for work. This provides very good scalability, as multiple CPUs can be in the dispatcher code searching their queues concurrently; it also reduces potential CPU-to-CPU synchronization. If there is no waiting thread on a CPU's queue, it will search the queues of other processors for work to do, which may result in thread "migrations". The dispatcher will also attempt to keep the queues depths relatively balanced across processors, such that there won't be a large difference in the length of the per-processor dispatch queues.

IRIX. IRIX 6.5 is an Operating System developed by SGI. The default IRIX scheduling is a time-sharing algorithm without priority. Each process has a guaranteed time slice (100 ms on a multiprocessors system and 20 ms on a uniprocessor system), which is the amount of time it is normally allowed to execute without being preempted. At the end of a time slice, the kernel chooses which process to run next on the same CPU. As long as a process has any affinity for a CPU, it is dispatched only on that CPU if possible. The affinity is decreased when processes are not on CPU. When its affinity has declined to zero, the process can be dispatched on any available CPU.

3.2   Model

Comparing the three schedulers it can be seen that Linux, Solaris and Irix give an advantage to a process which has any affinity for a processor. All algorithms are time sharing : a time slice is given to a process and finally only Linux and Solaris consider the priorities of processes. The model must be simplified because it must be used dynamically, its resolution must be quick. The scheduling is very complicate, but with high performance applications some hypotheses can be done:

- processes are long and a non-superuser can not improve its static priority so users keep the priority given by default
  $\Rightarrow$ dynamic priority are modified after each quantum and so on average the priorities do not matter during a long time
  $\Rightarrow$ a long process will finally access to every processor so the affinity is not very important in this case
- processes do many compute operations and a few input/output
  $\Rightarrow$ tasks input/output are neglected so the wait queue is ignored.

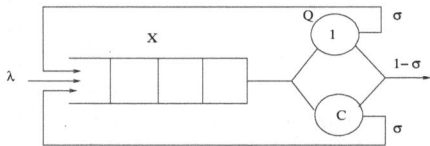

Fig. 2. Round robin model

So the model for the scheduling is a round robin queuing system (RR) without priority because on the whole, all processes have the same priority and will run on any processors. The system is composed of C servers. The process at the head of the queue will be executed by the first server which will become free. A job selected for operations is taken from the head of the ordered queue and is allocated a fixed amount Q of execution time. After those Q units, if the job requires additional processing time, it is fed back into the queue with the probability σ. Otherwise it departs from the system with the probability $1 - \sigma$. This model (figure 2) is simple and far away from a complex operating system like UNIX. Nevertheless, for coarse grain parallel applications with few input/output, the model is adequate. Processes arrive in the system at a Poisson rate λ. Each process leaves the system when it has received the CPU time it requires. The service time distribution is assumed geometric, the first moment of the service time distribution is given by equation (1) and the utilization factor ρ for the system is given in relation (1).

$$g_i = \sigma^{i-1}(1 - \sigma), \quad i = 1, 2, ..., \quad and \quad 0 < \sigma < 1$$

$$E(T) = \sum_{i=1}^{+\infty}(iQ) \cdot g_i = \frac{Q}{(1 - \sigma)} = \frac{1}{\mu}, \quad \rho = \frac{\lambda \cdot Q}{C(1 - \sigma)} \quad (1)$$

3.3   Expectation of the Number of Processes

The time quantum is assumed to be very small with respect to all other time values of the model. Hence, the probability to have a new process in the RR system during a quantum Q is equal to λQ. Let the state of the RR system at time t be the number of processes in the system at that time. This system is Markovian. The state diagram is depicted on figure 3, where state i represents the number of processes in the RR system.

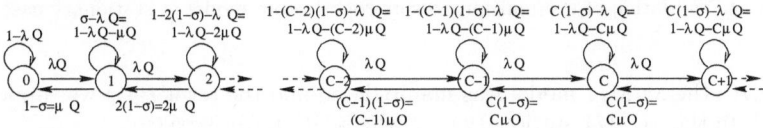

Fig. 3. Markov chain

Since it can be assumed there is a very small time quantum Q, this discrete time markov chain can be identified to a continuous time markov chain. Let $P_i(t)$ be the probability to have i processes in the system at time t. One can easily show that the transient probabilities are equivalent to an M/M/C queue and given by equation (2):

$$\text{for } 0 < i < C-1: \quad \dot{P_i}(t) = \frac{\partial P_i(t)}{\partial t} = \lambda P_{i-1}(t) - (\lambda + i\mu)P_i(t) + \mu(i+1)P_{i+1}(t)$$

$$\text{for i=0:} \quad \dot{P_0}(t) = \mu P_1(t) - \lambda P_0(t)$$

$$\text{for i} \geq \text{C:} \quad \dot{P_i}(t) = \lambda P_{i-1}(t) - (\lambda + C\mu)P_i(t) + C\mu P_{i+1}(t) \tag{2}$$

$X(t)$ is defined as the expected number of processes in the system. Biprocessors PC (LINUX 2.4.2) are artificially loaded. Processes are created with an incoming Poisson rate and their service times are exponentially distributed. The values of X^∞, the expectation number of processes at the stationary case and ρ the utilization factor are measured and then compared them with theoretical values given by the model M/M/C [12](equations: 3,1, figure 4). Some tests were done on IRIX and SOLARIS which gave as satisfying results as LINUX.

$$X^\infty = \frac{\rho^{C+1}P_0^\infty}{(C-1)!(C-\rho)^2} + \rho, \quad P_0^\infty = \frac{1}{\sum_{i=0}^{C-1}\frac{\rho^i}{i!} + \frac{\rho^C}{(C-1)!(C-\rho)}} \tag{3}$$

$\dot{X}(t)$ is defined as the derivative of X(t), it is easy to show that with equations (2), that $\dot{X}(t)$ obeys the fundamental following differential equation:

$$\dot{X}(t) = \frac{\partial X(t)}{\partial t} = \sum_{i=0}^{+\infty} i\dot{P_t}(i), \quad \dot{X}(t) = \lambda - (C\mu - \mu\sum_{i=0}^{C} P_i(t)(C-i)) \tag{4}$$

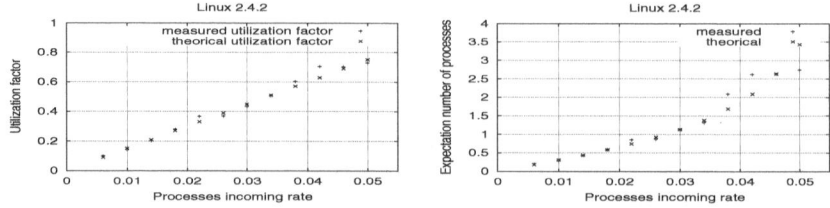

Fig. 4. Validation of the multiprocessors round robin model at stationary case

In [7] , the M/M/1 model was manipulated and the term $P_0(t)$ was approximated. In the M/M/1 stationary case, the relation (5) is true:

$$1 - P_0^\infty = \frac{X^\infty}{1 + X^\infty} \tag{5}$$

The idea in M/M/1 model is to approximate $(1 - P_0(t))$ with $\frac{X(t)}{1+X(t)}$. Such an approximation (called fluid approximation) was done for switching traffic [13] and revealed its accuracy. Here $C\mu - \sum_{i=0}^{C} P_t(i)(C - i)$ must be approximated to avoid infinite dimension which is not compatible with real time solution. The same approximation as M/M/1 is done and the number of servers (C) and a new coefficient called α are introduced. The value of α is chosen to ensure that the differential equation has the same value as X^∞ in the M/M/C model. Let $X_a(t)$ be the approximation of $X(t)$ (6).

$$\frac{\partial X_a(t)}{\partial t} = \lambda - C\mu\alpha \frac{X_a(t)}{1 + X_a(t)}, \quad \alpha = \frac{\lambda(1 + X^\infty)}{C\mu X^\infty} \tag{6}$$

A comparison between the approximation, the real value (solving the transient solution of the cut Markov chain) of the average number of processes in the system and a real execution on bipentium under Linux is depicted for $\lambda = 0.04$, $\mu = 0.033$ and $X(0) = X_a(0) = 0$ on figure 5.

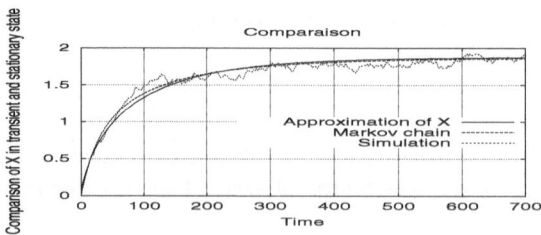

Fig. 5. Approximation of the average number of processes in the system

This autonomous differential equation always converges to the stationary solution and is also very accurate for the transient state. The differential equation represents the dynamical behavior of the load. Suppose that there are $X(t_0)$ processes at the observation time t_0. This differential equation will be able to predict the value of $X(t > t_0)$ with $X_a(t)$.

However, in real system λ and μ are not constant. Nevertheless, the system can be viewed piecewise stationary. In [7] the predictions of the values of λ and μ are explained in order to compute the expected number of processes at any time. The average observation of those parameters day to day and their values on the last few minutes are used. Depending on the behavior of machines the values of λ and μ in the future are estimated.

3.4   Prediction of the Expected Execution Time

At this point, the expected execution time of a deterministic process that is put in the stochastic round robin queue must be predicted. Let now consider a process requiring t_c units of computing time. Assume that this process arrives in the system at time t_0, while there are $X(t_0)$ processes in the run queue. This process will depart from the system at a random time t_r (due to the stochastic behavior of $X(t)$). $E(t_r)$ must be estimated. To this end, let first assume that the number of remaining processes will stay constant $(X(t > t_0) = X(t_0))$:

$$\text{if } (X(t_0) + 1 > C): \quad t_r = t_0 + \frac{t_c(1 + X(t_0))}{C}$$
$$\text{else:} \quad t_r = t_0 + t_c \tag{7}$$

This relation holds since UNIX uses a time sharing policy. Assuming now that $X(t)$ varies, the same argument can be applied to each time quantum. The relation between t_c and t_r thus obeys to the integral equation when $(X(t_0)+1 > C)$(8).

$$t_c = \int_{t_0}^{E(t_r)} \frac{C}{1 + X(t)} dt \tag{8}$$

Any numerical integration method enable to solve for $E(t_r)$ in the preceding equation (8). The expected completion time of a deterministic process competing for the processor with stochastic processes can now be predicted. If N processes have to be allocated at time t_0 (arrival time of the parallel application) to the same machine with $t_c^1 \leq t_c^2 ... \leq t_c^N$ and $t_r^0 = t_0$, the relation (9) can be proven by induction.

$$t_c^j = \sum_{i=0}^{j} \int_{E(t_r^{i-1})}^{E(t_r^i)} \frac{C}{((N - i + 1) + X(t))} dt \tag{9}$$

The piecewise approximation of X(t) enables to get analytical expression for the integral. Therefore the time spent to compute the values $E(t_r^i)$ is very small. This is essential if the mapping algorithms are implemented in a real time environment. The multiprocessors machines are simulated with round robin

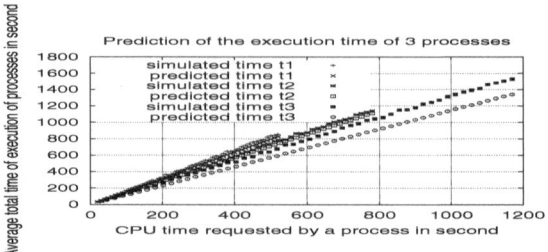

Fig. 6. Approximation of execution time

policy with a load of (ρ=0.09) . The measured and predicted execution times of three processes introduced at the same date are compared. They request different times of CPU ($t3 = t2 * 1.5 = t1 * 1.5 * 1.5$) (figure 6). The prediction provided by the algorithm is rather accurate. The mixing of deterministic and stochastic processes is well evaluated.

3.5 Task Mapping Algorithm

The previous algorithm allows to predict the expected execution times of several tasks on a workstation. It can be used to map the tasks of a parallel application in such a way that the application expected execution time is minimized.

The task mapping algorithm uses a modified version of the "Longest Processing Time First" algorithm [14]. The longest tasks are first mapped by minimizing the completion time. The completion time is predicted for each task on each workstation with the prediction algorithm. The model parameters are modified after each task mapping.

4 Conclusion

Network-Analyser is an observation and load balancing tool that provides several strategies for task allocation. Such a system is essential to obtain a good utilization of the global computational capabilities. It is running on different architectures (SUN, HP, IBM, PC). With its library, Network-Analyser is an open system that can be used by any software.

The essential point in the task allocation method developed in this paper is to introduce time (dynamic behavior of the system) in the decision model and to consider the whole distributed system as a stochastic system. It generalizes on multiprocessors the results found on uniprocessor. This work needs to be validated on real applications mapped on real machines and to be compared to different approaches.

Future work will concern the modeling of communication flows between tasks. First the work done for bus network will be integrated in the multiprocessors model. Secondly, more complex networks than a bus (Switched network like myrinet) will be considered. The approach assumes the knowledge of tasks CPU times t_c. If such values are unknown, a mechanism to estimate these values should be introduced. Therefore the resulting allocation problem will be more difficult and will take into account that t_c is a random variable.

References

1. A. Barak, R. Wheeler. *MOSIX: An Integrated Multiprocessors UNIX.* Proceeding of 1989 winter USENIX conference, San Diego, pp. 101-112, January 1989.
2. D.R. Cheriton. *The V Distributed system.* Communication of the ACM, vol. 31 No 3, pp. 314-333, mars 1988.
3. V.S. Sunderam, G.A. Geist, J. Dongarra, R. Manchek. *The PVM concurrent computing system : Evolution, Experience, and Trends.* Parallel Computing 20, pp. 531-545, 1994.
4. T. Monteil, J.M. Garcia, D. Gauchard, O. Brun. *Communication Kernel for High Speed Networks in the Parallel Environment LANDA-HSN.* IWCC99: IEEE International Workshop on Cluster Computing, pp. 63-70, Melbourne Australia 1999.
5. William D. Gropp, Ewing Lusk *User's Guide for mpich, a Portable Implementation of MPI.* Mathematics and Computer Science Division, Argonne National Laboratory, ANL-96/6, 1996
6. T. Monteil, J.M. Garcia *Task Allocation Strategies on Workstations Using Processor Load Prediction.* PDPTA97, International Conference on Parallel and Distributed Processing Techniques and Applications, pp. 416-421, Las Vegas USA, 1997
7. J.M. Garcia, D. Gauchard, T. Monteil, O. Brun *Process mapping given by processor and network dynamic load prediction* Euro-Par99 5th International Euro-Par Conference pp. 291-294, Toulouse France, 1999
8. T.L. Casavant, J.G. Kuhl. *A Taxonomy of Scheduling in General-Purpose Distributed Computing Systems.* IEEE Transactions on Software Engineering, vol. 14, No 2, February 1988.
9. Y.C. Chow, W.H. Kohler. *Models for Dynamic Load Balancing in a Heterogeneous Multiple Processor System.* IEEE Transactions on Computers, vol. c-28, No 5, pp.354-361, 1979.
10. C.Y. Lee. *Parallel machines scheduling with non simultaneous machine available time.* Discrete Applied Mathematic North-Holland 30 , pp 53-61, 1991.
11. F. Bonomi, A. Kumar. *Adaptive Optimal Load Balancing in a Non homogeneous Multi server System with a Central Job Scheduler.* IEEE Transactions on Computers, Vol. 39, No 10, pp. 1232-1250, October 1990.
12. L. Kleinrock *Queuing systems volume II: Computer Applications.* Wiley Interscience
13. J. M. Garcia, F. Legall, J. Bernussou. *A Model for Telephone Networks and its use for Routing Optimization Purposes.* IEEE journal on selected areas in communication; Special issue on communication network performance evaluation; Vol 4 No 6 pp 966-974, September 1986.
14. R. L. Graham. *Bounds on Multiprocessing Timing Anomalies.* SIAM J. Appl. Math.; Vol 17 No 2, march 1969.

Heterogeneous Dynamic Load Balancing

Tiberiu Rotaru and Hans-Heinrich Nägeli

Institut of Computer Science, University of Neuchâtel,
Rue Émile Argand 11, CH-2007 Neuchâtel, Switzerland,
{tiberiu.rotaru,hans.naegeli}@unine.ch

Abstract. The problem of fair data redistribution in heterogeneous environments is considered. Efficiently running applications based on adaptive computations on distributed systems requires adequate techniques for fair workload redistribution. A generalization of the diffusion algorithm for the case when the processors have different processing speeds is discussed. The worst case complexity of such an algorithm is theoretically analyzed and experimental results are reported.

1 Introduction

Running parallel applications on distributed systems requires efficiently using the available computational resources. As the slowest processor determines the execution time of the entire application, the workloads must be fairly distributed. From time to time, it may be necessary to proceed to a new repartition of workloads, as at runtime these can vary, often in an unpredictable manner. Parallel adaptive finite element applications arising in Computational Fluid Dynamics or Computational Mechanics were considered relevant for illustrating the need for dynamic load balancing [6,7], primarily in homogeneous systems. Such applications often rely on unstructured meshes, which are able to illustrate various general geometries and to easily reflect dynamic structural changes. Due to memory limitations and/or computational requirements the mesh redistribution process must preserve the data locality as much as possible. A fast method is necessary to apply after each adaptation phase in order to guarantee the load balance. Because generally the inter-processor communication is costly, the redistribution must be done with the least data migration and so that the computational dependencies between nodes residing on different processors is minimized. A centralized approach leads to heavy communication and it is not scalable. In the homogeneous case the diffusion schemes were successfully used to develop reliable dynamic repartitioning techniques like those provided by the popular packages ParMETIS and Jostle [7].

Less attention has been paid to dynamic load balancing in heterogeneous systems [4,11,8]. Although such environments offer multiple advantages, it is difficult to obtain the maximum benefit of their theoretical computing power. Contrary to the homogeneous case, the dynamic repartitioning of graphs in heterogeneous systems has not been yet satisfactory explored. In order to make

D. Grigoras et al. (Eds.): IWCC 2001, LNCS 2326, pp. 136–144, 2002.

things clear, we suppose we have to run a data-parallel application. The input data are initially distributed over the processors, which may have different processing speeds. We assume only that communication is slow compared to computing, so that it has a large impact on the overall execution time of a numerical algorithm. In our model, we abstract the speed of a processor by a real positive number called its *capacity*. A processor's workload is supposed to be infinitely divisible; hence it can be represented through a positive real number. Application-level load balancing techniques are considered here. Although it may need a larger number of steps than other schemes in a static framework, globally, using the generalized diffusion can be more appropriate when the communication topology changes dynamically.

2   Heterogeneous Dynamic Load Balancing

We consider a heterogeneous computing model $H = (G, l, c, \mathcal{A})$ in which

- $G = (V, E)$ represents the communication graph induced by the application $\mathcal{A}$ (which is mapped onto the set of processors V) and it is assumed connected; let $p = V$ and $q = E$;
- l is the vector of the processors' workloads;
- c is the vector of the processors' capacities; w.l.g. we can consider that $\sum_{1 \leq i \leq |V|} c_i = 1$.
- $\mathcal{A}$ is a given distributed application.

With these settings, the workload vector $\bar{l}$ corresponds to a *fair distribution* if

$$\frac{\bar{l}_i}{c_i} = \frac{\bar{l}_j}{c_j}, \text{ for all nodes } i \text{ and } j.$$

The problem to solve is to *determine the amount of workload to shift between adjacent nodes in H to obtain a fair data distribution with a certain minimal cost*. Obviously, in homogeneous systems a fair distribution is achieved when each processor has the same amount of work to perform.

Within such model, the generalized diffusion algorithm (shortly, *GDA*) was proposed for computing the minimal balancing flow [11,4]. As it name suggests, it is a generalization of the diffusion algorithm for the case when the processors have different speeds. If $l^{(0)}$ represents the initial workload vector, $l^{(n)}$ the workload vector after the n-th iteration, the algorithm can be expressed as an iterative process of the form $l^{(n+1)} = M \, l^{(n)}$, M being a $p \times p$ nonnegative matrix with the following properties:

$$\begin{cases} m_{ij} > 0, \text{ if and only if } ij \in E; \\ \sum_{i=1,p} m_{ij} = 1; \\ m_{ij} c_j = m_{ji} c_i, \text{ for all } i, j \in V. \end{cases} \tag{1}$$

A matrix satisfying the above properties will be referred to as the *generalized diffusion matrix* (shortly, *GDM*). The first condition means that in each iteration step the communication is allowed only between neighbors. The second constraint guarantees the conservation of the total workload in the system in the absence of external disturbances. The third condition is an expression of the fact that the communication links between two processing nodes do not loose their freight. The original diffusion algorithm was analyzed in the homogeneous case by Cybenko [3] and Boillat [1].

2.1 Convergence and Metrics

The following notations are used:

- e is the vector of size p, with all entries set to 1.
- $c^{1/2}$ is the *vector of the square roots of the capacities*;
- c_{max} and c_{min} are the *maximum* and the *minimum capacity*;
- D is the *diagonal matrix with the capacities on the main diagonal*;
- $\bar{l}$ is the workload vector corresponding to a fair distribution;
- $\|\cdot\|_q$ denotes the q-norm and $\|\cdot\|_{q,W}$ the weighted q-norm, that is $\|x\|_q = (\sum_{i=1}^{p} |x_i|^q)^{1/q}$ and $\|x\|_{q,W} = \|Wx\|_q$, for any vector $x \in \mathbb{R}^p$ and W a diagonal matrix with positive elements;
- d_i is the degree of vertex i in the graph G;
- $\Delta = \max_i d_i$;
- $e(G)$ is the edge connectivity of the graph G; it represents the minimum cardinal of a set of edges whose removal disconnects the graph [9];
- $\mathrm{diam}(G)$ is the diameter of G.

As it is column stochastic, a *GDM* has the spectral radius equal to 1. Furthermore, G being supposed connected, a *GDM* is primitive. The Perron vector of a nonnegative matrix is the eigenvector corresponding to its spectral radius with the sum of elements equal to 1 [10]. According to the Perron-Frobenius theorem, c and its multiples are the only eigenvectors of M with nonnegative entries [13]. For an arbitrary fixed heterogeneous model the following result holds:

Lemma 1. *The Perron vector of any GDM coincides with the vector of the processors' capacities.*

As a consequence, the workload vector corresponding to a fair distribution is the Perron vector multiplied by the total sum of the workloads, i.e. $\bar{l} = c(e^T l^{(0)})$.

Theorem 1. *A generalized diffusion matrix is diagonalizable and all its eigenvalues are real.*

Proof. Let M be a GDM and $D = \mathrm{diag}(c_1, ..., c_p)$. It is straightforward to verify that $M' = D^{-1/2} M D^{1/2}$ is real symmetric. Therefore, the eigenvalues of M' are real. As M and M' are similar, it follows that the eigenvalues of M are real, too.

As a consequence, one may assume that the eigenvalues of M are indexed so that

$$1 = \lambda_1(M) > \lambda_2(M) \geq \cdots \geq \lambda_p(M) > -1.$$

Let $\gamma(M) = \max\{|\lambda_2(M)|, |\lambda_p(M)|\}$. To be consistent with the homogeneous case [1], the term *convergence factor* will be used when referring to it.

The load imbalance in the system at a given time can be expressed using various metrics. The sequence of workload vectors $\{l^{(n)}\}_{n \geq 0}$ satisfies the following inequalities [11]:

$$\|l^{(n+1)} - \bar{l}\|_{2, D^{-1/2}} \leq \gamma(M) \cdot \|l^{(n)} - \bar{l}\|_{2, D^{-1/2}},$$
$$\|l^{(n+1)} - \bar{l}\|_{\infty, D^{-1}} \leq \|l^{(n)} - \bar{l}\|_{\infty, D^{-1}},$$
$$\|l^{(n+1)} - \bar{l}\|_1 \leq \|l^{(n)} - \bar{l}\|_1.$$

It can also be proved that

$$\|l^{(n)} - \bar{l}\|_{2, D^{-1/2}} \leq \gamma(M)^n \|l^{(0)} - \bar{l}\|_{2, D^{-1/2}},$$
$$\|l^{(n)} - \bar{l}\|_{\infty, D^{-1}} \leq \frac{\gamma(M)^n}{c_{min}} \|l^{(0)} - \bar{l}\|_{\infty, D^{-1}},$$
$$\|l^{(n)} - \bar{l}\|_1 \leq \frac{\gamma(M)^n}{c_{min}} \|l^{(0)} - \bar{l}\|_1.$$

The above relations show that after any iteration step, the distance to the fair distribution that is induced by the weighted 2-norm decreases. In the same time, the distances induced by the weighted ∞-norm and $1-$norm do not increase. Globally, the algorithm results in a geometrical reduction of all the above distances. As seen above, the convergence rate depends tightly on $\gamma(M)$, whatever metric is used. Therefore, adequate estimations should exist for it. The above results shows that a *GDA* completes in $O(1/|\ln(\gamma(M))|)$ steps. In the homogeneous case it was shown that the common diffusion schemes have an important property: they generate a balancing flow which is minimal w.r.t. a certain norm. This is also true in the heterogeneous for a large class of diffusion schemes [4,12].

2.2   Bounds for the Convergence Factor

Before deciding redistributing the workloads, one should be able to anticipate the maximum number of steps that a *GDA* will take to balance the system (and consequently, if it is worth to apply it). Adequate estimations of the convergence factor as a function of the characteristics of the communication graph should exist. As the graph induced by the current data distribution is often irregular and may change at runtime, the exact values of its spectra can not be given in advance. However, bounds can be formulated by analogy with the discrete time reversible Markov chains; the transposed of a *GDM* defines a random walk on the weighted graph G.

There is a close connection between the spectra of the Laplacian matrices of a graph and that of any *GDM* on this graph. Because M satisfies the set of conditions (1), the matrix $L = D - MD$ is a *weighted Laplacian* of G. On the other hand, one may consider the *generalized Laplacian* of G, expressed as $\mathcal{L} = D^{-1/2}LD^{-1/2}$. Bounds can be formulated for the second smallest eigenvalue of $\mathcal{L}$ using the Cheeger type inequalities involving the isoperimetric constant [2].

However, although such bounds are often tight, it is NP-hard to determine them. Following an alternative way, we generalized a result given in [5], expressed in the following theorem [11]:

Theorem 2. *Let M be an arbitrary GDM and $\theta(M) = \min_{ij \in E}\{m_{ij}c_j\}$. The following inequality holds:*

$$\lambda_2(M) \leq 1 - 4e(G)\frac{\theta(M)}{c_{max}} \sin^2\left(\frac{\pi}{2p}\right). \tag{2}$$

One is interested in finding diffusion matrices with a small convergence factor. When a single parameter is used, optimal matrices can be found in the homogeneous case for common topologies as the n-dimensional meshes or the n-dimensional tori [14]. In the heterogeneous case, because the capacities are different and the diffusion matrix is non-symmetric, finding optimal GDM's is much more difficult, even for simple cases. Instead, a relaxed condition can be used: *find GDM's which improve the inequality (2)*. One can notice that for any arbitrary M satisfying (1), $\theta(M)$ is upper bounded by $\min_i\{c_i/d_i\}$. The family of $M(\epsilon)$'s with the property

$$m(\epsilon)_{ij} = \min\left\{\frac{c_i}{d_i + \epsilon}, \frac{c_j}{d_j + \epsilon}\right\}\frac{1}{c_j} \tag{3}$$

for each edge (i, j) and uniquely determined when imposing the set of conditions (1) represents a family of GDM's. Having fixed

$$\epsilon_0 = 2e(G)\frac{c_{min}}{c_{max}} \sin^2\left(\frac{\pi}{2p}\right),$$

one can also show that

Theorem 3. *For all $\epsilon \geq \epsilon_0$, if $\lambda_p(M(\epsilon))) < 0$ then*

$$|\lambda_p(M(\epsilon))| \leq 1 - 2\frac{\epsilon_0}{\Delta + \epsilon}. \tag{4}$$

Therefore, as $\theta(M(\epsilon)) > c_{min}/(\Delta + \epsilon)$, one concludes that

Theorem 4. *For all $\epsilon \geq \epsilon_0$, if $\gamma_\epsilon = \max\{| \lambda_2(M(\epsilon) |, | \lambda_p(M(\epsilon) |\}$ then*

$$\gamma_\epsilon \leq 1 - 4\frac{e(G)}{(\Delta + \epsilon)}\frac{c_{min}}{c_{max}} \sin^2\left(\frac{\pi}{2p}\right). \tag{5}$$

As the right member of the above inequality is smaller when ϵ is smaller, too, the GDA based on $M^\star = M(\epsilon_0)$ potentially converges faster than any GDA based on a $M(\epsilon)$, with $\epsilon_0 \leq \epsilon$.

On the basis of the convergence properties given in the previous section and the above inequality, the following theorem can be stated:

Theorem 5. *The maximum number of iterations needed by the GDA based on $M^\star$ to balance the system belongs to $O((c_{max}p^2\Delta)/(c_{min}e(G)))$.*

In the homogeneous case, Boillat proposed a diffusion algorithm whose diffusion matrix can be expressed in our terms as $M(1)$ [1]. Above, we showed that a homogeneous diffusion based on $M(\epsilon_0)$ with $\epsilon_0 \simeq 1/2 \cdot e(G) \cdot \pi^2/p^2$ is potentially faster. Xu and Lau [14] found optimal diffusion matrices depending on a single parameter for common topologies that can be seen as members of the above considered family.

Polynomial diffusion schemes can be derived by similarity with the methods used in the matrix iterative analysis. However, such schemes often need knowledge at runtime of the eigenvalues of the generalized Laplacian [4]. They are effective when the communication topology does not vary, otherwise the computation of these eigenvalues will result in a significant overhead. Although it may need a relative large number of steps between two refinement/de-refinement phases, globally the use of the generalized diffusion can be more adequate as it can be restarted without further preparation.

2.3 Examples, Comparisons, Experimental Results

When the processing capacities are different it is difficult to give synthetic characterizations for the convergence factor, even for simple cases. From this point of view the obtained general bounds are useful. We simulated and tested various cases of heterogeneous diffusion. Test diffusion matrices with the entries corresponding to the edges of G defined as below were used:

$$m_{ij} = \min \left\{ \frac{c_i}{d_i + \epsilon}, \frac{c_j}{d_j + \epsilon} \right\} \frac{1}{c_j}, \ \forall \ ij \in E \tag{6}$$

$$m_{ij} = \frac{1}{\Delta + \epsilon} \frac{c_{min}}{c_j}, \ \forall \ ij \in E \tag{7}$$

$$m_{ij} = \frac{1}{\Delta + \epsilon} \sqrt{\frac{c_{min}}{c_{max}}} \sqrt{\frac{c_i}{c_j}}, \ \forall \ ij \in E \tag{8}$$

$$m_{ij} = \frac{1}{\Delta + \epsilon} \frac{c_i}{c_{max}}, \ \forall \ ij \in E \tag{9}$$

$$m_{ij} = c_i, \ \forall \ ij \in E. \tag{10}$$

The rest of the entries are considered 0, except those on the main diagonals which are uniquely determined by imposing the condition to the diffusion matrices to be column stochastic.

The tested topologies were binary trees with 15, 31 or 63 nodes and paths with 16, 32 or 64 nodes. It is well known that the paths are the topologies for which the diffusion has the worst convergence rate and for which the bounds for the convergence factor given in the previous section are reached(homogeneous case). Indeed, in the homogeneous case, for a path topology, $M^* = I - 1/(2 + \epsilon_0)L$. Therefore $\lambda_{M^*} = 1 - 4/(2 + \epsilon_0)\sin^2(\pi/2p)$. On the other hand, the inequality (2) reads in this case as

$$\lambda_{M^*} \leq 1 - 4\frac{1}{2 + \epsilon_0} \sin^2\left(\frac{\pi}{2p}\right). \tag{11}$$

In this case, we have equality in (11), therefore the bound exactly approximates the convergence factor. We considered the cases when the ratio $\alpha = c_{max}/c_{min} \in \{2, 5, 10\}$ and $\epsilon \in \{1, e(G)(c_{min}/c_{max})\pi^2/(2p^2)\}$. The results of the tests are summarized in table 1 and table 2. The numbers N_i represent the number of iterations performed by the diffusion algorithms based on the matrices defined by (6)- (10) and satisfying the set of conditions (1), until $\|l^{(n)} - \bar{l}\|_{2,D^{-1/2}} < 1$.

Table 1. Number of steps until convergence of a **GDA** on binary trees with 15, 31 and 63 nodes

p	α	ϵ	N1	N2	N3	N4	N5
15	2	ϵ_1	496	507	653	864	2275
		ϵ_0	371	380	489	648	2275
	5	ϵ_1	781	943	1364	2339	4330
		ϵ_0	568	707	1024	1756	4330
	10	ϵ_1	1325	1646	2912	6784	10517
		ϵ_0	963	1235	2186	5095	10517
31	2	ϵ_1	1117	1138	1435	1873	9847
		ϵ_0	837	853	1075	1404	9847
	5	ϵ_1	1483	1538	2921	5871	18206
		ϵ_0	1111	1153	2191	4404	18206
	10	ϵ_1	1623	2307	2450	4395	11761
		ϵ_0	1119	1730	1837	3296	11761
63	2	ϵ_1	2127	2196	2659	3328	34974
		ϵ_0	1595	1646	1994	2496	34974
	5	ϵ_1	3044	3588	5203	8734	50675
		ϵ_0	2224	2691	3902	6550	50675
	10	ϵ_1	4853	5505	11482	27410	116505
		ϵ_0	3549	4128	8612	20558	116505

The following conclusions can be drawn:

– The *GDA* based on $M^\star$ is better than all the other considered test diffusion algorithms, in terms of number of iterations.
– The number of iterations decreases when the parameter ϵ also decreases, for the considered test diffusion algorithms. When a parameter ϵ, with $\epsilon < \epsilon_0$, were used, no significant improvement in terms of number of iterations was detected.
– The upper bound fixed by (4) is tight, as in the case of a homogeneous diffusion on a path the equality holds.
– The choice of a diffusion matrix must be done carefully; the results for the diffusion defined by (10) serve as a bad example.

The generalized diffusion discussed here corresponds to a first order scheme. Diffusion techniques with an improved convergence rate like the second order

Table 2. Number of steps until convergence of a **GDA** on paths with 16, 32 and 64 nodes

p	α	ϵ	N1	N2	N3	N4	N5
16	2	ϵ_1	804	826	889	942	3461
		ϵ_0	536	551	593	628	3461
	5	ϵ_1	931	1119	1349	1918	4350
		ϵ_0	621	746	900	1280	4350
	10	ϵ_1	1439	2064	2259	2677	5356
		ϵ_0	960	1378	1508	1787	5356
32	2	ϵ_1	3819	3876	4551	5542	39744
		ϵ_0	2546	2584	3034	3695	39744
	5	ϵ_1	4754	5133	7076	10924	45896
		ϵ_0	3170	3423	4718	7285	45896
	10	ϵ_1	6132	7681	11527	21755	71800
		ϵ_0	4089	5122	7687	14509	71800
64	2	ϵ_1	12825	13158	15112	18015	255258
		ϵ_0	8550	8772	10075	12010	255258
	5	ϵ_1	13591	14157	23488	41731	269877
		ϵ_0	9061	9438	15659	27823	269877
	10	ϵ_1	13767	14401	30294	69426	266141
		ϵ_0	9179	9601	20197	46289	266141

schemes or polynomial schemes can be easily derived [4]. However such techniques require knowledge at runtime of the eigenvalues of the generalized Laplacian. Their computation may constitute a supplementary overhead when the communication topology changes. Typically, such changes may appear as a result of nodes migration. This imposes a recomputation of the parameters which are dependent on this topology. A generalized diffusion algorithm like that based on $M^\star$ has the advantage that it can continue straightforward after some minor update operations. The properties given in the previous section show that the load imbalance decreases after each iteration step, independently of the communication topology. Here we tried to answer to the question how bad the generalized diffusion can be? Additionally, we showed in [11] that a GDA has a better convergence factor than the hydrodynamic algorithm given in [8].

A scheme for dynamic repartitioning of adaptive graphs in heterogeneous systems using a GDA was derived. For the tests, a heterogeneous cluster of 10 SUN workstations running SunOS 5.7 was used. The execution times for dynamic repartitioning several adaptive graphs of different sizes are given in the table 3.

3   Summary and Conclusions

In the present paper a dynamic load balancing algorithm for adaptive simulations applicable in heterogeneous systems was discussed. We gave theoretical bounds for the maximum number of steps required by such an iterative process

Table 3. The execution time in seconds

Graph	number of vertices	number of edges	exec. time in sec.
simple	25	80	0.199s
grid20x19	380	1442	0.400s
stufe	1036	3736	0.719s
hammond	4720	27444	1.979s
shock	36476	142580	3.900s

to balance the system. The algorithm was integrated into a scheme for dynamic repartitioning of adaptive graphs in heterogeneous systems. Experiments were conducted within a heterogeneous cluster of workstations.

References

1. Boillat, J. E.: Load Balancing and Poisson Equation in a Graph. Concurrency: Practice and Experience, 2(4) (1990) 289-313.
2. Chung, F. R. K.: Spectral Graph Theory. CBMS Lecture Notes, AMS Publication (1996).
3. Cybenko, G.: Dynamic Load Balancing for Distributed Memory Multirocessors. Journal of Parallel and Distributed Computing 7 (1989) 279-301.
4. Elsässer, R., Monien, B., Preis, R.: Diffusive Load Balancing Schemes on Heterogeneous Networks. In G. Bilardi et al. (eds.), editor, 12th ACM Symposium on Parallel Algorithms and Architectures (SPAA), Vol. 1461 (2000) 30-38.
5. Fiedler, M.: Bounds for Eigenvalues of Doubly Stochastic Matrices. Linear Algebra Appl. 5 (1972) 299-310.
6. Hendrickson, B., Devine, K.: Dynamic Load Balancing in Computational Mechanics. Comp. Meth. Applied Mechanics & Engineering 184(2-4) (2000) 485-500.
7. Hu, Y. F., Blake, R. J.: Load Balancing for Unstructured Mesh Applications. To appear in Parallel and Distributed Computing Practice.
8. Hui, C. -C., Chanson, S. T.: Theoretical Analysis of the Heterogeneous Dynamic Load Balancing Problem Using a Hydrodynamic Approach. Journal of Parallel and Distributed Computing 43 (1997) 139-146.
9. Graham, R. L., Grötschel, M., Lovász, L.: Handbook of Combinatorics. Elsevier Science B.V., P. O. Box 211, 1000 AE Amsterdam, The Nederlands (1995).
10. Meyer, C. D.: Matrix Analysis and Applied Linear Algebra. SIAM (2000).
11. Rotaru, T., Nägeli, H.-H.: The Generalized Diffusion Algorithm. Techn. Rep. RT-2000/06-1, Institut d'Informatique, Université de Neuchâtel, June (2000).
12. Rotaru, T., Nägeli, H.-H.: Minimal Flow Generated by Heterogeneous Diffusion Schemes. In Interntional Conference On Parallel and Distributed Computing and Systems, Anaheim, USA, August 21-24 (2001).
13. Varga, R. S.: Matrix Iterative Analysis. Series in Automatic Computation, Prentice-Hall, Inc. Englewood Cliffs, New Jersey (1962).
14. Xu, C.: and Lau, F.: Load Balancing in Parallel Computers Theory and Practice. The Kluwer International Series in Engineering and Computer Science. Kluwer Academic Publishers (1997).

Multi-application Scheduling in Networks of Workstations and Clusters of Processors

D. Kebbal, E.-G. Talbi, and J.-M. Geib

LIFL, Université des Sciences et Technologies de Lille
59655 Villeneuve d'Ascq cedex -France-
{kebbal,talbi,geib}@lifl.fr

Abstract. In this paper, we present a framework for exploiting resources in Networks of Workstations (NOWs) and Clusters of Processors (COPs), in order to run multiple parallel adaptive applications. Adaptive model includes parallel applications capable to adapt their parallelism degree dynamically following availability of resources and changes in the underlying environment's state. Within the framework of the proposed environment, many components are developed. This includes fault tolerance, adaptive application building and scheduling and multi-application scheduling. In this paper, we focus our study on the multi-application scheduling problem. In the proposed multi-application scheduling model, each parallel adaptive application is controlled by its own scheduler, responsible for optimizing resources used by the application. A dynamic multi-application scheduler supervises all the applications and shares resources fairly among them, by means of a combined (time-sharing and space-sharing) scheduling algorithm.

1 Introduction

The increasing complexity of parallel applications, induced by the progress realized in many fields (telecommunication, etc.), has rapidly increased their computational power needs. Traditionally, parallel applications are executed on costly dedicated parallel platforms, such as MPPs, which quickly become obsolete. The recent and important emergence of networks of workstations (NOWS) and clusters of processors (IBM SP2/SP3, Alpha Farm, PC clusters) has provided efficient non-costly platforms for parallel and distributed processing. This is due to the proliferation of workstations with a constantly increasing performance/cost ratio and to fast communication networks. NOWs and COPs provide non-costly efficient processing platforms to these applications. However, these platforms are characterized by a number of properties making their exploitation sometimes difficult: dynamic and irregular load, heterogeneity, high failure frequency, etc. Moreover, the popular aspect of these platforms makes them attractive for many users which tend to use them simultaneously, in order to run multiple parallel applications. Therefore, tools for sharing resources and resolving conflicts between applications are required. Multi-application scheduling constitutes a solution for this problem.

D. Grigoras et al. (Eds.): IWCC 2001, LNCS 2326, pp. 145–155, 2002.
© Springer-Verlag Berlin Heidelberg 2002

Multi-application scheduling decides on how to affect the processes of a set of applications to the nodes of the system and how to control their execution. Multi-application scheduling techniques can be classified in time sharing, space sharing and combined techniques. Time sharing approaches consist of planning the execution of processes in the time (*gang scheduling* approaches [1]). Space sharing scheduling in opposite is based on partitioning the nodes of the system exclusively among the applications (IBM LoadLeveler/SP2 [2]). Combined scheduling is a combination of the two precedent categories, in that it decides at the same time of the placement of processes on the nodes and on their execution in the time [3]. Many scheduling systems use combined techniques in NOWs. Condor schedules multiple sequential applications in NOWs. MIST uses a gang scheduling-based algorithm which allows time sharing [4]. Piranha employs a combined approach for scheduling parallel adaptive applications in NOWS. The scheduling scheme is based on the prediction of availability periods of nodes [5]. In [6], a hierarchical multi-application scheduling approach is developed. The model comprises a number of global resource managers, responsible for allocating resources to applications. Each parallel application has at its disposal its own scheduler. Application schedulers interact with resource managers in order to request and release resources.

Combined techniques are promising solutions for resource exploitation in NOWs and COPs, because they intend to exploit the advantages of the two previous classes of techniques. The major part of the presented multi-application scheduling algorithms make some assumptions on applications' execution time or use predictive approaches. Moreover, there are a few work that have addressed the multi-parallel adaptive applications scheduling problem.

The remainder of this paper is organized as follows: the next section introduces briefly the parallel adaptive model. In section 3, we present our multi-application scheduling system. Section 4 presents the proposed multi-application scheduling algorithm. Section 5 addresses briefly the fault tolerance aspect. Then, some experimental results are presented in section 6. Finally, we present some concluding remarks in section 7.

2   Adaptive Applications

Adaptive scheduling systems allow parallel applications to change their parallelism degree[1] dynamically following the availability of resources. So, when new idle nodes are provided, the parallel application takes advantage of this availability by starting new computation on the provided nodes. Similarly, when some resources used by the application become unavailable, the application is requested to evacuate the computation which it has started on that nodes. Piranha [7], CARMI [8] and MARS [9] are examples of such systems.

A parallel application in MARS is composed of a master process and a set of workers. At the master level, some tasks (work units) which represent the

---

[1] The parallelism degree of an application means its number of processes.

computation are kept in its address space. A task consists of a data fragment and a function to be applied to that data. The master allocates the application tasks to workers and receives the results. If a node becomes overloaded or reclaimed by its owner, the application proceeds to withdraw the worker on this node. In this case, we say that the application is *folded*. Similarly, when a new node becomes available, the application creates a new worker on the provided node (application *unfolding*). In the case of application folding, the evacuated worker puts back the *partially processed task* to the master before dying, in order to be finished by another worker.

3   Multi-application Scheduling Model

In this section, we present our proposed multi-application scheduling system, which extends MARS to multi-application scheduling. Our aim is to develop a framework for managing multiple parallel applications and sharing resources among them. For this purpose, a multi-application scheduling module, having a global view on resources and applications, is developed.

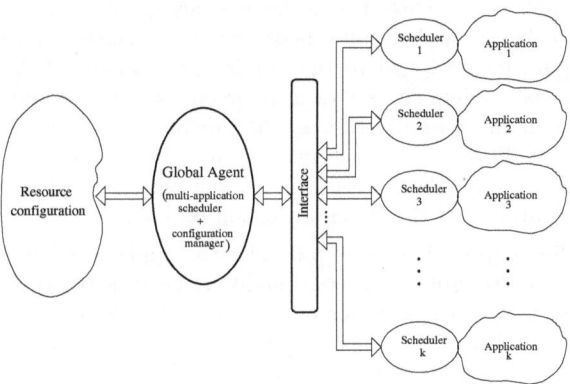

Fig. 1. Multi-application scheduling model

The proposed multi-application scheduling model (figure 1) uses a hierarchical scheduling approach [6]. An application scheduler controls each parallel adaptive application [10]. At the second level, a global agent manages the resource configuration and supervises the applications list. This approach allows efficient cooperation between the application schedulers and the global (multi-application) scheduler and is likely to increase the scheduling efficiency. A well-defined interface, specifying interaction protocols, permits the interaction between the application schedulers and the global scheduler.

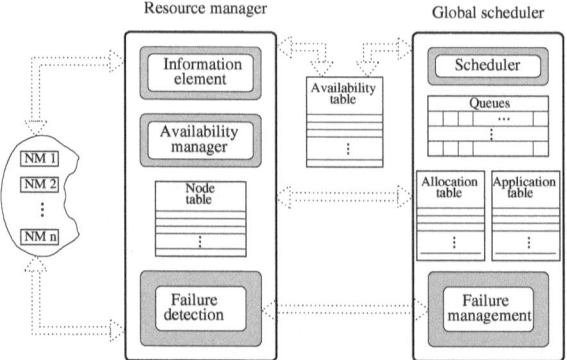

Fig. 2. System architecture

3.1 Application Schedulers

We adopted a model for building and scheduling parallel adaptive applications. The parallel application can be viewed as a collection of sequential tasks where the execution order is guaranteed by a dependency graph. The generated tasks are then handled by an application scheduler which ensures their allocation on the node configuration assigned to the application. Because MARS is a data-based model, a task is defined as a data fragment on which some actions must be applied. The parallel application is then defined as a set of tasks and a dependency graph. This model is relatively simple, because the application programming emphasizes on the computation which must be realized, rather than on the communication and the synchronization problems.

The scheduling approach tries to minimize the application's execution time, by maximizing the available work continually. Each task is assigned a priority value which depends on the number of its immediate successors in the dependency graph. The scheduling is preemptive, so, tasks with low priority values and running on fast nodes may be preempted in advantage of tasks with higher priority values and running on less powerful nodes.

3.2 Global Agent

The global agent is an important component in the multi-application scheduling model. So, it receives and satisfies the application requests and manages the resources. Therefore, we structured it into two agents: a *global scheduler* which supervises the submitted applications and makes the scheduling decisions; and a *resource manager* which manages the resource configuration. In addition, a *load state estimation element* is used in order to supervise the resource activities. The fault tolerance at the system level is reflected by two modules responsible for failure detection and transparent recovery of nodes and applications (figure 2).

Resource Manager. The resource manager locates and lists resources, controls their state and communicates the available ones to the global scheduler. On each node of the configuration, a *node manager* (NM) is started in order to control load state and user activities on the node [9]. The NM informs the resource manager when significant state changes occur. At the resource manager level, an *availability manager* continually determines the idle nodes and puts them at the global scheduler disposal, through the *availability table*.

Global Scheduler. The global scheduler receives and handles the requests of parallel adaptive applications submitted to the system. A well-defined multi-application scheduling scheme is used for this purpose. If the scheduler fails to satisfy the request of a submitted application, it puts it in a *queue* reserved to blocked applications.

4   Multi-application Scheduling Algorithm

The intent of the scheduling scheme is to satisfy the application resource needs and to resolve their conflicts. The scheduling policy is therefore influenced by the underlying environment characteristics and the application request types. Parallel adaptive applications may wish to use several resource types (classes): a set of workstations whatever their architecture type, a set of workstations of specified architecture types, or a set of specific resources other than workstations (nodes of clusters and MPPs, etc.). In this paper, we consider only the first class called *WORKSTATION*, given that the major part of existing parallel adaptive applications belong to this class.

The *WORKSTATION* request class indicates that the application wishes to use a set of workstations. The amount of requested resources is expressed by a range [*min-max*] which specifies the parallelism degree boundaries, outside of them the application efficiency can not be improved. The request must indicate the resource utilization mode: *multi-programmed* if the application allows mapping more than one of its processes on the same node and *mono-programmed* in the opposite case. The scheduling approach is dynamic and event-based; the considered events are: new application arrival, node overload, node availability, application termination, process termination, etc.

4.1   New Application

A new application arrival is accompanied by a request specifying the resource needs of the application. The request is then handled in three steps.

Request Verification. In this step, the request coherence is verified (validity of interval ranges, etc.).

Request Satisfaction. After the request verification, its satisfaction is tried. The scheduler determines the set of resources to be allocated to the application as follows:

– If the application doesn't enable mapping more than one of its processes on the same node, each idle node is considered one time. The resource amount to allocate to the application is determined by formula 1 (figure 3). This amount S_length must be: the mean parallelism degree of all running applications ($average$); or the number of available workstations ($avail$) and must belong to $[min,max]$ range. This formula allows to share resources fairly among applications through the $average$ parameter and to respect the parallelism degree boundaries of each application through the $[min, max]$ range.

$$S\_length = Min(Max(min, average, avail), max). \qquad (1)$$

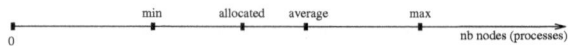

Fig. 3. Multi-application scheduling parameters

– The following algorithm determines S: the set of resources to be allocated to the new application:

for $i = 1$ **to** ws_types **do**
    while $n \in avail\_workstations(i) \wedge k < S\_length$ **do**
        $S = S \uplus [n]$
        $k = k + 1$
    end while
end for.

– If the application allows mapping more than one process on the same node, each workstation is considered many times.

Remapping. The goal of the remapping is to ensure a relatively fair resource sharing between applications. In this step, the scheduler tries to satisfy entirely the requests of applications that have not obtained the required amount of resources. If the amount of resources of S determined in the previous step is less than the required amount ($|S| < S\_length$), some resources used by running applications must be deallocated. The remapping algorithm consists of finding $nb = S\_length - |S|$ nodes used by other applications as follows:

s1: in this sub-step, the set of nodes already used by other applications is determined. That is the set of processes P running on nodes n which satisfy:

- if the new application doesn't enable mapping more than one of its processes on the same node, the node n must not be in S and must not host a process of the new application.

s2: the eligibility of each process P to be deallocated, is calculated (formula 2). This eligibility is defined using a "ranking" mechanism. Thus, the set of resources to be allocated SA and of processes to be deallocated SPD are determined as follows:

if $rank(appli) < rank(Appli(P))$ **then**
　　$SA = SA \uplus n.$
　　$SPD = SPD \uplus P.$
　　$update\_rank(Appli(P))$
end if.

For each process P, the eligibility (rank) value of the application owning that process is calculated and compared to the eligibility of the new application. The rank value depends on the current state of the application, the resource configuration which it exploits and its constraints.

$$rank(appli) = \alpha \times nb\_allocated + (1 - \alpha) \times (nb\_allocated - min). \quad (2)$$

Where $nb\_allocated$ is the number of processes currently owned by the application $appli$. $0 < \alpha < 1$, $\alpha = 0.5$ in the current implementation.

This formula allows to prevent applications from blocking by assigning high priority values to applications for which the number of allocated nodes is close to the min boundary. Each retreat of resources to an application is memorized and the application eligibility is recomputed for each new considered process.

s3: in this step, the exact resource amount needed, in the case that the defined amount is higher than the required one, is chosen.

Allocation. If the resource amount $S \cup SA$ is less than the min boundary ($|S \cup SA| < min$), the allocation is canceled and the application is blocked. Otherwise, the defined resource set is sent to the new application and the processes to be deallocated are stopped.

4.2   Node Overloading and Requisitioning

When a node becomes overloaded, the *node manager* informs the *resource manager* which forwards the information to the *global scheduler*. The ranking mechanism of the formula 2 is used to choose a process running on the overloaded node to evacuate it. If a node owner reclaims his workstation, all processes running on that node must be stopped.

4.3 Process and Application Termination

A process termination allows the scheduler to release its entry in the process table. However, if the number of the application's processes goes under the min boundary ($allocated < min$), the application must be suspended. The scheduler tries to allocate it some additional resources in attempt to prevent it from blocking. The above algorithms: request satisfaction and remapping are executed by considering the current amount of allocated resources ($allocated$) in formula 2. Application termination, in opposite, allows only the global scheduler to remove it from the application table.

4.4 Node Availability

When a new idle node is detected, the scheduler tries to restart some blocked applications. For each chosen application, the scheduling steps (request satisfaction and remapping) are executed. If no blocked applications can be restarted, the available node is allocated to the running applications which can extend their parallelism degree.

5 Fault Tolerance

Fault tolerance is an important aspect of NOWs and COPs, given their high failure frequency and the long lifespan of applications. The fault tolerance component is developed at two levels. At the application level, we provided parallel adaptive applications with a non-costly checkpointing/roll-back mechanism which allows them to handle the delicate failure problem. At the system level, we integrated to the system tools necessary for failure detection and recovery, through the *failure detection* and *failure management* modules (figure 2).

6 Performance Evaluation

We conducted some experiments using a synthetic parallel application from scientific computing in order to measure the performance of the proposed multi-application scheduling approach. The number of tasks, their duration and the application service time constitute the parameters of the scheduling policy. At each experiment, called *session*, a number of parallel adaptive applications of different service times are generated and executed using two scheduling policies: our *combined* approach and a dynamic partitioning-based (space sharing) approach. The key-points which characterize the experiments are: applications' service time, hardware configuration, scheduling policy used and inter-arrival times distribution. For each generated application i, we measure the following parameters: application response time (RT_i), application service time (sequential time, ST_i) and mean parallelism degree over the application's execution time. The experiments are conducted on a configuration of nodes composed of twenty SUN4 workstations connected by a 10Mbits/s Ethernet network. The system utilization rate is estimated following the load indicators (load average) and includes load induced by external processes. The experiments are executed in sessions of random duration. Applications arrive dynamically and inter-arrival times are exponentially distributed with a rate of λ. For each session s, we measure its average response time (formula 3).

$$MRT_s = \frac{\sum_{i=1}^{NbApplis_s} RT_i}{NbApplis_s} \cdot \qquad (3)$$

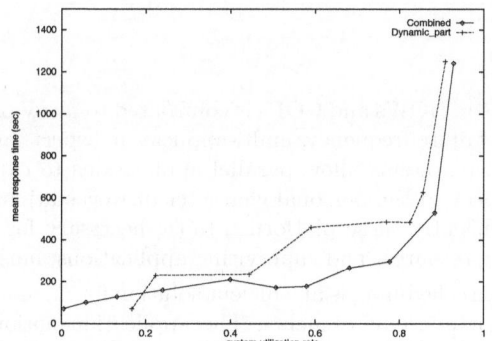

a) Mean response time versus system utilization rate

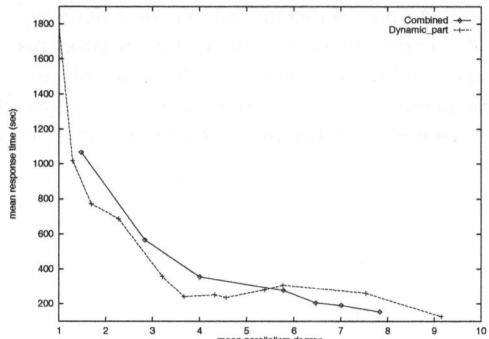

b) Mean response time versus average parallelism degree

Fig. 4. Mean response time versus different parameters

The results are average values of multiple runs. Figure 4a plots the mean response time (per session) versus the system utilization rate for the two scheduling approaches (Dynamic_part and Combined). This figure shows the performance of the combined approach which outperforms the space sharing one. Indeed, the combined approach benefits from its time sharing component which allows applications to exploit communication and synchronization periods of other applications. The performance gap between the two approaches is more important when the system is averagely used (between 0.4 and 0.6 on the figure).

The parallelism degree of parallel adaptive applications reflects in some way their evolution speed. Indeed, the high the mean parallelism degree, the high the evolution speed. On figure 4b, for small mean parallelism degree values (between 0 and 5), the Dynamic_part approach outperforms the combined one. In this situation, either the system is highly loaded, or there is a small number of applications with relatively low amount of work. In this case, the space sharing approach is more suited than the combined one.

7   Conclusion

Exploiting resources in NOWs and COPs is confronted to many problems such as heterogeneity, high failure frequency, multi-application aspect, interactive users, etc. Parallel adaptive systems allow parallel applications to exploit idle cycles in NOWs with respect to the personal character of workstations. Therefore, in order to exploit efficiently these platforms, tools, necessary for resolving these problems, managing resources and supervising applications, must be developed.

Multi-application scheduling is an efficient solution for managing and exploiting resources in dynamic environments. The application notion in scheduling permits to achieve some global objectives, such as fair resource sharing among applications, mean response time and resource utilization rate. The hierarchical scheduling approach used allows efficient cooperation between the global scheduler and the application schedulers, which results in good resource utilization. The performance results obtained show the contribution of multi-application scheduling. The combined scheduling policies achieve generally good performance, given the environment nature and the application constraints.

References

1. J. Ousterhout, D. Scelza, and P. Sindhu. Medusa: An experiment in distributed operating system structure. *Communications of the ACM*, 23(2):92–105, Feb 1980.
2. J. Skovira, W. Chan, H. Zhou, and D. Lifka. The easy - LoadLeveler API project. In D.G. Feitelson and L. Rudolph, editors, *Job Scheduling Strategies for Parallel Processing*, volume 1162. Springer Verlag, 1996.
3. B.B. Zhou, P. Mackerras, C.W. Johnson, D. Walsh, and R.P. Brent. An efficient resource allocation scheme for gang scheduling. In *IEEE International Workshop on Cluster Computing*, pages 187–194, Melbourne, Australia, Dec 1999.
4. K. Al-Saqabi, R. M. Proutty, D. McNamee, S. W. Otto, and J. Walpole. Dynamic load distribution in MIST. In *International Conference on Parallel and Distributed Processing Techniques and Applications*, Las Vegas, Nevada, USA, Jun 1997.
5. D. Gelernter, M. Jourdenais, and D. Kaminsky. Piranha scheduling: Strategies and their implementation. Technical Report 983, Department of Computer Science, Yale University, Sep 1993.

6. P. G. Raverdy. *Resource management and load balancing in large scale hetero-geneous systems: Application to mobile and parallel environments.* PhD thesis, University of Paris 6, 1996.
7. D. L. Kaminsky. *Adaptive Parallelism with Piranha.* PhD thesis, Yale University, 1994.
8. J. Pruyne and M. Livny. Interfacing Condor and PVM to harness the cycles of workstation clusters. *Journal on Future Generations of Computer Systems*, 12, 1996.
9. E-G. Talbi, J-M. Geib, Z. Hafidi, and D. Kebbal. *High Performance Cluster Computing*, volume I: Architectures and Systems, chapter MARS: An adaptive parallel programming environment, pages 722–739. Prentice-Hall, 1999.
10. D. Kebbal, E-G. Talbi, and J-M. Geib. Building and scheduling parallel adaptive applications in heterogeneous environments. In *IEEE International Workshop on Cluster Computing*, pages 195–201, Melbourne, Australia, Dec 1999.

The Parallel Algorithm of Conjugate Gradient Method

Andrzej Jordan[1] and Robert Piotr Bycul[2]

Technical University of Bialystok,
Department of Electrical Engineering,
Grunwaldzka 11/15,
15-893 Białystok, Poland

[1] jordana@cksr.ac.bialystok.pl, Tel. (+48 85) 7421651 ext. 123
[2] rpbyc@vela.pb.bialystok.pl, Tel. (+48 85) 7421651 ext. 115

Abstract. In this paper authors investigate parallel implementation of a conjugate gradient algorithm used for solving a large system of linear algebraic equations. Computations were carried out using a heterogeneous cluster of PCs, working under control of Windows 2000 operating system and an MPI library, as well as a massive parallel processor machine Hitachi SR-2201. The authors implemented two versions of the algorithm in cluster computations: an algorithm with equally distributed data among all processors, and another one with distribution depending on the speed of each PC processor. Speedup in all implementations was investigated and the conclusions were drawn.

1 Introduction

An electromagnetic field analysis is one of the most complex problems of physics. It results from the vector form of the Maxwell's equations, which "a priori" defines the electromagnetic field distribution in time and space domain. When analyzing the linear fields (μ = const, ε = const), the vector form of the Maxwell's equations after several transformations can be written in different forms, as presented in Fig. 1.

Among the models presented there the FDTD (Finite Differences Time Domain) method is worth mentioning because it enables direct integrating of the scalar form of Maxwell's vector equations in the time and space domain. It should be noted that a considerable number of methods applied for analyzing electromagnetic fields results in a set of linear algebraic equations:

$$\mathbf{Kx} = \mathbf{b} , \tag{1}$$

where $\mathbf{K}$ is a square coefficient matrix, $\mathbf{x}$ is an unknown vector and $\mathbf{b}$ is the right hand side vector. Following Fig. 1, the system (1) can be solved using direct or iterative methods. In this paper we present a parallel conjugate gradient algorithm, which is the most popular iterative algorithm in the electromagnetic field computations.

D. Grigoras et al. (Eds.): IWCC 2001, LNCS 2326, pp. 156-165, 2002.
© Springer-Verlag Berlin Heidelberg 2002

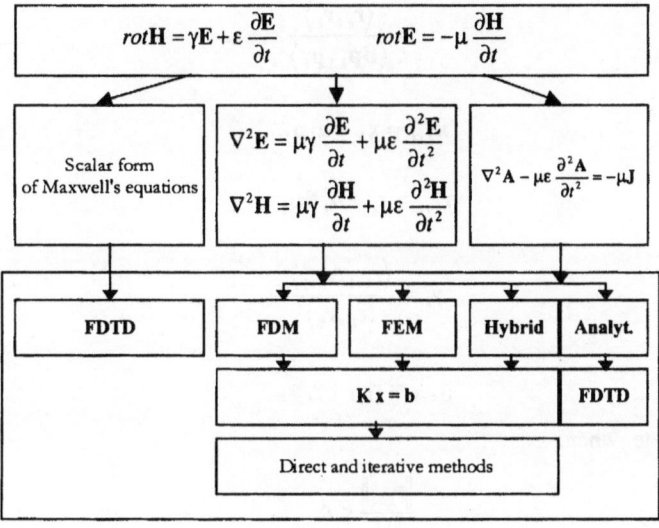

Fig. 1. Maxwell's equations and their modifications [4]

2 Sequential Conjugate Gradient Algorithm

A chosen version of the Sequential Conjugate Gradient Algorithm (SCGA) is convergent only if the coefficient matrix of the system of linear equations is symmetric and positive definite [3]. It is necessary to make the following operations for this condition to be fulfilled: multiplying both sides of the system (1) by transposed matrix $\mathbf{K}^{T}$ (it should be transposed and conjugate matrix $(\mathbf{K}^{*})^{T}$, when $\mathbf{K}$ is complex), we can rewrite system (1) in the following form:

$$\mathbf{B}\mathbf{x} = \mathbf{h}, \tag{2}$$

where $\mathbf{B} = \mathbf{K}^{T}\mathbf{K}$ (and it is symmetric and positive definite) and $\mathbf{h} = \mathbf{K}^{T}\mathbf{b}$. SCGA has now the following development:
We start with:

$$\mathbf{r}_0 = \mathbf{h} - \mathbf{B}\mathbf{x}_0, \tag{3}$$

$$\mathbf{p}_0 = \mathbf{r}_0, \tag{4}$$

where x_0 is the initial vector (for example, $x_0 = [0]^{T}$).
We iterate, for $k = 1, 2, 3, ...$:

$$\alpha_k = \frac{\langle \mathbf{r}_k, \mathbf{r}_k \rangle}{\langle \mathbf{Bp}_k, \mathbf{p}_k \rangle} \qquad (4a)$$

$$\mathbf{x}_{k+1} = \mathbf{x}_k + \alpha_k \mathbf{p}_k \qquad (4b)$$

$$\mathbf{r}_{k+1} = \mathbf{r}_k - \alpha_k \mathbf{Bp}_k \qquad (4c)$$

$$\gamma_k = \frac{\langle \mathbf{r}_{k+1}, \mathbf{r}_{k+1} \rangle}{\langle \mathbf{r}_k, \mathbf{r}_k \rangle} \qquad (4d)$$

$$\mathbf{p}_{k+1} = \mathbf{r}_{k+1} + \gamma_k \mathbf{p}_k \qquad (4e)$$

We terminate, when:

$$\frac{\|\mathbf{r}_{k+1}\|}{\|\mathbf{h}\|} < \varepsilon \qquad (5)$$

For example $\varepsilon = 10^{-12}$.
In the above algorithm

$$\|\mathbf{f}\| = \sqrt{\langle \mathbf{f}, \mathbf{f} \rangle} \qquad (6)$$

is an Euclidean norm and

$$\langle \mathbf{f}, \mathbf{g} \rangle = \sum_{i=1}^{n} f_i \cdot g_i \qquad (7)$$

is a vector inner product, $\mathbf{r}$ is a residual vector defined as $\mathbf{r} = \mathbf{b} - \mathbf{Kx}$. In the case when $\langle \mathbf{r}, \mathbf{r} \rangle = 0$, the solution of the system (2) is exact. Taking the round errors appearing in real computations into account, it is reasonable to apply equation (5), as a criterion of the solution accuracy. An ε denotes the tolerance, which specifies this accuracy. $\mathbf{p}_k$ is the search direction vector of the exact solution in the iteration number k. α_k and γ_k are real numbers. A more comprehensive description of this SCGA can be found in [3].

3 Matrix and Vector Operations in the SCGA

In the algorithm mentioned above we can identify basic matrix/vector operations that need to be performed in order to solve a large set of algebraic linear equations using SCGA:
- transposing matrix,
- matrix-matrix multiplication,
- matrix-vector multiplication,

– vector inner product,
– scalar-vector multiplication.

After many numerical investigations, parallel version of the algorithm was based on an assumption that the most time consuming and possible to parallelize operations are:

– matrix-matrix multiplication,
– matrix-vector multiplication,
– vector inner product.

We assumed that matrix transposition is not a suitable operation for computing in parallel, as it consists only of data moving operations, so the speed of computing the transposition is not gained when applying parallel computations. The scalar-vector multiplication is also too simple an operation to get speedup when computing in parallel.

4 Parallel Conjugate Gradient Algorithm (PCGA)

4.1 Data Vector Distribution

There are considerable number of methods of data decomposition and distribution in basic matrix/vector operations[1]. One of these methods is described in [1], where the distribution was called Physically Based Distribution. When referring to the example matrix-vector multiplication

$$y = Ax,\tag{8}$$

(where A is a matrix, and x, y are vectors) one should start from determining the distribution of vectors y and x among computing nodes. Then the distribution of matrix A should be consistent with the distribution of the vectors. Fig. 2 shows how the distribution of matrix A is induced from the vector distribution.

The subvectors of x and y are assigned to a logical 3x4 mesh of computational nodes. By projecting the indices of y to the left, we can determine the distribution of the matrix row-blocks of A. By projecting the indices of x to the top, it is possible to determine the distribution of the matrix column-blocks of A. The resulting distribution of the subblocks of A is given at the bottom of Fig. 2. More detailed information related to this distribution method can be found in [1].

In the computations presented in this publication we applied another method of data distribution, which can be called a "row distribution" as it distributes rows of a matrix. The method can be explained using the matrix-matrix multiplication. For example:

$$C = AB\tag{9}$$

---

[1] The basic matrix/vector operations are: matrix-matrix multiplication, matrix-vector multiplication and vector inner product.

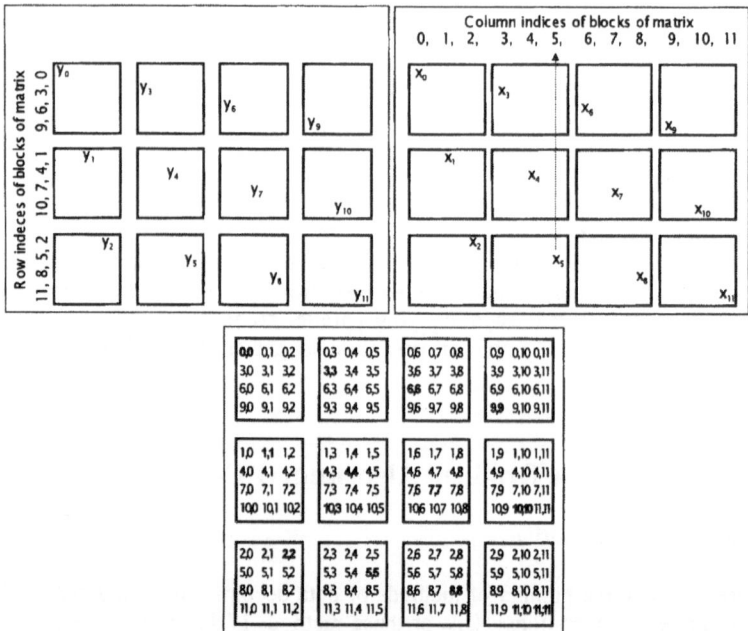

Fig. 2. Inducing a matrix distribution from vector distributions [1]

First, the resulting matrix **C** is partitioned into p sub-matrices, where p is a number of computational nodes. Fig. 3 shows the partitioning assuming 3 nodes: P_0, P_1, P_2 and 7x7 matrix **C** [2].

P_0	0,0	0,1	0,2	0,3	0,4	0,5	0,6
	1,0	1,1	1,2	1,3	1,4	1,5	1,6
P_1	2,0	2,1	2,2	2,3	2,4	2,5	2,6
	3,0	3,1	3,2	3,3	3,4	3,5	3,6
	4,0	4,1	4,2	4,3	4,4	4,5	4,6
P_2	5,0	5,1	5,2	5,3	5,4	5,5	5,6
	6,0	6,1	6,2	6,3	6,4	6,5	6,6

Fig. 3. Partitioning of the resulting matrix **C**

As we can see each node is to compute some number of the resulting matrix rows. The number is determined by the following equation:

$$D = INT\left(\frac{R}{p}\right), \tag{10}$$

---

[2] Fig. 3 illustrates matrix elements only as their indices. For example, "0,0" denotes the $C_{1,1}$ element, "0,1" – the $C_{1,2}$ element, etc. This denotation is also followed in Fig. 4.

where D is the mentioned number of rows, R is a number of all the rows[3] in matrix **C** and p is the number of nodes. INT means a function rounding D to an integer number. When the quotient R/p is not an integer number, one of the nodes has to compute more rows of the resulting matrix than others. This number can be determined using equation:

$$D' = D + R - p \cdot D = R + D(1 - p) \tag{11}$$

In the presented example p = 3, R = 7, so D = 2 and D' = 3. In the algorithm used on the SR-2201, the processor with the last rank number computes D' rows of the resulting matrix **C**, whereas in the version of algorithm with the data distribution depending on the speed of processors, the fastest processor computes D' rows.

The partitioning of matrix **C** induces the distribution of matrices **A** and **B**. It is known that the elements of the resulting matrix $\mathbf{C}_{mxl}$ are the inner products of matrix $\mathbf{A}_{mxn}$ rows by matrix $\mathbf{B}_{nxl}$ columns:

$$c_{ij} = \sum_{k=1}^{n} a_{ik} b_{kj} \qquad \begin{aligned} i &= 1,...,k \\ j &= 1,...,l \end{aligned} \tag{12}$$

As an example, for computing c_{11} element, we need to know the first row of matrix **A** and the first column of matrix **B**. For computing c_{12} element, we need the same row of matrix **A**, but the second column of matrix **B**, and so forth. Then, for computing the first row of matrix **C**, it is necessary to know the first row of matrix **A** and the whole matrix **B**. So only **A** and **C** matrices must be partitioned. Matrix **B** is not partitioned, so it must be sent as a whole to each processor at the beginning of parallel multiplying of the matrices.

Matrices **A** and **C** are distributed as in Fig. 4.

	A		**B**		**C**	

```
              A                             B                             C
     0,0 0,1 0,2 0,3 0,4 0,5 0,6   0,0 0,1 0,2 0,3 0,4 0,5 0,6   0,0 0,1 0,2 0,3 0,4 0,5 0,6
P0   1,0 1,1 1,2 1,3 1,4 1,5 1,6   1,0 1,1 1,2 1,3 1,4 1,5 1,6   1,0 1,1 1,2 1,3 1,4 1,5 1,6   P0
     2,0 2,1 2,2 2,3 2,4 2,5 2,6   2,0 2,1 2,2 2,3 2,4 2,5 2,6   2,0 2,1 2,2 2,3 2,4 2,5 2,6
P1   3,0 3,1 3,2 3,3 3,4 3,5 3,6 * 3,0 3,1 3,2 3,3 3,4 3,5 3,6 = 3,0 3,1 3,2 3,3 3,4 3,5 3,6   P1
     4,0 4,1 4,2 4,3 4,4 4,5 4,6   4,0 4,1 4,2 4,3 4,4 4,5 4,6   4,0 4,1 4,2 4,3 4,4 4,5 4,6
P2   5,0 5,1 5,2 5,3 5,4 5,5 5,6   5,0 5,1 5,2 5,3 5,4 5,5 5,6   5,0 5,1 5,2 5,3 5,4 5,5 5,6   P2
     6,0 6,1 6,2 6,3 6,4 6,5 6,6   6,0 6,1 6,2 6,3 6,4 6,5 6,6   6,0 6,1 6,2 6,3 6,4 6,5 6,6
```

Fig. 4. Distribution of A, B, C, matrices

The way of the data distribution in the matrix-vector multiplication is based on the partitioning of the resulting vector. The vector is partitioned into sub-vectors, one of D' elements, and remaining of D elements each. Matrix **A** is then distributed in an identical way to that in Fig. 4.

In the vector inner product the distribution of both vectors is identical to the distribution of the resulting vector in the matrix-vector multiplication.

The PCGA was implemented using C-programming language with an MPI library. The algorithm, as a whole, is sequential. Only the most time-consuming operations,

---

[3] When the matrix is square, R is equal to the size of the matrix.

mentioned in section 3 i.e. matrix-matrix multiplication, matrix-vector multiplication and vector inner product, are computed in parallel. The Master-Slave approach was used during the construction of the algorithm. The master processor performs all I/O operations, distributes data to slave processors, and stores computational results. It also has its own part of data to compute. The slave processors only receive data from the master, perform computing, using PCGA and then send the results back to the master processor.

4.2 Data Distribution Depending on the Speed of Processors

A computer cluster can often consist of computers of various computing power. In a typical heterogeneous cluster it is necessary to provide a possibility of uneven processor loading.

This version of the PCGA was used only in cluster computing because we assumed that the speed of the processors in the SR-2201 MPP differs so insignificantly that the difference can be neglected. The distribution was performed using the following equations:

$$D_i = INT(\frac{s_i}{\sum\limits_{i=1}^{p} s_i} \cdot n) \tag{13}$$

$$s_i = \frac{t_{max}}{t_i} \tag{14}$$

where D_i is an amount of data for processor number i, n is the size[4] of matrix $\mathbf{K}$, t_i is a computing time of the testing operation[5], which is performed at the very beginning of all the computations, to determine the speed of the i processor, and t_{max} is a computing time of exactly the same operation performed by the slowest processor.

This method of the data distribution differs from the one mentioned in section 4.1. Each processor gets a number of data, that depends on the processor speed, and the fastest processor, let it be k, gets $D_k + D'$ data to compute, where D' can be determined from equation:

$$D'= n - \sum\limits_{i=0}^{p} D_i . \tag{15}$$

---

[4] When the matrix is not square, n is a number of matrix rows.
[5] The testing operation was the vector inner product computed in sequential, repeated some number of times.

5 Speedup Analysis

5.1 Heterogeneous Cluster Implementation

Table 1 shows the basic characteristics of the PCs coupled in the cluster. The PCs were connected by the Fast Ethernet with maximal data transfer 100 Mbps. The sequence of the computers in the table is equivalent to the sequence of adding them to the cluster during speedup analysis.

Table 1. Basic characteristics of cluster PCs

No.	Processors' characteristics	Amount of RAM
1	Intel Pentium III 550 MHz	128 MB
2	Intel Celeron 400 MHz	128 MB
3	Intel Pentium III 650 MHz	256 MB
4	Intel Pentium 200 MMX	64 MB
5	Intel Pentium II 350 MHz	128 MB

Fig. 5 shows the speedup of parallel computations with equally distributed data, and Fig. 6 shows the speedup with data distribution depending on the speed of computers.

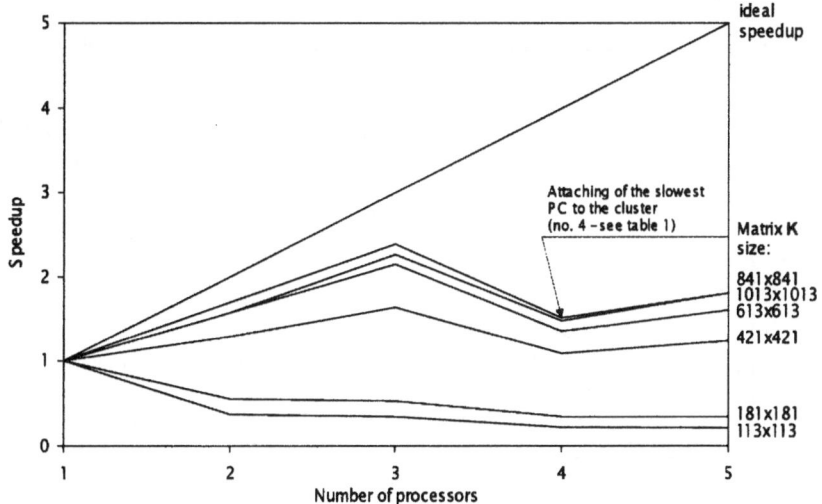

Fig. 5. Parallel computations speedup in the PC cluster with equally distributed data

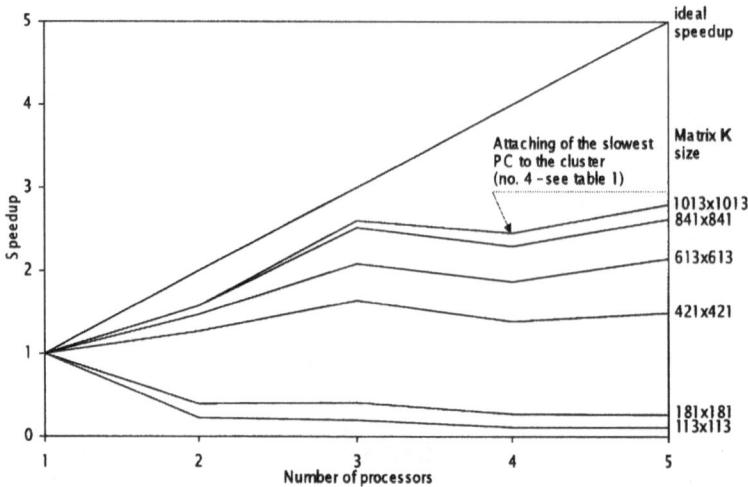

Fig. 6. Parallel computations speedup in the PC cluster with data distribution depending on the speed of the processors (Table 1)

5.2 Massive Parallel Processor Machine Hitachi SR-2201 Implementation

Fig. 7 shows the parallel computations speedup on the SR-2201 computer with equally distributed data.

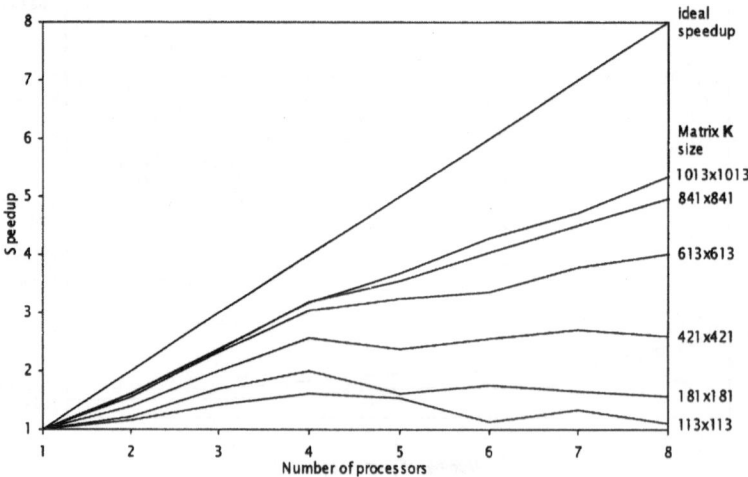

Fig. 7. Parallel computations speedup on the SR-2201 computer

6 Conclusions

The operation of multiplying both sides of the system (1) by the transposed coefficient matrix does not affect on the algorithm speed, when concerning to the generation of additional non-zero elements, because the algorithm was not optimized for the band matrices (which have been used as the coefficient matrices).

Although the presented algorithm is simple and not optimized, there is a visible speedup of computations. It is noticeable, that applying the distribution of the data depending on the computer speed in the cluster system has decreased the difference between the speedups from the SR-2201 computer and the cluster system.

It is evident that in a heterogeneous cluster system it is always better to apply a distribution of computational data that depends on the speed of each PC processor, because the slowest processor should do fewer computations than the fastest one. It is visible in the presented results that this way of distribution improved the speedup noticeably. This effect is more evident with greater differences between the speeds of the processors in the cluster. The large drop of the speedup caused by connecting the slowest, number 4 processor (Fig. 5) to the cluster is significantly reduced in the version of PCGA with the distribution of data depending on the processors' speed (Fig. 6).

What can be optimized in the presented parallel conjugate gradient implementation:

- Changing the sequential algorithm, especially by applying a preconditioning, so that the convergence could be improved,
- Applying better (faster) algorithms of matrices multiplication and matrix by vector multiplication – the algorithms used by the authors are very simple, and not optimal.

We are also planning to examine how would elimination of the zero-elements from the iterational process affect on the speed of the computations.

This work has been done in the frame of the statutes work No. S/WE/4/98.

References

1. A. Chtchelkanova, C. Edwards, J. Gunnels, G. Morrow, J. Overleft, R. van de Geijn: Towards Usable and Lean Parallel Linear Algebra Libraries. CS-TR-96-09, 1996.
2. A. Gupta, V. Kumar, A. Sameh: Performance and Scalability of Preconditioned Conjugate Gradient Methods on Parallel Computers. IEEE Transactions on Parallel and Distributed Systems, vol. 6, no. 5, pp. 455-469, 1995.
3. Jianming Jin: The Finite Element Method in Electromagnetics. John Wiley, New York, 1993.
4. A. Jordan: Theoretical Background of Parallel Electromagnetic Field Computations. The 10th International Symposium on Applied Electromagnetics and Mechanics, pp. 193-194, May 13-16, 2000, Tokyo, Japan.
5. P. S. Pacheco: A User's Guide to MPI. USFCA, 1998.
6. W. Peterson: Fixed point technique in computing eddy currents within ferromagnetic conductors exposed to transverse magnetic field. Archives of electrical engineering, Vol. XLVII, no. 1, pp. 57-68, 1998.

A Parallel Similarity Search in High Dimensional Metric Space Using M-Tree

Adil Alpkocak, Taner Danisman, and Tuba Ulker

Dokuz Eylul University
Department of Computer Engineering
35100 Bornova, Izmir, TURKEY
{alpkocak,danisman,ulker}@cs.deu.edu.tr

Abstract. In this study, parallel implementation of M-tree to index high dimensional metric space has been elaborated and an optimal declustering technique has been proposed. First, we have defined the optimal declustering and developed an algorithm based on this definition. Proposed declustering algorithm considers both object proximity and data load on disk/processors by executing a k-NN or a range query for each newly inserted objects. We have tested our algorithm in a database containing randomly chosen 1000 image's color histograms with 32 bins in HSV color space. Experimentation showed that our algorithm produces a very near optimal declustering.

1 Introduction

Similarity indexing is needed for many fields such as CAD, molecular biology, string matching and multimedia databases. In this study we focused on multimedia databases where each object (i.e., image, video, etc) is mapped into points in d-dimensional feature space. More specifically, an image in a multimedia databases is mapped into complex feature vectors representing color histograms, shape or textures descriptors, etc. and queries are processed against a database of those feature vectors. Similarity of two images is defined as a distance of their representing feature vectors in d-dimensional metric space. In image databases, a typical similarity query corresponds to a nearest-neighbor or range query in d-dimensional feature space.

To date, many of the similarity indexing structures has been proposed such as TV-trees, R-trees [5] [2], SS-tree [7], X-tree [3] and M-tree [4]. But, use of a similarity indexing is not generally fulfills the constraints about similarity searches. This is because, similarity indexing is both CPU and I/O bound due to the fact that the distance computations are CPU intensive tasks and image databases can be too large. To overcome these problems, there is an urgent need to parallel similarity indexing structures.

The core problem of designing a parallel similarity search algorithm is to find adequate declustering algorithm which distributes the data onto disks such that the data which has to be read in executing a query are distributed as equally as possible among disk. In the past, some declustering methods have been proposed [8]. In their

D. Grigoras et al. (Eds.): IWCC 2001, LNCS 2326, pp. 166-171, 2002.
© Springer-Verlag Berlin Heidelberg 2002

study, they have proposed four different approaches to decluster objects with two main categorizations: *Global* and *proximity based* allocation. Global allocation strategy contains two approaches: *round robin* and *random* while proximity based methods contains *simple* and *complex proximity*. The first group, global allocation, is the easiest method but does not take care the object proximity. The second group considers about object proximities but it has two major deficiencies. First, it does not consider data load at all and, the second, the proximity considerations operates only locally in an M-tree nodes children of the same parent. We therefore propose a new declustering method for parallel similarity search using M-tree in high-dimensional metric space. Our new approach guarantees a balanced load on disks and considers global proximity of whole objects in database. Our method produces an optimal declustering of objects for high-dimensional metric space.

In the remainder of the paper, first, we have given background information about M-tree indexing structure in next section and described the details of our approach in section 3. In section 4, we presented the results obtained from experimentation and give a comparison with related works.

2 M-Tree Indexing Structure

M-tree indexing structures was proposed in [4] and known as a dynamic and balanced access structure suitable to index generic metric spaces. Indexed objects are assumed to belong to a metric space and the similarity between the objects is calculated by a distance function satisfying the properties of *symmetry*, *positivity* and *triangle inequality* for any triple of objects.

An M-tree is a balanced tree with fixed-size nodes and all data appears in leaves. In each leaf node, except for entries in the root, the distance $d(O_i, P(O_i)$ from the object O_i to its parent object P(Oi) is also maintained in entries because the knowledge of this distance can easily be exploited to significantly increase search efficiency. Non-leaf nodes are also called *routing* objects, O_r since they represent sub-trees. Routing objects contain two additional items: (1) a pointer **ptr**$(T(O_r))$ to the root of the sub-tree $T(O_r)$, and, (2) the covering radius, $r(O_r)>0$, such that for all O_i from $T(O_r)$ the inequality $d(O_i,O_r) \leq r(O_r)$ is satisfied.

More formally it can be defined as follows:

$$(\forall N_x \forall i) \ (O_i \ni N_x) \textbf{ and } d(O_i, O_p)<=R_{NX} \textbf{ where } R_{NX} = \textbf{max}(d(O_i, O_p))$$

For a given specific metric defined by its distance, M-tree is able to support processing of two main types of queries. **Range Query**: *find all objects that are within a specific distance from a given object.* **Nearest Neighbor Query** (*k*-NN): find a specific number of closest objects to a given query object.

3 Objects Declustering

The main problem of designing a parallel similarity search is declustering of objects to exploit the both I/O and CPU parallelism. The declustering problem can be defined as an adequate distribution of the objects to disks/processors so that the objects that have to be read in executing a query are distributed as equally as possible among disks/processor. Furthermore, a declustering algorithm must take into consideration of object proximities, this is because, typical queries in high-dimensional metrics space fall into two categories either range or k-NN queries. Both type of query is processed according to their overall proximities in given metric space. Therefore, we concentrated on proximity based object declustering.

More formally, for a given multicomputer architecture with m disks/processors, assuming that Q is a query, RS is the result set of query Q and OP_i is the set of objects for query Q found on disk i, an optimal declustering condition can be defined as follows:

$$(\forall i) \, (\mathbf{count}(OP_i \cap RS) \cong (\mathbf{count}(RS) \, / \, m) \quad \text{where} \ (1 \leq i \leq m, \ \mathbf{count}(RS) \gg m)$$

This condition summarizes the best case and, if a declustering algorithm satisfies the above condition we say that this declustering algorithm is optimal. On the other hand, the worst case for a declustering algorithm can be defined as follows:

$$(\forall i \ \text{except} \ j) \, (\mathbf{count}(OP_i \ \cap \ (RS - OP_j)) = \varnothing \,) \quad \text{where} \ (1 \leq i \leq m, \ 1 \leq j \leq m, \ \mathbf{count}(RS) \gg m)$$

In another say, $RS - OP_j = \varnothing$

According to the definitions above, a declustering algorithm must address two issues: (1) the load of each disk/processor must be balanced among disk/processors and (2) this must be done by considering objects overall proximities. Therefore, we concentrated on these issues and proposed a declustering algorithm. Our algorithm works as follows. After inserting the newly added object, a range query is performed for the newly added object. In this query, newly inserted object's distance to parent routing object is given as a radius.

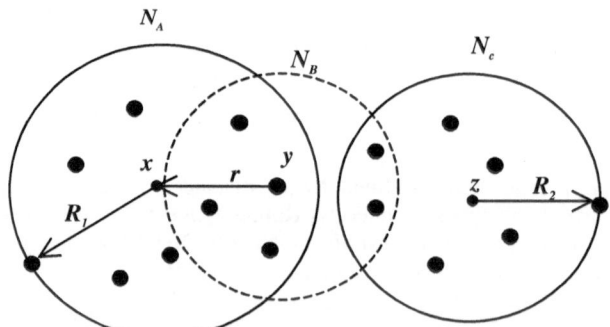

Fig. 1. Proximity checking for newly added object.

In Figure-1, two M-tree nodes, N_A and N_C, are shown in 2-dimensional space. In order to equally distribute objects in a *RS* among a number of disks/processors, we need to find closer objects to the currently inserted object. If an object O_y is inserted as a sibling of N_A, then its distance to its parent object O_p, is defined as $d(O_y, O_p) = r$. After the insert operation succeeds, a range query is performed with a threshold value of r. This is shown with dashed-lines in Figure-1. For the objects that far away from its parent object, the probability of having a closer neighbor object from another M-tree node increases with the increasing value of the r. The range query allows us to find the closest objects to the current object and the object processor ID. After successfully processing of the range query, the processor that has minimum number of objects is selected for newly inserted objects. More formally, assuming that P is the number of processors, the processor selection algorithm can be defines as follows:

$$(\forall_i) \ (\text{Select } P_i \ \text{ where } \ (1 \le i \le m, \ \textbf{count } (OP_i \cap RS) \text{ is minimum})$$

In this way, we always select the processor that has minimum number of objects in result set *RS*. This mechanism provides an optimal declustering strategy by considering both object proximity and processors load. *RS* can also be obtained by a k-NN. In this case the value of k can be the number of processor in the cluster.

4 Experimentation Results

In order to evaluate our declustering algorithm we did a series of experimentation on a database containing randomly chosen 1000 image's color histograms. For color histogram, HSV color space is divided into 32 subspaces (32 colors: 8 ranges of H and 4 ranges of S). In the resulting histogram, the value in each dimension in a color histogram of an image represents the density of each color in the entire image. Histogram intersection was used to measure the similarity between two images feature vectors. We used a modified multithreaded implementation of M-tree to index high-dimensional color vectors.

First, we have run the system using random distribution (round-robin) and, then used our algorithm with two alternatives, k-NN queries and Range queries. After successfully creating the index, we run 100 successive k-NN queries on three different indexes for different distribution schemes for the varying size of processors for 2, 4 and 8 and. Experiments repeated for varying k values. Then, we have observed the standard deviation of processor loads, according to given optimal declustering definition, for each combination step. Figure-2 shows the experimentation results obtained.

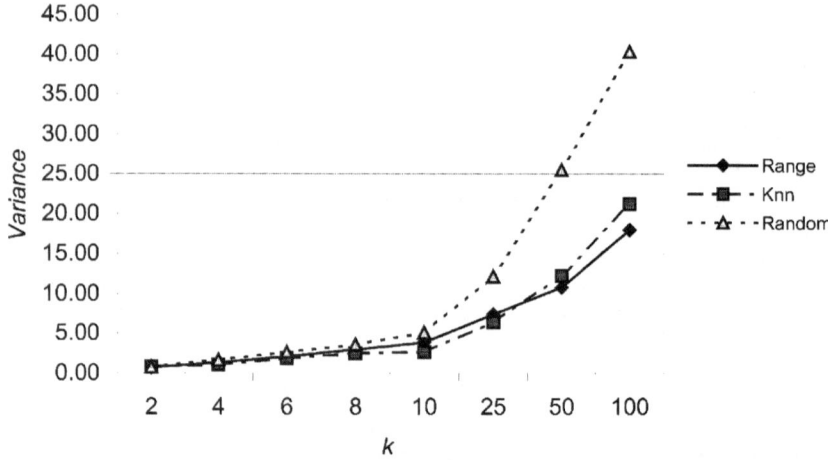

Fig. 2. Comparison of Declustering Methods

5 Conclusion

In this study, parallel implementation of M-tree to index high dimensional metric space has been elaborated and an optimal declustering technique has been proposed. First, we have defined the optimal declustering and developed an algorithm based on this definition. Our declustering algorithm considers both object proximity and data load on disk/processors by executing a k-NN and range query for each newly inserted objects.

We have tested our algorithm in a database containing randomly chosen 1000 image's color histograms with 32 bins in HSV color space. As a distance function, the Euclidian distance is used to evaluate the object similarities.

As a result, our algorithm produced a good declustering very near to optimal. Using Range query in our algorithm resulted a better declustering against of k-NN query. But the cost of range query is more than range query. Besides, random declustering method is also a good in CPU times, which is 7 times less then our algorithm. However, if we consider that the query processing response time is more important than database population time, our algorithm can be used to exploit both I/O and CPU parallelism for query processing in high dimensional metric space.

References

1. Berchtold, S., Böhm, C., Braunmüller, B., Keim, D.A., Kriegel, H.P. : "Fast Parallel Similarity Search in Multimedia Databases", *Proc. Of Int. Conf. On Management of Data,* 1997, ACM SIGMOD, Tuscon, AZ, (1997)

2. Beckman, N. , Kriegel, H.P. : The R*-tree: "An Efficient And Robust Access Method For Points And Rectangles", *Proc. of ACM SIGMOD Conference*, (1990) 332-331
3. Berchtold, S.,   Keim, D.A., Kriegel, H.P. : "The X-tree: An Index Structure for High-Dimensional Data", *Proc. of the VLDB Conference.*, (1996) 28-39
4. Ciaccia, P., Patella, M. , Zezula, P. : "M-tree: An Efficient access method for similarity search in metric spaces", In *Proceedings of the 23rd VLDB International Conference*, Athens, Greece, August (1997) 426-435
5. Gutman, A. : "R-Trees: A Dynamic Index Structure For Spatial Searching", *Proc. of the ACM SIGMOD Conference*, (1984) 44-57
6. Linn, K., Jagadish, H.V., Faloutsos, C. : "The TV-Tree : An Index Structure For High Dimensional Data", *VLDB Journal,* Vol.3, No.4, (1994) 517-542
7. White, D.A.,   Jain, R. : "Similarity Indexing with the SS-tree", *Proc. of 12th IEEE International Conference on Data Engineering*, New Orleans, Louisiana, February (1996) 516-523
8. Zezula, P., Savino, P., Rabitti, F., Amato, G., Ciaccia, P. : "Processing M-Tree with Parallel Resources", In *Proceedings of the 6th EDBT International Conference*, Valencia, Spain, March, (1998)

A User-Level Interface for Clustering Mathematical Software Kernels

Dana Petcu, Horia Popa, and Dorin Ţepeneu

Western University of Timişoara, B-dul V.Pârvan 4, 1900 Timişoara, Romania,
{petcu,hpopa,dorinte}@info.uvt.ro,
http://www.info.uvt.ro/~petcu

Abstract. We shortly describe a software prototype allowing the cooperation between several Maple processes running on different processors
of a cluster. Two examples, a graphical one, and another which is concerning with the numerical solution of a large mathematical problem,
sustain the idea of an improvement of Maple's capabilities to deal with
intensive computational problems.

1 Introduction

Very often scientific applications need more computing power than a sequential
computer can provide. A viable and cost-effective solution is to connect multiple processors together and coordinate their computational efforts. In the last
decade there has been an increasing trend to move away from expensive and specialized proprietary parallel supercomputers towards networks of workstations.
The use of clusters to prototype, debug, and run applications is becoming an increasingly popular alternative to using specialized parallel computing platforms.
An important factor that has made the usage of clusters a practical proposition
is the standardization of many tools and utilities (like Parallel Virtual Machine,
shortly PVM [5]) used by parallel applications.

Originally, mathematical software was designed as educational aid and tool
for prototyping algorithms which would then be translated into a programming
language. Today, mathematical software offers an interactive way of working,
programming and rapid prototyping for many users finding that a degradation
in speed by a small factor is more than made up an improvement of programming easy by a greater factor. To improve the time performances of such a kind
of software or to improve the capabilities by coupling different mathematical
software kernels, several user-interfaces have been designed recently. For example, NetSolve [1] is designed to solve computational science problems over a
network using a wide collection of mathematical software, including Matlab and
Mathematica.

We present in this paper two examples of using the recently developed prototype of a user-interface in Maple, PVMaple (Parallel Virtual Maple), allowing
the inter-connection of several Maple processes running on different processors
of a parallel computer, a cluster, or a network of workstations. Efficiency tests
have been performed on a cluster of dual-processor SGI Octanes linked by three

D. Grigoras et al. (Eds.): IWCC 2001, LNCS 2326, pp. 172–178, 2002.
© Springer-Verlag Berlin Heidelberg 2002

10-Mbit Ethernet sub-networks. Section 2 reviews shortly prototype's main characteristics and Section 3 describes the two examples.

PVMaple was presented for the first time in [10]. Several tests with PVMaple have been reported also in [13]. PVMaple is one the four basic tool of PaViS (Parallel Virtual Solver, [12]) allowing the inter-connection of different mathematical software kernels (at this moment Maple, Matlab, Mathematica and EpODE – ExPert system for Ordinary Differential Equations – a numerical solver of initial value problems [9]). Several comparative tests done relative to the most closest tool, Distributed Maple [14], have reveal the advantage of using PVMaple in the case of a network of PC's and in the solving process of some large mathematical problems [11].

2   Prototype Overview

Parallel Virtual Maple is an extension of Maple capabilities to distributed computations for workstations grouped into a parallel virtual machine, providing also facilities for post-execution analysis of a distributed computing session. PVMaple's aim is to interface the flexible process and virtual machine control from PVM system with several Maple processes, allowing also the cooperation between Maple processes. The main goals of the tool are the following ones: to be a public domain tool designed for anyone who want to solve a problem requiring a large amount of computer resources (download from http://www.info.uvt.ro/~petcu/pvmaple), to be faster than previous designed systems, and to allow parallel programming within Maple (the user interacts with the system via the text oriented Maple front-end).

PVMaple was created following the ideas of the previously build-up tool, Distributed Maple. Therefore there are many similarities between these two distributed computing environments. Several benchmarks concerning Distributed Maple and PVMaple can be found in [11]. Other similar tools are reported in Table 1.

Note that DPToolbox [8] is also very close to PVMaple's idea to maintain the PVM-function syntax into the user interface within the CAS. It realizes a multi-instance approach to support a convenient development of distributed and parallel Matlab applications. It uses PVM for process communication and control. Matlab instances are coupled via DPToolbox on heterogeneous computer clusters and parallel computers.

Table 1. Parallel and distributed Maple: different versions

Version	Built upon	Type	Parallel	Cluster	Reference
Sugarbush	Linda	Maple extension	+	-	[3]
‖Maple‖	Strand	Maple extension	+	-	[15]
Maple for Paragon	New kernel	New Maple	+	-	[2]
FoxBox	MPI	Maple extension	+	+	[4]
Distributed Maple	Java	Maple extension	-	+	[14]

Table 2. PVMaple components and dependencies

Component type	PVMaple	
	Component	Format
CAS	Maple V 4.0-6.0	binary
Communication	pvmd	binary
CAS library	pvm.txt/pvm.m	Maple text/internal
Binding	commandm	binary
Paths	paths.txt	text

The task scheduler is the PVM daemon lying on each machine which participates to the distributed computing. The applications cannot be started in the absence of the public domain software which support the scheduler. The binding between the Maple process and the daemon is done by a special binary, namely command-messenger. Table 2 presents more details about the tool structure.

Typical functions for message passing paradigm are provided inside Maple: process creation, send and receive primitives, procedure for stopping the parallel virtual computing machine. Table 3 presents such functions. Details about the function syntax can be found in [10].

In order to reduce the network traffic, the send and receive command in PVMaple have been constructed in such a manner to allow multiple commands to be send once to all or a specific remote task. The user must write a string of commands (by concatenation, for example). Moreover, using string of commands, the described Maple expressions will be remotely evaluated. A second application of the fact that strings of commands are used for send/receive functions is that the remotely Maple kernels (slaves of the master Maple process which has started them) can cooperate between them by sending and receiving data or commands.

The active time periods are registered by PVMaple into some text file which remains in a temporary directory after the virtual machine has been stopped and can be used also by PVMaple time function or other programs in further time diagram processing.

Table 3. Process control and inter-communications via Maple function library pvm.m

Meaning	PVMaple
Create local or remote Maple processes	spawn
Send commands to Maple processes	send
Receive results from Maple processes	receive
Stop distributed computing	exit
Time measurement	settime, time
Components identification	ProcID, MachID, TaskId, Tasks

3   Experiments

Numerous tests have been done in order to test PVMaple's efficiency in solving computational intensive problems. We present here only two different examples of Maple's improvement via PVMaple due to the inter-connection between several kernels. The tests have been performed on a cluster of dual-processor SGI Octanes linked by three 10-Mbit Ethernet sub-networks.

The first example is concerning with the recursive process of constructing a computer image of a known fractal curve, the snowflake. The initial curve is presented in the left part of Figure 1. The result of the first level of segmentation

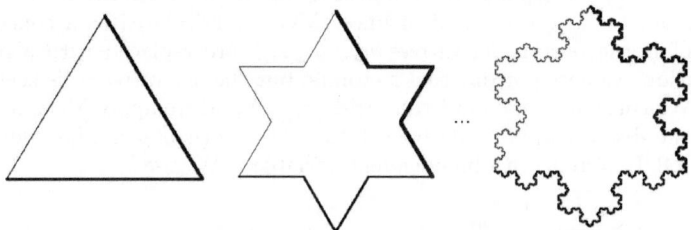

Fig. 1.   Snowflake recursive generation using Maple's plotting commands

is the curve from the middle. The number of curve points increases dramatically with the recursion levels: $3 \cdot 2^{2n-1}$ points where n is the recursion level. After $n = 6$ levels of segmentation the curve image is similar to that from the right part of Figure 1. The plot structure can be constructed in the current version of Maple, only for $n \leq 7$ (unreasonable time requested in the case of a greater n value). To construct a more refined image, for example for $n = 8$, we can divide the plot structure construction into smaller tasks, starting from the initial curve. In our case, we can easily divide the initial curve into three segments (different thickness values for each segment, in Figure 1). Using PVMaple to compute the curve points on three different processors of the cluster, for $n = 7$, the mean time (mean of several tests) necessary to generate and draw the snowflake was $T_3 = 18.08$ s, while the mean time to generate it on one processor without task division, was $T_0 = 36.93$ s, i.e. a speed-up of 2.04. For $n = 8$ it was possible to draw the snowflake in the mean time $T_3 = 79.81$ s using three Maple kernels on different processors, while it was impossible to draw it using one Maple kernel within at least 5 minutes. For $n < 7$ the usage of several Maple kernels is not justified since the time necessary to exchange the Maple's commands and results dominates the computation time of the curve points.

The second example is concerning with the simulation of a plate loading due to the movement of a car passing over it which is necessary for example in a plate design process. The mathematical model is described by the following partial differential equations [6]:

$$u_{tt} + \omega u_t + \sigma \Delta\Delta u = f(t, x, y),$$

where $u\big|_{\partial\Omega} = 0$, $\Delta u\big|_{\partial\Omega} = 0$, $t \in [0,T]$ on x-axis, $u_t(0,x,y) = 0$, where $(x,y) \in \Omega = [0,l_x] \times [0,l_y]$, and the load f is the sum of two Gaussian curves on y-axis, with four wheels moving in the x-direction. More precisely we take the following particular values for the problem parameters:

$$\Omega = [0,2] \times [0,4/3], \ \omega = 1000, \ \sigma = 100, \ t \in [0,7]$$

$$f(t,x,y) = \begin{cases} 200(e^{-5(t-x-2)^2} + e^{-5(t-x-5)^2}) & \text{if } y = 4/9 \text{ or } y = 8/9, \\ 0 & \text{otherwise.} \end{cases}$$

The basic procedure for the classical finite-difference, finite-element or finite-volume methods for PDEs starts by establishing two grids, on t and x. The partial derivatives are replaced with algebraic approximations evaluated at different grid points. In the method of lines (MOL) t is treated as a continuous variable. Thus the partial derivatives u_x, $u_{xx}, \ldots$ are replaced with algebraic approximation evaluated at different x-points, but the derivative u_t is keept unmodified. We construct an equidistant grid (x_i, y_j) and we apply MOL in order to obtain the discrete approximative solution $u_{ij} \approx u(\cdot, x_i, y_j)$. This procedure lead to an ODE system with independent variable t. We use

$$\Delta\Delta u(\cdot, x_i, y_j) \approx \frac{1}{\Delta^2 x} \frac{1}{\Delta^2 y}[20u_{ij} - 8(u_{i-1\,j} + u_{i+1\,j} + u_{i\,j-1} + u_{i\,j+1}) +$$

$$+2(u_{i-1\,j-1} + u_{i+1\,j-1} + u_{i-1\,j+1} + u_{i+1\,j+1}) + u_{i-2\,j} + u_{i+2\,j} + u_{i\,j-2} + u_{i\,j+2}]$$

If we take the step size $\Delta x = \Delta y = 2/9$, we have a 8×5 grid points and 80 ODEs of the following form:

$$(U^{(k)})_t = F^{(k)}, \qquad k = 1\ldots 80$$

where

$$U^{(k)} = \begin{cases} u_{ij}, & k = 5i+j, \\ (u_t)_{ij}, & k = 40 + 5i + j, \end{cases} \quad i = 1\ldots 8, j = 1\ldots 5,$$

$$F^{(k)} = \begin{cases} U^{(k+40)}, & k = 5i+j, \\ -\omega U^{(k-40)} - \sigma\Delta\Delta U^{(k-40)} + f(t,x_i,y_j), & k = 40 + 5i + j. \end{cases}$$

If we take the step size $\Delta x = \Delta y = 1/9$ we have 17×11 grid points and 374 stiff ODEs. The stiff property of this system make impossible the use of simple integration methods like Euler's explicit rule or standard Runge-Kutta method; we must use step-by-step implicit methods which are more complicated.

Solving ODEs obtained by MOL can be an intensive computational problem which cannot be often dealt by current sequential computers. A reasonable solution is to appeal to the more powerful networks of workstations or parallel computers. There are many theoretical ways to solve ODE using multi-processing. Here we consider parallelism across the integration method. We take for example the Runge-Kutta method [7]:

$$U_{n+1} = U_n + \Delta t[a(k_1 + k_2) + (1/2 - a)(k_3 + k_4)]$$
$$k_1 = F(U_n + \Delta t(ck_1 + (1/2 - b - c)k_2)), \ a = 3/2,$$

$$k_2 = F(U_n + \Delta t((1/2 + b - c)k_1 + ck_2)), \ b = \sqrt{3}/6,$$
$$k_3 = F(U_n + \Delta t(dk_3 + (1/2 - b - d)k_4)), \ c = 5/12,$$
$$k_4 = F(U_n + \Delta t((1/2 + b - d)k_3 + dk_4)), \ d = 1/2.$$

At each integration step, the k_1 and k_2 values (vectors) can be computed on one processor and meanwhile, k_3 and k_4, on another processor.

The integration process of the discretized plate problem using the above described Runge-Kutta method needs a time of minute orders in the case of 80 ODEs and respectively a time of hour orders in the case of 374 ODEs using either Maple or a faster numerical solver than Maple (like EpODE [9]). The Maple integration time can be reduced using a supplementary and cooperative Maple kernel, for example to solve the system in k_3 and k_4 at each step. Moreover, in order to solve the implicit equations we can use Maple's numerical solving procedure giving an approximate solution with a guaranteed high precision. The tests on the cluster system reveal a speed-up closes to the ideal value: 1.68 for 32 ODEs, 1.92 for 80 ODEs. The numerical solution in the case of 374 ODEs can be used for an animated simulation of the loading (Figure 2 sketches three frames of a such animation in Maple).

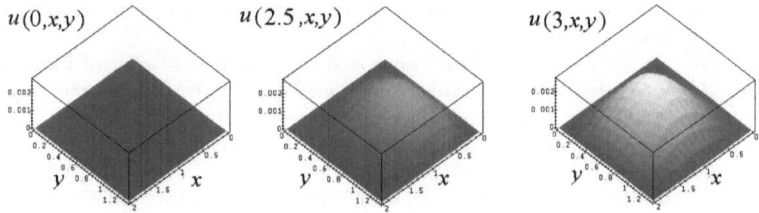

Fig. 2. Loading simulation: plate under the pressure of a car passing over it ($u \equiv 0$ in the first picture, $\max_{x,y} u(3, x, y) \approx 0.0025$ in the last picture)

Further examples and test results concerning PVMaple can be found in [10] and [13].

4   Conclusions

The results of two different experiments sustain the idea that parallel virtual extensions to known computing environments, like PVMaple, can improve the capabilities of the basic environments, in our case Maple, at least by extending the domain of problems to be solved or by reducing the response time of different solvers. PVMaple is potentially useful also for education in parallel programming, for prototyping algorithms and for fast and convenient of easily parallelizable computations on multiple processors. It is an evolving project at an early stage of development and there is definitely room for improvement.

References

1. Arnold, D. et al., NetSolve-1.3 Primer, http://www.cs.utk.edu/netsolve/ (1998).
2. Bernadin, L., Maple on a Massively Parallel, Distributed Memory Machine. In *PASCO '97: Second International Symposium on Parallel Symbolic Computation*, eds. M. Hitz, E. Kaltofen, ACM Press, New York (1997), 217-222.
3. Char, B.W., Progress Report on a System for General-Purpose Parallel Symbolic Algebraic Computation. In *ISSAC '90: International Symposium on Symbolic and Algebraic Computation*, ACM Press, New York (1990), 96-103.
4. Diaz, A., Kartofen, E., FoxBox: a System for Manipulating Symbolic Objects in Black Box Representation. In *ISSAC '98: International Symposium on Symbolic and Algebraic Computation*, ed. O. Gloor, ACM Press, New York (1998), 30-37.
5. Geist, Al, Dongarra J. et al., Parallel Virtual Machine, http://www.epm.ornl.gov/pvm/pvm_home.html (1992).
6. Hairer E., Wanner G., *Solving ordinary differential equations II. Stiff and differential-algebraic problems*, Springer-Verlag, 1991.
7. Iserles A., Nørsett, S.P., On the theory of parallel Runge-Kutta methods, *IMA J. Num. Anal.* **10** (1990), 463-488.
8. Pawletta S. et al., Distributed and Parallel Application Toolbox for use with Matlab, http://anson.ucdavis.edu/~bsmoyers/parallel.htm (1997).
9. Petcu, D., Drăgan, M., Designing an ODE solving environment, *LNCSE* **10**: *Advances in Software Tools for Scientific Computing*, eds. H.P. Langtangen et al, Springer (2000), 319-338.
10. Petcu, D., PVMaple: a distributed approach to cooperative work of Maple processes, *LNCS* **1908**: *Recent Advances in Parallel Virtual Machine and Message Passing Interface*, eds. J. Dongarra et al, Springer (2000), 216-224.
11. Petcu, D., Working with Multiple Maple Kernels Connected by Distributed Maple or PVMaple, Preprint RISC 18-01, Linz, 2001.
12. Petcu, D., Connecting scientific computing environments, Proceedings *CSCS-13*, eds. I. Dumitrache, C. Buiu, 2001, Ed. Politehnica Press, 388-393.
13. Petcu, D., Solving initial value problems with parallel Maple processes, *LNCS* **2150**: *7th International Euro-Parallel Processing*, eds. R. Sakellariou et al, Springer (2001), 926-934.
14. Schreiner, W., Developing a distributed system for algebraic geometry, *EuroCM-Par'99: 3rd Euro-conference on Parallel and Distributed Computing for Computational Mechanics*, ed. Topping, B., Civil-Comp. Press, Edinburgh (1999), 137-146.
15. Siegl, K., Parallelizing Algorithms for Symbolic Computation Using ‖Maple‖. In *4th ACM SIGPLAN Symposium on Principles and Practice of Parallel Programming*, ACM Press, San Diego (1993), 179-186.

Implementing Multithreaded Protocols for Release Consistency on Top of the Generic DSM-PM² Platform

Gabriel Antoniu and Luc Bougé

LIP, ENS Lyon, 46 Allée d'Italie, 69364 Lyon Cedex 07, France
`Gabriel.Antoniu@ens-lyon.fr`

Abstract. DSM-PM² is an implementation platform designed to facilitate the experimental studies with consistency protocoles for distributed shared memory. This platform provides basic building blocks, allowing for an easy design, implementation and evaluation of a large variety of *multithreaded* consistency protocols within a unified framework. DSM-PM² is portable over a large variety of cluster architectures, using various communication interfaces (TCP, MPI, BIP, SCI, VIA, etc.). This paper presents the design of two multithreaded protocols implementing the release consistency model. We evaluate the impact of these consistency protocols on the overall performance of a typical distributed application, for two clusters with different interconnection networks and communication interfaces.

1 Introduction

Traditionally, Distributed Shared Memory (DSM) libraries [7,10,11,6] allow a number of separate, distributed processes to share a global address space, based on a *consistency protocol* which implements the semantics specified by some given *consistency model*: sequential consistency, release consistency, etc. The processes may usually be physically distributed among a number of computing nodes interconnected through some communication library. The design of the DSM library is often highly dependent on the selected consistency model and on the communication library. Also, only a few of them are able to exploit the power of modern thread libraries and to provide multithreaded protocols, or at least to provide thread-safe versions of the consistency protocols.

The main objective of the DSM-PM² project is to provide the programmer of *distributed, multithreaded applications* with a flexible and portable implementation platform where the application and the consistency protocol of the underlying DSM can be *co-designed* and tuned together for performance. The programmer can select the consistency protocol best suited for his application, or can even program his own consistency protocol using basic blocks provided by the platform. Multiple consistency models are supported and protocols can be easily implemented for these models through alternative mechanisms available in DSM-PM². Comparative experimentations can be carried out on different cluster architectures, since the platform is portable across most UNIX-like systems

D. Grigoras et al. (Eds.): IWCC 2001, LNCS 2326, pp. 179–188, 2002.

and supports a large number of communication interfaces: TCP, MPI, BIP [12], SCI [5], VIA [4], etc. Finally, an important feature is that the platform is operational in a multithreaded context: distributed threads can safely access shared data and concurrency-related problems are adressed directly by the consistency protocols.

In this paper we present the design of the multithreaded versions of two consistency protocols for the *release consistency* model. We describe their integration to DSM-PM^2 and we compare their performance using a multithreaded version of a FFT kernel from the SPLASH-2 [13] benchmark suite.

2   The DSM-PM^2 Platform

DSM-PM^2 [1] has been designed as an experimental implementation platform for multithreaded DSM consistency protocols. It relies on the PM^2 (*Parallel Multithreaded Machine*, [9]), a runtime system for distributed, multithreaded applications. PM2 provides a POSIX-like programming interface for thread creation, manipulation and synchronization in user space, on cluster architectures. PM2 is available on most UNIX-like operating systems, including Linux and Solaris. For network portability, PM2 uses a communication library called Madeleine [2], which has been ported on top of a large number of communication interfaces: high-performance interfaces, like SISCI/SCI and VIA, but also more traditional interfaces, like TCP and MPI. DSM-PM^2 inherits this portability, since all its communication routines rely on Madeleine. An interesting feature of PM^2 is that it allows threads to be preemptively and transparently migrated across the cluster nodes. DSM-PM^2 provides these mobile threads with the abstraction of a uniformly shared memory on top of the distributed architecture exploited by PM^2.

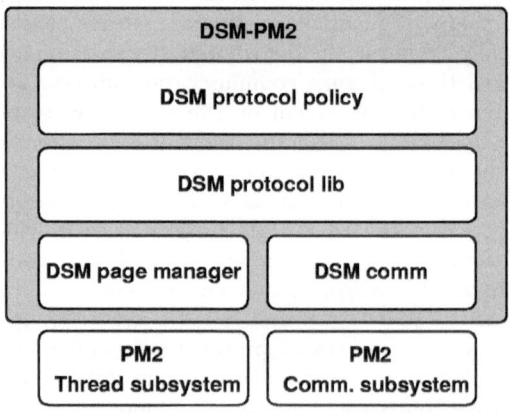

Fig. 1. The architecture of DSM-PM^2.

DSM-PM^2 is structured in layers. At the top level, the *DSM protocol policy* layer allows consistency protocols to be built out of common library routines, provided by the *DSM protocol library* layer. These routines rely on DSM-PM^2's main generic components: the *DSM page manager* and the *DSM communication manager*. The former handles the access rights to the shared pages on each node, using a distributed page table. The latter provides common communication routines, like sending a page request, sending a page, sending an invalidation request, etc. These generic components have been designed in order to facilitate the implementation of new consistency protocols. The main feature of all elements of the architecture is their design for a use in a multithreaded context.

Table 1. Eight routines which define a DSM protocol in DSM-PM2.

Protocol function	Description
`read_fault_handler`	Called on a read page fault
`write_fault_handler`	Called on a write page fault
`read_server`	Called on receiving a request for read access
`write_server`	Called on receiving a request for write access
`invalidate_server`	Called on receiving a request for invalidation
`receive_page_server`	Called on receiving a page
`lock_acquire`	Called after having acquired a lock
`lock_release`	Called before releasing a lock

DSM-PM^2 currently provides 6 protocols. The application can select one of them via a function call at the initialization of the application:

```
pm2_dsm_set_default_protocol(li_hudak);
```

The user can also create new protocols by defining 8 functions which specify the behavior of the DSM system for some generic DSM events. These functions are listed in Table 1. The 8 functions are grouped into a protocol via a simple function call:

```
int new_proto;
new_prot = dsm_create_protocol
  (read_fault_handler, write_fault_handler,
   read_server, write_server,
   invalidate_server, receive_page_server,
   acquire_handler, release_handler);
pm2_dsm_set_default_protocol(new_prot);
```

3   Two *Multithreaded* Protocols for Release Consistency

Historically, DSM systems have first used *sequential consistency*. Li and Hudak [7] have proposed several MRSW protocols (*Multiple Readers, Single Writer*) for this model, based on page replication to serve read accesses and page migration to serve write accesses. One of these protocols, relying on a dynamic distributed page manager [7], has been adapted by Mueller [8] to a multithreaded context. A variant of this protocol is available in DSM-PM^2 under the name li_hudak.

Relaxed consistency models, such as *release* consistency have been introduced in order to allow more efficient DSM implementations, at the price of stricter constraints on the use of the shared data. In these models, consistency actions may be delayed till synchronization operations with locks or barriers. Many implementations have illustrated the advantages of these models with respect to performance, nevertheless most efforts were limited to the *single-threaded* case: a unique, sequential execution flow runs on each cluster node. The main reason is the lack of integration of the DSM libraries with the thread libraries, which came out more recently.

DSM-PM^2 is an original platform which integrates both aspects: *multiple* threads can run concurrently on the each node and keep sharing global data. Within this framework, multithreaded consistency protocols can be designed, implemented and evaluated. Such multithreaded protocols may be derived from classical, single-threaded protocols, but also original protocols can be designed, relying for instance on thread migration or implementing a semantics based on the thread concept (like Java consistency).

We present below two multithreaded protocols for realease consistency, derived from classical, single-threaded protocols.

3.1   A MRSW, Invalidation-Based Protocol: erc_sw

The erc_sw protocol (*Eager Release Consistency, Single Writer*) is a MRSW protocol implementing *eager* release consistency: consistency actions are taken immediately on exiting a critical section (lock *release*), as opposed to *lazy* protocols which may delay such actions until another node enters a critical section (lock *acquire*). In erc_sw, the *acquire* routine takes no consistency action. Pages are manages using a dynamic distributed manager, as in li_hudak. Each page may be modified by a single node at a time (the *owner*). The other nodes may require read-only copies of the page from this node. On modifying the page, the owner sets a flag. At the exit of the critical section, the *release* operation invalidates all copies of the pages whose flags are set. Thus, any node which subsequently reads the page will need to ask for an up-to-date copy. If a node needs to write to the page, it musk ask the page to the owner, together with the page ownership.

The general scheme of this protocol is classical and has been implemented in other DSM systems [3]. Our contribution consists in providing a more complex, multithreaded version, which efficiently handles concurrent acccesses on a page on each node. Traditionally, single-threaded systems process page faults sequentially on each node: no page fault is processed until the previous page fault is completed. In a multithreaded environment, the hypothesis of the *atomicity* of page fault handlers is not valid any longer. Threads waiting for a page need to give hand to other threads, in order to allow an efficient overlap of the page transfer by computation. Consequently, multiple threads may produce page faults to the *same* page and the accesses need to be served concurrently in an efficient way, by minimizing the number of page requests. For instance, a single page request may suffice to serve several page accesses. Also, in erc_sw, page requests may be concurrent with invalidation requests. The implementation guarantees that the consistency constraints are observed, while allowing a high degree of concurrency. Handling these aspects makes the design of multithreaded protocols more difficult than in the single-threaded case.

3.2   A Home-Based Protocol Using Multiple Writers: hbrc_mw

The hbrc_mw protocol (*Home-based Release Consistency, Multiple Writers*) implements a *home-based* approach: each page is statically associated to a node which is in charge of always keeping an up-to-date copy of that page. As in the previous protocol, the *acquire* routine takes no action for consistency. When a thread needs to *read* a shared page, an up-to-date copy is brought from the home node. For a *write* access, a page copy is brought in if necessary, then a *twin* page is created. The thread can then modify the page. On exiting the critical section, each modified page is compared word-by-word with its twin and the modifications detected (called *diffs*) are eagerly sent to the home node, which applies them to the reference copy and then sends invalidation requests to all nodes which keep a copy of the page. In response to these invalidations, the other nodes which have concurrently modified the page compute and send their diffs to the home-node.

As opposed to the previous protocol, hbrc_mw allows a page to be concurrently modified on multiple nodes. This avoids the ping-pong effects produced by erc_sw protocol when two nodes concurrently write to disjoint addresses on the same page (*false sharing*). Also, the twinning technique reduces the communication overhead, since only the modified data is sent to the home-node, instead of whole pages. On the other hand, more processing time and more memory is required (for twin creation and diff computation). The tradeoff between these aspects depends on the access patterns to shared data, which vary from one application to another.

Here again, our contribution consists in designing a *multithreaded* protocol based on the scheme presented above. The protocol routines are not atomic, as is usually the case in single-threaded systems. As in the case of the erc_sw protocol, accesses to the *same* page, on the *same* node, are processed *concurrently* in an efficient way. Concurrency also needs to be carefully handled for *release* operations: the *release* function may be called concurrently by multiple threads, but diffs related to the same page are sent to the home node only once. Also, a release operation can run concurrently with an invalidation request sent by the home node (as a result of receiving diffs from some other node). The concurrent release and invalidation may require that the local diffs for the *same* page be sent to the home node, but the two operations need to synchronize so that the diffs be sent only once. These race situations are illustrated below.

3.3   Implementation in DSM-PM²

The two protocols have been implementated in the C language and use the programming interface of DSM-PM²'s basic components (the DSM page manager and the DSM communication manager). Figure 2 illustrates the *release* operation of the `hbrc_mw` protocol. The code has been slightly simplified, for the sake of clarity. It illustrates a typical situation of concurrency, specific to a multithreaded context. This function is activated by DSM-PM² on exiting a critical section.

The main loop of this function traverses the list of the pages modified since the last entry to a critical section. For each page, if the local node is the home node of the page, invalidations are sent to all nodes having a copy of the page. Otherwise, the function computes the diffs between the modified page and its saved twin and sends these diffs to the home node. Once the home node acknowledges their application, the function goes on to the next page.

The multithreaded implementation of this protocol needs to guarantee that concurrent calls to this function by different threads on the same node can proceed correctly. The `dsm_pending_release` function detects such a race. If a thread calls the release function while another thread is executing it and has already sent the diffs, then the second thread does not send the diffs again; it only waits for the diffs sent by the first thread to be acknowledged (`wait_for_release_done`).

Another situation of concurrency occurs when this release function is called by two threads on two *different* nodes $N1$ and $N2$. If the threads have modified the same page, both need to send the diffs to the home node. On receiving the first diffs, say from node $N1$, the home node will send an invalidation to node $N2$. The node $N2$ then has to respond by sending its own diffs. Independently of this, the *release* operation on node $N2$ also requires that the diffs for the same page be sent to the home node. The implementation guarantees that the diffs are sent only once, while allowing both operations on node $N2$ (release and invalidation) to proceed concurrently. This is achieved thanks to the the test `diffs_to_send`.

4   Experimental Results

We have studied the behavior of our two protocols for release consistency using a 1D FFT kernel extracted from the SPLASH-2 [13] benchmark suite, which we adapted for a multithreaded execution. The program uses two shared matrices $\sqrt{n} \times \sqrt{n}$ distributed on processors by blocks of lines. Communication takes place during 3 transpose operations and involves all-to-all communication. Transpose

```
void dsmlib_hbrc_release () {
  if(!dsm_test_and_set_pending_release_or_wait()) {
    int index = remove_first_from_list (&page_list);
    while (index != NULL) {
      dsm_lock_page(index);
      if (get_owner (page) == dsm_self ())
        invalidate_copyset (page);
      else {
        if diffs_to_send(page) {
          send_diffs (page, get_owner (page));
          set_access (page, NO_ACCESS);
          free_twin (page);
          send_invalidate_req
              (get_owner (page), page);
          wait_ack (page);
        }
      }
      dsm_unlock_page(index);
      page = remove_first_from_list (&page_list);
    }
    clear_pending_release_and_broadcast_done();
  }
}
```

Fig. 2. The `lock_release` functionof the `hbrc_mw` protocol.

operations are blocked in a pipeline fashion: processor i first transposes a sub-matrix from processor $i + 1$, then a submatrix from processor $i + 2$, etc. Our experiments have been carried out on two different platforms: 1) a cluster of 200 MHz Pentium Pro PCs under Linux 2.2.13, interconnected by Fast Ethernet under TCP; 2) a cluster of 450 MHz Pentium II PCs interconnected by a SCI network handled by the SISCI interface. The costs of the basic operations are given in Table 2.

Table 2. Cost of elementary operations (μs).

Operation	TCP/Fast Ethernet (PPro 200 MHz)	SISCI/SCI (PII 450 MHz)
Page fault	23	11
Transmit request	370	38
Page request	3900	119
Page protection	22	12

In Figures 3 and 4 we compare the two protocols for release consistency to the li_hudak protocol provided by DSM-PM^2, which implements sequential consistency. The comparison has been done on our two clusters, using 4 nodes, with one application thread per node. The execution on the SCI cluster is about 20 times faster than on the Fast Ethernet cluster, because of the relative performance of the two networks in terms of bandwidth and latency. In both cases, the erc_sw and hbrc_mw protocols produce much more efficient execution times than the li_hudak protoco. This illustrates the benefits of release consistency compared to sequential consistency in the presence of read/write false sharing, which occurs here (i.e., one node writes a page while another one reads it). The figures obtained on TCP illustrates the superiority of the hbrc_mw protocol compared to erc_sw, thanks to its multiple writers, which results in a reduced number of page transfers. The less performant the network, compared to the processors, the more important this advantage.

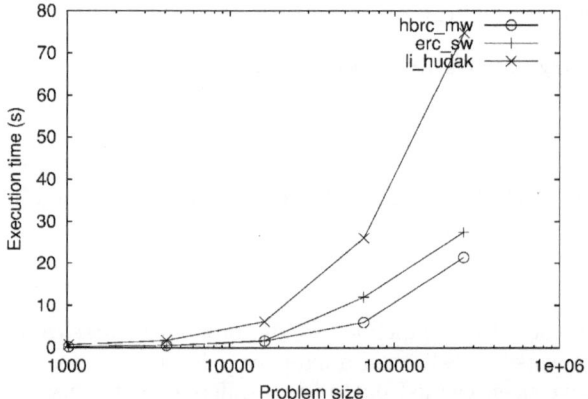

Fig. 3. FFT on TCP/Fast Ethernet (4 nodes).

Table 3. FFT on TCP/Fast Ethernet (seconds).

Threads/node	1	2	4	8
li_hudak	74.8	54.8	54.4	57.5
erc_sw	27.2	21.0	19.6	24.1
hbrc_mw	21.4	20.9	20.9	21.1

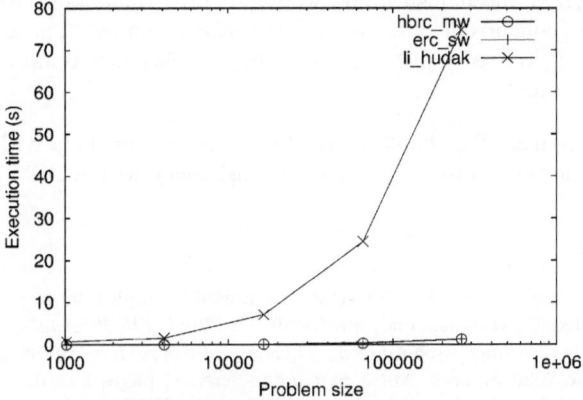

Fig. 4. FFT on SISCI/SCI (4 nodes).

Table 4. FFT on SISCI/SCI (seconds).

Threads/node	1	2	4	8
li_hudak	79	57	44	36
erc_sw	1.3	1.3	1.4	1.4
hbrc_mw	1.2	1.2	1.2	1.2

We have also studied the influence of multithreading on the efficiency of the protocols, by varying the number of threads per node for a given problem size (256 kB) and for a fixed number of nodes (4). The execution times are presented in Tables 3 and 4. First, let us note that the overhead due to multithreading is not significant. On the other hand, when the communication-to-computation ratio is high (i.e., for a low-speed network and for consistency protocols which involve a lot of communications), using more than one application thread per node may improve performance, thanks to the overlap of communication by computation. A finer analysis of these phenomena is currently in progress.

5   Conclusion

We have illustrated how *multithreaded* protocols can be designed, implemented and evaluated within the unified framework provided by DSM-PM^2. This platform appears as an interesting tool for developers of distributed, multithreaded applications using a shared memory model, since it facilitates DSM protocol implementations by providing a lot of common, basic components. In this paper, we focused on two protocols implementing the *release consistency* model through alternative mechanisms, and we highlighted some issues related to the higher degree of concurrency due to a multithreaded context. The approach presented can be generalized to other consistency models (such as Java consistency, or scope consistency).

Acknowledgments. We thank Vincent Bernardi for his help with the implementation of the two protocols for release consistency within DSM-PM^2.

References

1. G. Antoniu and L. Bougé. DSM-PM2: A portable implementation platform for multithreaded DSM consistency protocols. In *Proc. 6th International Workshop on High-Level Parallel Programming Models and Supportive Environments (HIPS '01)*, volume 2026 of *Lect. Notes in Comp. Science*, pages 55–70, San Francisco, April 2001. Held in conjunction with IPDPS 2001. IEEE TCPP., Springer-Verlag.
2. L. Bougé, J.-F. Méhaut, and R. Namyst. Efficient communications in multi-threaded runtime systems. In *Proc. 3rd Workshop on Runtime Systems for Parallel Programming (RTSPP '99)*, volume 1586 of *Lect. Notes in Comp. Science*, pages 468–482, San Juan, Puerto Rico, April 1999. Springer-Verlag.
3. J. B. Carter. Design of the Munin distributed shared memory system. *Journal of Parallel and Distributed Computing*, 29:219–227, 1995. Special issue on distributed shared memory.
4. Dave Dunning, Greg Regnier, Gary McAlpine, Don Cameron, Bill Shubert, Frank Berry, Anne-Marie Merritt, Ed Gronke, and Chris Dodd. The Virtual Interface Architecture. *IEEE Micro*, pages 66–75, March 1998.
5. IEEE. *Standard for Scalable Coherent Interface (SCI)*, August 1993. Standard no. 1596.
6. L. Iftode and J. P. Singh. Shared virtual memory: Progress and challenges. *Proceedings of the IEEE*, 87(3), March 1999.
7. K. Li and P. Hudak. Memory coherence in shared virtual memory systems. *ACM Transactions on Computer Systems*, 7(4):321–359, November 1989.
8. F. Mueller. Distributed shared-memory threads: DSM-Threads. In *Proc. Workshop on Run-Time Systems for Parallel Programming (RTSPP)*, pages 31–40, Geneva, Switzerland, April 1997.
9. R. Namyst. *PM2: an environment for a portable design and an efficient execution of irregular parallel applications*. PhD thesis, Univ. Lille 1, France, January 1997. In French.
10. B. Nitzberg and V. Lo. Distributed shared memory: A survey of issues and algorithms. *IEEE computer*, 24(8):52–60, September 1991.
11. J. Protic, M. Tomasevic, and V. Milutinovic. Distributed shared memory: concepts and systems. *IEEE Paralel and Distributed Technology*, pages 63–79, 1996.
12. Loïc Prylli and Bernard Tourancheau. BIP: a new protocol designed for high performance networking on Myrinet. In *1st Workshop on Personal Computer based Networks Of Workstations (PC-NOW '98)*, volume 1388 of *Lect. Notes in Comp. Science*, pages 472–485. Springer-Verlag, April 1998.
13. S. C. Woo, M. Ohara, E. Torrie, J.P. Singh, and A. Gupta. The SPLASH-2 programs: Characterization and methodological considerations. In *Proc. 22nd Annual Int'l Symp. on Comp. Arch.*, pages 24–36, Santa Margherita Ligure, Italy, June 1995.

Communication Balancing for Wireless Nodes in a LAN-WAN Cluster

Cosmina Ivan

Technical University of Cluj-Napoca
Department of Computer Science
26-28, Baritiu Str., Ro 3400 Cluj-Napoca, Romania
tel: +40-64-294835, fax:+40-64-194491
cosmina.ivan@cs.utcluj.ro

Abstract. In the past, the most common way of network-based computing was through wired networks. However, with advances in wireless communication technology, the Wireless Local Area Network (WLAN) has become a viable option for performing distributed computing. Taking this into account, we present in this paper a cluster based on wireless and wired nodes. The wireless nodes can attach and detach dynamically in a controlled way based on a high-level communication protocol. The goal is to achieve an efficient load balance, a reasonable execution and communication time within the cluster .

1 Introduction

In recent years, high-speed networks and new generation of processors are making network of workstations (NOW) an appealing vehicle for parallel and distributed computing. Clusters/networks of workstations built using commodity hardware or software are playing a major role in redefining the concept of Supercomputing [1][2]. Applications appropriate for clusters are not restricted to those traditionally running on supercomputers or other high-performance systems [3]. In recent LANs, the communication speed of wired Local Area Networks (LANs) can be of the order of Gigabits per second based on high performance communication devices. On the other hand, with the rapid evolution of wireless communications, it is an explosion of communication devices and mobile systems. With these advances, the Wireless Local Area Network (WLAN) has become rapidly a crucial component of computer networks.

While clusters based on LAN and WLAN offer the most competitive cost/performance figures, their management is not an easy task. In this respect, we have developed a technique for parallel programming for this kind of clusters, based on the idea of overlapping computations with communications. We suggest a communication protocol that considers the load and communication balancing of programs. This protocol is the basis of our novel programming model for the WLAN-LAN based cluster.

The rest of the paper is organized as follows: in section 2, the chosen cluster architecture is defined, in section 3 we propose a programming model, and in section 4, a theoretical evaluation of the communication time is explained. Finally, we present some conclusions and future work.

D. Grigoras et al. (Eds.): IWCC 2001, LNCS 2326, pp. 189-196, 2002.
© Springer-Verlag Berlin Heidelberg 2002

2 The Cluster Organization

At the present, there are a lot of different technologies for LANs and WLANs, the most widely used technology in LANs being Ethernet, with rates from 10 Mbps up to 1 Gbps (Gigabit Ethernet). On the contrary, in WLAN lower communication speed can be achieved because two different physical technologies are used, infrared radiation and radio signal. Although the computing over LAN is up to now more efficient than computing over WLAN due to its higher communication speed, we focused our scope to a "short" area network over wireless and wired links. Moreover, we study the influence of the portability of the wireless nodes, which in any moment can be or not connected to the wired network. We consider a cluster with one wired Ethernet segment and an arbitrary amount of portable nodes. For this cluster model, the parallel programs are more difficult to design due to portability. For this reason, we have designed a general strategy for parallel programs implementation. The proposed architecture presents more flexibility, the wired nodes are connected through any typical wired interconnection and the wireless ones employ Network Interface Cards (NICs), which are connected to an external radio or infrared transmitter. The interconnection of both types of nodes is done by an access node, which is connected to both networks using wired and wireless NICs. The access node makes the following actions:
• the dynamic distribution of data to each node present in the cluster (by sending packets of data);
• the reception of results;
• the coordination of the wireless medium access implementing a Point Coordination Function (similar to that defined by the IEEE 802.11 standard);
• the invocation of the association and disassociation services to allow that the wireless nodes can appear and disappear dynamically in the cluster in a controlled manner, to make an efficient load balancing.

3 The Programming Model

In order to develop an efficient programming strategy, it is important to take into account the high transmission latency of the wireless media. For that reason, we hide this communication latency overlapping communications and computations. To do this we have identified two different overlapping strategies. One is at the access node level, that overlaps its computations with its communications. The second consists in overlapping the computations and communications of wireless and wired nodes. We will assume a logical communication bus or ring connecting the wired nodes and another one connecting the wireless nodes.

While the former strategy is not difficult to implement, the latter is a hard task and several studies for efficient dynamic data distribution have to be undertaken. In our present work, we consider the first type of overlapping. Because the wireless nodes connect and disconnect in a dynamically way, we cannot distribute data among nodes (wired and wireless) at the compilation time. The number of wireless nodes is unknown. As some classical methodology only distributes data at compilation time, in this paper we present a new dynamic data redistribution methodology, at the execution time, and the corresponding code generation methodology.

Figure 1 shows a high level communication protocol that makes feasible the first type of overlapping described previously. Notice that computations made by the access node, e.g. computations made with the results coming from the wired and wireless nodes, can be overlapped with communications. The parameters np and nw represent the number of wired and wireless nodes respectively. While the former is a constant value, the latter can vary during the execution time of the parallel algorithm due to the association and disassociation of wireless nodes. For example, initially in the association point there are new wireless nodes associated with the cluster. This number of nodes can increase or decrease in the association/disassociation point. Both parameters np and nw can change their values from application to application. The parameters gp and gw represent the data packet sizes in bytes, which are sent to the wired and wireless nodes. Their values are variable during the execution time of the parallel algorithm to let the access node perform an efficient load balancing.

The access node starts the program execution sending an association message to wireless nodes and data message size gp to the wired ones. In this protocol there can be also several association and disassociation messages.

The final message is an end one, meaning that the access node has finished the program execution. Let us mention that the wireless communications are slower than the wired ones. Therefore, in order to reduce the communication latency, we can consider some different communication strategies. For example, the access node could send data to the wireless nodes first. After this task is finished it would send data to the wired ones. Another strategy could be based in one of the processes

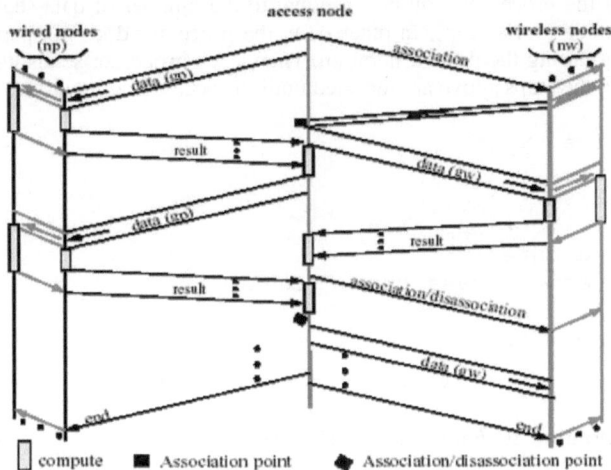

Fig. 1. High-level communication protocol.

scheduling techniques known as the first shortest job: the access node sends data to the wired nodes and finally data are sent to the wireless ones, that is, it does communications inversely than the previous strategy. This technique is better than the previous one because the nodes (wired and wireless) wait less time to receive data from the access node on average. Both strategies are sequential, without overlapping between wired and wireless communications. It is possible to run two threads in the access node and make the communications concurrently.

There are a lot of overlapping policies. For example, intervals of equal length could be assigned to each thread. If we throw first the thread that take less time to finish the communications (the first shortest job technique) on average, then the nodes again will wait less to get data. Therefore, in any case, with or without communication overlapping, the first shortest job must be applied. On the other hand, if the access node was a computer with two processors, then two threads could throw, so the communications to the wireless and wired nodes could be made in parallel. Of course, this would be the best technique of communication to be applied in the proposed cluster.

Following, the general skeleton of the algorithm to be implemented by the wired nodes, the wireless stations and the access node respectively is introduced. It is used for the implementation of iterative parallel algorithms.

3.1 Programming Skeleton for the Wired Nodes

Initially, the wired nodes determine the identifier my_id, with $1 < my\_id < np$. Following, each node waits to receive data. The access node sends p data segments, each consisting of k elements, so that $gp = p*k$, with $1 < p < np$.

The processor with identifier 1 (P1) works with the first segment received, P2 with the second, etc. The processor i makes computation with the i-th data segment if the identifier of the processor is minor or equal to the number of data segments sent by the access node (variable p). In other case, the processor does not participate in the computation during the present iteration. Then, each processor sends its results to the access node; the steps above are repeated until the access node sends no more data.

```
determine my_id
repeat
   receive (data, p)
   if my_id <= np then
       compute()
       send (access_node, result)
   endif
until no more data.
```

Fig. 2. Algorithm for wired nodes.

3.2 Programming Skeleton for the Wireless Nodes

Initially, the wireless nodes try to associate to the cluster after they have received an association message sent by the access node. During the association interval, the wireless stations contend to gain access to the wireless medium using CSMA/CA protocol. The station which gains the medium sends a message to the access node, which replies to it by sending another message that contains the processor identifier (initially 1). When the association interval finishes, the access node knows the number of wireless nodes present at the cluster. Notice that it could be possible the existence of more wireless nodes, which are not able to associate to the cluster (because the current association interval has concluded before these stations had been able to gain the medium), and these stations must wait the next association interval to try again the association.

Next, the wireless nodes previously associated receive data from the access node. We cannot consider that the associated i processor computes the i-th data received due to the presence of disassociations. If a processor with identifier smaller than i, is disassociated, then the processor i computes the (i-1)-th data segment. Because the disassociation process is implemented in a centralized manner (like the association process), only the access node knows the identifiers (processors) active. For that reason, together with the data sent, the access node sends a vector of integers, denoted by ID, where ID[j] equal to 1 means that station with identifier j is associated and it participates in the computations. On the contrary, if ID[j] is 0 means that station j does not take part in the calculations, and consequently it is a disassociated node. By this vector, processor i detects its data segment. It could happen that the processor i does not receive a data segment to work with, i.e. for this processor the expression Σ ID[j] > p is true (p represents the total data segments sent by the access node to wireless stations). This value could be different from the number of data segments that the wired nodes receive). In this case, processor i does not participate in the current iteration of the computation process.

In other situation, it takes part actively and receives data for computing. Later, a polling interval takes place to gather results and for this interval the access point assigned turns to the stations that have participated on the computations. Immediately later, a disassociation interval starts and during this period, one or more stations can try to disassociate the cluster. The complete algorithm presented above is repeated until the access node sends no more data.

```
repeat
    while not(associated) and
        not (end association interval) do
        receive an association message
        if medium==free then
            send association request
            receive identifier
        end if
    end while
        if associated then
            receive (data, p, ID)
            if data to compute with then
                make computations
                receive a polling message
                if my turn then send results
                else wait my turn
            end if
        end if
        if disassociation then
            receive a disassociation message
            send a disassociation request
        end if
    end if
until no more data or disassociated
```

Fig. 3. Algorithm for the wireless nodes

3.3 General Skeleton for the Access Node

Initially, the access node determines the number of wired and wireless nodes present at the cluster. The former can be read from a configuration file, and the latter can be calculated after the association interval finishes. For each association request, it generates a new identifier (initially 1), which is sent to the applicant wireless node and updates the ID vector.

At the same time the access node receives these requests, it sends data to the wired nodes. After the association interval ends, the access node sends data plus ID vector to the wireless nodes. It also receives results coming from wireless processors.

The access node sends data plus ID vector to the wireless nodes, and also receives results coming from the wired nodes. The access node initiates a period of polling in which it receives data coming from wireless processors. After that, a disassociation interval takes place in which the wireless nodes contend for the medium if they want to request its disassociation of the cluster. For each request received, the access node updates the number of wireless nodes and the vector ID. At the end of this interval, the algorithm is repeated until there are not more data to be distributed to the wired and/or the wireless network.

```
Compute number of wired nodes (np)
  repeat
  do parallel
   for wireless network
          send an association message
          receive requests, update ID and send
   identifiers
          compute number of wireless nodes (nw)
          send data + ID to wireless nodes
          send a polling message
          receive results
          initiate a disassociation service
          update number of wireless nodes and vector ID
   end for
    for wired network
          send data
          receive results
    end for
  end do parallel
  until no more data to be distributed
```

Fig. 4. The algorithm for the access point

4 The Theoretical Evaluation of the Communication Time

In this section we present a theoretical evaluation of the communication time between access node and the wired and wireless nodes. We analyze the different communication strategies that we have presented in section 3.

Let $t_{comm}(k) = t_{wles}(k_1) + t_{wred}(k_2) + t_{ad}$ be the communication time for sending k bytes in the parallel algorithm, where $k=k_1+k_2$, $t_{wless}(k_1)$ is the communication time to send bytes to the wireless nodes, $t_{wred}(k_2)$ is the communication time to send bytes to the wired nodes, and t_{ad} is the
time spent in the association and disassociation of wireless nodes. In general $t_{wles}(k_1)$ can be calculated as $t_{wles}(k_1) = A_1 + k_1A_2$, and $t_{wred}(k_2)$ as $t_{wred}(k_2) = B_1 + k_2B_2$, where A_1 and B_1 represent the message startup overhead in the wireless and wired communications respectively, and A_2 and

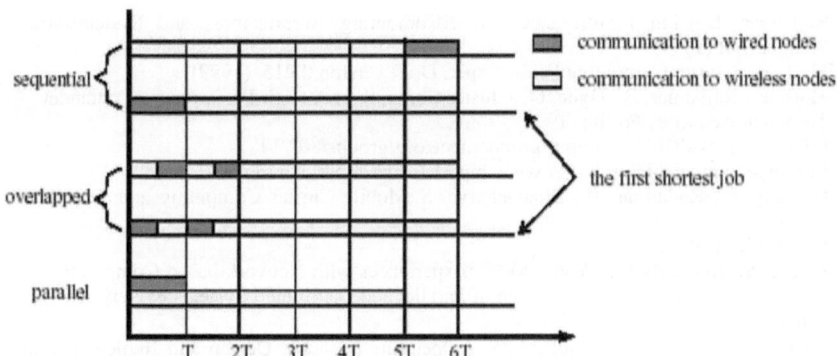

Fig. 5. Different communication techniques.

B$_2$ are the transfer times for a byte. In Fig. 5 it is shown the communication time spent by the access node taking different communication strategies into account. In this figure, we consider a 10 Mbps transmission speed in the wired network and 2 Mbps in the wireless one. We assume that the access node sends the same amount of data to the wireless and wired nodes, that is, the parameter k_1 is equal to k_2, so if we make $t_{wred}(k_2)$ equal a T, then $t_{wles}(k_1)$ would be equal a 5T. As a conclusion , the better communication technique is running both communications in parallel. In this way, the wireless and wired nodes must wait less time to get data to work with. If the communications cannot be made in parallel (only sequential or concurrent communication is possible), then the better choice is the "first shortest job" technique. In this way, it is simple to observe that in order to minimize the communication time of the program it is necessary to send more data to the LAN. To balance the communication latency of the wireless network, k_2 must be at least 5 times greater than k_1. The remaining problem is to determine how high or low must be the term k_2 (or k_1) such as the terms A_1, B_1, and t_{ad} become not important in the communication time above.

5 Conclusions and Future Work

With the recent advances in wired and wireless LANs, it is apparent that it could be feasible to perform distributed computing over such heterogeneous networking environment. In this paper we have presented a WLAN-LAN based cluster, where the wireless nodes can associate and disassociate from the cluster during the parallel algorithm execution. A programming model for iterative applications on the above architecture was also presented and we are in process of testing the programming model proposed and evaluating the optimal number of messages to be sent to the wired and wireless nodes to balance the communications.

References

1. Rajkumar, B.:High Performance ClusterComputing Architectures and Systems,vol.1. PrenticeHall (1999)
2. Mark, B. :Cluster Computing White Paper. Draft version 0.915, (1999).
3. Mark, B., Rajkumar, B., Hyde, D. :Cluster Computing: A High-Performance Contender
4. Technical Activities Forum (1999) 79-83.
5. Information available in: http:// grouper.ieee.org/groups/802/11
6. Information available in: http:// www.hiperlan.com/hiper_white.pdf.
7. Haihong, Z., Rajkumar, B., Bhattacharya, S.:Mobile Cluster Computing and Timeliness Issues.
8. Informatica (1999) 17.
9. Janche, S., Lin, C-H M., Wang, M-C. :Experiences with Network-based Computing over Wireless Links. International Journal of Parallel and Distributed Systems & Networks, vol. 2, no. 2. (1999) 79-87.
10. Tannenbaum, A. S., Woodhull, A. S. : Operating Systems. Design and Implementation, 2nd Edition. Prentice Hall (1997).

An Architecture and Task Scheduling Algorithm for Systems Based on Dynamically Reconfigurable Shared Memory Clusters

Marek Tudruj and Lukasz Masko

Institute of Computer Science, Polish Academy of Sciences
01–237 Warsaw, ul. Ordona 21, Poland
{tudruj, masko}@ipipan.waw.pl

Abstract. The paper presents proposals of a new architecture and respective task scheduling algorithms for a multi–processor system based
on dynamically organised shared memory clusters. The clusters are organised around memory modules placed in a common address space.
Each memory module can be accessed through a local cluster bus and a
common inter–cluster bus. Execution of tasks in a processor is done according to a specific macro dataflow model. It allows task execution only
if all data needed by a task have been loaded into processor data cache.
The data cache pre–fetching and single assignment data move principle
enable elimination of cache thrashing and cache coherence problem. An
extended macro dataflow graph representation is introduced that enables
modelling of data bus arbiters, memory modules and data caches in the
system. A task scheduling algorithm is proposed that defines mapping
of program tasks into dynamic processor clusters on the basis of a program graph analysis. The algorithm is based on a modified Dominant
Sequence Clustering approach and defines such dynamic structuring of
clusters that minimises program execution time.

1 Introduction

Shared memory systems are under strong development since they offer high
computing power at low cost. Unfortunately, such systems still show degradation
of communication efficiency with the increase of the number of processors and
also high time overhead due to functioning of parallel data caches. Decomposition
of computations and communication into parallel processor clusters helps very
much in solving the efficiency problem. There exist quite many commercial or
experimental implementations of shared memory cluster systems [1,2,3,4,5,6,7].
In these implementations, a cluster is a set of processors that share a certain
memory address subspace that can be accessed by a local memory bus, multi–bus
or crossbar switch. The clusters are connected by larger external networks like
busses, meshes, tore and hyper–cubes. In existent implementations, the quantity
and the size of clusters are fixed and not too big. The data cache problem consists
in the coherence control of data caches and avoidance of reloads of the same
data (thrashing). Both problems are a focus of intensive research [1,2,11,12,13].

D. Grigoras et al. (Eds.): IWCC 2001, LNCS 2326, pp. 197–206, 2002.

Analytical models of communication in shared memory multi–bus systems were studied in many papers [8,9,10]. However, no detailed architectural features or program execution paradigms were discussed in these publications.

This paper presents a proposal of the shared memory system architecture based on dynamically reconfigurable processor clusters together with automatic task clustering algorithms for the proposed system. The proposed architecture addresses problems of shared memory systems, enumerated above. In the domain of communication and computational scalability, dynamic processor clusters enable fitting system structure to program needs. It permits to decompose communication traffic among local cluster networks to reduce contention in the global network. Dynamic structures of clusters enable optimisation of the use of system resources: processors, data busses and memory modules. The architecture enables switching processors between clusters with data contained in their data caches. The architecture addresses also the problem of data caching efficiency. It assumes data pre–fetching into caches and loading cluster memory modules according to the single assignment principle that eliminates the cache coherency problem. The proposed program execution paradigm requires that all data required for a task are present in the cache before task activation. The tasks are so determined to eliminate data cache loads and thrashing during task execution. Such paradigm can be called a cache controlled macro dataflow model. Additional problem addressed in the proposed architecture is memory access parallelism. Both data caches and memory modules are accessed by a dual system of busses for intra– and inter–cluster communication.

The paper presents an algorithm for automatic decomposition of program execution into dynamic processor clusters with the heuristic minimisation of the total program execution time. The algorithm assumes an original modification of the Dominant Sequence Clustering (DSC) heuristics [14,15,16]. It includes a new program representation that is adequate for time analysis of shared memory clusters based on bus communication. It enables modelling of the behaviour of bus arbiters, data caches and memory modules. The notion of the dominant sequence and also task clustering rules are modified adequately to the new program graph representation and the underlying system architecture. The algorithm first finds program decomposition into unlimited number of clusters and then adjusts the number of clusters and processors to the parameters of a real system.

The paper is composed of three parts. In the first part, the proposed system architecture is described. In the second part, the program graph clustering algorithm is presented. In the third part an algorithm for mapping logical clusters into real system is given. An example illustrates the proposed algorithms.

2   System of Dynamically Configurable SMP Clusters

The general structure of the system is shown in Fig. 1. Processors use separate memories for instructions and data placed in separate address spaces. Processors are organised in dynamic shared memory clusters. The processors in a cluster uses data from the same data memory module via an Intra–Cluster Bus. The address space of a cluster module is linear. It is placed in the common address space. During computations, processors access data from data caches. A processor can pre–load data to its cache from the cluster memory module (Cache Pre–fetch instruction). An additional Inter–Cluster Bus connects processors with memory modules in other clusters. By using it, processor can also move data to its cluster memory module and at the same time to its data cache from a distant module (Move instructions). Computations do not start in a processor unless all data move and cache pre–fetch instructions, which precede a task code, are completed. The data moves and cache pre–fetches should be consistent with the cache size. During task execution processors send computation results only to the data cache, without up–dating the memory module. To update the memory, a processor performs a special Write–Module instruction. The results, which are meant for other processors, are written using new addresses. Such single assignment principle avoids data consistency problems for copies of data in caches used by many processors. A memory controller arbitrates accesses to a memory module through the inter–cluster bus and intra–cluster busses. If dual ported memory modules are applied, the reads are parallel. Write accesses are done sequentially. To enter a cluster, a processor performs a Connect–Bus instruction. It removes the processor from a cluster it belonged to. The processor is switched from using one memory module to using another. Such change done at the end of a computation, just before the computation results are written from the data cache to a memory module, will enable writing the results to a new memory module. In this way, a processor can be switched to a new cluster to provide common new data from its data cache. Data exchange based on shared memory

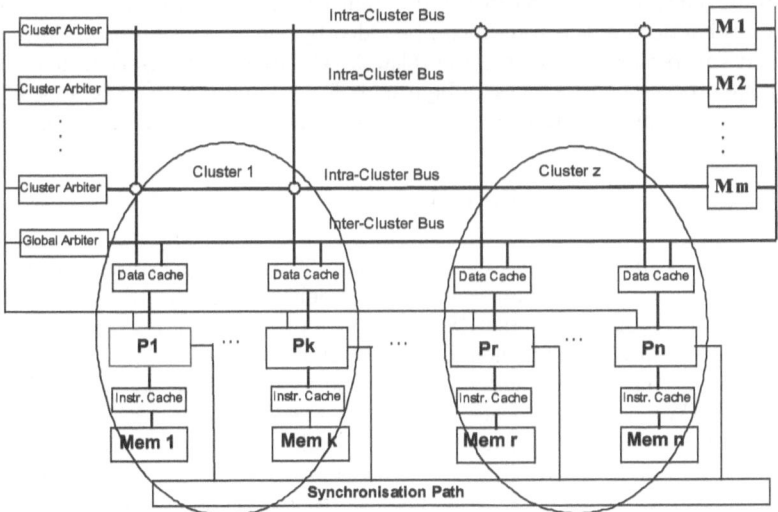

Fig. 1. General structure of the system

is synchronised by availability bits stored with data in memory modules. Before data are ready, the availability bits are set to Empty. They are set to Ready when data are written. Simultaneous reads of the same data to many memory modules are possible after synchronisation of all reading processes. It concerns also parallel fills of data caches. Each processor snoops addresses sent over data busses in a similar way as in [13]. When the address on a bus equals to the source address of a move or cache pre–fetch request in its queue, it reads data from the bus. If the transmission on the bus is shorter than needed, the processor can complete the transfer by the request in the queue with changed source address.

Each bus in the system is provided with an arbiter that controls data transfers. Read or write requests coming from a program are stored in each processor in separate queues according to their priorities. Write requests have higher priority than reads. The requests have priorities that correspond to the length of the data. All arbiters are fed with the highest priority requests coming from all involved processors. Each arbiter allows the processor with the highest priority request to perform the transmission. If it is a memory read, the processor starts transmission from respective memory with checks of data availability bits on the fly. It proceeds if all the data are ready. If they are not, the read is suspended and the processor performs next read request from the given priority queue. Each completed transmission or a failure to complete the granted transmission is acknowledged to the arbiter. If all read attempts failed in all requesting processors in a cluster at a given priority level, the arbiter allows to send requests from the lower priority queues from the requesting processors of the cluster. The highest priority is requested again after a write has been performed in the cluster, since it can make some new data available for reads. The global bus arbiter synchronises accesses of processes in different clusters to the memory modules. The control actions in the system can be aided by the Synchronisation Path, see Fig. 1. It can perform a barrier, a eureka, AND/OR synchronisation dedicated to a single processor. A barrier can be used before switching sets of processors to clusters, or to support data exchange between processors belonging to a cluster.

3   Task Clustering Algorithm

Standard macro dataflow representation of parallel programs is extended in this paper, to enable a realistic analysis of program behaviour in shared memory clusters based on a system of busses. Special kinds of nodes are introduced in the program graph: intra–cluster memory bus arbiter nodes (CA), the inter–cluster global memory bus arbiter node (GA), memory read nodes (R) and memory write nodes (W). Usually, an arbiter node has several incoming and outgoing communication edges that come from read and write nodes. They represent transmission requests. Each arbiter node has a pre–defined request selection and activation strategy. The activated node executes and sends a token back to the arbiter. This makes the arbiter resume the request selection procedures. Read and write nodes have weights that represent volumes of data transferred. Arbiter nodes introduce delays that correspond to the latency of the selection and activa-

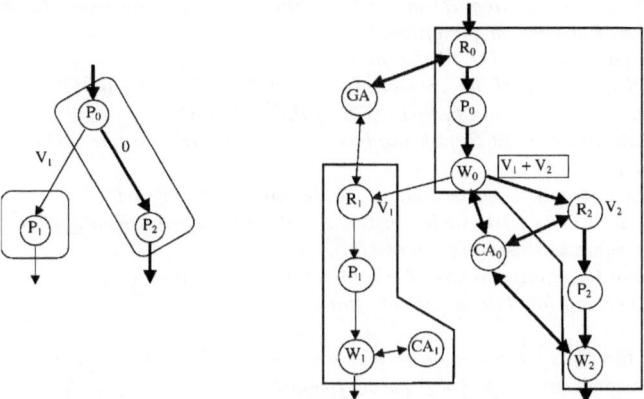

Fig. 2. Clustering in macro dataflow graphs (left) and extended macro dataflow graphs (right)

tion procedure. An exemplary extended macro dataflow graph (EMDFG) representation as opposed to standard macro dataflow graph representation (MDFG) is shown in Fig. 2 (data transfers between task nodes: P0, P1, P2 where P0 and P2 are located in the same cluster).

We propose a two–phase heuristic algorithm that allocates tasks of the EMDFG to SMP clusters. In the first phase, a task clustering algorithm minimises the total program execution time. In the second phase, the task clusters are mapped into a real system. Task clustering is understood here in a different way, comparing the literature [11,12,13]. Tasks are placed in a cluster by allocation to processors that share the same memory module. Tasks performed by a processor are defined so as not to need data cache loads during execution. During task clustering, the algorithm can allocate parallel tasks to a processor only if the resulting joint data volume fits the data cache capacity. A task can be performed only if all necessary data are brought to the processor data cache i.e. all read nodes are performed. Task results are sent to the cluster memory module by write nodes. Initially all tasks in a are assigned to different single processor clusters. We find the Extended Dominant Sequence (EDS) as the path going from the initial node(s) to the end node(s) whose execution time is the longest. The EDS includes task nodes, write nodes, read nodes but also the global (inter–cluster) bus arbiter and local (intra–cluster) bus arbiters concerned with the read/write nodes (thick arrows in Fig. 2). In the program graph, we will identify subgraphs composed of a write node, read node, task node, and arbiter node(s) that implement communication between two of adjacent task nodes executed in sequence. We call such subgraphs Elementary Communication Subgraphs (ECS). The task clustering algorithm based on the Extended Dominant Sequence heuristics is presented in Fig. 3.

Allocate each task in the program graph to a different single processor cluster.
Compute the initial EDS in the graph.
Compute the parallel time PT of the graph.
Mark all ECSs in the graph as unexamined. Set PT as the current PT.
WHILE *there exists an unexamined ECS of the EDS* **DO**
  Select the unexamined ECS with the largest execution time in the EDS to be
  the current ECS
  (1.)**IF** *the selected ECS write node has only one successor node*
      Unify the ECS's write node cluster and the ECS's read node cluster
      on the same processor (sequentially).
      Evaluate the improvement of PT for obtained tentative graph
      with checking for data cache overflows.
  ELSE
      Unify the ECS's write node cluster and the ECS's read node cluster
      on the same processor (in a parallel way).
      Evaluate the improvement of PT for obtained tentative graph
      with checking for data cache overflows.
      Unify the ECS's write node cluster and the ECS's read node cluster
      by placing the latter on a separate processor.
      Evaluate the improvement of PT for obtained tentative graph
      with checking for data cache overflows.
  END_IF
  FOR_ALL *unexamined ECSs that delay in arbiters the read node*
      of the current ECS
    Select them one–by–one and for each execute actions given in 1.
  END_FOR_ALL
  FOR_ALL *unexamined ECSs that maximally delay the read nodes*
      that belong to the EDS and do not belong to the current ECS
    Select them one–by–one and for each execute actions given in 1.
  END_FOR_ALL
  Among all clusterings performed above validate one which has resulted
  in the biggest improvement of the parallel time of the graph
  (including the zero improvement).
  IF *the validated clustering action has reduced the current PT*
      and no cache overflow due to it was observed
    Replace in the program graph the unified clusters by the cluster
    obtained as the result of the validated clustering action.
    Set the current PT to the PT of thus transformed graph.
  END_IF
  Mark the current ECS as examined.
  Find a new EDS in the transformed graph.
END_WHILE

Fig. 3. Task clustering algorithm

4   Allocation of Task Clusters to Processor Clusters

The clustering phase results in logical task clusters bound to shared memory
modules. We can directly assign task clusters to processor clusters in a real sys-

Find all connected components of the clustered program graph.
Denote their number as CC.
IF *CC is not bigger than the number of memory modules*
    Assign connected components to memory modules.
    IF *the point–wise width of the clustered program graph in any point of time*
        exceeds p
      Reduce the point–wise width of the clustered program graph
      not to exceed p in any point of time by merging tasks in parallel
      processors in some clusters such as to possibly balance the parallel
      time of all processors in these clusters.
    END_IF
ELSE
    Compute the parallel time of each connected component of the clustered graph.
    Reduce the number of connected components of the clustered program graph
    not to exceed m by merging of components which have the smallest parallel
    times so as possibly not to increase (or to increase to the smallest extent)
    the parallel time of the program.
    Assign connected components to memory modules.
    IF *the point–wise width of the clustered program graph in any point of time*
        exceeds p
      Reduce the point–wise width of the clustered program graph not to exceed p
      in any point of time by parallel merging of tasks in processorsin some clusters
      if no cache overflow occurs or by sequential merging in the opposite case, so as
      to possibly balance the parallel program time in all processors in these clusters.
    END_IF
END_IF

Fig. 4. Task cluster merging algorithm

tem only if the number of memory modules available in the system is sufficiently big. Otherwise, we have to perform task cluster merging, to obtain the final number of task clusters equal to the number of physical memory modules with possibly balanced program execution time in all processor clusters. During cluster merging, bus arbiters are merged into joint arbiters. By the point–wise width of the program graph we understand the sum of the numbers of processors in all clusters which co–execute in a given point of time. If a point–wise width of the program graph exceeds the number of available processors then tasks have to be merged inside processors in clusters. The merging algorithm principles, Fig. 4, are similar to those described in [14]. The algorithm first groups the connected components of the graph in larger clusters to obtain their number equal to the number of memory modules in the system. If the number of processors required for execution exceeds the real number of processors, loads of processors in clusters are merged. The two actions are done with optimisation that tries to equalise program execution time in all processors of the clusters.

5   Example

The clustering and merging algorithm steps for an exemplary program graph are shown in Fig.5. In these figures, polygons inside other polygons denote processors inside clusters. If a cluster contains a single processor, the internal polygon is not shown. Bold arrows denote the extended dominant sequence. The clustering has been performed in three steps. The program parallel execution time PT is reduced from 11310 to 8200. Merging of process clusters is done for the system with 2 processor clusters. Task cluster merging has increased the PT by 11%.

6   Conclusions

A proposal of a new architecture for a multi–processor system based on dynamically organised processor SMP clusters has been presented in the paper. The clusters are based on local intra–cluster busses that connect processors and their data caches to memory modules. Programs are performed according to a cache controlled macro dataflow model that allows for task execution only if all required data are brought to the data cache. This eliminates data thrashing in caches. Data reads to caches are done according to the single assignment principle that eliminates cache coherence problems. Bus contention effect can be reduced by decomposition of communication traffic among many intra–cluster busses. Processors with data caches can be dynamically switched between clusters. Together with multiple read facility based on bus snooping, this can much reduce traffic on the bus.

A task scheduling algorithm has been next presented that assigns program tasks into reconfigurable processor clusters to optimise program execution time. The algorithm is based on the analysis a new program graph representation. It is a macro dataflow graph extended by additional nodes that represent actions of bus arbiters, data caches and memory modules. The algorithm is composed of two phases: task clustering that minimises program execution time and mapping task clusters into available system resources. The task clustering algorithm is based on a modified Dominant Sequence approach. It includes a heuristics that implements balancing of the communication traffic of dynamic cluster busses together with reduction of the total program execution time. Tasks are added to clusters only if the data exchange traffic on the intra–cluster busses due to inclusion of a task to a cluster decreases program parallel time. Parallel tasks can be allocated to the same processor if no cache overflow results. The process cluster mapping adjusts the number of task clusters and the number of processors used in the clusters to the real number of memory modules and processors in the system. The dominant sequence approach provides a polynomial complexity of the scheduling algorithm.

All evaluations of parallel program time are done by symbolic execution of the extended macro dataflow graphs proposed in this paper. It enables assuming different strategies for the functioning of bus arbiters as well as different control of memory modules and data caches. Checking against data cache overflows is performed on the fly with parallel program time evaluation, so it does

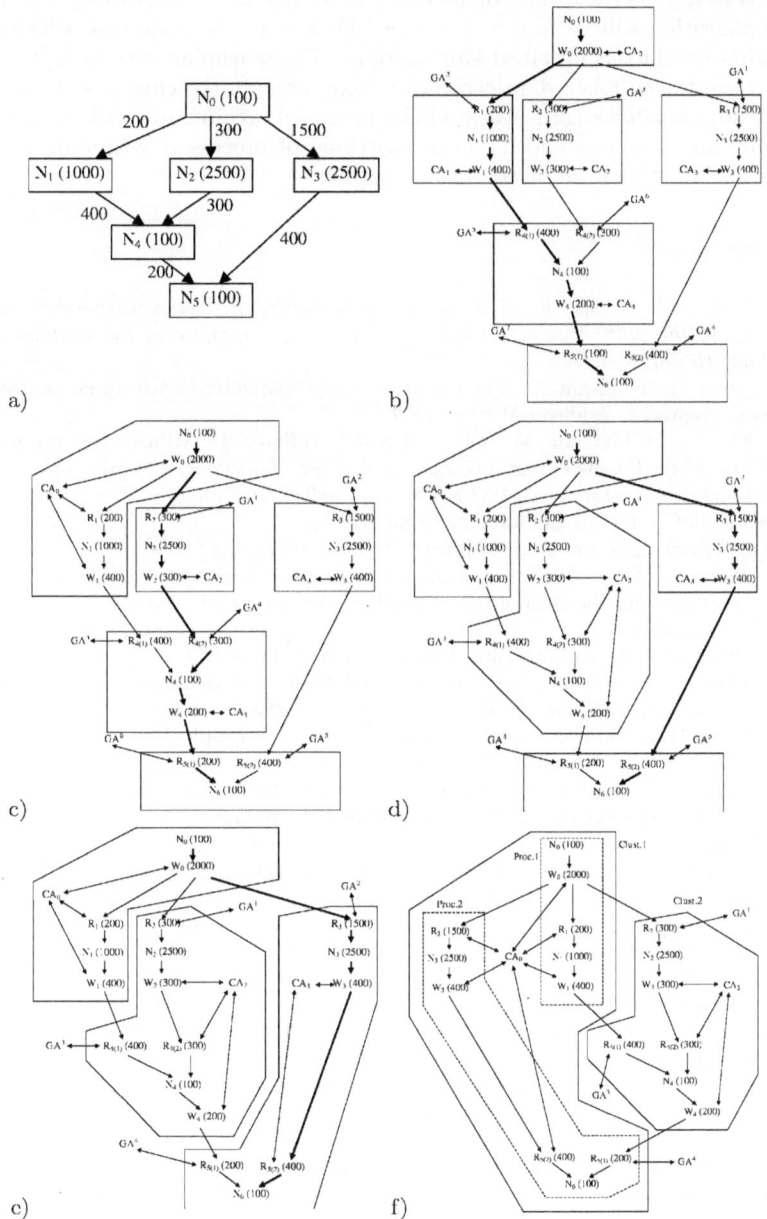

Fig. 5. a) The initial MDFG (left), b) EMDFG (right), PT = 11310, (c–e) consecutive clustering steps, PT = 8200; f) the EMDFG mapped into 2 clusters, PT = 9110

not excessively increase the polynomial complexity of the algorithm. The proposed algorithm will be further developed by a more elaborate task scheduling algorithm for clusters obtained after merging. The redefining of tasks (splitting) will be considered when data cache overflows occur in the clustering phase. In further works, additional features of the proposed architecture such as parallel reads by bus snooping and dynamic switching of processors with data caches will be included into the scheduling algorithms.

References

1. J. Protic, M. Tomasevic, V. Milutinovic: A Survey of Shared Memory Systems, *Proc. of the 28th Annual Hawaii International Conference of System Sciences, Maui, Hawai, Jan. 1995*, pp. 74–84.
2. D. Sima, T. Fountain, P. Kacsuk: *Advanced Computer Architectures; A Design Space Approach*, Addison–Wesley, 1997.
3. Y. Kanaka, M. Matsuda, M.Ando, K. Kazuto, M.Sato: "COMPaS": A Pentium Pro PC–based SMP Cluster and its Experience, *IPPS Workshop on Personal Computer Networks of Workstations*, LNCS 1388, pp. 486–497, 1998.
4. "Scalable Clusters of Commodity Computers",
   http://www.csag.cs.uiuc.edu/projects/clusters.html
5. *Multimax Technical Summary*, Encore Computer Corporation, March 1987.
6. D. Lenoski et al: The Stanford Dash multi–processor, *IEEE Computer*, Vol.25, N.3, 1992, pp. 63–79.
7. Convex Exemplar Architecture, *Convex Press*, 1994, p. 239.
8. T. Lang et al.: Bandwidth of Crossbar and Multiple–Bus Connections for Multiprocessors, *IEEE Trans. on EC*, Vol.C–11, N.12, 1982, p. 1237–1234.
9. C.R. Das, L.N. Bhuyan: Bandwidth Availability of Multiple–Bus Multiprocessors, *IEEE Trans. on Computers*, Vol.C–34, N.10, Oct. 1985, pp. 918–926.
10. Q. Yang, L.N. Bhuyan, Performance of Multiple–Bus Interconnections for Multiprocessors, *Journal of Parallel and Distributed Computing 8*, (March 1990), pp. 267–273.
11. D.M. Tullsen, S.J.Eggers: Effective Cache Pre–Fetching on Bus Based Multiprocessors, *ACM Trans. on Comp. Systems*, Vol.13, N.1, Feb. 1995, pp. 57–88
12. D.A, Koufaty et al: Data Forwarding in Scaleable Shared Memory Multi-Processors, *IEEE Trans. on Parallel and Distr. Technology*, Vol.7, N.12, 1996, pp. 1250–1264.
13. A. Milenkovic, V. Milutinovic: Cache Injection: A Novel Technique for Tolerating Memory Latency in Bus–Based SMPs, *Proc. of the Euro–Par 2000*, LNCS 1900, 2000, pp. 558–566.
14. T. Yang and A. Gerasoulis: PYRROS: Static Task Scheduling and Code Generation for Message Passing Multiprocessors, *Proc. of 6th ACM Int'l Conf. on Supercomputing (ICS92)*, 1992, pp. 428–437.
15. Y.K. Kwok, I. Ahmad: Dynamic Critical–Path Scheduling: An Effective Technique for Allocating Task Graphs to Multiprocessors, *IEEE Transactions on Parallel and Distributed Systems*, Vol.7, N.1, January 1996, pp. 46–55.
16. A. Gerasoulis, T. Yang: A Comparison of Clustering Heuristics for Scheduling Directed Acyclic Graphs on Multiprocessors, *Journal of Parallel and Distributed Computing*, Vol.16, 1992, pp. 276–291.

Distributed Rendering Engine

Nicolae Tapus, Emil Slusanschi , and Tudor Popescu

Computer Science Department, POLITEHNICA University Bucharest
Splaiul Independentei 313, Bucuresti, Romania
ntapus@cs.pub.ro; olorin@cs.pub.ro;   popele@yahoo.com

Abstract. This paper present aspects of architecture of a cluster of workstations developed using ATM and FastEthernet technology and some of the basic principles of distributed memory programming, based on message-passing. The team used an application called Parallel POV-Ray rendering engine to show the viability of the "PoliCluster". This paper will describe the performance improvement that the Cluster architecture brought to this particular application. A significant role in choosing this particular application as an example was the natural parallelism of the rendering engine.

1.   Introduction

The demand for better performance from a given application is a typical characteristic of modern time automatic computation. To do this, there are three fundamentally different solutions: the use of a high-performance mono-processor system, the use of a massive parallel platform such as Cray T3E or IBM SP-3, and lastly, the use of a Cluster Of Workstations. The performance of dedicated parallel computer is excellent but the price will be accordingly high. A new approach of developing a high performance computing is based on a cluster of standard commercial systems. A cluster is a group of independent computer systems which forms a loosely coupled multiprocessor system. An independent interconnection infrastructure provides inter-processors communication.

Clusters, built using commodity-off-the-shelf (COTS) hardware components and free, or commonly used software, are playing a major role in solving large-scale science, engineering and commercial applications. Cluster computing has emerged as a result of the convergence of several trends, including the availability of inexpensive high performance microprocessors and high speed networks, the development of standard software tools for high performance distributed computing, and the increasing need of computing power for computational science and commercial applications. To prove the viability of the Cluster architectures, a rendering application was chosen as an example. The Cluster was used because it is the best suited This paper will show the performance increase that this structure brings for this kind of applications and the fact that the use of a dedicated parallel computer will not be necessarily the best solution, as scalability and portability could not be obtained so easily on those architectures.

D. Grigoras et al. (Eds.): IWCC 2001, LNCS 2326, pp. 207-215, 2002.

2. Environment of the Parallel Implementation

2.1 Hardware Structure, PoliCluster

A cluster is a type of parallel or distributed processing system that consists of a collection of interconnected stand-alone computers working together as a single, integrated computer resource[5]. In theory, a node can be a single or multiprocessor computer, such as a PC, workstation, or symmetric multiprocessor. Each node has its own memory, I/O devices and operating system. The nodes are usually connected using a high speed networks like Fast Ethernet, ATM or Myrinet. Our cluster uses PC's that run WinNT, Linux or other distributions of Unix O.S. The server node controls the activity of the whole cluster and acts as a fileserver for the client nodes, it is also the console of the whole system and it represents the interface of the Cluster with the outside world.

The first step was to build this parallel architecture. It all started with 8 computers which had Windows Workstation NT4, WMPI 1.2 installed, and support for the ATM-Link 155 3c975 (3COM) network adapters linked through a Cisco Lightstream 1010 ATM Switch. The team proudly named this small Cluster: "PoliCluster", Fig 1.

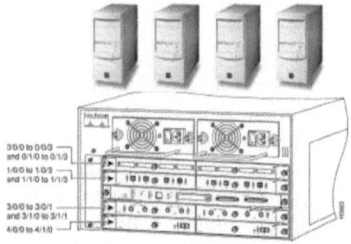

Fig. 1. Demo PoliCluster infrastructure

From the multitude of applications that were suited to parallel approaches, the developers stopped to a method of obtaining high-resolution images using a rendering technique named ray tracing. As the team documented the project they found that this procedure can produce high quality pictures and, at the same time was a method that required a lot of processing power and it took a lot of time when building such images. In other words this is exactly the kind of application that would demonstrate the performance of the Cluster architecture. The application is part of an open project built by the POV-team (Persistence Of Vision). Starting from their sources the team developed a parallel version that would be able to run on our Cluster and use its 8 systems instead of just one as the original application. The idea is that it is possible to increase the number of computers in the cluster and the only thing that has to be done is to change the configuration files.

2.2 Software for Parallel Processing

The software that provides the support for the communication can be the Parallel Virtual Machine (PVM) or Message Passing Interface (MPI). The team chose MPI as a standard as it is more suited to the needs of the project and it provides cross platform compatibility.

The project goals are: the shortening of the generation time of high-resolution images, using a Cluster structure described below with the ray-tracing method; the use of parallel systems specific network communication techniques, in this case message passing; to prove the viability of the COW structure and to make a performance analysis.

By shortening the time taken to generate the final images, the quality of those images is maintained. The desired image is obtained in a smaller amount of time but with the same characteristics as the image that was rendered on a single machine. The time spared can be used to generate other images, which together can be used to obtain spectacular animation sequences.

The system is composed of a Windows console and one or more DOS clients. The Ray-tracing engine is POV-Ray. The reason for the existence of the DOS clients is that they work faster. The MPI release on the Win32 platforms is WMPI 1.2, which is based mainly on Mpich 1.1.1.

3.   Parallel Ray-Tracing

3.1. POV-Ray

Ray-tracing is a rendering technique that generates an image by simulating the way that the light rays travel in the real world. Still, the method by which the image is obtained is exactly the opposite of the real-life phenomenon. In reality, the light rays are emitted by a light source towards any object that surrounds it. The light reflects on the objects that it encounters or passes through the object if it is transparent. The light that is reflected or refracted by the objects contained in a scene, is noticed by the human eye, or, by an optical device such as a video camera or a photographic camera.

Now, as the observer does not notice the majority of the light rays, it would take too long to generate an image in the way it really happens in reality. An example would be the following, lets assume that someone enters a dark room and the light is turned on. The image that the person observes is only the part of the room that is touched by light rays. So, only a certain amount of the light rays emitted by the source reach our eyes. Therefore analyzing each light-ray would not be enough.

Ray-tracing programs like POV-Ray start with their simulated camera and trace rays backwards out into the scene. The user specifies the location of the camera, light sources, and objects as well as the surface texture properties of objects, their interiors (if transparent) and any atmospheric effects such as fog, haze, or fire.

For every pixel in the final image one or more viewing rays are shot from the camera, into the scene to see if it intersects with any of the objects in the scene. These "viewing rays" originate from the viewer, represented by the camera, and pass through the viewing window (representing the final image).

Special features like inter-diffuse reflection (radiosity), atmospheric effects and area lights make it necessary to shoot a lot of additional rays into the scene for every pixel.

Ray tracing is not a fast process by any means, but it produces very high quality images with realistic reflections, shading, perspective and other effects. What deserves to be noticed is that the rendering engine used is the same for all the operating systems for which there are available source codes, and therefore portability is easily obtained.

Now here are some of the features that POV-Ray has to offer to the user:

- Easy to use scene description language;
- Standard include files that pre-define many shapes, colors and textures;
- Very high quality output image files (up to 48-bit color);
- 15 and 24 bit color display on many computer platforms using appropriate hardware;
- Many camera types, including perspective, panorama, orthographic, etc;
- Spotlights, cylindrical lights and area lights for sophisticated lighting;
- Inter-diffuse reflection (radiosity) for more realistic lighting;
- Atmospheric effects like atmosphere, ground-fog and rainbow;
- Particle media to model effects like clouds, dust, fire and steam;
- Several image file output formats including Targa, PNG and PPM;
- Basic shape primitives such as ... spheres, boxes, quadrics, cylinders, cones, triangles and planes;
- Advanced shape primitives such as ... Torii (donuts), bezier patches, height fields (mountains), blobs, quartics, smooth triangles, text, fractals, superquadrics, surfaces of revolution, prisms, polygons, lathes and fractals;
- Shapes can easily be combined to create new complex shapes using Constructive Solid Geometry (CSG). POV-Ray supports unions, merges, intersections and differences;

3.2. Parallel POV-Ray

Now here is a description of the transformations that were made to the engine so that it passed from single-processor to multi-processor generation of the image, on the PoliCluster.

At any given time, in the system, there is only one console of the POV-Ray application, that is the WinNT version that was modified by the team so that it can be used as the master node of the entire Cluster. There is a menu that is used to configure the execution, if this menu is not used, the execution will be made locally on the computer where the console resides, exactly as the original POV-Ray. If one chooses to use the Parallel Rendering version then he must select the Tools menu, and then select the Configure Parallel Rendering submenu. The User can choose the number of computers used, the names of the computers and the resolution of the image.

The master, or the console initiates the clients through an MPI-Init call (each client Workstation should have a MPI daemon running on them so that the MPI could work). The master sends the file with the image specifications to the clients as well as the parameters with which the remote engine should be called in order to process the proper region of the image. The idea is simple, each pixel in the image is independent of the others and therefore each processor can build a fragment of the big image without the need to communicate with them. This implementation is a Master-Slave model. At this particular point, each client, starts to generate the image fragments according to the users requests. After the client has finished rendering the line, he sends the line back to the master. The master will copy the line into a file and he will send a new line to the free client. From this point onward it all depends on the system where the engine is implemented (network quality, processor speed, storage capacity etc).

The communications between the clients and the master is synchronous and serialized for the sending of the image description files as well as for the rendered images in order to prevent any loss of data as this will bring to the failure of the whole process. It is assumed that the Parallel-rendering engine will be used to generate high-resolution images and not normal (lower than 1280x1024) virtual images that can be obtained in a reasonable amount of time on a mono-processor machine.

3.3. Code Examples

Here is one significant fragment of code taken from the application. The fragment present an MPI Sequence that is used to distribute the image specification file to the MPI clients:

```
filestruct fis_struct; int myrank, ranksize; int i;

// MPI initialization

MPI_Init (&argc, &argv);

// the current rank

MPI_Comm_rank (MPI_COMM_WORLD, &myrank);

// the size of the MPI systemMPI_Comm_size
(MPI_COMM_WORLD, &ranksize);

MPI_Barrier (MPI_COMM_WORLD);

if (myrank == 0){// if this is the master send the
configuration file

  fis_struct->fname=malloc(sizeof(&nume_fisier));
```

```
    fis_struct->size=malloc(get_file_size( &nume_fisier));

      for (i=1; i<ranksize,i++){

        MPI_Send (&fisier_struct->fname, 1,

        MPI_CHAR,  i, 98, MPI_COMM_WORLD);

        MPI_Send (&fisier_struct->size,
        sizeof(fisier_struct->size), MPI_CHAR, i, 99,
        MPI_COMM_WORLD);

      } // end for

  } // end master else{

    // this is the slave code receive configuration file

      MPI_Recv (&fisier_struct->fname, 1,

        MPI_CHAR, 0,98, MPI_COMM_WORLD, &status);
MPI_Recv (&fisier_struct->size,

          sizeof(fisier_struct-  >size), MPI_CHAR, 0,

          99, MPI_COMM_WORLD, &status);

      // create the file

      create_file(&fisier_struct- >fname);

      copy_file(&fiser_struct->size)

    } // end slave code

  MPI_Barrier (MPI_COMM_WORLD);

  MPI_Finalize ();
```

4.   Performance Increase

Two different aspects must be taken into account here. First of all, for the rendering process the speed-up is almost equal to the number of processors used, the overhead of the communications is minimal if the size of the image is bigger than 1280x1024. Therefore, if 16 processors were used a gain of between 9.5 – 13.9 times can be obtained. As it can be seen from the table the gain increases as the size of the image grows. Secondly, the hardware resources, network adapters, time needed to transmit

Resolution	16 processors	8 processors	1 processors
6400x4800	3675	8240	50308
3200x2400	1015	2012	10040
1280x1024	357	815	1815
1024x768	278	418	1084
800x600	267	362	668
640x480	265	279	430

Fig. 2. Table with time, in seconds for various resolutions/number of processors

the lines back from the clients to the master, rebuilding of the final image from pieces must be taken into account. All these variables come to add to the overhead of the process. As can be seen from the table presented in Figure 2., and the graph from Figure 4., as the image grows, the speed-up grows as well as expected.

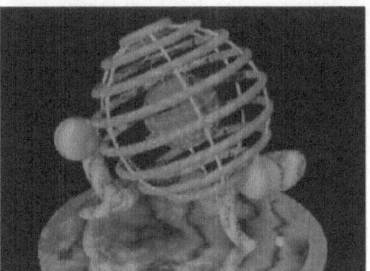

Fig. 3. "piece2.pov" image

The platform used initially in the PoliCluster was based on Pentium computers. The network used is either a normal Ethernet, or a Local LAN using ATM network adapters and a Cisco ATM Lightstream 1010 Switch. The results presented in Figure 2 were taken on the ATM Network using the "piece2.pov" image file specification. The source file for this image was taken from the POV-Ray package.

From the tests that were made for small dimensions of the data packets, the performances of the Ethernet and ATM networks are comparable, for big packets, the ATM is slightly faster. The numbers in the table from Figure 2 are in seconds and the graph from Figure 4 is depicted in a logarithmic base so that it can be better observed. The data presented is obtained for the mono-processor, 8 and 16 processors systems.

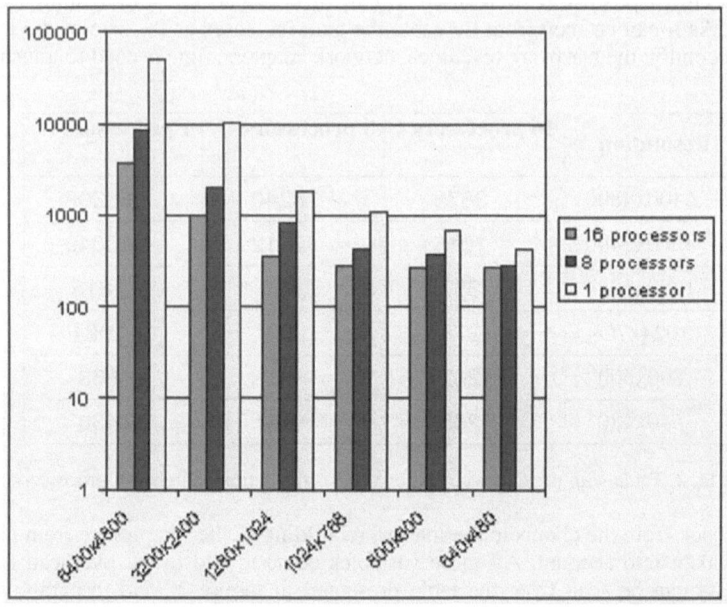

Fig. 4. Graph describing the data from Figure 2 on a logarithmic scale

5. Conclusions

Due to the fact applications need more and more processing power it is natural to build parallel architectures. We used a Cluster Of Workstations because such a system uses components that we can find in any university laboratory and because the cost of a massive parallel computer is much too often too high. The paper has demonstrated that the Cluster of Workstations is capable of significant improvements in performance, even employing modest workstations as clients. So we can easily say that Clusters are a viable alternative to dedicated parallel systems. For such a system the existence of qualified personnel to develop and maintain these kind of applications and the resources available it's a must.

The standardization effort for the message–passing architectures must be noted, MPI is offering the actual standard for the message-passing systems. The main variables that determinate the performances are the hardware qualities and the algorithms employed to minimize network transfer. From the programmers point of view the problems are those regarding synchronization. The parallel-rendering engine tried to employ as little synchronization as possible, so actually it only synchronizes at the beginning and at the end of the rendering process.

From the observations that were made using this application, one can draw the conclusion that the Cluster of Workstations is a viable structure, first from the economic point of view, as they are cheap and easy to build and maintain. These Workstations can be used during daytime as normal Workstations for labs and programming and then at night or during designated hours, they can be used in Cluster architectures to solve CPU-bound problems such as the one presented in this paper. The communication support is offered by the MPI standard. A very important aspect is that this kind of system is able to make a link between completely different operating systems such as Windows, Macintosh and Unix platforms, and so the users, which after all are interested in performance, are able to get that performance out of every computer available. It is almost certain that in the future these systems will thrive and develop at an ever-increasing rate, because they offer performance comparable with the dedicated parallel machines at an accessible price.

Interesting result in areas like modeling of climatic changes over big periods of time, the evolution of galaxies, the atomic structure of materials, the efficiency of a certain engine, the air flux over the body of an automobile, the destruction determined by violent impacts, the behavior of microscopic electronic devices and, last but not least, as is the case with this work, generation of high resolution virtual images and of high-resolution animation are obtained using more than 100 PCs connected by a high speed interconnection.

References

1.   Cisco Online Documentation - http://www.cisco.com/support/ (2001)
2.   Hennessy, J., Patterson, D. : Computer Architecture - a quantitative approach , Morgan Kaufmann, NewYork, (1992) 582-585
3.   McDysan, D., Spohn, D. : ATM Theory and Application. McGraw-Hill, NewYork, (1998)
4.   Sima, D., Fountain, T., Kacsuk, P. : Distributed Memory Systems Arhitectures. Advanced Computer Architectures - a design space approach , Addison – Wesley, NewYork, (1997) 587-592
5.   Buyya, R. (ed.) : High Performance Cluster Computing: Programming and Applications, Prentice Hall, (1999)
6.   Kumar,V., Grama, A., Gupta, A., Karypis, G. : Introduction to Parallel Computing: Design and Analysis of Algorithms, Benjamin/Cummings, (1994)
7.   Pacheco, P.: Parallel Programming with MPI. Morgan Kaufmann Publishers, (1996)
8.   MPI Software – http://www-unix.mcs.anl.gov/mpi/mpich/
9.   Sterling, T., Salmon, J., Becker, D., Savarese, D. : How to build a Beowulf, MIT Press, (1996)
10. POV-Ray Foundation – www.povray.org

A Distributed Application for Monte Carlo Simulations

Nicolae Tapus, Mihai Burcea, and Vlad Staicu

Faculty of Computers and Automatics
Computer Science Dept.
Polytechnic University of Bucharest
{ntapus, burceam, vlads}@cs.pub.ro

Abstract. The present paper implements a cluster of workstation (COW) structure and also an application that will demonstrate the advantages and benefits of such a structure. The application is a message – passing – based parallel program, which simulates in parallel the propagation of photons through various environments. The simulation is based on the Monte Carlo principle of 'throwing the dice'. Performance of both the application and the communication structure is evaluated by using parallel profiling tools.

1. Introduction

For more than a decade now the performance of the computing systems has been growing at an alarming rate. This is due both to the development of the VLSI technologies, and to the design and architecture of the computers, which allows for the actual and effective utilization of this pure hardware potential and helps translate it into performance. The most important aspect here is the parallelism, running in parallel as many applications as possible on our system, and getting as much as possible out of our resources.

Parallelism is a concept that applies to all levels of a computer system, depending on the technological layer and at the same time interacting with several architectural concepts, such as bandwidth, data locality, latency, and synchronization.

The purpose of this paper is to implement a cluster of workstations and adopt a parallel application to run on this structure with the intention of showing the benefits and advantages of using such an architecture. The conclusions will be drawn based upon the evaluation of the application's performance.

The base platform on which the application was run consisted of several workstations interconnected through a high – speed ATM switch, and several versions of MPI were used in order to take advantage of the intrinsic parallelism of the application. The performance was evaluated using parallel profiling tools, such as Vampir and VampirTrace.

The communication layer is based on the use of Ethernet, Fast Ethernet and ATM, with the prospective use of Gigabit Ethernet in a later phase.

D. Grigoras et al. (Eds.): IWCC 2001, LNCS 2326, pp. 216-223, 2002.
© Springer-Verlag Berlin Heidelberg 2002

2. Choosing the Architecture

One might be tempted to sit and ponder which is best, a single ultra – performance computer system, or a multi – processor one, each of them taken separately less performance than the first option, but offering the ability to run tasks in parallel. The second choice is obviously the preferred one, and here are a few reasons for this: processor speeds double every 18 months, but the same thing cannot be said about the media access speed (hard drives and other storage devices), and usually the processing power is not the bottleneck in a system, but the access to stored data and communication – related issues; computations done in parallel try to compensate at least in part for these drawbacks; besides, parallel computing can speed an application up to hundreds and thousands of times, depending on its nature.

Even so, there was a choice to be made between a parallel supercomputer, and a cluster of workstations. This was made in favor of the latter, and here is why: with respect to the kind of applications that can be run on them, in a COW system the bandwidth may still represent a bottleneck. For this reason, COWs are best suited for applications that do not involve extensive communication, but are rather CPU – intensive. Besides the most appropriate application type to be run on them, the two types of architectures differ in complexity also: usually a COW consists of several workstations, which are regular PCs, and some (preferably solid) communication / interconnection support, usually a fast interconnection network or switch, as illustrated in the figure below.

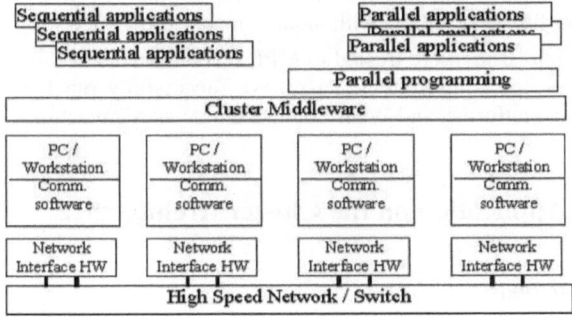

The network interface hardware usually consists of a Fast Ethernet / ATM network interface card. The fact that all of the cluster's components are regular components, bought 'off the shelf', tremendously reduces the price of the entire system. Also an important factor for the price aspect is the fact that for a cluster you only need one console, therefore, one display will do.

At the same time, this standardization of the components offers the system a better fiability and dependability, and greater hardware scalability – it is far easier (and cheaper !) to insert a few more workstations in your cluster than to buy another board for your SMP, and to upgrade both your memory and communication buses. And we must not forget the ease of installation and maintenance of a cluster.

The dependability of the system is not a factor one should ignore. If a random workstation from your cluster fails, all you need to do is to replace or buy the new component (or even an entire workstation), all this time the cluster being perfectly functional, and just offering fewer computing resources. On the other hand, you will go through a great deal of trouble should one of your processors in your SMP fail, and the costs for recovery will be considerably higher.

However, a cluster is definitely more difficult to program than a multiprocessor system. This is because in the case of a cluster, the programmer must explicitly handle all communication aspects, while in a parallel system there is both hardware and software support for this implemented at the OS level.

In a cluster of workstations, each workstation can run its own OS, independently, among which we usually find Linux or WinNT, thus the system being single – processor oriented, and not having support for communication. This way, the communication issue is often one that requires time and skills from the programmer.

To try and level the balance, several parallel programming paradigms have evolved over the time. Different approaches and technologies implemented above or even inside the operating system try to take over as much as possible of the communication management responsibility. Some of the more popular solutions are message – passing – based technologies (such as PVM and MPI), and Distributed Shared Memory (DSM) systems.

Our implementation makes use of a very performance ATM switch for the communication infrastructure, a Cisco LightStream 1010 with self – configurable hot – swappable modules. The switch supports 5 removable modules, each with 2 sub modules, and each of these can manage either 4 OC-3 links (CAT 5 UTP or fiber optic), or one OC-12 link (622 Mbps) with mono – mode fiber optic.

The communication issues were trusted to MPI, several flavors of this having been used on the different operating systems : we have successfully run LAM MPI and MPICH on the Linux platforms, and WMPI on the Windows NT machines.

3. The Parallel Application on the Cluster Architecture

3.1 Monte Carlo Methods

What exactly is a Monte Carlo method ? Monte Carlo refers to any method of simulation that involves random numbers.   Monte Carlo methods are used in simulating natural phenomena, experimental simulations, numerical analysis, etc.

3.2 Monte Carlo Methods for Simulating Radiations Propagation

Monte Carlo methods for radiations propagation represent a powerful method of solving an impressive number of problems, from designing and testing nuclear reactors, to modeling nuclear experimental devices, and computing coefficients needed in prediction of the effects of iradiating biological matter; for many complex problems, Monte Carlo modeling is the only acceptable choice.

Basically, the Monte Carlo method for radiation propagation simulation consists of a more or less interactive simulation of the successive interactions that occur when the radiations propagate through substance and matter; the simulation process starts with the emission of the particles from a source, and follows the particles until a certain stage of their evolution. The simulation takes place by building an abstract model of the physical system. A number of representative cases is selected out of the total of the possible trajectories of the particles. The decisions are made based upon the selection values which are pseudo randomly generated with adequate probability densities.

Consequently, we can conclude that solving a problem in the Monte Carlo way involves both general aspects related to generating pseudo random variables, and aspects specific to the given problem.

3.3 Monte Carlo Methods for Generating Random Numbers

Very large sequences of random numbers are quite often needed in scientific applications; randomly generated numbers are not the best thing we can get, since they would incur unreproductible results, thus making the debugging process very difficult. The solution is given by the pseudo randomly generated numbers.

In this paper we are using a random number library called SPRNG (Scalable Parallel Random Number Generator), developed at NCSA, UIUC.

3.4 Generating Pseudo Random Sequences on Parallel Structures

The reason why this is a self – standing section of this paper is that generating in parallel sequences of pseudo random numbers is a very important part of the application. In particular, sequences of random numbers are used for establishing the direction in which a photon will be emitted by the source, for establishing the kind of interaction a photon will suffer, for establishing the new direction after the interactions, etc.

Besides, the photon source is distributed, in that it is separately simulated on each processor in part. The alternative would have been to generate all the photons on one processor, and transmit them with their properties over to all the other processors, but that was not a viable solution because if the immense number of messages that would be sent over the network (we simulate millions and tens of millions of particles); also it is possible that the slaves finish their work on the received data and hang around idle until they receive the next set of data through the network (the transmission of the data may take longer than the work on the data for datasets of certain sizes).

Besides that, the reason we need a distributed parallel pseudo random generator becomes obvious, because a 'regular' pseudo random generator may generate appropriate sequences each by itself, the *entire* sequence, the one generated *in ensemble*, may not satisfy our criteria. Essential features of a parallel pseudo random generator would be, without getting into details: randomness, reproducibility, speed, a period as long as possible.

The great advantage that Monte Carlo simulation methods offer is coarse granularity in the case of parallelizing applications of this sort, because coarse – grained parallel algorithms are the best solution for architectures based on message – passing. In this case, the accurateness of the simulation and of the results obtained depends in a high degree upon the number of simulated particles, which in our application is of tens of millions. This aspect puts our application in the calculus – intensive applications class, destined to be solved by the means of parallel computing.

3.5 Implementation Details

The idea behind the application is to simulate the physical interactions that take place at the propagation of photons through various types of material. This involves modeling and simulating the emitting source, the photons themselves, the interactions that may take place, and their consequences, with their new resulting particles or losses of particles, as the case may well be.

The basic steps of the algorithm can be summarized as follows:
- model the emission of a photon from the source
- model the trajectory until the first interaction
- determine the coordinates of the interaction (which is a probabilistic event)
- determine the type of the interaction (which is also a probabilistic event)
- if a Compton interaction took place, then compute the photon's energy and trajectory first in the local coordinates system, then in the global one, and go to step 2.
- if a photoelectric interaction took place, end the simulation for that photon. The same happens if the photon exits the limits of the simulation environment (which can also be limitless)
- if a electron – positron emission took place, then decide the direction of the resulting two particles and go to step 2 for each of the resulting photons.

3.6 Parallel Implementation Issues

The simulation of a photon together with all its descendants will be done on the same processor, for the purpose of keeping at an overall low the inter – processor communication overhead. The granularity of the algorithm is given by the sum of the sequential steps described above. The granularity of the parallel application is large, because the communication between the workstations only takes place in the beginning and at the end of the simulation. The application architecture consists of one master processor (i.e. workstation) which distributes the work to the other slave nodes, and also does a piece of the work itself afterwards, and at the end of the simulation the master collects the results from the slaves, and computes various statistics out of the gathered data. So what we basically do is distribute the number of photons on the available workstations.

Although there is no explicit dynamic load balancing of the available processors' load, a certain degree of load balancing is insured by the parallel pseudo random number generator: probabilistically speaking, there is no reason for a processor to generate more electron – positron pairs than the others, thus leading to a higher load of that processor. Also due to the criteria that our parallel pseudo random number generator must meet, a uniform repartition of the photons and of the physical phenomena that take place is insured.

As previously stated, the emitting source is not local to the master node, it is distributed and simulated locally on each processor, thus preventing the network from becoming overloaded with small messages running from the master to the slaves (keep in mind that we are dealing with millions and tens of millions of particles, and even though one may think aggregation of the messages, this would still imply a somewhat continuous communication, because we are dealing with a dynamic, on – going process). The accuracy of doing so (i.e. of 'distributing' the source) is assured once again by the pseudo random number generator.

When there are no more particles to simulate, each processor sends its results to the master node, which computers the overall statistics and displays them in a friendly format.

4. Performance Evaluation

Experience shows that it is considerably more difficult to debug and profile a parallel application, rather than a sequential one, which only has one unique instruction flow. The far greater space taken by the application's state at one certain moment in time, and the communication that is taking place between the composing processes, both give a higher degree of difficulty in trying to analyze the behavior of a parallel application.

A common situation would be that on some parallel architecture, some parallel application just doesn't behave, and has poor performance. The best that the usual programmer can get in order to identify the bottleneck is to obtain a trace file (more often than not overwhelmingly huge), and realize that the solution is *somewhere* inside of it. The last but definitely the easiest task would be to identify that piece of information inside the enormous amount of raw information available.

This is where our profiling tools came in. Vampir offers the entire set of operations needed in such a situation: profiling, counters and event tracing, all in nice visual formats. Vampir converts the trace info in a variety of graphical visions, such as timelines showing the state of the processes in the system at certain moments in time, profiling statistics that show the execution durations of miscellaneous routines, communication statistics that offer the amount of sent and received data, as well as the communication rates, etc. The profiling and communications statistics help locate the bottlenecks, and the timeline displays together with the possibility of 'zooming in' on the time scale offer the explanation for it.

Vampir together with the trace generator VampirTrace helped us obtain several valuable graphics and statistics, of which we will only reproduce here a few, mentioning that the results regarding the speedup and scalability of the application are really impressive.

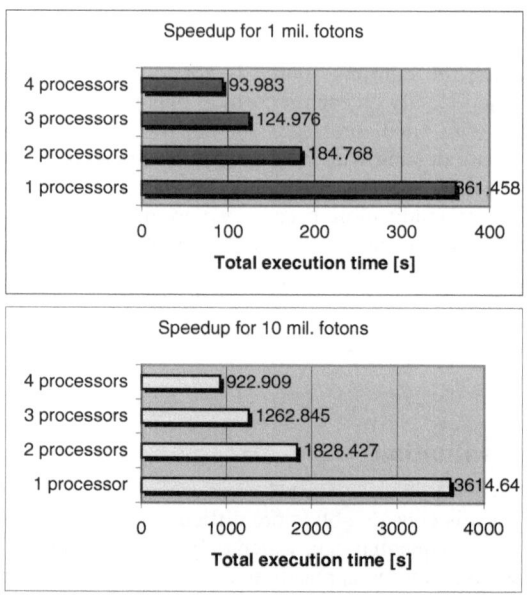

5. Conclusions

With an impressive speedup factor of 3.9165 out of 4, and an efficiency factor of 0.9791, one can draw several conclusions about the application and the infrastructure. Before that one must take into consideration several factors, such as the type of the implemented application – an parallel application (i.e. with a high degree of intrinsic parallelism). The coarse granularity offered by the implementation goes very well with the parallel paradigm that was chosen: message passing, because it involves a really small amount of communication overhead, taking full advantage of the facilities offered by this paradigm.

Even so, an efficiency factor of 97% is not something to look over, especially since when while at small dimensions of the problem the performance improvement is not very impressive, as the size of the problem grows, the efficiency factor comes very close to the theoretical value (the ideal value); this means that the application scales very well, and can be explained through the fact that the communication overhead is insignificant in comparison with the computing process, and grows at a much slower rate than the time spent in computations.

The extensive exploit of parallelism can be noticed in the snapshots taken with the Vampire tool on the Linux systems.

One should also remark the high degree in which the performance of the system depends on the quality of the interconnecting communication network or switch.

All these being said, one can draw the conclusion that for certain types of applications (i.e. calculus – intensive), a parallel system is the definite solution, and among these we notice the clusters of workstations as being the cheapest, most flexible, and the one with the best performance / price factor architecture present on the market at this time, and with the continuously increased support both from vendors and software developers, clusters will almost gain more and more market share.

References

1.   O. Sima – "Simularea Monte Carlo a transportului radiatiilor", ALL (1999)
2.   Computational Physics Class at Carleton University, CA,
     http://www.physics.carleton.ca/courses/75.502/
3.   Nicolae Tapus – Local Area Networks – lecture notes, Faculty of Automatics and Computers, CS Department
4.   A. S. Tanenbaum – "Structured Computer Systems", Agora (1999)
5.   A. S. Tanenbaum – "Computer Networks", Agora (1997)
6.   David McDysan, D. Spohn – "ATM Theory and Application", McGraw – Hill, (1998)
7.   Cisco Online Documentation, http://www.cisco.com/support/
8.   Valentin Cristea – Program Systems for Computer Networks – lecture notes, Faculty of Automatics and Computers, CS Department
10. Designing and Building Parallel Programs, by Ian Foster
     http://www-unix.mcs.anl.gov/dbpp/text/book.html
11. The MPI Forum & MPICH home, http://www-unix.mcs.anl.gov/mpi/
12. Scallable Parallel Random Number Generators at University of Illinois, at Urbana – Champaign, www.ncsa.uiuc.edu/Apps/CMP/RNG/www/toc.html
13. Kai Hwang – "Advanced Computer Architecture", Mc Graw – Hill (1993)
14. "Parallel Computer Architecture", Morgan Kaufmann (1997)
15. Random Number Generators
     http://www.ncsa.uiuc.edu/Apps/CMP/RNG/www/toc.html
16. MPI Tutorial, http://www-unix.mcs.anl.gov/dbpp/text/node107.html
17. Tools for evaluating performance of parallel programs:
     http://www.cs.utk.edu/~browne/perftools-review/
18. Evaluating performance of MPI:
     www.cs.purdue.edu/homes/markus/research /pubs/mpi-perf/node4.html
19. Designing and Building Parallel Programs, by Ian Foster, Performance Tools section.,
     http://www-unix.mcs.anl.gov/dbpp/text/node110.html
20. VAMPIR User's Guide and VAMPIRTRACE User's Guide, http://www.pallas.de/vampir/

A Model for Accessing Resources of the Distributed File Systems

Sabin C. Buraga

Faculty of Computer Science, "A. I. Cuza" University of Iaşi
G-ral. Berthelot Str., 16, Iaşi, Romania
busaco@infoiasi.ro

Abstract. The modern operating systems must integrate various Internet services, especially World–Wide Web facilities to access different Web resources using file system mechanisms. In this paper we present a high-level model to access via Web the resources of a distributed file system. The proposed description is based on *Resource Description Framework* (*RDF*) recommendation of the World–Wide Web Consortium, a standardized foundation for processing metadata.

1   Introduction

A *distributed system* is a collection of loosely coupled computers interconnected by a communication network. As far as a specific computer in a distributed system is concerned, the rest of the machines (also known as *hosts*) and their respective resources are remote, whereas its own resources are local.

An important part of a distributed operating system, the *file system* provides file services to clients (other hosts of the network). A client interface for a file service is made of a set of primitives, called *file operations*, such as opening a file, removing a file, reading from a file, writing to a file, and so on.

A *distributed file system* is a file system whose clients, servers, and storage devices (e.g., disks) are dispersed among the interconnected computers of a distributed system [10].

At present and in the near future, the operating systems must integrate various Internet services, especially World–Wide Web facilities to remotely access Web files (resources) using file system mechanisms. The general requirements for such distributed and Internet-enabled file systems are: scalability, support for client/server architecture, location-transparent global organization of files, on-line administration, log-based recovery/restart, safe replication, security [8].

To facilitate this integration, we propose a high-level model for accessing resources of a distributed file system. The proposed model is using *Resource Description Framework* (*RDF*), a basis for processing metadata. RDF provides interoperability between applications that exchange machine-understandable information on the WWW.

To express various file properties, we can use an XML-based language, called *XFiles* language [4]. The elements of XFiles language will be used to specify different RDF statements about the components of a distributed file system or about the relationship between these components.

D. Grigoras et al. (Eds.): IWCC 2001, LNCS 2326, pp. 224–230, 2002.

2   Resource Description Framework

Resource Description Framework (RDF) is a standardized basis for processing metadata [9]. RDF consists in a model for the representation of named properties and property values. RDF properties may be thought of as attributes of resources and in this sense correspond to traditional attribute–value pairs. RDF properties also represent relationships between resources and therefore a RDF model can resemble an entity–relationship diagram. In object-oriented design terminology, resources correspond to objects and properties correspond to instance variables.

To facilitate the definition of metadata, RDF is based on *classes*. A collection of classes, typically designed for a specific purpose or domain, is called a *schema*. Through the sharability of schemas, RDF supports the reusability of metadata definitions. The RDF schemas may themselves be written in RDF.

2.1   RDF Model

The basic model of RDF consists of three object types:

Resources. All objects being described by RDF expressions are called *resources* and they are always named by *Uniform Resource Identifiers (URI)* [1,5] plus optional anchor identifiers. Using URI schemas (i.e. `http`, `ftp`, `nfs`, or `file` schemas), every type of resource can be identified in the same manner.

Properties. A *property* is a specific aspect, characteristic, attribute, or relation used to describe a resource, as stated in [9]. Each property has a specific meaning, defines its permitted values, the type of resources it can specify, and its relationship with other properties (via RDF Schema).

Statements. A specific resource together with a named property, plus the value of that property for that resource is an RDF *statement*. These three individual parts of a statement are called, respectively, the *subject*, the *predicate*, and the *object*. The object of a statement (e.g., the property value) can be another resource or a literal.

The RDF data model provides an abstract, conceptual framework for defining and using metadata. The concrete RDF syntax is based on *Extensible Markup Language (XML)* [2,5] – a platform independent, World–Wide Web Consortium standardized meta-language.

Using RDF syntax, we can represent in XML the following assertion about the owner of a particular file:

```
<rdf:RDF>
  <rdf:Description about="file:///home/busaco/article.tex"
    <f:Owner>
      <rdf:Description about="http://www.infoiasi.ro/~busaco/">
        <o:Login>busaco</o:Login>
        <o:Group>profs</o:Group>
        <o:Name>Sabin-Corneliu Buraga</o:Name>
      </rdf:Description>
    </f:Owner>
  </rdf:Description>
</rdf:RDF>
```

In this example, we express the following assertion: "The individual referred to `http://www.infoiasi.ro/~busaco/` is named Sabin-Corneliu Buraga and he has as login name `busaco` and his user group is `profs`. The resource (file) `/home/busaco/article.tex` is owned by this individual".

The namespace prefix f refers to a specific namespace prefix chosen by the author of the RDF expression and defined in an XML namespace declaration such as `xmlns:f="http://some.host/files-schema"`. The *rdf* namespace is defined by World–Wide Web Consortium to be specified in every RDF statement. The XML namespaces [3] are used to avoid parsing conflicts for identical elements or attributes names included in the same XML document.

Also, RDF defines three types of container objects:

- *Bag* – an unordered list of resources or literals,
- *Sequence* – an ordered list of resources or literals, and
- *Alternative* – a list of resources or literals that represent alternatives for the single value of a property.

The collections can be used instead of *Description* element.

For example, to specify the user configuration files of the `thor.infoiasi.ro` machine (this host has 193.231.30.225 as IP address), we can write:

```
<rdf:Bag id="ConfigFiles">
  <rdf:li resource="file:///etc/passwd" />
  <rdf:li resource="file:///etc/shadow" />
</rdf:Bag>
<rdf:Description aboutEach="#ConfigFiles">
  <f:Location dns="thor.infoiasi.ro">193.231.30.225</f:Location>
</rdf:Description>
```

The containers may be defined by an URI pattern. RDF can also be used to make statements about other RDF statements (higher-order statements).

2.2   Formal Model for RDF

The RDF data model can have three equivalent representations: as 3-uples, as a graph, and in XML. Formally, the RDF data model is defined as follows [9]:

1. There are three sets called *Resources*, *Literals*, and *Statements*.
   There is a subset *Properties* $\subset$ *Resources*.
   Each element $s \in$ *Statements* is a triple $s = \{pred, sub, obj\}$, where $pred \in$ *Properties*, $sub \in$ *Resources*, and $obj \in$ *Literals* $\cup$ *Resources*.
2. The *reification* of a $\{pred, sub, obj\} \in$ *Statements* is a new resource $r \in$ *Resources* as follows:
   - $s_1 : \{\mathsf{type}, [r], [RDF : Statement]\}$
   - $s_2 : \{\mathsf{predicate}, [r], [pred]\}$
   - $s_3 : \{\mathsf{subject}, [r], [sub]\}$
   - $s_4 : \{\mathsf{object}, [r], [obj]\}$

where s_1, s_2, s_3, $s_4 \in$ *Statements* and type, predicate, subject, object $\in$ *Properties*.

3. There is an element of *Properties* known as *RDF* : *type*. Members of *Statements* of the form { *RDF* : *type, sub, obj* } must satisfy the following condition: *sub* and *obj* are members of *Resources*.

4. There are three elements of *Resources*, not contained in *Properties*, known as *RDF* : *Seq*, *RDF* : *Bag* and *RDF* : *Alt*. There is a subset *Ord* $\subset$ *Properties* corresponding to the ordinals $(1, 2, 3, \ldots)$. We refer to elements of *Ord* as RDF_i, where $i = 1, 2, 3, \ldots$

3   RDF Description of Distributed File Systems

To represent RDF statements about various file characteristics we can use an XML-based language to store file properties, called *XFiles* language. In [4] we present an XML schema for this language. The XML schema is used for validation and parsing purposes.

The root element of an *XFiles* document is the *Properties* element. This element may contain, in any order, the following child elements:

- the *Type* element reflects the file type: ordinary, directory, pipe, symbolic or hard link, character or block device, or socket, on Unix-like systems; the *mime* attribute specifies the MIME (Multipurpose Internet Mail Extensions) type for a file (i.e. `text/html`, `image/gif` or `application/executable`);
- the *Location* element represents the IP address of the host on which a certain file resides; the *dns* attribute is used to specify the Domain Name System (DNS) entry for the given IP address;
- the *Auth* element specifies the authentification method to access a given file (e.g. basic or digest user authentification);
- the *Owner* element includes the information about the owner of a file: login name, password, group, real identity etc.; it is possible to have multiple owners for a single given file;
- the *Size* element specifies the actual file size; *max* attribute denotes the maximum permitted size for a file;
- the *Permissions* element reflects the set of file permissions, e.g. *read*, *write*, *execute* (on Unix) [6] or *Full Control, Change Permissions, Read*, or *Take Ownership* (on Windows) [12]; also, this parameter can be used to store NFS file modes [7];
- the *Timestamp* element gives the possibility to track the access, modification or status-change time of a specific file;
- the *Version* element can be used in a Concurrent Versions System (CVS) environment, for versioning purposes;
- the *Parse* element denotes the application(s) used to process a file (e.g. file editors, compilers, viewers etc.); the *params* attribute can be used to pass additional options to a program.

3.1   Our Proposal and Existing Distributed File Systems

Sun Microsystems defined a remote file access mechanism known as *Network File System* (*NFS*) [7,13]. NFS allows a computer to run a server that makes some of its files available for remote access, and allows various applications on other machines to access those files. NFS uses many of the Unix file system definitions and assumes a hierarchical naming system. Another approach is *Network Information Service* (*NIS*) [14], formerly known as Yellow Pages, used on Linux systems. Our proposed RDF model can be used to describe different remote file hierarchies (multiple hierarchies in an NFS server).

Microsoft proposed *Active Directory* [12] on Windows 2000/XP systems to provide directory service functionality, including a means of centrally organizing, managing, and controlling access to network resources. Active Directory, like NIS, makes the physical network topology and protocol transparent and offers support for management of distributed PCs, network services, and applications. Our proposal can express partial information about the logical structure of Active Directory (domains, organizational units, etc.).

Other approaches are *Prospero* [15] – an Internet-compatible virtual system model based on Uniform Resource Identifiers (URI) and *Coda* [8] – an experimental file system developed at Carnegie Mellon University.

Examples. We give a couple of examples of RDF constructs about the resources of a distributed file system:

To specify an ownership property and a password-based authorization method to access a set of files stored on the local machine and on a remote host, we can define the following RDF assertions:

```
<rdf:RDF>
  <rdf:Bag ID="myfiles">
    <rdf:li resource="file:///tmp/article.tex" />
    <rdf:li resource="ftp://ftp.tuiasi.ro/pub/src/gaen" />
  </rdf:Bag>

  <rdf:Description about="#myfiles">
    <f:Properties>
      <f:Auth>Basic</f:Auth>
      <f:Owner>
        <rdf:Description
          about="http://www.infoiasi.ro/~busaco">
          <f:Login uid="714">busaco</f:Login>
          <f:Password>NU74b33cs</f:Password>
        </rdf:Description>
      </f:Owner>
      <f:Permissions>
        <f:Permission>User-Read</f:Permission>
        <f:Permission>User-Write</f:Permission>
        <f:Permission>Group-Read</f:Permission>
      </f:Permissions>
```

```
    </f:Properties>
  </rdf:Description>
</rdf:RDF>
```

We express the fact: "For the given collection of files, the owner of these files is the user busaco. The files will be accessed by providing a password and only the owner will be able to read and write them. The owner's group members will be able only to read them." The f namespace corresponds to all elements and attributes of our defined *XFiles* language.

The next RDF document specifies the alternatives for a remote execution of an application (an XML parser):

```
<rdf:RDF>
  <rdf:Description about="file://localhost/article.xml">
    <f:Properties>
      <f:Type mime="text/xml">ordinary</f:Type>
      <f:Owner uid="714">busaco</f:Owner>
      <f:Parser params="-q">
        <rdf:Alt>
          <rdf:li>
            <rdf:Description about="file:///sbin/expat">
              <f:Type mime="application/executable">
                ordinary
              </f:Type>
              <f:Location dns="localhost">
                127.0.0.1
              </f:Location>
            </rdf:Description>
          </rdf:li>
          <rdf:li>
            <rdf:Description about="nfs://host/xmled.exe">
              <f:Type mime="application/octet-stream">
                ordinary
              </f:Type>
              <f:Location dns="it2.infoiasi.ro">
                193.231.30.228
              </f:Location>
            </rdf:Description>
          </rdf:li>
        </rdf:Alt>
      </f:Parser>
    </f:Properties>
  </rdf:Description>
</rdf:RDF>
```

In this example, we can observe the use of RDF statements to specify two applications (defined as RDF *Alt* elements), one on the local machine, the second on a Windows file system accessed via NFS. One of these applications will be executed to process the given file (in our example, an XML source file).

4   Conclusions and Further Work

In this paper, we have proposed a RDF description for distributed file systems. Our XML-based approach is platform and implementation independent and can be used for any particular (distributed) file system. The proposed RDF model can be validated and manipulated by *Simple RDF Parser and Compiler (SiR-PAC)* [16], a freely available Java servlet based on Megginson's SAX (Simple API for XML) processor. An implementation of our RDF model can be also based on the *Document Object Model (DOM)* [5,11] specification.

Currently, we are developing a Java servlet that generates various RDF statements about the files of the Linux *ext2fs* file system. We intend to experiment another implementation on Microsoft *.NET* Framework using C# language.

Also, the proposed RDF description of distributed file systems needs to be enriched by formal RDF schemas.

References

1. Berners-Lee, T. et al. (eds.): Uniform Resource Identifiers (URI): General Syntax. Internet Standard, IETF RFC 2396 (1998)
2. Bray, T. et al. (eds.): Extensible Markup Language (XML) – version 1.0 (updated). W3C Recommendation, Boston (2000): `http://www.w3.org/TR/REC-xml`
3. Bray, T., Hollander, D., Layman, A. (eds.): Namespaces in XML. W3C Recommendation, Boston (1999): `http://www.w3.org/TR/REC-xml-names`
4. Buraga, S.: A RDF Description of Distributed File Systems. Scientific Annals of the "Al. I. Cuza" University of Iaşi, Computer Science Series, tome IX (2000) 27–46
5. Buraga, S.: Web Technologies (in Romanian). Matrix Rom, Bucharest (2001)
6. Buraga, S, Ciobanu, G: Programming Workshop on Computer Networks (in Romanian). Polirom Publishing House, Iaşi (2001)
7. Comer, D., Stevens, D.: Internetworking With TCP/IP, Vol. III: Client-Server Programming And Applications. Prentice Hall, New Jersey (1993)
8. Kramer M.: Distributed File Systems. IBM White Paper, Boston (1996)
9. Lassila, O., Swick, R. (eds.): Resource Description Framework (RDF) Model and Syntax Specification. W3C Recommendation, Boston (1999): `http://www.w3.org/TR/REC-rdf-syntax`
10. Silberschatz, A., Peterson, J., Galvin, P.: Operating Systems Concepts. Addison-Wesley, Reading MA (1992)
11. Wood, L. (ed.): Document Object Model (DOM) Level 1 Specification. W3C Recommendation, Boston (1998): `http://www.w3.org/TR/REC-DOM-Level-1`
12. * * *: Microsoft Active Directory (2001): `http://msdn.microsoft.com/`
13. * * *: Network File System (NFS). Internet Standard, IETF RFC 1094 (1991)
14. * * *: Network Information Service (NIS): `http://www.suse.de/~kukuk/nis/`
15. * * *: Prospero Website: `http://www.cuhk.hk/guides/earn/prospero.html`
16. * * *: Simple RDF Parser and Compiler (SiRPAC): `http://www.w3.org/RDF/Implementations/SiRPAC`

Coarse-Grain Parallelization of Test Vectors Generation on Multiprocessor Systems

Felicia Ionescu, Mihail Ionescu, Cristina Coconu, and Valentin Stoica

University Politehnica of Bucharest,
Splaiul Independentei 313, Bucharest, Romania
{fionescu, mionescu, cristina, vstoica}@atm.neuro.pub.ro

Abstract. The paper describes parallel implementation of automatic test vectors generation on multiprocessor systems using Boolean Difference Algorithm. The analysis of the algorithm points out that coarse-grain parallelization involves two types of data-dependencies that require different techniques for removing them: circuit model replication and mutual exclusion mechanisms. Toward balancing load of the work among processors, static and dynamic partitioning of computational task is studied. For each parallelization strategy, the theoretical speedup is estimated in order to select the most efficient implementation. The estimated and measured results show that the speed of automatic test generation can be significantly increased with parallel approach and this is an important achievement in the present technological context, with wide availability of multiprocessors stations.

1 Introduction

Automatic test vectors generation for combinational circuits is intensively studied, since this technique can also be used to test sequential circuits. The test vectors generation algorithms involve searching among the set of input vectors of the circuit that differentiate a fault-free circuit from the faulty one, for a given set of faults. The test vectors generation problem for combinational circuits is NP-complete: no deterministic algorithm with a polynomial time complexity is known to exist [1].

Among test vectors generating techniques, the *algebraic algorithms* use Boolean difference method to test all possible input vectors in order to determine the vectors that can detect a given fault [2]. Boolean Difference Algorithm has exponential complexity time with respect to number of primary inputs and can be used for circuits with many gates but with a small number of primary inputs. Other algorithms use branch-and-bound method to explore search space of possible solutions. In such algorithms every signal is considered as a decision point (like in D-algorithm, [2]), or only input signals are considered as decision points (like PODEM algorithm, [3]) and some heuristics are used to determine next decision point, using topological structure of the circuit.

D. Grigoras et al. (Eds.): IWCC 2001, LNCS 2326, pp. 231-240, 2002.

Automatic test vectors generation for large circuits is a very computational intensive problem. To reduce the execution time, parallel processing is not only required, but also possible, due to the distributed nature of the problem.

The basic objective of the present work is to develop a parallel test vectors generation algorithm in which the speedup increases almost linearly with the number of processors in a multiprocessor system. In multiprocessors systems, processes (or threads) running on different processors communicate with each other by means of shared memory: processes (or threads) can share and concurrently update identical memory locations.

2   Boolean Difference Algorithm

For analysis of Boolean Difference Algorithm (BDA), we consider a combinational circuit with r gates, n signals, m primary inputs and q primary outputs. Logic circuits are modeled as interconnections of gates, with several input signals and one output signal. Signals that are not the output signals of any gate in the circuit are called *primary inputs*. Signals that realize the output functions of the circuit are called *primary outputs*.

A fault is a fabrication failure that can be detected by the functional basis (the output functions of the circuit). One of the most used model of the fault is the model which assumes that a fault causes the inputs or output of logic gates to be permanently "stuck" at logic 0 or 1 (commonly called SA0 or SA1). A fault XSAv is a fault on line (signal) X, which is "stuck at v", where v can be 0 or 1 logic. It can be observed that a circuit with n signals can have 3^n - 1 possible faults, since each signal can be SA0, SA1, or fault free. If it is assumed that only one stuck-at fault will be present at every time, then the number of faults in a circuit with n signals is $F = 2n$.

2.1   Basic Sequential Boolean Difference Algorithm

In object-oriented approach, the circuit model consists in a set of two types of objects, gates and signals, which are instances of two basic classes (Gate and Signal). Gate and signal objects and the interconnections among these objects represent the *topology* of the circuit and this description is unchanged for all tests for a given circuit. All signals in the circuit are shared objects: the value of a signal is set by a gate, when its response to an input vector is evaluated, and all other gates connected to the output of this gate uses this value. The concurrent accesses to signal shared objects will be analyzed for data-dependencies removal in parallel implementation of the algorithm.

An input vector is a test vector if it satisfies the *controllability condition* and the *observability condition*. An input vector, for which the value of signal X is the inverse of v, accomplishes the controllability condition of the fault XSAv. For a fault on line X to be observable, the response of the circuit (the array of primary outputs, Q) must be different at least in one position for the signal X forced at 0 and, respectively, at 1.

The C-like pseudo-code of the sequential *Boolean Difference Algorithm* is:

```
/* Function OneVector() tests if t is a test vector */
OneVector (int t, Signal X, int v){
   for (g=0; g<r; g++)
      Compute the output of gate g;
   if ((X is the output of gate g)&&(X == v)
      return;                 /* Controllability condition is
                                 not satisfied */
   X = 0;
   for (g=0; g<r; g++)
      Compute the output of gate g;    /* Results Q(0) */
   X = 1;
   for (g=0; g<r; g++)
      Compute the output of gate g;    /* Results Q(1) */
   if (Q(0) != Q(1))    /* Observability condition
                           is satisfied*/
      Add t in test vectors list for fault XSAv;
}
BDA(){
   for (f=0; f<2n; f++ ){
      Fault f: XSAv (v=0 or v=1);
      for (t=0; t<2^m; t++)
         OneVector(t, X, v);
   }
}
```

The outer loop (with loop-counter f) of the algorithm processes all $F = 2n$ faults in the circuit. For every fault, the set of 2^m input vectors is searched in order to identify the test vectors in the medium loop (with loop-counter t) of the algorithm. For every input vector, the controllability and observability conditions are evaluated in the function `OneVector()`.

2.2 Sequential Execution Time of BDA

The execution time necessarily to determine if an input vector is a test vector for a given fault has different number of steps (basic operations), depending on the position of the fault in the circuit.

The gates in a combinational circuit can be ordered on several layers, in such a way that a gate from layer k requires signals only from layers 0, 1,...(k-1) [1]. In this ordering, the first layer is the layer of gates connected only at primary inputs and the last layer is the layer that contains only primary outputs

A basic operation in this algorithm is the computation of the output of one gate and has an execution time denoted with t_g. When the fault is on the first layer of gates, the minimum number of basic operations for an input vector is 1 (if the input vector did not satisfies the controllability condition), and the maximum number of basic operations equals $2r +1$(if the input vector satisfies the controllability condition). Results the minimum and maximum execution time for an input vector:

$$T_{V\min} = t_g; \quad T_{V\max} = (2r+1)*t_g. \tag{1}$$

For such a fault, the execution time has a minimum value given by the sum of execution time for all input vectors, which is approximated using medium execution time of input vectors and, with the assumption that $r \gg 1$, has the expression:

$$T_{F\,min} = 2^m * \left(T_{V\,min} + T_{V\,max}\right)/2 = 2^m * (r+1) * t_g = r * 2^m * t_g \,. \tag{2}$$

When the fault is on the last layer of gates, the minimum number of basic operations for an input vector equals r, if the input vector did not satisfy the controllability condition. The maximum number of operations equals $3*r$, if the input vector satisfies the controllability condition. In this situation, the minimum and maximum execution time for an input vector are given by the equations:

$$T_{V\,min}^{'} = r * t_g \,; \quad T_{V\,max}^{'} = 3r * t_g \,. \tag{3}$$

For such a fault, the execution time has a maximum value, given by the sum of execution time for all input vectors, and has the expression:

$$T_{F\,max} = 2^m * \left(T_{V\,min}^{'} + T_{V\,max}^{'}\right)/2 = 2r * 2^m * t_g \,. \tag{4}$$

For a circuit with m primary inputs, r gates and n signals, the sequential execution time T_s is given by the sum of execution time of all faults and has the expression:

$$T_S = 2n * \left(T_{F\,min} + T_{F\,max}\right)/2 = 3n * r * 2^m * t_g \,. \tag{5}$$

If the medium number of signals per gate is q, than the number of the circuits signals is $n = q*r$, and the equation of sequential execution time becomes:

$$T_S = 3n * r * 2^m * t_g = O\!\left(n * r * 2^m\right) = O\!\left(q * r^2 * 2^m\right). \tag{6}$$

This equation reveals an exponential growth of execution time with number of primary inputs (m), a linear growth with the medium number of signals per gate (q) and a quadratic growth with the number of gates (r).

3 Parallelization of Boolean Difference Algorithm

Like other many test vectors generation algorithms, Boolean Difference Algorithm (BDA) presents several levels of parallelism, due to its distributed nature.

Parallelism levels in BDA are pointed out by the nested loops of the algorithm, represented pseudo-code of BDA. Each loop of the algorithm can be distributed among different threads for concurrent execution if the iterations of that loop are data-independent or synchronization mechanisms are provided. These parallelization techniques correspond to coarse-grain parallelization (fault-level, in the case of outer loop distribution), medium-grain parallelization (input vector-level, in the case of medium loop distribution) and, respectively, fine-grain parallelization (gate-level, in the case of inner loops distribution) of the BDA.

In present work, coarse-grain parallelization of BDA on shared-memory multiprocessors is investigated. In this approach, the degree of parallelism equals the number of circuit faults $(2n)$, which, for large circuits, is large enough to allow efficient utilization of processors available in today multiprocessor systems (Silicon Graphics Origin2000 has maximum 128 processors, IBM RS/6000 Model 370 has maximum 14 processors, a. s.o.).

In this parallelization approach, computational tasks are partitioned and distributed to a number of P threads that are concurrently executed on P processors of the system. Two types of partitioning will be considered: static and dynamic. In *static partitioning*, every thread (running on a processor) receives a constant number of tasks (a partition of the faults set) and executes until it finishes the allocated partition. In *dynamic partitioning*, all threads concurrently exploit a shared list of computational tasks (faults list). Each thread extracts one task and executes it; when the current task is finished, the thread extracts a new available task; the execution finishes when all tasks in the tasks list where executed. In order to select the most appropriate parallelization strategy, the parallelization requirements and the performances that can be obtained must be analyzed and compared.

3.1 Coarse-Grain Parallelization of Boolean Difference Algorithm

In *coarse-grain parallelization*, the faults set is distributed among threads, by distribution of the iterations of the outer loop of the algorithm. This loop is data-dependent because in different iterations, the same signal objects are written with different values corresponding to the considered fault.

The solution for concurrent execution of the threads in fault-level parallelism is the replication of the signal objects. For P threads, P replicas of the signal objects are needed and this replication removes the dependencies between iterations: each thread (for a partition of faults set) writes in a different replica of signal objects.

3.2 Static Partitioning of Faults

In static partitioning of the faults, each thread computes test vectors for a partition of $2n/P$ faults, and this partition is established at the start of the algorithm. The program starts with one thread (main thread) which creates P worker threads, with indexes (id) from 0 to $P-1$. A worker thread with index id computes the iterations of outer loop for faults from $f = 2id{\times}n/P$ to $f = 2(id+1){\times}n/P$ on its own circuit model, executing the function `BDStaticThreadFunction()`. In static partitioning of the faults, threads compute equal partitions of iterations ($2n/P$ iterations), but the execution time for different partitions varies because the execution time for an iteration (corresponding to a fault) is not constant (equations 2 and 4 give the minimum and maximum execution time for one fault).

The function BDStaticThreadFunction()is:

```
BDStaticThreadFunction(int id){
    for (f=2*id*n/P; f<2*(id+1)*n/P; f++ ){
    Fault f: XSAv (v=0 or v=1);
    for (t=0; t<2ᵐ; t++)
        OneVector(t,X,v);
    }
}
```

In Fig. 1, a situation with 20 faults, static partitioned among 4 threads, each thread computing 5 iterations (for 5 faults), is represented.

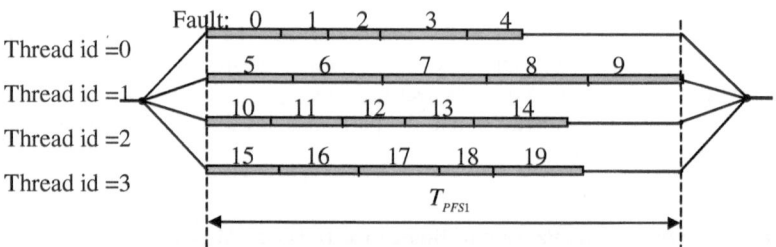

Fig. 1. Load-imbalance in static partitioning of faults.

The parallel execution time has two components. The first component, T_{PFS1}, is the execution time needed for test vectors computation and is given by the thread that works on worst-case (maximum) execution time partition:

$$T_{PFS1} = \frac{2n}{P}T_{F\max} = \frac{4n*r*2^m*t_g}{P}. \tag{7}$$

All other threads, which work on smaller execution time partitions, wait for this thread terminates the work. This waiting time, due to unbalanced load of threads, represents a parallel overhead.

The second component of the parallel execution time, T_{PFS2}, is given by the time spent by the system for threads' creation and scheduling. Supposing that t_c is the medium time required for one thread creation and scheduling and that total creation and scheduling time increases linear with the number of threads, T_{PFS2}, is:

$$T_{PFS2} = P*t_c. \tag{8}$$

Parallel execution time (T_{PFS}) and speedup (S_{FS}) have the expressions:

$$T_{PFS} = T_{PFS1} + T_{PFS2} = \frac{4n*r*2^m*t_g}{P} + P*t_c. \tag{9}$$

$$S_{FS} = \frac{T_S}{T_{PFS}} = \frac{P}{1.33 + \dfrac{P^2 * t_c}{3n * r * 2^m * t_g}}. \tag{10}$$

From equation 10, it is obvious that the speedup increases when one or more of circuit parameters (n, r and m) increase, because the denominator of the ratio decreases. Experimental measurements (presented in the last section) confirm this behavior of the speedup. To study speedup behavior with respect to number of processors (P), the speedup equation is written in a general form as:

$$S = \frac{P}{1 + D(P,n,r,m)}. \tag{11}$$

The speedup (S) increases with number of processors (P) if the derivative of S with respect to P is positive, i.e. $dS/dP > 0$. From equation 11, we can write:

$$\frac{dS}{dP} = \frac{1 + D - P\dfrac{dD}{dP}}{\left(1 + D^2\right)}. \tag{12}$$

The condition $dS / dP > 0$ becomes:

$$P < 2\sqrt{n * r * 2^m * \frac{t_g}{t_c}}. \tag{13}$$

Equation 13 establishes that, for a given circuit complexity, the speedup increases when the number of processors increases, only if the number of processors remains below a limit value. Considering the ratio t_g/t_c as a constant (depending on multiprocessor system) with a value near unit (1), the condition 13 is fulfilled almost always. So, for a relative small circuit (with $n = 32$, $r = 8$, $m = 4$), for limit number of processors is 128. For a large circuit (with $n = 4096$, $r = 1024$, $m = 10$) the limit number of processors is 2^{17} (131072), which is a huge value, unreached by today available multiprocessor systems.

3.3 Dynamic Partitioning of Faults

Because the iterations of the loop that are distributed in fault-level parallelism approach have different execution time, static partitioning involves a load-imbalance overhead: all threads except one wait the termination of those thread that processes worst-case execution time partition. This overhead can be eliminated with a dynamic partitioning of the faults set. In dynamic partitioning, all faults are arranged in a list, shared accessed by all threads. The threads concurrently access this list and every thread extracts an available task (a fault for which the test vectors will be determined) from the list and executes it.

The operation of extracting a fault from the faults' list is a critical section because two or more threads concurrently update the faults' list status. For correct execution of the critical section, a synchronization object (a mutual exclusion object- *mutex*) is used. From all concurrent threads, only the thread that acquires the mutex (with lock_mutex operation) can access the shared faults list, while all other threads must wait until the mutex is released (with unlock_mutex).

The function executed by a thread in dynamic partitioning of the faults is:

```
BDDynamicThreadFunction() {
  while(status<2*n) {
    lock_mutex;
    f = fault_list[status];      /* f = XSAv; */
    status++;
    unlock_mutex;
    for (t=0; t<2^m; t++)
      OneVector(t,X,v);
  }
}
```

Parallel execution time in fault-level parallelism with dynamic partitioning of faults set is constituted of 3 components. The first component (T_{PFD1}) is the time spent by threads to determine the test vectors for all possible faults. Due to the fact that no thread wait another threads to finish, the execution time for all faults (T_s) is evenly distributed to the threads, so that:

$$T_{PFD1} = \frac{T_S}{P} = \frac{3n*r*2^m*t_g}{P}.$$ (14)

The threads can compute different number of faults, but their execution time is nearly perfect balanced. At most one fault execution time imbalance occurs, when a thread processes last fault, while all others have finished the work, but this load-imbalance can be neglected.

The second component (T_{PFD2}) of the parallel execution time is the time needed for threads creation and scheduling and has the same expression like for static partitioning (equation 8).

In dynamic partitioning, a new component of the parallel execution time appears (T_{PFD3}), namely the time consumed by threads in synchronization accesses to shared faults list. If time amount t_s is needed for mutex acquiring and release, the time spent for mutex accesses for $2n$ faults extraction operations from the faults list is:

$$T_{PFD3} = 2n*t_s .$$ (15)

The total parallel execution time T_{PFD} and speedup (S_{FD}) in dynamic partitioning of faults are:

$$T_{PFD} = T_{PFD1} + T_{PFD2} + T_{PFD3} = \frac{3n*r*2^m*t_g}{P} + P*t_c + 2n*t_s .$$ (16)

$$S_{FD} = \frac{T_S}{T_{FDP}} = \frac{P}{1 + \dfrac{P^2 * t_c}{3n * r * 2^m * t_g} + \dfrac{2P * t_s}{3r * 2^m * t_g}}. \qquad (17)$$

Like for static partitioning of faults set, if the number of processors is constant, the speedup increases with the number of gates (r), number of signals (n) and the number of primary inputs (m) and these results are confirmed by measurements presented in the last section. The behavior of the speedup with respect to number of processors is similar with the previous case: the speedup increases with the number of processors (P) if P remains below a limit value and this value is enough large to be fulfilled by all available multiprocessors systems. To compare the speedup in dynamic partitioning with that obtained in static partitioning, the terms D (P,n,r,m) of the speedup equations are compared. From equations 10 and 17, it can be written:

$$D_{FS} = 0.33 + \frac{P^2 * t_c}{3n * r * 2^m * t_g}; \quad D_{FD} = \frac{P^2 * t_c}{3n * r * 2^m * t_g} + \frac{2P * t_s}{3r * 2^m * t_g}. \qquad (18)$$

Results that $D_{FD} < D_{FS}$ and $S_{FD} > S_{FS}$ if:

$$P < \sqrt{n * r * 2^m * \frac{t_g}{t_c}}. \qquad (19)$$

The condition 19 is fulfilled almost always, which means that dynamic partitioning is more efficient then static partitioning of faults set.

4   Experimental Results and Conclusions

Fig. 2. presents the experimental results obtained on IBM RS/6000 multiprocessor, under AIX V4.3 operating system and POSIX threads.

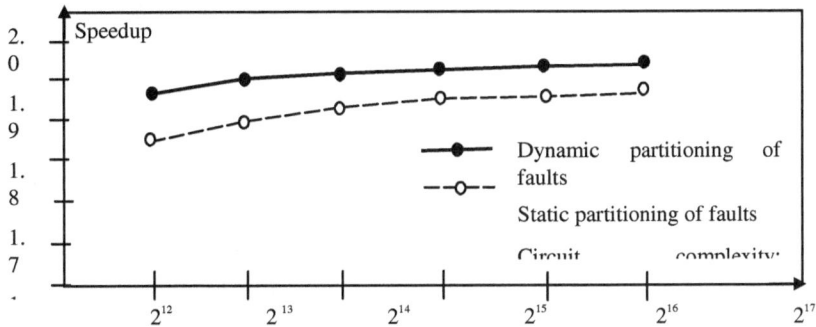

Fig. 2. Speedup as function of circuit complexity (number of inputs m, number of gates r), for $P = 2$, $q=4$, and different parallelization strategies

The dynamic partitioning of tasks is better that static partitioning, due to load balancing of the work, which involves lower parallel overhead. Dynamic partitioning of tasks needs a shared tasks list, concurrently accessed and updated by all threads, but this requirement is efficiently accomplished in multiprocessors systems with shared memory.

The results of this study show that significant speedups can be obtained for test vectors generation for combinational circuits through coarse-grain parallel processing on multiprocessors system and this is an important aspect in the present context, with wide availability of multiprocessors systems.

References

1. *Chakradhar, S., Agrawal, V.D., Bushnell, M.* - Neural Models and Algorithms for Digital Testing, Kluwer Academic, Boston, 1991.
2. *Abramovici, M., Breuer, M.A., Friedman, A.D.* – Digital Systems Testing and Testable Design, Computer Science Press, New York, 1990.
3. *Goel, P.* - An implicit enumeration algorithm to generate tests for combinational circuits, IEEE Transactions on Computers, vol. 30, no.3,March 1981.
4. Kramer, G.- Employing Massive Parallelism in Digital ATPG Algorithms, Proceedings of the IEEE International Test Conference, 1983, pp.108-112.
5. Siennicki, J., Bushnell, M.L., Agrawal, P., Agrawal, V.D., An asynchronous Algorithm for Sequential Circuit Test Generation on a Network of Workstations, Proceedings of the 8-th International Conference on VLSI Design, January 1995, pp.37-42.

OpenMP/MPI Programming in a Multi-cluster System Based on Shared Memory/Message Passing Communication

Adam Smyk and Marek Tudruj

Polish - Japanese Institute of Information Technology,
ul. Koszykowa 86, 02-008 Warsaw, Poland
{asmyk,tudruj}@pjwstk.edu.pl

Abstract. The paper presents parallel implementation of the *FDTD* method that is used for computer simulation of high frequency electromagnetic field propagation. The parallel implementation is based on simultaneous application of message passing communication in distributed memory multi-processor environment (*MPI* library) and communication by shared variables in the environment with shared memory (*OpenMP* library). The methodology of mixed communication mode with message passing and shared memory is presented. Parallel versions of the *FDTD* computation programs were tested in the system composed of four shared memory processor clusters additionally connected by message passing networks. Program execution efficiency measurements and comparisons for different communication versions are presented.

1 Introduction

This paper concerns parallel computer modeling of electromagnetic wave propagation in two-dimensional space using the *FDTD* (*Finite Difference Time Domain*) method [1]. Some *FDTD* implementations in different parallel systems have been already described [2]-[4]. In our paper, special attention is put on the communication model that has been used in the *FDTD* programs. Our experiments were carried out using a system composed of four computer clusters, which were built of four processors that shared a common memory. Such systems are very popular today [5]-[7] and have the following advantages: flexible structure, adjustable functional characteristics, easy scalability and low cost. The system has inter-processor communication composed of two paradigms: message passing and access to a shared memory [8]. Shared memory clusters contained in the system are connected using two message passing networks with different data throughputs. The *FDTD* programs in *C* language are parallelised using data and code distribution among different processors. Data, which describe electromagnetic wave propagation states, are distributed among parallel processors of the clusters. Parallel processing inside processor clusters was based on multi-threading technique organized by using the *OpenMP* library [9]. Communication between processes in processors from different clusters was implemented by message passing with the use of the *MPI* (*Message Passing Interface*) library [10].

D. Grigoras et al. (Eds.): IWCC 2001, LNCS 2326, pp. 241–248, 2002.

Program execution speed-up was evaluated for different parallelisation methods and for different kinds of communication. The combination of two kinds of parallel libraries, shared memory *OpenMP* and message passing *MPI*, provides better speed-up than the unique use of the *MPI*. The use of the very fast *Myrinet* network [11] for message passing was studied against the mixed communication with slower *FastEthernet* [12] network.

The paper is composed of four main parts. In the first part, some methodology for mixing message passing and shared memory communication is presented. In the second part, the analysed parallel application is described. The third part presents details of the program code design. The last part described the experiments and discusses their results.

2   Mixing the *MPI* and *OpenMP* Libraries

The *MPI* is a very popular communication library based on message passing. The *OpenMP* library is used for parallel applications based on multi-threading with shared memory communication. Both libraries can be used in programs written in *Fortran, C* and *C++*. The idea of "mixed communication mode" programming consists in joining an available message passing executive environment with a shared memory environment [11] that enables an efficient use of advantages of both environments, Fig. 1. At first, the sequential code is analyzed to detect its properties useful for execution in the multi-processor distributed memory environment including such features as code scalability and load balancing.

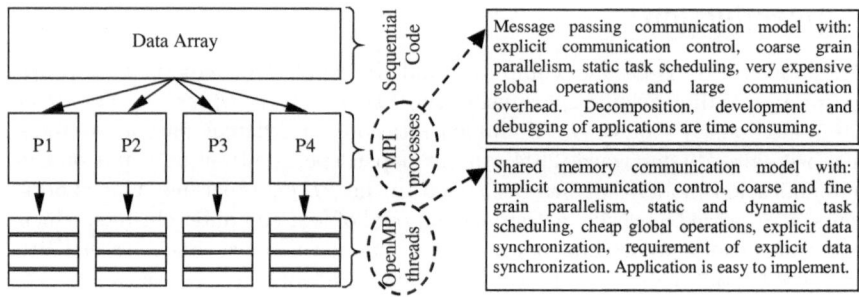

Fig. 1. Mixed mode programming.

Then, the parallel code is prepared using available communication libraries (*MPI, PVM*) and the program design tools (such as graphical program design environment *GRADE* [16]). Next, taking into account that each parallel process can (at a limit) execute a different part of the sequential code, parallel processes have to be individually modified by inclusion of respective directives and functions of the *OpenMP*. Special attention should be put to inter-process communication and synchronization functions performed by message passing (*MPI*). Such communication should be located in code performed by a single thread. If for some reasons, the communication has to be placed in a parallel region, the communication has to be performed in sections critical, master or single, otherwise synchronization of processes placed on different *SMP* nodes can be difficult. Fig. 1 presents also main features of the *MPI* and *OpenMP* libraries, which should be considered while writing applications based on distributed and shared memory communication environments. The main problem that appears in the case of distributed environment, is the scalability of applications and the balancing of computational loads of processors (load balancing). It is particularly important in fine-grain parallel applications where an increase of the number of used processors should speed-up computation (good scalability). This is not obvious, since more intensive communication due to the increased number of parallel processes assigned to different processors, may involve too-big communication time overhead, which can eliminate the speed-up resulting from parallel computation. If the application code scales well in the shared memory environment, then the mixed mode can increase the computation speed-up providing that the distributed memory environment is used for the coarse-grain computation parallelisation and the shared memory environment is used for fine-grain parallelisation of computational loops. Next feature, which makes universal parallelisation difficult, is the necessity to define the number of processors before program execution. It makes that dynamic control of involved parallel processes is impossible or can be achieved by introduction of additional conditional, communication and synchronization instructions that result in the strong complication of the code and the increase of communication, which reduces the expected speed-up. In such case, on each *SMP* node there should be organized a process that will be generating additional threads during program execution, depending on the size of the problem and the number of available processors.

3   Parallel Computation Method

High frequency electromagnetic field propagation is described by Maxwell equations that determine values of electric and magnetic field in each point of the area under analysis. For computer modeling based on the *FDTD* method, the physical area in which the propagation of the electromagnetic field is analysed and described using a set of *Yee* cells [13] placed at intersections of a two-dimensional 2D mesh. The area contains the source of the electromagnetic wave (antenna) and a dielectric. Taking into account the *Mur* boundary conditions [14], the values of the electric and magnetic fields in given cells depend on physical properties of these cells and the field values in neighbouring cells. Parallel computation is used for the *FDTD* method to reduce computation time. The applied parallelisation technique, Fig. 2, is based on decomposition of the program into many processes assigned to separate processors and on further decomposition of processes into parallel threads executed in different processors sharing the same memory. All the analyzed area has been mapped into a two-dimensional data matrix. The elements of the matrix contains descriptions of the physical properties of the cells. The data matrix is decomposed into sub-matrices assigned to parallel processes. The inter-process communication is performed by message passing. Parallel processes compute vectors Ez, Hx and Hy that correspond to sub-sets of *Yee* cells, using the respective data matrix parts. The processes can be programmed in such a way that, during computation, internal computation threads are created for parallel execution of the most time-consuming loops in functions. Threads of a process are assigned to processors of the same *SMP* node to which the process is assigned. Threads communicate by common variables in the shared memory of the node.

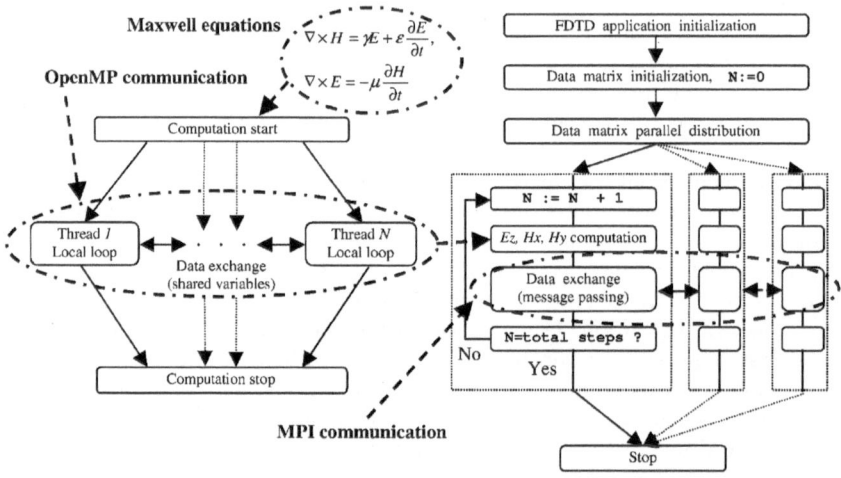

Fig. 2. FDTD computation scheme (*MPI* processes and *OpenMP* threads distribution).

4   Design of the *FDTD* Program Code

The main parallel program design problems are: scalability and balancing of computational loads of processors. It is especially important for fine-grain parallel applications where increasing number of processors should not deteriorate speed-up of computation per processor. The schematic of the 2D *FDTD* program based on the joint use of *MPI* and *OpenMP* libraries is presented in Fig. 3. First several lines of the code perform initialization of the *MPI* library with stating of the number of parallel processes (numbcpu), reading of input data and initialization of the *OpenMP* library for a number of threads (THREAD_NUMBER). The essential part of the code that is copied in parallel processes, constitutes a for loop (with NR_STEPS iterations that correspond to the number of time steps) based on a sequence of execution phases. The functions in the phases perform computations and *MPI* communication between parallel processes. Mixed mode communication is used in implementation of functions that compute the initialisation of the antenna (WaveSource(n)), the boundary *Mur* conditions, computing electric and magnetic field vectors. Two versions of the code for evaluation

of the electric field vector **Ez** in each cell of the analyzed area are presented in
Fig. 3 (right side). The **Ez** function is composed of two nested computation loops
that are executed for a given scope of cells (**X** and **Y**), which is determined for the
assumed number of *MPI* processes. These loops are computationally intensive.

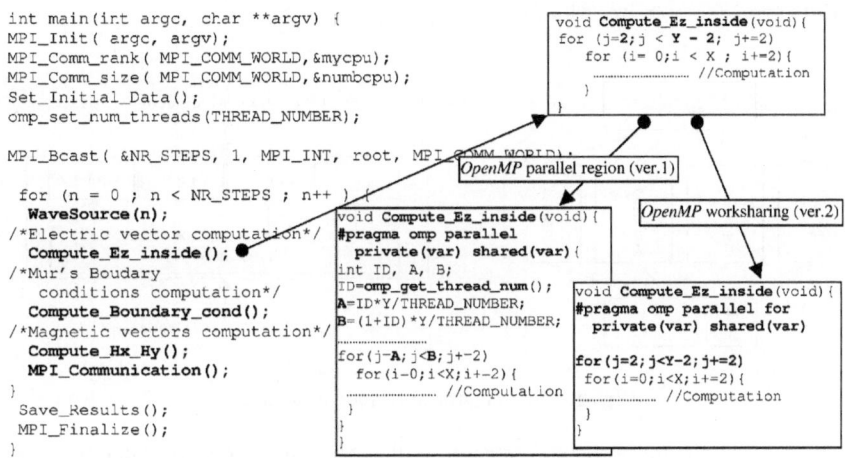

Fig. 3. FDTD computation scheme (Application program scheme.)

The *OpenMP* library is used to distribute data and computations between parallel threads. In Fig. 3 (ver.1), a parallel region is created which will be computed
by dynamically created threads in this region (**#pragma omp parallel**). Each
thread computes a distinct sub-area of cells, so the new data scopes (**A** and **B**)
are assigned for each thread. In Fig. 3 (ver.2), the worksharing facility of the
OpenMP library (**#pragma omp parallel for**) is used. It results in automatic
distribution of the external loop between a determined number of threads. In the
second case, the possibility of taking a wrong decision is very small since there
is no change of the original code as opposite to the first case (the loop structure
and the rest of the code are not changed).

5   Experimental Results

The described *FDTD* application has been tested in an *SMP* cluster based on four
SMP computers connected using *FastEthernet* and *Myrinet* external networks,
Fig. 4(*left*). Each *SMP* computer (DELL PowerEdge 6300 PC-Server) consisted
of four processors Pentium-II Xeon 450 MHz, which shared a common memory
(2GB EDO-DRAM per node), Fig. 4(*right*). The experiments were carried out
for constant dimensions of the analyzed area (2500x500 cells). The numbers of
time steps were 10, 100, 1000 and 10000. Inter-processor communication inside
SMP nodes was tested for three cases: shared memory, the *MPI* and *OpenMP*
libraries. Communication between *SMP* nodes was done in *MPI*. The experiments

were performed for two different methods of parallel computation decomposition and different mappings of communication into physical system networks. The first method consisted in assigning one process to each separate processor in the system (16 processes, four processes on each *SMP* node). In this case, each process contained a single thread, all communication was in *MPI* and included 15 data transfers per iteration.

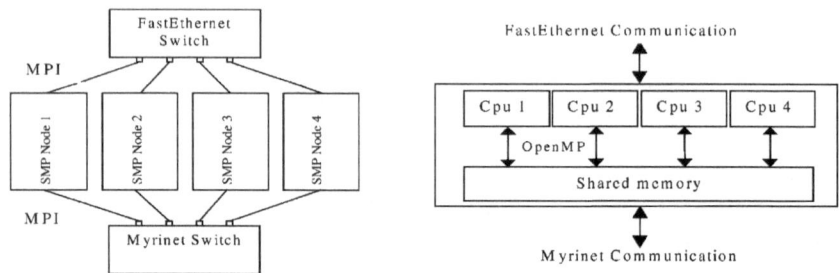

Fig. 4. SMP cluster and node schemes.

With the second method, one process, which contained four parallel threads, was allocated to each *SMP* node, with each thread on a different processor. In this case, the inter-process communication was done in *MPI* and inter-thread communication was done in *OpenMP*. The *MPI* communication included only 3 data transfers per iteration. Program execution speed-up measurements are shown in Fig. 5(*left*). With allocation of up to 16 processes to different processors (single *OpenMP* threads), *MPI* communication and *FastEthernet* external network (100Mbits/sec), the maximal speed-up was 5. With the similar allocation scheme but a much faster *Myrinet* network (800Mbits/sec), the maximal speed-up was equal to 10.

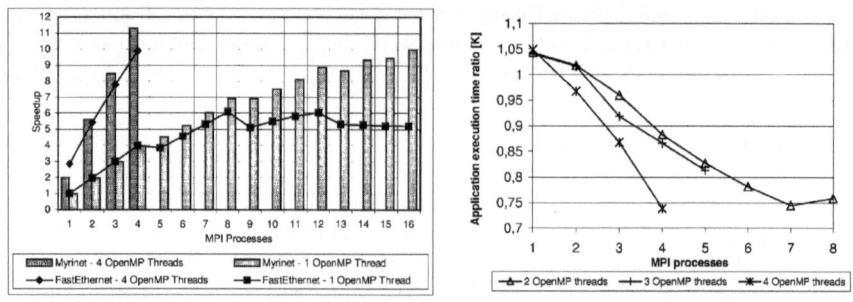

Fig. 5. FDTD program speed-up and program execution time ratio.

With such decomposition of computation, the speed-up for both types of networks is comparable for the number of processors not bigger than 8. For bigger number of processors, the speed-up obtained for the *Myrinet* network was much better, with a maximal factor of 2. With the "mixed mode" communication and decomposition of computation into up to 4 *MPI* processes on each *SMP* node, each of which creates 4 *OpenMP* threads, the speed-up with the *FastEthernet* network was equal from 3 to 10. The similar computation decomposition method for the *Myrinet* network gave the speed-up from 2 to 11. Thus, for mixed mode communication, the speed-up for different speeds of external network was approximately the same. A comparison of the process-based computation decomposition and *MPI* communication with mixed decomposition into processes with multiple threads and mixed mode communication shows that for the same number of threads and the *Myrinet* network, the obtained speed-up is very similar. It means that the use of 15 times faster *Myrinet* network is equivalent to the use of a better, mixed mode communication. Similar comparison for the *FastEthernet* network showed the superiority of the mixed communication mode with the factor of about 3.

The ratio (K) of execution time for parallel application versions with two different strategies of program decomposition of threads as function of number of *MPI* processes is shown in the Fig. 5(*right*). K represents the ratio of the execution time of the program based on *OpenMP* parallel regions (`#pragma omp parallel`) and the execution time of the same program based on worksharing (`#pragma omp parallel for`). In the first case, decomposition into threads is explicitly defined by the programmer, while in the latter case, it is done automatically by *OpenMP* system. We can see, that the execution time with *OpenMP* parallel regions is even up to 25% shorter than execution time with *OpenMP* worksharing. So, the programmer contribution to implementation of *OpenMP* parallel regions is important for the efficiency of the program.

6   Conclusions

The paper presented an evaluation of parallel implementation of the *FDTD* method in a system based on dual communication: message passing and shared memory. Communication by message passing was done through the *MPI* library. Shared memory communication was based on the *OpenMP* library. The biggest computing speed-up, slightly better than 11, was obtained with mixed communication based on 4 *MPI* processes with 4 *OpenMP* threads, each process allocated to an *SMP* computer connected by the *Myrinet* network. This speed-up was bigger than the speed-up obtained with exclusively *MPI* communication and 16 processors. The application of the very fast *Myrinet* network enabled to obtain the comparable speed-ups for the *MPI* and mixed mode communication for the same total number of threads. So, the 15 times higher communication speed of the *Myrinet* network (with the reduced *MPI* communication in the application program) permitted to match the advantages of the mixed communication mode. The experiments have proved that the optimization done by the programmer can give better results than the automatic loop parallelisation provided by *OpenMP*.

When the maximal efficiency of the produced code should be obtained, the decomposition of loops into parallel threads should be implemented by using the *OpenMP* parallel region facility. When the speed and low cost of the program design are important, one can use automatic parallelisation facility (*OpenMP* worksharing should be applied). However, in this case, one can expect less efficient programs (up to 25%) comparing the case of a manual design of parallel regions.

This work has been done in the frame of the KBN research grant 8T10A 050 18 and an internal research grant of PJIIT.

References

1. K.S.Kunz, R.J.Luebers: *The Finite Difference Time Domain Method for Electromagnetics*, CRC Press Inc., 1993.
2. A.Jordan, B.Butrylo: Parallel Computations of Electromagnetic wave Propagation, Int. Conf. On Parallel computing in Electrical Engineering, *PARELEC '98*, pp. 296-300, Bialystok, 1998
3. L.Nicolas, C.Volaire, A Survey of Computational Electromagnetics on MIMD Systems, Int. Conf. On Parallel computing in Electrical Engineering, *PARELEC '98*, pp. 7 - 19, Bialystok, 1998
4. J.Forenc, A.Skorek, Analysis of High Frequency Electromagnetic Wave Propagation Using Parallel MIMD Computer and Cluster System, International Conference on Parallel Computing in Electrical Engineering, *PARALEC'2000*, Trois-Rivieres, Quebec, Canada, 27-30 August 2000
5. Y.Kanaka, M.Matsuda, M.Ando, K.Kazuto, M.Sato: COMPaS: A Pentium Pro PC-based SMP Cluster and its Experience, *IPPS Workshop on Personal Computer Based Networks of Workstations*, LNCS 1388, pp. 486-497. 1998.
6. *Pentium Pro Cluster Workshop*, http://www.scl.ameslab.gov/workshops/.
7. *Scalable Clusters of Commodity Computers*, http://www.csag.cs.uiuc.edu/projects/clusters.html.
8. B.Wilkinson, M.Allen: *Parallel Programming Techniques and Applications using Networked Clusters of Workstations and Parallel Comp.*, Prentice Hall 1999, pp 450.
9. *OpenMP*, http://www.OpenMP.org.
10. M.Snir et al.: *MPI, The Complete Reference*, The MIT Press, 1998.
11. N.J.Boden, D.Cohen et al. *Myrinet - Gigabit-per-second Local-Area Network, IEEE MICRO*, Vol. 15, No.1, 1996, pp. 29-36.
12. *Ethernet Technologies*, http://www.cisco.com/univercd/cc/td/doc/cisintwk/ito_doc/ethernet.htm.
13. K.S.Yee: *Numerical Solution of Initial Boundary Value Problems Maxwell's Equations in Isotropic Media, IEEE Trans. On Antennas and Propagation*, Vol. AP-14, N. 3, pp. 302-307, (1966).
14. G.Mur: *Absorbing Boundary Conditions for the Finite-Difference Approximation of the Time-Domain Electromagnetic Field Equations*, IEEE Trans. on Biomed. Eng., Vol. BME-34, N. 2, pp. 148-157, (1987).
15. L.Smith, M.Bulk: Development of Mixed Mode *MPI/OpenMP* Applications, *WOMPAT 2000*, San Diego Supercomputer Center, California, July 6th-7th, 2000.
16. *P-GRADE, A Professional Graphical Parallel Programming Environment*, http://www.lpds.sztaki.hu/projects/p-grade/.

Expressing Parallelism in Java Applications Distributed on Clusters

Violeta Felea[1], Nathalie Devesa[1,2], Bernard Toursel[1,2], and Pierre Lecouffe[3]

[1] LIFL (UPRESA CNRS 8022) - University of Science and Technology of Lille
59655 Villeneuve d'Ascq CEDEX - FRANCE
{felea,devesa,toursel}@lifl.fr, lecouffe@iut-info.univ-lille1.fr
[2] École Universitaire d'Ingénieurs de Lille (EUDIL)
[3] Institut Universitaire de Technologies A (IUTA) - Lille

Abstract. Java threads allow to express parallelism of a Java application. However, integrating parallelism in the context of distributed object systems, namely in the Java RMI context, raises problems at both conceptual and implementation levels. This article presents an useful tool, the distributed collection, which allows the expression of parallelism and an easy recovery of the results. The parallelism proposed associates the two approaches: the data parallelism, through fragmented data and the task parallelism using asynchronous calls. We show the interest of distributed collections, evaluating the facility in the conception of distributed and parallel Java programs.

1 Introduction

Distributed object computing is a computing paradigm that allows objects to be distributed across heterogeneous networks and allows each of the components to interoperate as a unified whole. Three of the most popular distributed object paradigms are: Microsoft's Distributed Component Model (DCOM [10]), OMG's Common Object Request Broker Architecture (CORBA [11]) and JavaSoft's Java Remote Method Invocation (Java/RMI [12]). All of these techniques are similar as they consider the server-client architecture model. Consequently, the programming models for these paradigms are using a server-client programming model. At the same level, of the conception, in the Java/RMI programming model, synchronous remote calls constitute a drawback in performances. On the execution level, deploying applications over the execution platform is neither automatic not optimal.

The ADAJ environment (Adaptive Distributed Applications in Java) proposes strategies in the conception of distributed and parallel applications and mechanisms to improve execution of distributed processing on a cluster of workstations, in the context of distributed Java RMI objects.

In order to make execution more efficient, load balancing mechanisms are to be introduced at the middleware level. These mechanisms are based on information issued from an observation tool [2] of the relations between objects, proposed by ADAJ. This tool analyses the behavior of applications as well as of

D. Grigoras et al. (Eds.): IWCC 2001, LNCS 2326, pp. 249–258, 2002.

the platform during the execution. This approach is associated to the conception tools proposed in order to improve the efficiency of the execution and in order to make an automatic distribution of applications over the cluster.

In this article, we present a conceptual approach in order to easily express parallelism in programs executing in a distributed environment. Based on the structure of distributed collections, this approach integrates both data and task parallelism in the conception of applications. Data parallelism consists of processing different data in parallel. This possibility is offered by data fragmentation and distribution. Task parallelism, independently of the data placement, enables processing different tasks on the same data.

The article is structured into 9 sections: the second one describes briefly the ADAJ programming and execution environment and presents the expression of parallelism in ADAJ, introducing the concept of distributed collection; the concept is explained later, at a functional level in section 3 and at an implementation level in section 6. The fourth section presents the functionalities attached to the distributed collection, and section 5 deals with the recovery of the results. Section 7 partially evaluates the distributed collections, while section 8 makes comparisons with other related works. We conclude in section 9.

2   Expressing Parallelism in ADAJ

ADAJ is designed as a programming and execution environment for distributed and parallel object oriented applications. It is dedicated to cluster computing, over heterogeneous platforms, but oriented homogeneous programming provided by the Java language. This environment uses the concept of distributed class introduced by the JavaParty project [1]. A distributed class extends a classical Java class on a distributed environment. It groups objects, named *remote* objects, of a same class, which can be instantiated on different machines. Consequently, a distributed class makes remote objects' creation possible and the distribution of objects throughout the network. These objects appear as though they were local within the application. ADAJ introduces the *global* objects, an extension of the *remote* objects, which can be remote accessible, can migrate and are observable (considered by the observation tool [2]). Classical Java objects are supported by the ADAJ applications, as *local* objects; they have the Java object's semantics, being neither remote accessible, nor can migrate.

The aim of ADAJ is to improve the efficiency of task execution, which can be explicitly decomposed in independent sub-tasks, in a multithreading system. ADAJ addresses problems about the conception of a parallel program, offering a simple expression of parallelism. ADAJ also proposes an implicit data distribution and exploits the data parallelism.

2.1   Data Parallelism

In the presented environment, our objectives can not be achieved either by using the JGL libraries of the Voyager project [4] which do not take advantage of multithreading, or by the remote vectors of the first version of JavaParty (not developed in the second) that do not offer any possibility of data processing.

Our objectives could be achieved through the JavaParty vectors, that are equivalent to the Java vectors in distributed system, but data scattering is source of inefficiency in the execution. ADAJ proposes a hierarchical structure, named *distributed collection*, which groups objects in fragments; data parallelism is obtained by parallel activations of threads on fragments. Exploiting data parallelism through fragmented data has first been introduced in the ACADA project [9], implemented in C++.

The sequential processing of a fragment takes advantage of the locality of data in a fragment. In this way, the distributed collections propose a methodology of programming for expressing parallel processing. ADAJ offers a design tool for the conception of parallel programs, proposing parallel and distributed operators, and also synchronous operators applied to the "future object" (see section 5) which allow the deferred recovery of the results.

The fragments are distributed according to the implicit distribution strategy proposed by ADAJ which considers static information (static analysis of code) as well as dynamic information, as the load of the machines for the instantiation, or information issued from the observation tool (the relations between objects) for the redistribution. The distribution of the objects in the fragments is explicit; in this way, the distributed collection allows to control the granularity of parallelism, through the quantity of data in fragments. Activation of a parallel task on all objects is replaced with activation of parallel tasks on fragments. This mechanism is completely transparent for the user. The distribution of fragments contributes to the adaptability of the application to the evolution of computation and to the modifications of the execution platform.

2.2   Task Parallelism

In ADAJ project, the expression of a conventional task parallelism is achieved through asynchronous calls on global objects. This is a more general technique used to achieve parallelism, already proposed by the Jacob [7] and the ProActive PDC [3] Java projects. Asynchronous calls on global objects are also used to anticipate results. This facility creates parallel programs which integrate task parallelism. In this article, we detail the data parallelism achieved through the distributed collections.

3   Hierarchy of the Distributed Collection

The local Java collections [5] are not appropriate structures from two points of view: on one hand, the locality of all data is not adapted for a distributed environment and on the other hand, local collections do not offer a suitable framework for the distribution of tasks. ADAJ intends to distribute its applications on the JVMs (Java Virtual Machine), in order to have efficient parallel processing execution. Therefore, integrating the Java collection framework in a distributed environment, ADAJ proposes a hierarchical structure, the distributed collection. Its root is a *fragmented object*. On the second level there are the *fragments*, containing data.

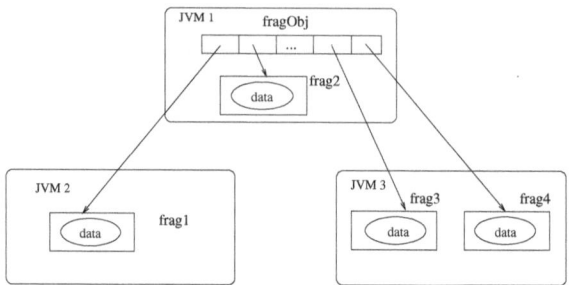

Fig. 1. The structure of a distributed collection

Figure 1 presents the structure of a distributed collection, on two levels: the first one is composed of a fragmented object, *fragObj*, located on the first JVM (JVM1), and the second level is composed of four fragments (*frag1, frag2, frag3* and *frag4*) respectively, distributed on the Java machines 2, 1 and 3. The fragments contain data. We note that we can have several fragments on the same JVM and the fragmented object and fragments can be placed on the same JVM. The hierarchical structure of a distributed collection will allow distribution of data processing, associated to the data placement.

3.1   Fragmented Objects and Fragments

The fragmented object is a global object, because it needs to be remote accessible. It offers the same functionalities as a Java vector object, allowing: to get information about its size (the number of fragments), to find a fragment or the index of a given fragment, to manipulate fragments by their numerical position, or to iterate on the fragments.

The fragments are also global objects, consequently, they are observable objects and can migrate. They can contain either local or global objects. The fragment and the objects it contains should be on the same virtual machine, in order to give locality for the parallel processing. Moreover, if objects in the fragment are local, a migration of the fragment, in the case of load imbalance, does not generate auxiliary remote communication because of the local object's semantics (copies of local objects are created on the machine that receives the fragment).

The amount of data contained in the fragments is decided by the user. Consequently, granularity of parallelism is controlled by the user through the distributed collection.

The number of fragments which are created is correlated to the number of machines in the cluster. When having several fragments on the same virtual machine, the load balancing can be efficient.

The cyclic placement of fragments on the JVMs and the explicit mechanism of migration proposed by the JavaParty project are only tools for redistributing objects. An adaptive placement, taking into account the loads of the machines, and an implicit decision of migration could improve performances of execution whether a load imbalance is detected.

In ADAJ, basing ourselves on the default mechanism of migration offered by JavaParty, we intend to integrate another migration tool, specific to fragments. Active fragments (for which one method is being executing) will be able to migrate; this is not possible for the moment in the current JavaParty version. This new tool of migration is under development and it uses a technique of postcompilation [16].

4   Parallel Processing Distribution

Invoking a parallel task on each data contained in the distributed collection leads to a small granularity of parallelism. The distributed collection, through its structure, controls the granularity of parallelism. The activation of parallel tasks on all objects is replaced by the activation of parallel tasks on the fragments.

Thus, the *distribute* primitive, attached to the distributed collection, iterates over and applies a specified task on all fragments of the distributed collection; doing this sequentially is inefficient; moreover, it slows the execution by the overload due to the construction of such a structure. In order to allow parallelism, this primitive invokes asynchronously the specified task on each fragment. Besides, as a task may return results, these are automatically recovered in a particular structure presented in section 5.

The *distribute* primitive needs the following information: the distributed collection, the task to be executed on every fragment, the parameters needed by the task and a particular structure, named *collector* (presented in the next section), which allows to recover the results.

The left part of figure 2 presents an example of a call of a *distribute* primitive on the distributed collection whose root, the *fragObj* object, is placed on the first JVM. Threads (T in the figure), one per fragment, are launched on the JVM1 in order to achieve asynchronism. They spawn the specified task on the corresponding fragment; one JVM can support several fragments (the RMI threads in the figure are part of the RMI protocol of remote task execution).

5   Result Recovery

Parallel tasks on fragments may return different results, as they are executing on different fragments containing several data. In order to recover these results, a reception structure for the results recovery and processing is introduced: the *collector* (see the right part of figure 2).

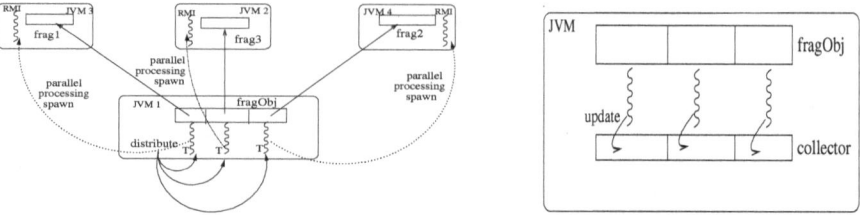

Fig. 2. The processing distribution and the result recovery

A *collector* is associated to a *distribute* call and stores all the results of the parallel tasks activated on fragments. As the results could arrive in a random order, generally different from the order of task activations, the *collector* is similar to the concept of future data, used in the ACADA project, and also proposed in the Ajents project [8]. In ProActive PDC [3], this object acts as a place-holder for the result of a not-yet-performed invoked task.

The *collector* gathers the results (for tasks returning results), and assures of the end of tasks (for tasks which do not return results), thus it has a double functionality. Different primitives attached to the *collector* allow the access to all results (*getAll*), to a first available result, not yet treated (*getOne*) or to a result issued from a certain fragment (*getI*). A not yet treated result is an available result, which has not yet been used. When no results are returned, another primitive, *waitEnd*, assures of the end of the execution of all parallely spawned tasks.

The results which are returned (one for the *getI* and *getOne* primitives and an array for the *getAll* primitive), pack auxiliary information as the fragment on which the task was activated, and its index in the fragmented object. These information are added in order to avoid new communications when searching the fragment for which a result was returned.

6   Implementation

The distributed collection is implemented in Java language, making the ADAJ applications completely portable; it uses the mechanism of Java threads (in order to provide asynchronous remote calls) and the ADAJ transparent object distribution.

The distributed collection is implemented as a hierarchy whose root is a fragmented object; on the second level are the fragments. Distributed collections are instances of the *DistributedCollection* class, while fragments are instances of the *RemoteFragment* class. In the library, other classes which extend this class are offered: *VectorFragment* or *StackFragment*, which facilitate the use of fragments as vectors or stacks. The user can define his own fragment, extending the *RemoteFragment* class or any other of its subclasses. The hierarchy of the library classes and of the user classes for fragments is shown in the next figure:

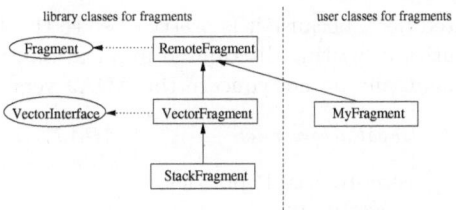

Fig. 3. Diagram of library classes and user classes for fragments. The classes are marked in rectangles and the interfaces they implement in ellipses. The "extend" link is continuous, while the "implement" link is dotted.

A distributed collection is constructed specifying the type of fragments it contains:

```
DistributedCollection distrCol = new DistributedCollection(
                                    "MyFragment");
```

where the class *MyFragment* designs a fragment declared in the following manner:

```
class MyFragment extends RemoteFragment{
      public void methodVoid(...) { ... }
      public Object methodRes(...) { ...; return ...;}
   }
```

If a *methodRes* method (which returns a result) is defined in the *MyFragment* class, the *distribute* primitive can be invoked:

```
Collector c = DistributedTask.distribute(distrCol, "methodRes",
                                    args);,
```

where **args** is an array of parameters for the *methodRes* method. If the method does not take any parameter, then the invocation of the *distribute* primitive is:

```
Collector c = DistributedTask.distribute(distrCol, "methodRes",
                                    null);
```

For a method as *methodVoid* (which does not return any result), the syntax is:

```
Collector c = DistributedTask.distributeV(distrCol,
                                    "methodVoid", args);
```

7   Evaluation

In this section we present a partial evaluation of the distributed collections concerning their use in the conception of an ADAJ application.

In the following table we present the modifications to be made on a sequential program in order to obtain its distributed version (JavaParty) (bold) and its ADAJ version using the distributed collections (italic). An intermediate RMI version is not presented here, because it is pretty close to the JavaParty version. Moreover, some facilities in writing distributed applications are already gained by the JavaParty version and do not concern the ADAJ version.

sequential version	JavaParty version	ADAJ version using distributed collections

classPopulation
  extends Vector {
    public void task(){
      add(...);
    }
}
	remote class Population {
	  Vector v;
	  public void task(){
	    v.add(...); // use of v
	  }
	}
		remote class Population
		  extends *VectorFragment*{
		    public void task(){
		      add(...);
		    }
		}

The example is extracted from the application of an evolutionary genetic algorithm to the traveling salesman problem. The distributed version uses an island model, in which individuals are divided into several subpopulations assigned to concurrent processes which perform local genetic operations, and the best solutions are exchanged by immigration between subpopulations. Communications between subpopulations for the JavaParty version are centralized, while for the ADAJ version, they can be easily made distributed, aspect enabled by the tools offered by the distributed collections.

The tasks over the subpopulations in the sequential version (or in the RMI and JavaParty versions) can be invoked in the following manner:

```
Population[] pop = ... ; // initialisation
for (i = 0; i < n; i++)  // n is the number of subpopulations
    pop[i].task();
```

Taking into account the synchronism of the remote calls, in the RMI case, as in the JavaParty version, the user has to develop mechanisms which deal with asynchronous calls, in order to improve efficiency:

```
class ThreadAsync extends Thread{
        Population pop;
        public ThreadAsync(Population pop){ this.pop = pop; }
        public void run(){ pop.task(); }
    }
```

The parallel code inspired from the RMI (or JavaParty) version would be:

```
Population[] pop = ... ; // initialisation
for (i = 0; i < n; i++){
    Thread task = new ThreadAsync(pop[i]);  // task creation
    task.start();                           // task spawn
}
```

On the other hand, generally, the user would provide non generic tools to recover results.

Using the distributed collections proposed in ADAJ, the construction of a population and the invocation of some task on all subpopulations can be done easily as:

```
DistributedCollection distrCol = new DistributedCollection (
                                        "Population");
Collector c = DistributedTask.distribute(distrCol,"task",
                                        null);
```

This short examples shows the facility of expressing distributed and parallel processing using the distributed collections (even though the mechanism of result recovery, through the collector, is not shown).

8 Related Work

In this section, we briefly describe several Java parallel programming environments which are related to our work.

Designed before the introduction of the collections framework in the Java language [5], the Do! project [13] developed its own collection library, which contains the minimal functionalities necessary for the project. Parallelism is achieved through the "operators pattern" as well as through the concept of *active object*. Our approach tries to remain as closely as possible to the classical Java conception of programs.

ProActive PDC [3] is a 100% Java library which provides transparent remote objects as well as asynchronous two-way calls. Thanks to ProActive PDC, all method calls between the application modules are asynchronous, which provides efficient communication-calculation overlapping. "Active objects" are also used, their location being explicitly defined by modifying the instantiation code.

The DPJ library [14] concerns data parallel programs using the SPMD model of parallel execution and MPI as communication library. Different distributed containers are proposed in order to introduce data distribution on the network. The main goal of the research is the development of parallel execution control, as well as facilities for distribution and data exchange among nodes. DPJ lacks transparent location of objects, as well as asynchronous remote calls, a way of expressing parallelism.

Other Java distributed environments have been proposed, on a different level, as in the cJVM project [15], which aims to obtain a single system image of a traditional JVM in a cluster.

Targeted towards and implemented on clusters of workstations, the JavaParty project [1] proposes a distributed class, equivalent to the classical Java class in one JVM. Designed as a layer over the RMI protocol, it does not offer, as in the first version, some collection implementations, as the vector or the stack.

9 Conclusion

Distributed collections allow expression of parallelism for the ADAJ applications, which give the user the possibility of controlling the granularity of parallelism.

Distributed fragments encapsulate asynchronous task calls. Thus, task parallelism is added to data parallelism through parallel processing and distribution of fragments.

Parallel tasks take advantage of Java multithreading programming while fragment distribution is based on the concept of global object, which is a remote accessible Java object, that can migrate and is also observable. The property of observability for global objects is required as they participate in redistribution of objects, in the case of load imbalance.

Distributed collections are introduced with no modifications of the Java Virtual Machine or of any element of the Java environment. Global objects are however introduced by the keyword *remote*, using a precompiler.

The conceptual approach of distributed collections will be associated, at the execution level, with observation and security mechanisms during execution, in order to increase efficiency of distributed and parallel Java processing.

References

1. M. Phillippsen, M. Zenger: JavaParty - Transparent Remote Objects in Java. ACM 1997 Workshop on Java for Science and Engineering Computation (1997)
2. A. Bouchi, E. Leprêtre, P. Lecouffe: Un mécanisme d'observation des objets distribués en Java. In RenPar'12, 171–176 (2000)
3. D. Caromel, W. Klauser, J. Vayssiere: Towards Seamless Computing and Metacomputing in Java. In Concurrency Practice and Experience, Vol. 10 (1998) http://www-sop.inria.fr/sloop/javall
4. ObjectSpace: Voyager - JGL libraries. http://www.objectspace.com, v3.1 (1996)
5. Sun Products - JDK1.2: Collections JDK 1.2. http://java.sun.com/products/jdk/1.2/docs/guide/collections/index.html
6. Sun Products - JDK1.2: API & Language Documentation. http://java.sun.com/products/jdk/1.2/docs/api/overview-summary.html
7. DS&0 Research Team: Jacob Software - Active Container of Object for Java. http://jccf.labri.u-bordeaux.fr/jodo/
8. M. Izatt, P. Chan, T. Brecht: Ajents: Towards an Environment for Parallel, Distributed and Mobile Java Applications, ACM 1999 Java Grande Conference
9. L. Verbièse, B.Toursel, P. Lecouffe: Distribution and Load Balancing in ACADA, Parelec'98, October, Poland
10. E. Frank, I. Redmond: DCOM: Microsoft Distributed Component Object Model, IDG Books worldwides (1997)
11. Object Management Group Inc.: The Common Object Request Broker: Architecture and Specification. OMG Document Revision 2.2, February (1998)
12. Sun Products - JDK1.2: Remote Method Invocation. http://java.sun.com/products/jdk/1.2/docs/guide/rmi/index.html
13. P. Launay, J.L. Pazat: Écrire parallèle, exécuter distribué. Technique et science informatique, 19, number 9, 1193 – 1221 (2000)
14. V. Ivannikov, S. Gaissaryan, M. Domrachev, V. Etch, N. Shtaltovnaya: DPJ: Java Class Library for Development of Data-parallel Programs. Institute for System Programming, Russian Academy of Sciences (1997). http://www.ispras.ru/~dpj
15. Y. Aridor, M. Factor, A. Teperman: cJVM: a Single System Image of a JVM on a Cluster. 1999 IEEE International Conference of Parallel Processing (ICPP-99)
16. Byte Code Engineering Library. http://bcel.sourceforge.net/

Advanced Collaboration Techniques between Java Objects Distributed on Clusters

Florian Mircea Boian and Corina Ferdean

{florin,cori}@cs.ubbcluj.ro

Abstract. The purpose of this paper is to propose possible solutions to some problems and requirements concerning the interaction between Java objects spread across clusters of machines. The problems we consider include requirements concerning location transparency and high-availability of Java distributed objects. Thus, an object should be able to access another remote object without knowing where that object resides. This location transparency induces also migration transparency. The enhanced properties of services offered by Java server objects are provided by duplicating the active Java objects, also transparently, for the clients. In order to achieve our aims for supporting reliable Java distributed applications, we developed a framework based on JNDI and LDAP, as the protocol to access the directory service where the references to the Java shared objects are stored.

1 Introduction

Basically, every distributed system implies two or more active entities (processes, threads, active objects) performing computations, in different address spaces, potentially on different hosts. Thus, these active execution entities should be able to communicate and, also, their interaction requires properties like reliability and high-availability of the active entities involved.

Even if the basic communication mechanisms like *sockets* or *RPC* (Remote Procedure Call) are flexible and sufficient for general communication, distributed object systems, have supplementary requirements. In such systems, the semantics of object invocation is achieved using *remote method invocation* or RMI between program-level objects residing in different address spaces and possible on different hosts.

This paper focuses on the interaction between objects implemented using the Java language and spread across clusters of machines. The general approach used for this purpose is Java RMI, a uniform mechanism integrated in the Java standard, as we'll show in the section 2 of this paper. Although useful, this mechanism has its limits in terms of providing location-transparent and high-available remote server objets. Nevertheless, the Java standard offers language constructs and APIs –like JNDI, with support for LDAP- which we exploited in order to provide a practical solution to the required properties –location and migration transparency, high-availability, reliability- of Java remote objects. This solution adapts and implements on the Java platform, a

D. Grigoras et al. (Eds.): IWCC 2001, LNCS 2326, pp. 259-270, 2002.

fault-tolerance replication model, which we called *hybrid replication model* and which combines the classical passive replication of servers objects with a method of choosing the primary copy dynamically, based on a specified criterion like: current servers charges, a simple random or FIFO technique, etc.

The rest of the paper is structured as follows: in section 2 we'll present shortly the standard Java RMI mechanism, in section 3 we'll show how the limits of this approach can be overcome, by implementing a hybrid replication model using Java standard technologies and the LDAP protocol. The section 4 mentions related works and finally, section 5 ends the paper with a conclusion.

2 Java RMI Mechanism

Java RMI (Remote Method Invocation) offers a distributed object model for the Java Platform. Thus, the Java RMI system assumes the homogeneous environment of the Java virtual machine (JVM), and it uses the standard Java object model, extending it into a distributed context.

RMI is unique in that it is a language-centric model that takes advantage of a common network type system. In other words, RMI extends the Java object model beyond a single virtual machine address space.

The underlying communication protocol used in Java RMI mechanism is JRMP. This protocol allows the object methods to be invoked between different Virtual Machines across a network, and the actual objects can be passed as arguments and return values during method invocation. Java RMI could be described as a natural progression of the procedural RPC, adapted to an object-oriented paradigm for the Java platform environment.

Without further details, we mention that the communication between remote objects, using Java RMI mechanism, is structured in a layer hierarchy, as depicted in figure 1.

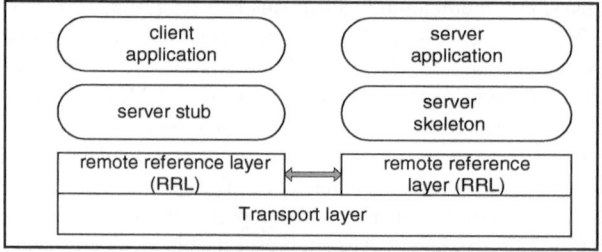

Fig. 1. RMI Architecture

For more details concerning the Java RMI mechanism, we give the following references [10].

3 Providing Java Distributed Objects with Support for Location Transparency and High-Availability

A natural question, which arises in the case of Java distributed objects interaction, is how it would be possible for a client object to access a remote object, without having to know a priori the server object location. This feature of location independence becomes a fundamental requirement if it is assumed that Java server objects could change their location, migrating between different hosts.

Another problem is to ensure that the services provided by a Java server objects remain still available, even if it crashes.

Neither of the two problems are solved by the standard Java RMI mechanism (as it is known, the client `lookup` method requires the server rmi URL as the parameter).

Our paper comes with a practical solution to these problems, by implementing a fault-tolerance replication model using standard technologies based on Java and the LDAP protocol.

In the following, we'll describe both the underlying model and its implementation, resulting in an uniform framework, with APIs to be used on the client and server side.

3.1 The Hybrid Replication Model

Our approach adapts and implements on the Java platform, a fault-tolerance replication model, which we called *hybrid replication model*. This model combines the classical passive replication of servers objects with a method of choosing the primary copy dynamically, based on a specific criterion like: the current servers charge, a simple random or FIFO technique, etc.

In order to give a more formalized specification of the model, we note: $rso=(\{<attr_i>_{i=1,na}\ ,\ <met_j>_{j=1,nm}\}, ref\_name, loc\_host)$ a remote server object, with an internal state –attributes $<attr_i>_{i=1,na}$ and methods $<met_j>_{j=1,nm}$, a name *ref_name* to be used by the clients to get a reference of the object, and the location *loc_host* of the machine hosting the object.

In our model, we replicate the object on *n* hosts, obtaining a set of n coherent copies $\{copy\_rso_{c,c=1,n}\}$, a primary copy and *n-1* secondary copies, where $copy\_rso_c=(\{<attr_i>_{i=1,na}\ ,\ <met_j>_{j=1,nm}\}, ref\_name, loc\_host_c), \forall c, c=1, n.$

The invocation mechanism forwards the client request to the primary copy, it chooses dynamically based on a pre-established criterion, like those mentioned above. The primary copy treats the request and communicates the results to the secondary copies, so they could update their internal state and remain coherent.

The figure 2 illustrates the remote invocation mechanism in the case of the hybrid replication model.

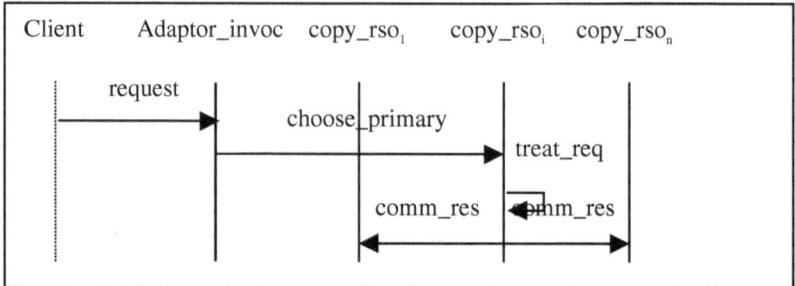

Fig. 2. The remote invocation mechanism for the hybrid replication model

3.2 Using JNDI and LDAP to Extend Java Distributed Computing

As we said before, in order to provide fault-tolerant Java server objects, independent of their location, we implemented the underlying hybrid replication model on the Java platform. We used standard technologies like JNDI (Java Naming Directory Interface) and LDAP (Light Directory Access Protocol), as the protocol to access the directory service where the references to the Java server objects are stored [9, 13].

For a presentation of these technologies, we'll indicate the following references: [4,12], for JNDI and [6,7,11,14], for LDAP.

In the Java distributed computing context, LDAP provides a centrally administered and possibly replicated service for use by Java applications spread across the network. For example, an application server might use the directory for registering objects that represent the services that it manages so that a client can later search the directory to locate those services as needed.

The JNDI provides an object-oriented view of the directory, thereby allowing Java objects to be added to and retrieved from the directory without requiring the client to manage data representation or location execution issues.

There are different ways in which Java applications can use the directory to store and locate objects. Thus, an application might store (a copy of) the object itself (it could be a `Remote` object), a reference to an object, or attributes that describe the object.

In this survey, we'll use the second method. Storing references instead of Java objects have several advantages, like: saving storage space, allowing concurrent access to active shared objects, providing persistence facilities and secure access to the objects (only through methods of its interface).

JNDI offers the `javax.naming.Reference` class, which makes it possible to record address information about objects not directly bound to the directory service. The reference to an object contains the following information [1]:
The class name of the referenced object

A vector of `javax.naming.RefAddr` objects that represents the addresses, identifying the connections to the object

The name and location of the object factory to use during object reconstruction `javax.naming.RefAddr` is an abstract class containing information needed to contact the object (e.g., via a location in memory, a lookup on another machine, etc.) or to recreate it with the same state. This class defines an association between content and type. The content (an object) stores information required to rebuild the object and the type (a string) identifies the purpose of the content.

The relation between a `Reference`, `RefAddr`, Type, and Content is represented in figure 3.

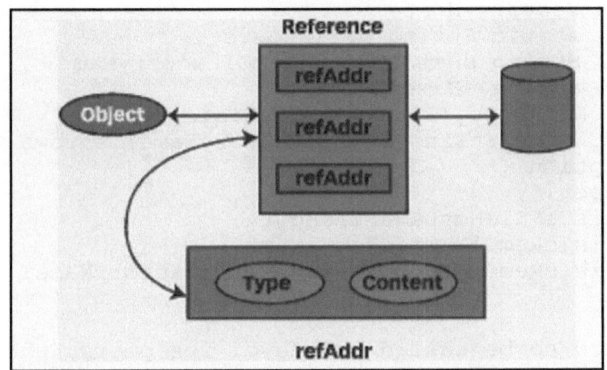

Fig. 3. The relation between a Reference, RefAddr, Type, and Content

The vector of `RefAddress` instances, from the `Reference` object, represents the key to our solution of providing location transparency and high-availability in the case of Java distributed objects.

We'll describe our model in the context of the framework we developped to support the applications with special requirements for the Quality of Service.

This framework contains Java classes and interfaces, grouped in the `javaDO-JndiLdap` package, to be used both on the server and client-side. The textual descriptions are followed by a representative source fragment from the corresponding `javaDOJndiLdap` class.

The `RefRemObj` class, extended from `UnicastRemoteObject`, represents the superclass for the reliable remote server objects that we proposed to implement.

This class implements two interfaces:

1. The `Referenceable` interface, with the `getReference()` method, which defines and returns an object of type `Reference`, to be bound to the directory service.

In this `Reference` object, we define as the vector of `RefAddress` instances, the hosts where the remote object and its backups are running (as rmi objects registered with `rmiregistry`). The list of machines hosting active shared object is read from a text file, configured a priori.

2. The `RefRemote` interface is extended from the standard `Remote` interface and contains one method `updateState()`. This method is called by one of the server

objects peers, when that replica changes its state and wants to propagate the new state
(current members data values) to the others backups.

```
package javaDOJndiLdap;
//import ...

//superclass for the remote server objects
public class RefRemObj extends UnicastRemoteObjec
          implements Referenceable, RefRemote {
          Vector vHosts;
          static String sFileHosts;
          String sRemClName,sRemClFactoryName;
          String sName2Bind;
   public RefRemObj(String sFileHosts,String
     sRemClName,String sRemClFactoryName) throws Remote
     Exception {
        super();
        this.sFileHosts=sFileHosts;
        this.sRemClName=sRemClName;
        this.sRemClFactoryName=sRemClFactoryName;
     }

//method to be called by one of its peers, when this
//one changes its state
public void updateState() {
     //particular to every server object implem.
}

//read the file with the server hosts in vHosts
public void getRemObjHosts() {
}

//method which provides a reference to the server
//object; the ref. will be stored into directory
public Reference getReference() throws NamingExcep
   tion {
     getRemObjHosts();
     Reference ref=null;
     ref=new Reference(sRemClName,new
      StringRefAddr("HOST",
      (String)vHosts.get(0)),sRemClFactoryName,null);
     for (int i=1;i<vHosts.size();i++)
      ref.add(new StringRefAddr("HOST",
      (String)vHosts.get(i)));
     return ref;
}
//bind the server object, with the sName2Bind name,
//to rmiregistry on localhost
public void bind2rmireg(String sName2Bind,
   RemoteObject remobj) {
     try {
```

```
         System.setSecurityManager
         (new RMISecurityManager());
         try {
          java.rmi.registry.LocateRegistry.
          createRegistry(1099);
         }
         catch (java.rmi.server.ExportException ee) {}
         catch (RemoteException re) {}
         String sLocHost=InetAddress.getLocalHost()
          .getHostName();
         Naming.rebind("rmi://"+sLocHost+"/"
          +sName2Bind,remobj);
        }
        catch(Exception e){System.out.println(e);

   }
   //...
 }
```

The ldapBinder class contains one method bind2ldap(), which binds a
server object (in fact its reference), given its name, to the directory service running on
the specified host and port.

The function is invoked on the server side and it makes the binding of the Reference to the object into the directory service, transparently, without knowing where
the new created object, will be running. As we mentioned above, this is encapsulated
in the getReference() method.

The binding operation also records into directory an Attributes objects, to keep
the last invoked server index (relative to the list from the hosts file).

```
package javaDOJndiLdap;
//import ...
public class ldapBinder {
   //binds a server object, given its name, to the
   //directory service on the specified host and port
   public void bind2ldap(String hostLdap, String
      port,String rootEntry, String sName2Bind,
      RemoteObject remobj) {
        //set up environ for creating the initial context
        Hashtable env = new Hashtable();
        env.put(Context.INITIAL_CONTEXT_FACTORY,
         "com.sun.jndi.ldap.LdapCtxFactory");
        env.put(Context.PROVIDER_URL,
         "ldap://"+hostLdap+":"+port+"/"+rootEntry);
        try {
         //create the initial context
         DirContext ctx = new InitialDirContext(env);
         //constructs an Attributes objects,
         BasicAttributes ba=new BasicAttrib
```

```
      utes("svInd","0");
      //bind a reference to the obj to the directory
      ctx.rebind("cn="+sName2Bind, remobj,ba);
      ctx.close();
      }
      catch (NamingException e) {}
   }}
```

The ldapFinder class provides the findFromldap() method, to be used on the client-side, in order find a server object, bound to the directory service running on the specified host and port. The client has to know only the name, the server object was bound with, and not its hosting machine(s). Besides the location, the server object duplication is also transparent to the clients.

```
package javaDOJndiLdap;
//import ...
public class ldapFinder {
   //finds a server object, with a given name, bound
   //to the directory service
   public RemoteObject findFromldap(String hostLdap,
      String port,String rootEntry, String sName2Bind) {
      RemoteObject remobj=null;
      //set up environment, as for the bind operation
      try {
       DirContext ctx = new InitialDirContext(env);
       //find the object by its name
       remobj=(RemoteObject)ctx.lookup
         ("cn="+sName2Bind);
       ctx.close();
      }
      catch (NamingException e) {}
      return remobj;
   }
}
```

The DirContext.lookup() method (called from findFromldap()) instantiates transparently a RemObjFactory object (this class was also defined in our model) and calls its getObjectInstance() method.

This method uses a user-defined criterion (for example a ChSvCriterion instance) to find an available server object and to reconstructs it from its Reference, stored into the directory service.

In order to provide load balancing, it uses the stored Attributes object, with which it starts the quest, in the circular manner. So, the duplicated available server objects are provided each time, after a round-robin strategy.

```
package javaDOJndiLdap;
//import ...
class ChSvCriterion {
```

```
            RemoteObject remobj=null;
//establish a criterion to choose an available server
//with the required quality of service
public Object chooseAvailServ(Reference ref,String
  name,Context ctx) {
    try {
        //..
        Attributes attr=((DirContext)ctx).
         getAttributes(name);
        //get from attr the index of the next server obj
        //to call
        //look an avail obje server, in the RR manner
        for (i=ind;i<noAddr;i++) {
            //...
            remobj=(RemoteObject)Naming.lookup
            ("rmi://"+(String)addr.getContent()+"/"+nam);
            //...
        } //for
        for (i=0;i<ind;i++)
            //...
            //set new attributes (the index of the next
            //server obj to contact)
    }
    catch(Exception e){}
    return remobj;
    }
}

public class RemObjFactory implements ObjectFactory {
    //constructor
    //reconstructs the server object, given its reference
    //use a ChSvCriterion for that porpose
    public Object getObjectInstance(Object obj, Name
      name, Context ctx,Hashtable env) throws Exception {
        if (obj instanceof Reference) {
            Reference ref = (Reference)obj;
            ChSvCriterion crit=new ChSvCriterion();
            return crit.chooseAvailServ(ref,name.get(0),ctx);
        }
        return null;
    }
}
```

The client uses the remote reference it received, in the usual way, invoking methods published in the interface of the server object. If the called methods are not idempotent, the client should invoke the updateState() method for the target server, in order to ensure duplicated objects consistency.

The RemObjFactory class corresponds to the Adaptor_invoc from our hybrid replication model.

We mention that, in order to avoid the multicast `updateState()` primitive, a possible solution is to keep into the directory service an attribute with the index of the server which has the most recent state (a kind of primary server between the replicas). The rest of duplicate servers, when called by the clients, could have update their members from the primary. But for each client call, there is a supplementary overhead because of the update redirection, and, besides, if the primary server fails, the most current and correct state is lost.

Example

In order to exemplify the support provided by the framework described above, we implemented a sample application, in which the generic `RefRemObject` was extended by a particular remote object of `Hello` type.

This shared object provides the `sayHello()` method to be called by the clients.

```
import javaDOJndiLdap.*;
public class HelloImpl extends RefRemObj implements
Hello {
  public HelloImpl() throws RemoteException {
    super("fileHosts","HelloImpl",
    "javaDOJndiLdap.RemObjFactory");
  }
  public String sayHello() throws RemoteException {
    //...
  }
}
```

The server object registration and lookup are done by myLdapServer, myLdapClient objects, respectively and they are based on javaDOJndiLdap.ldapBinder and javaDOJndiLdap.ldapFinder, and the operations these classes provide.

This example was tested on cluster of Sun workstations, on one of which the LDAP director server was running and on some of the others workstations the replicated server objects were active.

As our experimental results showed, even if some of the server objects crashed, the service they provide, remains available as long as at least one object copy is still active. Further work of this project concerns automatically activating crashed object copies (when their hosting machine is still alive).

However, our experimental results showed also a significant performance decrease in terms of response time, than in the case of a classical Java RMI call. This is caused by the indirection level of the LDAP server storing object references. This problem can be alleviated using the "nearest" server object to be invoked and caching mechanisms (also, subjects of further work).

Nevertheless, there is a tradeoff between a fast response time and the degree of availability of the server objects. Choosing the optimal parameters –like numbers of replicas- depends on the concrete applications and on the criticality of the interacting Java server objects.

The full sources of the javaDOJndiLdap package and the sources of this sample together with a Rational Rose UML model can be retrieved from
http://www.cs.ubbcluj.ro/~cori/download/helsamp.zip

4 Related Work

The model presented in this paper is not intended to be a competitive alternative to other powerful solutions, like those proposed by CORBA implementations: Visibroker with its dynamic, distributed directory service ORB Smart Agent –osagent-[15] or Electra ORB [3]. Instead, we provided a pure Java solution using facilities included in the standard JDK.

As related Java projects we mention *JGroup* (University of Bologna, '99) [8] and *FilterFresh* (Bell Laboratories, '98) [2]. They both are based the object group paradigm, but FilterFresh uses primary-partition group communication services (GCS) and JGroup uses a partitionable GCS.

Replicated remote objects –forming a group- cooperate in order to provide a dependable and high available service to their clients. GCS enables the creation of dynamic groups of objects, communicating through reliable multicast primitives. Clients transparently interact with an object group as with a single non-replicated entity.
JGroup adapts view synchrony, typically defined for message-based group communication systems to remote method invocations on objects.

The registry service included in JGroup is composed by a distributed collection of remote objects, which maintain a database of bindings: *(name, group of remote objects)*. The remote objects forming a JGroup registry cooperate using GCS provided with JGroup, and may be invoked as a single RMI registry.

The FilterFresh software was integrated into Java RMI, and provides support for building fault-tolerance into replicated Java server objects by implementing an underlying *Group Communication* mechanism, using a `GroupManager` object. This class also maintains the correctness and integrity of replicated servers. The Group Managers use a *Group Membership* algorithm to maintain a consistent group view and a *Reliable Multicast* mechanism to communicate with other Group Managers.

The `GroupManager` class was used to construct a fault-tolerant RMI registry called `FTRegistry`, a group of replicated RMI registry servers.
The package also included the implementation of the `FTUnicast`, a client-side mechanism that tolerates and masks server failures below the stub layer, transparent to the clients.

And finally, as related work, we mention the thesis project *GLOBE - Global Object Exchange* (University of Copenhagen, 2001) [5].
It extended the tuplespace Linda paradigm by providing dynamic fault-tolerance to ensure availability and dynamic scalability for better performance. A prototype of GLOBE has been implemented using JavaSpaces and Jini. The conclusion was that the distributed tuplespace, in spite of the trade-off between fault-tolerance, scalability and performance, is more efficient that the centralized tuplespace under high workload conditions.

5 Conclusion

This paper focused on the interaction between distributed objects implemented using the Java language. Although the standard approach Java RMI provides remarkable features in terms of usage simplicity and transparent remote call semantics, it doesn't threat requirements like location and migration transparency and high-availability for the Java server objects.

Our paper proposed a solution to these problems, based on a fault-tolerance hybrid replication model, which combines the classical passive replication of server objects with a method of choosing the primary copy dynamically, by specifying a user criterion. We adapted and implemented this model on the Java platform, using standard technologies like JNDI (Java Naming Directory Interface) and LDAP (Light Directory Access Protocol), as the protocol to access the directory service where the references to the Java server objects are stored. The developed framework provides APIs to be used both on the client and server side, to configure the fault-tolerance properties of the Java server objects, by hiding the underlying implemented mechanism.

References

1. Advanced JNDI, http://www.javaworld.com/javaworld/jw-03-2000/jw-03-howto.html
2. Baratloo A., FilterFresh: Hot Replication of Java RMI Server Objects, Technical Report, Bell Laboratories, (1998)
3. The Electra Object Request Broker, www.softwired-inc.com/people/maffeis/electra.html
4. JNDI Tutorial, http://java.sun.com/products/jndi/tutorial/
5. The GLOBE project, http://www.diku.dk/students/eglarsen/GLOBE
6. LDAP: A Next Generation Directory Protocol,
   http://www.intranetjournal .com/foundation/ldap.shtml
7. LDAP and JNDI: Together forever, http://www.javaworld.com/javaworld/jw-03-2000/jw-0324-ldap_p.html
8. Montresor A., Davoli R., Babaoglu O., Group-Enhanced Remote Method Invocations, Technical Report, Univerity of Bologna April (1999)
9. Referenceable Objects and References,
   http://java.sun.com/products/jndi/tutorial/objects/storing/reference.html
10. Remote Method Invocation Specification,
    http://java.sun.com/products/ jdk/1.1/docs/guide/rmi/spec/rmiTOC.doc.html
11. RFC LDAP, http://www.ietf.org/rfc/rfc2713.txt
12. RMI Registry Service Provider JNDI,
    http://sunsite.ccu.edu.tw/java/jdk1.3 /guide/jndi/jndi-rmi.html#USAGE
13. Schema for Representing Java Objects in an LDAP Directory,
    http://www-4.ibm.com/software/network/directory/library/publications/jndidoc/doc/draft-ryan-java-schema-00.txt
14. SLAPD Daemon, http://www.umich.edu/~dirsvcs/ldap/doc/guides/slapd/1.html#RTFToC1
15. The Visibroker's Smart Agent,
    http://www.cs.huji.ac.il/support/docs/java/vbroker/vbj/pg/noframes/chap10.htm

Java Tools for Measurement of the Machine Loads

A. Bouchi, R. Olejnik, and Bernard Toursel

LIFL - UPRESA CNRS 8022
Laboratoire d'Informatique Fondamentale de Lille
Université des Sciences et Technologies de Lille
59655 Villeneuve d'Ascq Cédex
France
Tél. 33 (0)3 20 43 45 39 , Fax: 33 (0)3 20 43 65 66
{bouchi, olejnik, toursel}@lifl.fr
http://www.lifl.fr/

Abstract. This article presents an observation mechanism of the evolution of the machine load. These machines form an execution platform for irregular distributed applications which are developed in Java/RMI. This observation mechanism is entirely designed in Java. It is thus entirely portable. We developed this mechanism in the form of a measuring tool of load and a tool for diffusion of the load information. We also present the various experiments we have done in order to validate these tools.

1 Introduction

The development of distributed applications, using a great number of computers inter-connected by a network and in particular by internet, becomes a rapidly developing field of research. In this context, the Java language gives some interesting features to the distribution management, heterogeneity and security [1]. Java has known a rapid success. The Java compiler provides an intermediate code handled by the virtual machine (Java Virtual Machine or JVM). The JVM runs on the majority of workstations and PCs. The pair formed by the language Java and the virtual machine JVM can be considered as one of the key platforms for large-scale applications. This approach presents two major advantages. The first advantage is the large diffusion of this platform. The second advantage lies in the fact that all Java virtual machines consist of a homogeneous base for the development of such applications.

The effective execution of the distributed applications requires one to adopt mechanisms which ensure the automatic adaptation of the execution as a fonction of the computing evolutions and the re source availability modifications. These requirements need to have both the information relating to machine load evolution, and the knowledge of the dynamical relation between the objects, which have already been described in [2].

D. Grigoras et al. (Eds.): IWCC 2001, LNCS 2326, pp. 271–278, 2002.

This work enters within the project ADAJ (Adaptive Applications Distributed in Java) which is realised by the Paloma team of LIFL laboratory. The project ADAJ attempts to provide some answers for designing applications [3] and efficient executions concerning distributed treatments on the network. ADAJ works in the context of distributed object systems built around Java/RMI and JavaParty [4].

2   The Observation

The execution of an irregular application can generate an imbalanced load which impairs the effectiveness of the system. Moreover, in a multi-user context, the computing potential available for a given computer varies during the execution. Because of this problem, a strategy of adequate observation will be set up. This observation is based on two aspects:

- Observation of the relations between the objects.
- Observation of the load on the various nodes and the network.

The mechanism of load balancing uses the information provided by these observations. The observation mechanism of the relations between the objects [2] is based on the counting of the called methods between the objects.

The observation of node load implies the realization of two mechanisms. The first is a measurement mechanism which computes the local load in a node. In a permanent way or on demand, it gives load information for each machine. The second is a diffusion mechanism which sends the load indications to every other machine. So each one of them can estimate its own load and can compare it to the whole of the execution platform. The rest of this article presents the estimate tool of the workstation and PC load.

3   The Mechanism of Load Estimation

We fixed some constraints for the choice of the load estimation mechanism. Our constraints are the effectiveness and the simplicity. Under these conditions, the tool must be independant of the computer power and of the scheduling strategy. A study and a precise calibration of this tool allow one to validate that although our tool is simple. All the previously evoked aspects are really taken into account.

The tool for estimate of the local load in a machine is implemented using a Java thread. This thread runs in each JVM belonging to the execution platform. The load computing mechanism is based on the computing of average waiting time for the CPU, after having yielded it explicitly. We assume that the average time is small, if there are no other threads ready to be scheduled either in the JVM, or in the computer. In the opposite case, average time is larger. This assumption is checked by the various experiments described in this article.

For reasons of effectiveness and speed we choose to use a simple algorithm. This simplicity allows one to obtain load information without excessive overcost of computing which could disturb the execution of the other applications running on the machine. In addition, as we have mentioned in the introduction, the use of a Java platform ensures a complete portability of this algorithm.

This algorithm is based on a Java thread. It contains two phases:

- a phase of estimation of waiting time for the CPU. This phase uses the method *yield()* of the java class *Thread*. The thread which executes this method gives back the CPU to the scheduler and waits being awaken again by the scheduler. The waiting time of the thread depends directly on the computer load. To eliminate the instantaneous effects of machine load variations, we repeat this operation several times (controlled by the parameter *Iteration_Nbr*). Finally, the average time (*TimeInterval / Iteration_Nbr*) which is calculated in the algorithm computes directly a reliable estimation of the load. So, in the rest of this article, the unit used to describe the load is the millisecond.
- a phase of storage of these data is implemented with a queue (*cpuLoadList*), which allows one to smooth the data over greater periods of time and avoid taking into account short and exceptional phenomena.

```
loadEstimation(Iteration_Nbr, cpuLoadList){

    // waiting time estimation phase
    t1 = System.currentTimeMillis(); // read the computer time
    for(int i=0; i<Interation_Nbr ; i++)
      yield(); // restore the CPU
    t2 = System.currentTimeMillis();
    TimeInterval = t2 - t1;

    // compute the average load
    loadValue = TimeInterval / Iteration_Nbr ;

    // storage phase
    cpuLoadList.enqueue(loadValue);  // write in the queue
}
```

The average of the stored values in the queue *cpuLoadList* gives the machine load.

We want to determine now the influence of the various parameters on the taken measures: the iteration count *Iteration_Nbr* and the queue size *cpuLoadList*. The following experiments are done on several Sun/Solaris machines of various powers.

3.1   Choice of the Iteration Count

We start two threads in a JVM. The first thread estimates the load. The second one produces a computing load on the computer. The latter runs 30 seconds after the beginning of the testing program. The obtained results following the modification of the iteration count (1, 2, 5 and 10) are presented in the figure (1.1). The load detection appears slower for a greater iteration count (5 or 10) because the loop takes more time to terminate. In these experiments, the queue size is fixed at 20. As we do not use instantaneous measurements, but already smoothed measurements of load, a stairway effect appears in the figure (1.1).

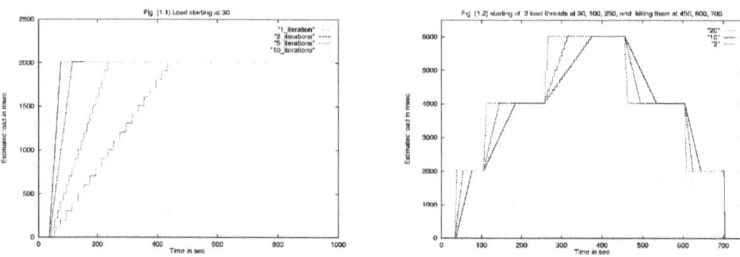

Fig. 1. The effects of the iteration count and the queue size

3.2   Choice of the Queue Size

The figure (1.2) presents the effects produced by the queue size *cpuLoadList* modifications. This queue is used to store the various measurements of load taken within a JVM (queue containing 2, 10 and 20 measurements). This JVM contains three threads which are used to load the computer. They are started at the moments of 30, 100 and 250 seconds. Then these threads are killed at the moments corresponding to 450, 600 and 700 seconds. The results presented in figure (1.2) show several stages. The value of the queue size controls the arrival to these stages.The more the queue size is small, the more the rise is fast. Consequently, choosing a small queue size is preferable. However, this choice lead to a strong reactivity with the fast variations of the load.

4   Validation of the Tool on Various Platforms

The execution platform of the distributed applications includes several architectures of different types supporting the JVM. We thus tested the load estimation tool on these various architectures which are Solaris, Linux and Windows/NT.

4.1   Internal Observation of the Load in JVM

We observed the evolution of the JVM load under the influence of several threads loading the machine and being started after 30 seconds from the begining of the program. Throughout this experiment, the physical machine did not contain any other active process. Placed in three different contexts (system Solaris, Linux and Windows NT), the obtained results are presented in the figure 2. To ensure us of the validity of these results, we used several machines of each type. The results show that the computed load value is linear with the number of running threads:

$$loadvalue = k * n \tag{1}$$

where :

– k : is a constant value which depends of the machine used. For Solaris systems this value is 2010 milliseconds, 10 milliseconds for Linux and 20 milliseconds for Windows/NT.
– n : is the number of running threads.

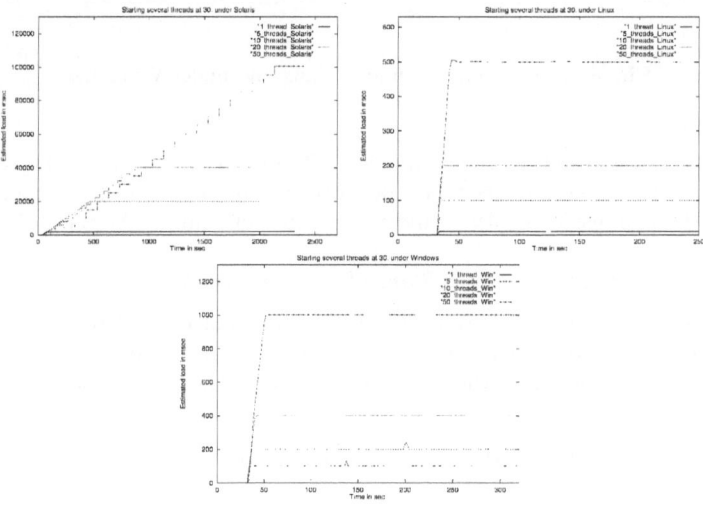

Fig. 2. Observation under Solaris, Linux and Windows

4.2 Load Observation inside a Computer

We observe the load of a computer which contains several JVMs. The first contains a thread which computes the load and five threads being used to load the computer. Each one of other JVMs contains a load thread. The figure (3.1) presents the obtained results under Linux. The results of these experiments show that the load value can be calculated by the following formula:

$$loadvalue = 10 * Int\_Thr\_Nbr * (1 + Ext\_Pro\_Nbr) \qquad (2)$$

where :

– Int_Thr_Nbr is the number of running threads in the JVM.
– Ext_Pro_Nbr is the number of JVMs launched in the site.

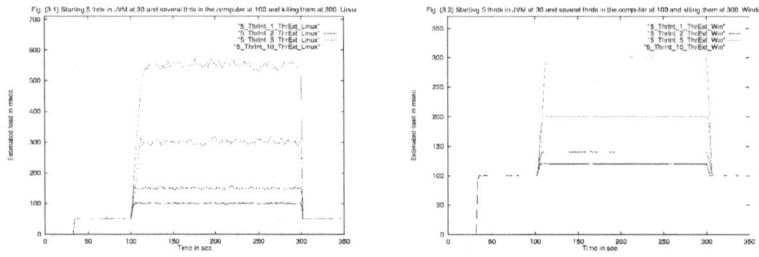

Fig. 3. The observation under Linux and under Windows

The obtained results under Windows/NT are presented in the figure (3.2). The estimated value appears to be proportional to the sum of the number of running threads inside the JVM and the number of running JVMs.

$$loadvalue = (Int\_Thr\_Nbr + Ext\_Pro\_Nbr) * 20 \qquad (3)$$

All these experiments show that the measurement of load reacts indeed to the introduction and the suppression of treatments in the computer, as well as inside the JVM which does the measurements as in the other processes.

5   Information Diffusion Mechanism

After having the estimated information of local load in each node, diffusing this information is necessary. That enables us to compare the load of a given node to the load of the other nodes belonging to the same execution platform. Four protocols for the information diffusion are possible [5] :

– Explicit exchange: A "on-demand mechanism" is used. The response time is the main disadvantage of this method. A distribution of load between all the computers can be done only after all of them receive the load values of the other computers.
– Periodic exchange: It is made spontaneously by all the computers. Each of them periodically diffuses the value of their own loads on the network. The disadvantage of this diffusion method is that it generates a constant and significant load on the network, sometimes unnecessarily.

- Relative exchange: It is done only when there is a variation higher than a certain value of the load. The choice of the threshold from which the load is transmitted constitutes the key point of this method. This operating mode allows one to reduce considerably the quantity of exchanged information.
- Implicit exchange: it is carried out in a transparent way. Information on the load is added to the messages which circulate between the machines. This method implies that there are indeed regular communications between the machines.

Because of its good ratio between effectiveness and load network, we chose the third protocol (relative exchange) to develop our tool.

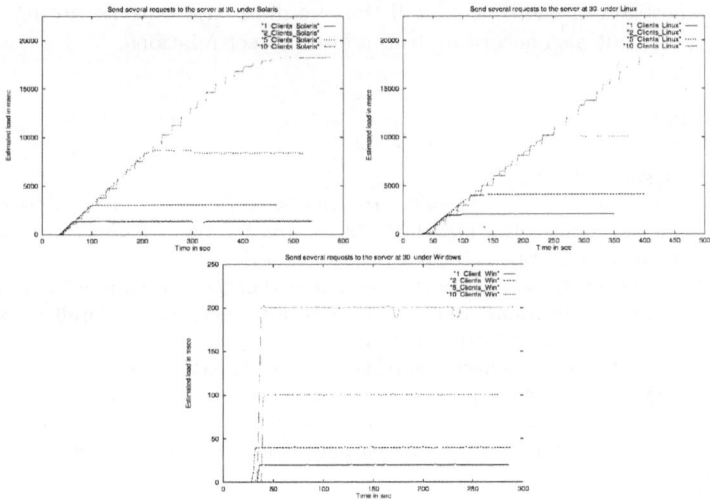

Fig. 4. Observation of a server

6   Experiments from a Program

We observed an application of client/server type. A server is waiting for the client requests. At the request reception, the server starts a thread which carries out an infinite loop and waits for news requests. The clients run on different and homogeneous machines (either Sun/Solaris, or Linux, or Windows/NT). Connection is done through Java/RMI.

Figure 4 shows various obtained results under these systems. On each of them, the results clearly show that the load of the computer where is located the server increases with the number of clients (1, 2, 5 and 10). This confirms the correct working of our load estimator.

7   Conclusion and Future Works

In this article we have presented an estimation tool which measures effectively
the load of all the computers of an execution platform for Java distributed applications. This tool is implemented by using a thread which executes a simple
algorithm. It does not generate significant overcost computing. We have presented various experiments which validate this tool.

Measurements have also shown a strong dependence on the kind of the system
used. A calibration of this tool on the various systems is essential. Another work
in progress is to extend this tool to the measurement of the network load.

Finally, in ADAJ project, the presented tools supplement a distribution system of objects between the various machines of a platform. This last system
considers the relations between the objects of the application. The distribution
and the migration of the objects will thus be done, not only according to the
machine loads, but also according to the inter-object relations.

References

1. http://java.sun.com/docs/.
2. Bouchi (A.), Leprêtre (E.) et Lecouffe (P.).An observation mechanism of distributed
   objects in Java. RenPar'12 : French Conference on Parallel Architectures and Systemes. Besançon 2000, pp. 171-176.
3. Felea (V.), Toursel (B.) et Devesa (N.). Distributed collections : a tool for the design
   of Java parallel applications. RenPar'13 : French Conference on Parallel Architectures and Systemes. Paris 2001, pp. 97-102.
4. Philippsen (Michael) et Zenger (Matthias). – JAVAPARTY. A Distributed Com-
   panion to Java. http://wwwipd.ira.uka.de/JavaParty/.
5. Talbi (E.) - Dynamic allocation of process in the distributed and parallel systems.
   State of the art. Laboratoire d'Informatique Fondamentale de Lille. report 162.
   January 1995.

The Parallel FDTD Algorithm and Its Application to the Analysis of Complex Structures

Boguslaw Butrylo

Bialystok Technical University, ul. Grunwaldzka 11/15,
15-893 Bialystok, Poland
Bogb@cksr.ac.bialystok.pl

Abstract. The properties of the approximated methods applied in the analysis of electromagnetic phenomena are presented. The detailed description of restrictions and advantages of the FDTD method is given. The principles of parallel implementation and the properties of the distributed FDTD algorithm are discussed. Analysis of the parallel processing performance is carried out. The presented parallel FDTD algorithm calculates the propagation of electromagnetic wave in the semi-infinite space.

1   Introduction

Experimental investigation of the electromagnetic (EM) field distribution is the basic tool in the analysis of electromagnetic compatibility in some complex systems (e.g. some antenna systems, microwave circuits, systems of mobile telephones, medical equipments) [3], [7], [11]. The performance of the typical sequential computers is not sufficient for the analysis of electromagnetic phenomena in a large model.

Development of the computer technology and stable enlargement of the performance of computer systems enable to simulate the complex electromagnetic phenomena. The distributed, high performance computing (MIMD computers and clusters of workstations) is an alternative and cost effective method in the analysis of the realistic, approximate models of the complex systems. High performance numerical simulation enables to change the methodology of EM field analysis:

- The distribution of EM field inside the complex system can be analyzed.
- The simulation of interaction EM field with biological structure can be realize without direct exposure on the electromagnetic radiation.
- The numerical optimization and *what-if* analysis are possible.
- Advanced computer aided engineering methods can be applied for the electromagnetic equipment.

2   Numerical Estimation of Electromagnetic Fields

All electromagnetic fields (including incident and direct, low, medium and high frequency) are governed by the Maxwell equations. The time-dependent Maxwell's curl equations describe the distribution of an electric field intensity

D. Grigoras et al. (Eds.): IWCC 2001, LNCS 2326, pp. 279-286, 2002.
© Springer-Verlag Berlin Heidelberg 2002

$\mathbf{E}=E_x\cdot\mathbf{1}_x+E_y\cdot\mathbf{1}_y+E_z\cdot\mathbf{1}_z$ [V/m] and a magnetic field intensity $\mathbf{H}=H_x\cdot\mathbf{1}_x+H_y\cdot\mathbf{1}_y+H_z\cdot\mathbf{1}_z$ [A/m] in the vector form

$$rot\ \mathbf{H} = \gamma\,\mathbf{E} + \varepsilon\frac{\partial\mathbf{E}}{\partial t}\,, \tag{1a}$$

$$rot\ \mathbf{E} = -\mu\frac{\partial\mathbf{H}}{\partial t}\,, \tag{1b}$$

where γ [S/m], ε [F/m], μ [H/m] represents electrical conductivity, permitivity and permeability of the medium respectively.

A finite approximation is applied to solve the equations (1) in numerical analysis of EM fields. The scheme of numerical integration of Maxwell's equations designates the properties of the implemented method (table 1).

Table 1. Properties of the approximated methods in the analysis of electromagnetic field [8]. The results were estimated for a homogeneous cubic model. The model was divided into N finite elements (or cells) on each edge. The coefficients C_1, ..., C_4 depend on representation of float-point numbers in the computer system, and the coefficients C_5, ..., C_8 depend on numerical implementation of the approximated method.

The approximated method	Number of unknowns	Required size of the memory	Number of float-point number operations in a time step
Finite-Difference Time-Domain Method (FDTD)	$6N^3$	C_1N^3	C_5N^5
Finite Element Method (FEM), direct solver	$6N^3$	C_2N^5	C_6N^7
Finite Element Method (FEM), iterative solver	$6N^3$	C_3N^3	$C_7N^{4\ldots6}$
Boundary Element Method (BEM)	$24N^2$	C_4N^4	C_8N^6

One of the numerical methods used in the analysis of the electromagnetic phenomena is FDTD (Finite-Difference Time-Domain) method [11]. The cell proposed by Yee makes it possible to carry out numerical calculation of electromagnetic fields [12]. The algorithm described by Yee divides the analyzed space into elementary cubes. The E_x, E_y, E_z, H_x, H_y, and H_z components of the electric and magnetic field intensity are linked to each Yee cell. On the basis of the structure of the Yee cell, the Maxwell's equations are integrated both in the time and space domains. The leapfrog scheme is applied in the computations. The components of electric field are calculated in the even time steps, whereas the components of magnetic field in the odd time steps [4], [11].

The following advantages cause the wide application of the FDTD method in the analysis of complex structures, including bio-electromagnetic analysis [1], [2], [5], [10], [11]:

♦ It is possible to build the FDTD model by the data transfer from the others computer systems. For example, the data from medical imaging systems (MRI –

magnetic resonance imaging, CT – computer tomography) can be easily adapt to the FDTD model (Fig. 1).

♦ The Yee cells enable to prepare the complex model. The complexity of a biological body can be reflected in the constructed model: geometry and some details of the anatomy, a structure of the tissues and thin layers, non-homogeneity and anisotropy of some materials.
♦ Direct numerical integration in time domain enables to simulate the electromagnetic impulses and discharges.
♦ The analysis of transient state and its direct, step-by-step visualization are possible.
♦ Miscellaneous field phenomena in the scattered and incident fields can be simulated (e.g. selective absorption and dispersion of EM wave).
♦ The absorption boundary condition (ABC) enables to simulate the open boundary models (i.e. wave propagation in the infinite space). There are some schemes of ABC in the FDTD method (e.g. Mur's BC, PML, RT, Liao's BC) [6], [11].

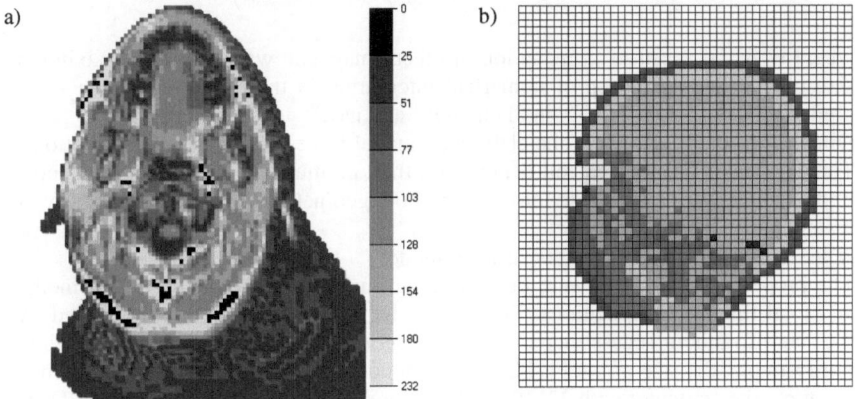

a)   b)

Fig. 1. a) Isometric 3D view of the FDTD model of human head with axial cross-section. No material data agglomeration was made. The colors of the cells correspond to the relative results of MRI scanning. b) The sagittal cross-section of the FDTD model of the human head. The number of Yee cells was reduced by agglomeration of the cells. The set of 52 MRI images was used to create the model.

3   Restrictions of the Analysis

The structure of the FDTD mesh is very simple and well ordered. The following limitations should be taking into account, when the realistic FDTD model is generated:

A. The lower limitations of the constructed model

♦ Nyquist's restriction. The maximum size of the Yee cell (Δx, Δy, and Δz) cannot exceed the half of length of the electromagnetic wave λ in the analysed case

$$(\Delta x \leq 0.5 \cdot \lambda) \wedge (\Delta y \leq 0.5 \cdot \lambda) \wedge (\Delta z \leq 0.5 \cdot \lambda). \tag{2}$$

The electromagnetic field distribution is calculated in the selected points of the created model. The approximated mesh determines the distribution of the points. The maximum distance between the points has to assure proper sampling of the propagated electromagnetic wave. The maximum dimensions of the Yee cells comply the limitation

$$(\Delta x \leq 0.1 \cdot \lambda) \wedge (\Delta y \leq 0.1 \cdot \lambda) \wedge (\Delta z \leq 0.1 \cdot \lambda) \qquad (3)$$

in the elaborated FDTD models.
- Numerical accuracy and convergence of the approximated method are the function of parameters of the model. Courant's condition should be regard in the FDTD models [11]

$$\left(\Delta t \leq \frac{\Delta x}{w \cdot c_0}\right) \wedge \left(\Delta t \leq \frac{\Delta y}{w \cdot c_0}\right) \wedge \left(\Delta t \leq \frac{\Delta z}{w \cdot c_0}\right), \qquad (4)$$

where c_0 is the speed of propagation of electromagnetic wave, Δt – the maximum size of the time step (step of numerical integration in the time domain), w – the predefined coefficient ($w=3^{0.5}$ in 3D models, and $w=2^{0.5}$ in 2D models).
- Dimensions of the details of the elaborated model force the additional assumptions. The maximum size of Yee cell depends on the minimum dimensions of the details in the model. We have to take into account both geometry details and complexity of material structure of the model.

B. The upper limitations of the constructed model
- The properties of the hardware determine the maximum size of the FDTD model and total time of computations. The approachable size of the model is limited by the size of random access memory in the *in-core* version of the FDTD algorithm. For example, the size of the FDTD model cannot exceed ~500 000 Yee cells, when we apply the computer with 32MB RAM memory. The maximum size of the FDTD model can be easily enlarge in the distributed, multi-processor implementation of the algorithm

$$N_{Yee} = N_S \cdot N_{Yee,1}, \qquad (5)$$

where N_{Yee} – the maximum number of Yee cells in the distributed system, N_S – the number of computing nodes (workstations), $N_{Yee,1}$ – the maximum number of Yee's cells in the single computing node (workstation).

4   Distributed Implementation of the FDTD Method

Distributed implementation of the FDTD method can be applied in a natural way for the analysis of electromagnetic wave propagation [4], [9], [11]. The distributed implementation of the FDTD method is based on the direct data decomposition (Fig. 2).

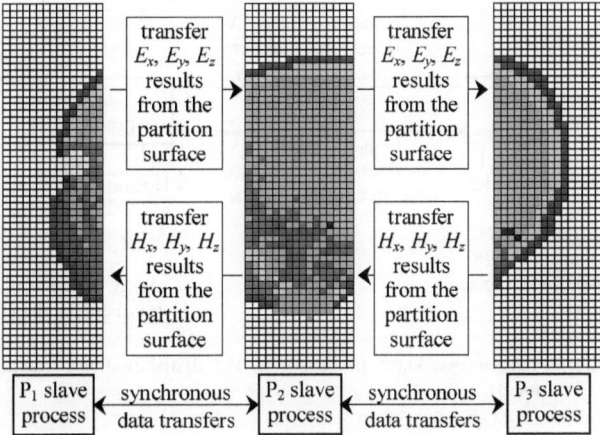

Fig. 2. The method of domain decomposition in the distributed implementation of the FDTD algorithm. The exemplary model (Fig. 1) was divided into 3 sub-domains.

The domain decomposition (shape and size of the sub-domains) can be determining flexible at the beginning of computation procedure. Each FDTD model can be divided for the sub-models. Each sub-model was calculated in one workstation or processor unit. Number of the sub-models should be less than the number of workstations in a cluster (number of slave processes). Depending on the needs, the number of computing units and sub-domains can be matched.

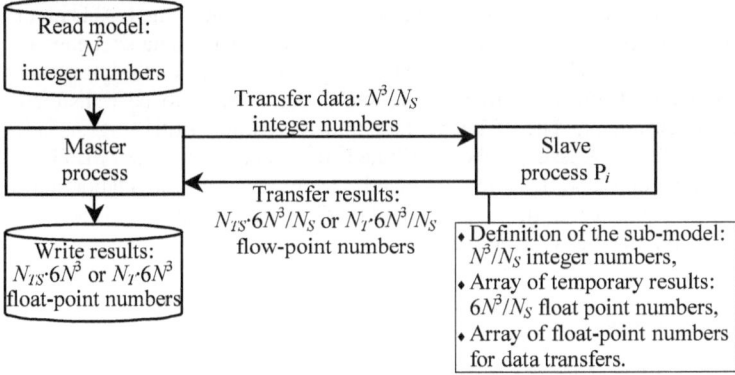

Fig. 3. The relation between the master and slave processes in the distributed implementation of the FDTD algorithm (3D model): $N_{Yee}=N^3$ – the number of Yee cells in a cubic model (uniform meshing in 3D space), N_S – the number of slave processes (workstations), N_T – the total number of time steps, N_{TS} – the number of time steps when the results are transferred to the master process.

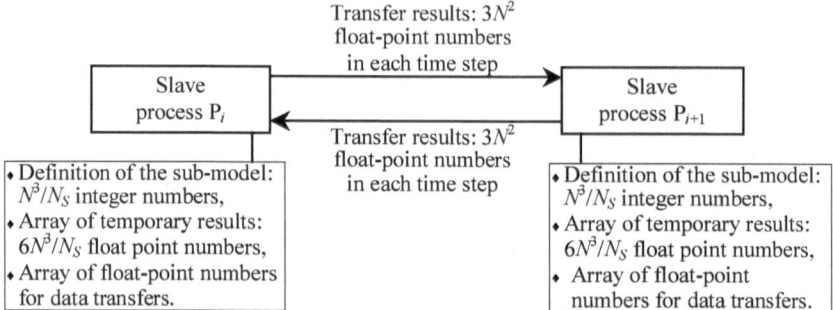

Fig. 4. The relation between two slave processes in the distributed implementation of the FDTD algorithm (3D model).

As the result of 3D model decomposition we obtain: 3D data set for material data, 3D data set for temporary results of computations, and auxiliary 2D data set for communication between processing units.

The correct domain decomposition should fulfill two general conditions:

• Load balancing of the computers (processors). The uniform decomposition of the model can be applied in the homogeneous network.
• Minimization of time of data transfers between slave processors.

The speedup and efficiency of the distributed FDTD algorithm are limited by performance of the data transfer between computers. The shape and material structure have no influence on the efficiency of the distributed version of the FDTD algorithm.

Numerical integration of Maxwell's equations requires the data exchange between adjacent workstations (Fig. 3, Fig. 4). The temporary values of the electromagnetic field components from the border of the sub-domains have to be transferred from computer to computer. The efficient data transfer from partitioning surfaces is a critical, and bottleneck issue in the distributed implementation of the FDTD method. The blocking send and receive commands were used in the elaborated FDTD algorithm. In that case the algorithm is self-synchronized and no additional synchronization messages are necessary.

5   Conclusions

The fundamental influence on the total time of computations is exerted by the real time of computations and the time of data transfer between computing units (Fig. 5). It was noted that with the increase of the number of processors there was a linear increase of the exchanged information. According to the self-synchronization scheme and method of domain decomposition, some information is processed simultaneously between processing units.

The concurrent calculation of electromagnetic wave propagation, making use of the FDTD method, speeds up the computations. According to the principle of domain decomposition (multiple data stream), relative time of electromagnetic field computations is reduced (Fig. 6). The calculations are slowed down as a result of data transfers. This aspect of the algorithm still remains to be improved.

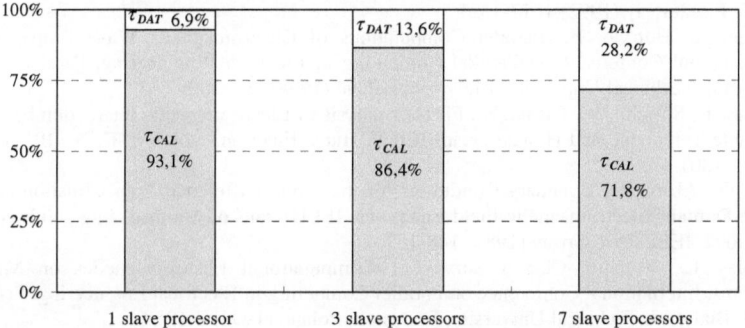

Fig. 5. Confrontation of the relative time of computation (τ_{CAL}) and relative time of data transfers (τ_{DAT}) in the elaborated distributed version of the FDTD algorithm. The absolute time of the task (computation or data transfer) was divided by the total time of computation. The Alex AVX MIMD computer was used [4].

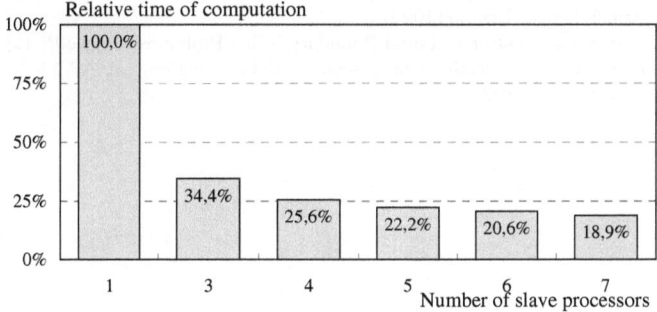

Fig. 6. Correlation between the relative time of computation and number of computing units. The total time of computation with N_S processing unit was related to the total computation time of sequential algorithm. The results were obtained in the analysis of the electromagnetic field distribution on the MIMD, multiprocessor Alex AVX computer.

This work has been done in the frame of the KBN grants No 8T10A 050 18 and W/WE/3/99.

References

1. Elsherbeni, A.Z., Taylor, C.D. Jr., Rahmat-Samii, Y.: Real Time Simulation of the Interaction of Electromagnetic Wave with a Human Head. http://sepwww.stanford.edu /seg/books/3dem/elsher/elsher.html

2. Gandhi, O.P.: FDTD in Bioelectromagnetics: Safety Assessment and Medical Applications, Chapter 11 in Advances in Computational Electromagnetics: The Finite-Difference Time Domain Method. Edited by A. Taflove, Artech House, Dedham (1998) 613-651
3. Hoefer, W.J.R.: Time Domain Electromagnetic Simulation for Microwave CAD Applications. IEEE Transactions on Microwave Theory and Techniques, vol. 40, No. 7. IEEE, Piscataway (1992) 1517-1527
4. Jordan, A., Butrylo, B.: Parallel Computations of Electromagnetic Wave Propagation. International Conference on Parallel Computing in Electrical Engineering, Parelec 1998. Bialystok Technical University, Bialystok, Poland (1998) 296-300
5. Masao, T., So-ichi, W., Toshio, N.: FDTD Analysis of Electromagnetic Interaction between Portable Telephone and Human Head. IEICE Trans. Electron., vol. E79-C, No.10. (1996) 1300 - 1307
6. Mur, G.: Absorbing Boundary Conditions for the Finite-Difference Approximation of the Time-Domain Electromagnetic Field Equations. IEEE Trans.on Biomed. Eng., Vol. BME-34, No. 2. IEEE, Piscataway (1987) 148-157
7. Nicolas, L., Vollaire, Ch.: A Survey of Computational Electromagnetics on MIMD Systems. International Conference on Parallel Computing in Electrical Engineering, Parelec 1998. Bialystok Technical University, Bialystok, Poland (1998) 7-19
7. Quick Wave – User's Guide. Qwed, Warsaw (1997)
8. Rodohan, D.P., Saunders, S.R.: Parallel implementations of the FDTD method. 2nd International Conference on Computation in Electromagnetics. IEE (1994) 367-370
9. Sullivan, D.M., Gandhi, O.P., Taflove A.: Use of the Finite-Difference Time-Domain Method for Calculating EM Absorption in Man Models. IEEE Transactions on Biomedical Engineering, vol. 35, No. 3. IEEE, Piscataway (1988) 179-186
10. Taflove, A.: The Finite-Difference Time Domain Method - Computational Electro-dynamics. Artech House, Boston (1999)
11. Yee, K.S.: Numerical Solution of Initial Boundary Value Problems Maxwell's Equations in Isotropic Media. IEEE Transactions on Antennas and Propagation, vol. AP-14, No 3. IEEE, Piscataway (1966) 302 – 307

A Theoretical Application of Feedback Guided Dynamic Loop Scheduling

Tatiana Tabirca[1], Len Freeman[1], and Sabin Tabirca[2]

[1] University of Manchester, Computer Science Department, CNC
Oxford Road, Manchester, M13 9NG, England
{tabircat,lfreeman}@cs.man.ac.uk
[2] University College Cork, Computer Science Department
College Road, Cork, Ireland
s.tabirca@cs.ucc.ie

Abstract. In this paper we briefly describe the Feedback-Guided Dynamic Loop Scheduling (FGDLS) algorithm that was proposed in Bull et al. [2] and Bull [1]. The FGDLS algorithm uses a feedback mechanism, based on measured execution times, to schedule a parallel loop within a sequential outer loop. We compare the FGDLS algorithm with other scheduling algorithms for a simple model problem — the parallel computation of the inverse of a triangular matrix.

1 Introduction

Load imbalance is the most important overhead in many parallel applications. Because loop structures represent the main source of parallelism, the scheduling of parallel loop iterations to processors can have a significant effect on minimising load imbalance. Among many algorithms for loop scheduling (see [13] for a classification), Feedback Guided Dynamic Loop Scheduling (FGDLS) is one that was suggested recently. The algorithm was introduced by Bull [1], and successively developed by Bull, Ford, Freeman and Hancock [3,6]; it was applied successfully in several practical applications, including Numerical Weather Prediction [2].

Finding the inverse of a unit diagonal, lower triangular matrix is a frequently studied problem in Numerical Analysis. Several methods, both sequential and parallel, have been proposed for its solution (see, for example, [5], [8], [10]). A straightforward parallel algorithm is obtained when the $n \times n$ unit diagonal, lower triangular matrix A is written as $A = I_n - B$, where B is strictly lower triangular. In this case the inverse matrix is given by $A^{-1} = \sum_{i=0}^{n-1} B^i$ (see Stewart [14], p. 112) and this sum can be computed by several different approaches. In the following, we show how the FGDLS algorithm can be used to schedule the computation of the inverse of the unit diagonal, lower triangular matrix A using this sum of powers of the matrix B. (Note that the restriction to unit diagonal, lower triangular matrices is convenient, but not necessary; the algorithms are applicable to any non-singular, triangular matrix.)

D. Grigoras et al. (Eds.): IWCC 2001, LNCS 2326, pp. 287–292, 2002.
© Springer-Verlag Berlin Heidelberg 2002

2   FGDLS Method

In this section we review the important features of the FGDLS method. More information about the method can be found in [1], [3] and [6]. We assume that the loop structure of Figure 1 is to be scheduled for a parallel machine with p processors $P_1, P_2, \ldots, P_p$. We

---

do seq $t = 1, m$
    do par $i = 1, n$
        call `loop_body(i)`
    end do
end do

Fig. 1. The loop structure

also assume that the workload associated with the subroutine `loop_body(i)` is given by $w_i, i = 1, 2, \ldots, n$. FGDLS gives a block partitioning of the parallel loop such that the total workload is approximately equally distributed onto the processors at any time t (on the outer sequential iteration t). Let l_j^t and h_j^t be the lower and upper bounds of the loop block assigned to processor j at time t. These bounds satisfy the simple equations

$$l_1^t = 1; \quad l_{j+1}^t = h_j^t + 1, j = 1, 2, \ldots, p - 1; \quad h_p^t = n. \tag{1}$$

FGDLS starts with the initial, arbitrarily chosen, loop bounds $(l_j^1, h_j^1)_{1 \leq j \leq p}$. New loop bounds $(l_j^{t+1}, h_j^{t+1})_{1 \leq j \leq p}$ are calculated from the bounds $(l_j^t, h_j^t)_{1 \leq j \leq p}$ as follows. We assume that the execution time of each processor at time t (the accumulated execution time for `loop_body(i)`, $i = l_j^t, l_j^t + 1, \ldots, h_j^t$) is given by $T_j^t, j = 1, 2, \ldots, p$. A piecewise constant approximation of the workload at time t is then given by

$$w_i^t = \frac{T_j^t}{h_j^t - l_j^t + 1}, \quad l_j^t \leq i \leq h_j^t, \ j = 1, 2, \ldots, p. \tag{2}$$

New loop bounds, $l_j^{t+1}, h_j^{t+1}, j = 1, 2, \ldots, p$, are calculated so that this piecewise constant workload $w_i^t, i = 1, 2, \ldots, n$, is approximately equally distributed over the p processors:

$$\sum_{i=l_j^{t+1}}^{h_j^{t+1}} w_i^t \simeq \frac{1}{p} \cdot \sum_{i=1}^{n} w_i^t = \overline{W}. \tag{3}$$

A simple way to solve this approximate equi-distribution problem is to calculate the loop upper bounds as follows

$$h_j^{t+1} = h \quad \Leftrightarrow \quad \sum_{i=l_j^{t+1}}^{h} w_i^t \leq \overline{W} < \sum_{i=l_j^{t+1}}^{h+1} w_i^t.$$

The loop lower bounds are then given by

$$l_{j+1}^{t+1} = h_j^{t+1} + 1, \ j = 1, 2, \ldots, p - 1.$$

3   Inverting a Lower Triangular Matrix

In this section we present a classical method for inverting a unit diagonal, lower triangular matrix. Consider $A \in M_n(R)$, where the elements of A satisfy

$$A_{i,i} = 1, \ i = 1, 2, \ldots, n$$

$$A_{i,j} = 0, \ i < j,$$

and where $M_n(R)$ denotes the set of square real matrices of order n. Since $\det(A) = 1$, the matrix A is invertible. Let $B \in M_n(R)$ be the matrix such that

$$A = I_n - B. \tag{4}$$

The matrix B satisfies $B_{i,j} = 0, \ \forall i \leq j$ — it is *strictly* lower triangular. It is known [10] that

$$B^n = 0_n \tag{5}$$

where 0_n represents the $n \times n$ null matrix, and thus that

$$A^{-1} = \sum_{i=0}^{n-1} B^i. \tag{6}$$

Equation (6) offers several opportunities for the parallel computation of A^{-1}. Lakshmivarahan and Dhall [10] present several parallel algorithms for evaluating a polynomial on the matrix space $M_n(R)$. One, based on Horner's method, produces a parallel computation by partitioning the matrices into sub-matrices. A variant of this method [8] is used in the following:

1. Initialise $A_1 = I_n$.
2. For $t = 1, 2, \ldots, n - 1$, repeat

$$A_1 = B \cdot A_1 + I_n. \tag{7}$$

At the end of this computation, the matrix A_1 contains A^{-1}. If Equation (7) is rewritten by columns we find that

$$c_i(A_1) = B \cdot c_i(A_1) + c_i(I_n), i = 1, 2, \ldots, n. \tag{8}$$

where $c_i(A)$ represents the ith column of A. The resulting algorithm for computing A^{-1} is presented in Figure 2.

Computing $c_i(A_1) = B \cdot c_i(A_1) + c_i(I_n)$ is the dominant calculation in the above algorithm. Because B is strictly lower triangular and A_1 is lower triangular, we find that this calculation can be executed in

$$1 + 2 + \cdots + (n - i) = \frac{(n - i)\ (n - i + 1)}{2}$$

operations. Since the different iterations of the parallel loop have different execution times, it is difficult to find an efficient static schedule. Therefore, dynamic loop scheduling algorithms are suitable for scheduling this computation.

Inputs: n - the matrix order.
          A - the matrix.
Output: A_1 - the inverse matrix.
procedure inverse(n,A,A_1)
   do par $i = 1, n$
      do par $j = 1, n$
         if $i > j$ **then** $B(i,j) = -A(i,j)$
              else $B(i,j) = 0$
         end if
         if $i = j$ **then** $A_1(i,j) = 1$
              else $A_1(i,j) = 0$
         end if
      end do
   end do
   do seq $t = 1, n - 1$
      do par $i = 1, n$
         $c_i(A_1) = B\, c_i(A_1) + c_i(I_n)$
      end do
   end do
end

Fig. 2. The parallel algorithm for computing A^{-1}

4   Implementation and Numerical Results

The algorithm inverse was implemented on a Silicon Graphics Origin 2000 parallel computer with 16 R10000 processors (running at 195 MHz). The implementation used the following scheduling algorithms: block scheduling (B), self-scheduling (SS), affinity scheduling (AS) and feedback guided dynamic loop scheduling (FS).

The block scheduling algorithm is the simplest; it divides the parallel loop into p equal-sized blocks or chunks. This schedule can lead to load imbalance, although the computation cost of the scheduling algorithm is small, and there are no synchronisation overheads.

The self-scheduling algorithms use a central queue of iteration indices. When a processor finishes the computation associated with a given iteration index, it removes the next loop iteration index from the queue and executes the associated computation. The simple block self-scheduling algorithm [9] allows a processor to take a chunk of k iterations from the queue; this reduces the contention of multiple processors accessing the shared queue, but can lead to some load imbalance. To avoid this poorer load balance, guided self-scheduling algorithms, see [11], dynamically change the chunk size, starting from a large size and making it progressively smaller. The way in which the chunk size decreases gives rise to several different guided self-scheduling algorithms: adaptive guided self-scheduling [4], factoring [7] and trapezoid self-scheduling [15]. Trapezoid self-scheduling was used for the results given in Table 1.

Affinity scheduling algorithms [12], [16] use an iteration queue for each processor in order to reduce the contention to the shared queue of self-scheduling algorithms —

each processor manages its own queue. The main advantage of affinity scheduling is that temporal locality of data is maintained, thereby reducing the associated overheads.

Table 1. Execution times

	$p = 1$	$p = 2$	$p = 4$	$p = 8$	$p = 16$
B	24.835	18.082	16.594	12.173	8.096
SS	24.894	16.794	12.091	8.450	5.289
AS	24.881	15.106	11.487	7.043	3.275
FS	24.859	13.652	7.206	4.569	2.791

The algorithms were evaluated with a matrix with 1000 rows and columns. The execution times for different numbers of processors ($p = 1, 2, 4, 8$ and 16) are shown in Table 1 and Figure 3. Several remarks can be drawn by analysing the results. The longer execution times for schedule B are mainly due to the poor load balance of a static schedule. Using dynamic scheduling (SS, AS, FS), the load imbalance is reduced leading to shorter execution times. The schedule FS results in the shortest execution times.

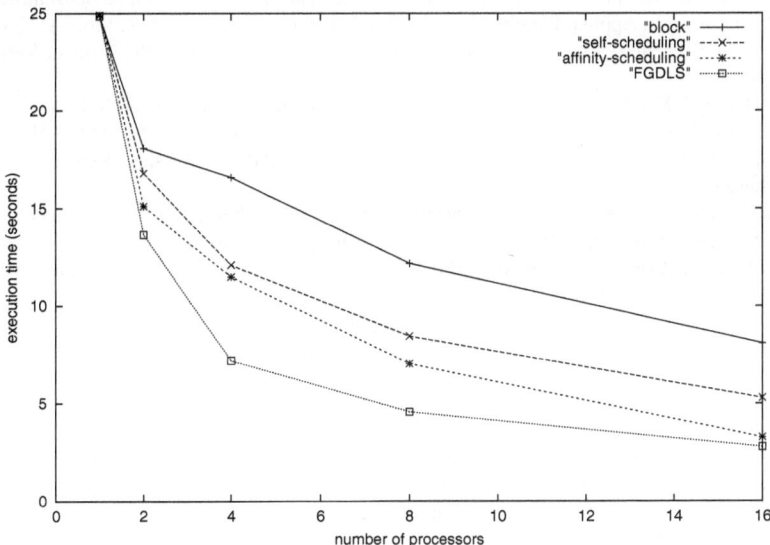

Fig. 3. Performance of the Algorithms.

5   Conclusions

FGDLS has been proven to be a useful loop scheduling algorithm. This algorithm uses measured execution times to guide subsequent schedules of the parallel loop. This article has shown how the FGDLS algorithm can be used to schedule the computation of the inverse of a lower triangular matrix. Moreover, comparison with several other scheduling algorithms has confirmed the efficiency of the FGDLS algorithm.

References

1. J.M.Bull (1998) Feedback Guided Loop Scheduling: Algorithm and Experiments, Proceedings of Euro-Par'98, Lecture Notes in Computer Science, Springer Verlag.
2. J.M.Bull, R.W.Ford and A.Dickinson (1996) A Feedback Based Load Balance Algorithm for Physics Routines in NWP, Proceedings of Seventh Workshop on the Use of Parallel Processors in Meteorology, World Scientific.
3. J.M.Bull, R.W.Ford, T.L.Freeman and D.J.Hancock (1999) A Theoretical Investigation of Feedback Guided Loop Scheduling, Proceedings of Ninth SIAM Conference on Parallel Processing for Scientific Computing, SIAM Press.
4. D.L.Eager and J.Zahorjan (1992) Adaptive Guided Self-Scheduling, Technical Report 92-01-01, Department of Computer Science and Engineering, University of Washington.
5. T.L.Freeman and C.Phillips (1992) Parallel Numerical Algorithms, Prentice Hall, New York.
6. T.L.Freeman, D.J.Hancock, J.M.Bull and R.W.Ford (2001) *Feedback Guided Scheduling of Nested Loops*, In Applied Parallel Computing, ed. T. Sørevik, F. Manne, R. Moe, A. H. Gebremedhin, Lecture Notes in Computer Science, vol. 1947, pp. 149–159, Springer-Verlag, Berlin.
7. S.F.Hummel, E.Schonberg and L.E.Flynn (1992) Factoring: A Practical and Robust Method for Scheduling Parallel Loops, Communications of the ACM, vol.35, no.8, pp.90–101.
8. J.Jájá (1992) An Introduction to Parallel Algorithms, Addison-Wesley, Reading, Massachusetts.
9. C.P.Kruskal and A.Weiss (1985) Allocating Independent Subtasks on Parallel Processors, IEEE Trans. on Software Engineering, vol.11, no.10, pp.1001–1016.
10. S.Lakshmivarahan and S.K.Dhall (1990) Analysis and Design of Parallel Algorithms: Arithmetic and Matrix Problems, McGraw-Hill, New York.
11. C.D.Polychronopolos and D.J.Kuck (1987) Guided Self-Scheduling: A Practical Scheduling Scheme for Parallel Supercomputers, IEEE Trans. on Computers, vol.36, no.12, pp.1425–1439.
12. S.Subramanian and D.L.Eager (1994) Affinity Scheduling of Unbalanced Workloads, Proceedings of SuperComputing 94, IEEE Comp. Soc. Press, pp.214–226.
13. R.Sakellariou (1997) On the Quest for Perfect Load Balance in Loop-Based Parallel Computation, PhD Thesis, Department of Computer Science, Manchester University.
14. G.W.Stewart (1973) Introduction to Matrix Computations, Academic Press, New York.
15. T.H.Tzen and L.M.Ni (1993) Trapezoid Self-Scheduling Scheme for Parallel Computers, IEEE Trans. on Parallel and Distributed Systems, vol.4, no.1, pp.87–98.
16. Y.Yan, C.Jin and X.Zhang (1997) Adaptively Scheduling Parallel Loops in Distributed Shared-Memory Systems, IEEE Trans. on Parallel and Distributed Systems, vol.8, no.1, pp.70–81.

DIM – A Distributed Image Processing System, Based on ISO IEC 12087 Image Processing Standard

Paulina Mitrea

"Avram Iancu" University, Applied Sciences Faculty, Cluj Napoca- ROMANIA
paulina.mitrea@art-net.ro, mitpola@yahoo.com

Abstract. The amount of computing in the vast majority of image processing applications is high, leading to a high interest in reducing execution time. Following our line in developing complete and general purpose Image Processing tools, succeeding to a Multithreaded Image Processing System conceived for single processor systems, we develop now a Distributed Image Processing System, which will implement the ISO IEC 12087 Image Processing Standard with Cluster Computing methods. The final aim of this work is to obtain a complete image-processing library for Cluster Computing. Some basic notions, followed by the presentation of the most important methods implemented in order to generate the distributed algorithms, will be presented in this paper.

1 Introduction

The amount of computing in the vast majority of image processing applications is high, leading to a high interest in reducing execution time. This is the reason why this domain has known a spectacular development, especially in the last years. There are various distributed Image Processing environments now, which are often designed explicitly for some important domains (such as medicine, robotics, earth physics, astrophysics, industry etc). Such a system, one of the most known, is *DIPE – a Distributed Environment for Medical Image Processing*, that provides image processing services over integrated teleradiology services networks [5]. This environment dates from 1997. Another one is *DIPS – Distributed Image Processing Shell*, which is a software tool, developed at the Computer Graphics and Vision unit of the Graz University of Technology in Austria [8]. *IPARS – Integrated Parallel Accurate Reservoir Simulators* - is a framework for developing parallel models of subsurface flow and transport through porous media. It was developed at the "Center for Subsurface Modeling", at the University of Texas' Institute for Computational and Applied Mathematics [9]. More recently, in April 2001, at the Workshop on Parallel and Distributed Computing in Image Processing at San Francisco (PDIVM'2001), new systems were presented, more and more powerful, using various Cluster Computing and Parallel Computing technologies.

Following our line in developing complete and general purpose Image Processing tools, succeeding to a *Multithreaded Image Processing System* conceived for single computer systems within a collaboration with Dynamic Imaging from Norway, we

D. Grigoras et al. (Eds.): IWCC 2001, LNCS 2326, pp. 293-307, 2002.
© Springer-Verlag Berlin Heidelberg 2002

develop now a *Distributed Image Processing System*. The aim is to implement now
the ISO IEC 12087 Image Processing Standard with Cluster Computing methods. The
final aim of this work is to obtain a complete image-processing library for Cluster
Computing.

2 Image Processing Basic Principles and Terminology

Our works respects the Programmer's Imaging Kernel System imaging model,
represented bellow by his four major parts, which are: data objects; operators, tools
and utilities; system mechanisms; import and export.

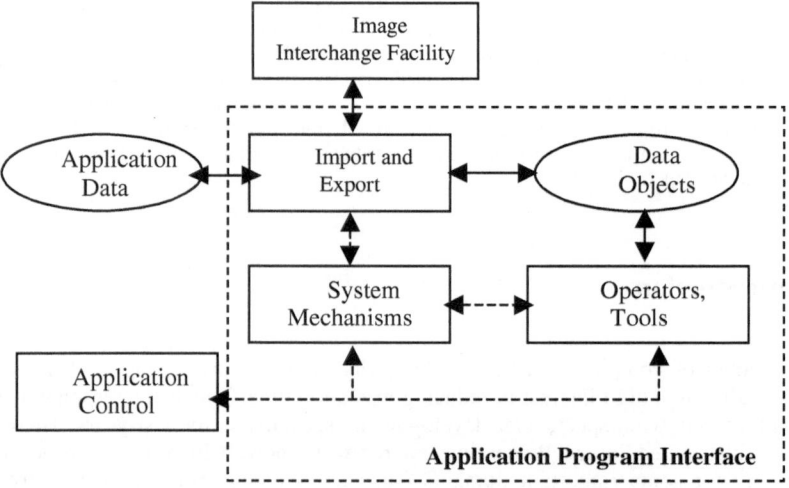

Fig. 1. Programmer Imaging Kernel System imaging model

In the most general acceptation, in the case of the 3-dimensional space, the image
data objects are defined to be five-dimensional arrays with ordered indices denoted
by: x – as horizontal index, y – as vertical index, z – as depth index, t – as time index,
b – as color band index. A two-dimensional array involving only two indices is called
a pixel plane [see 10]. Conceptually, a five–dimensional image object can be
considered as being organized as a set of depth, time and band pixel planes [10]. In
this case, *a single source image* is expressed as a five-dimensional array
SRC(x,y,z,t,b), and the p-th source image in a set of P images is expressed as
$SRC_p(x,y,z,t,b)$, where $1 \leq p \leq P$. Analogically, *a single destination image* is expressed
as a five-dimensional array DST(x,y,z,t,b), and the q-th destination image in a set of
Q images is expressed as $DST_q(x,y,z,t,b)$, where $1 \leq q \leq Q$.

According to the Image Processing Standard ISO/IEC [see 10], certain dimensional subsets of a general five-dimensional image object have the following semantic meanings: monochrome, volumetric, temporal, colored, spectral, volume-temporal, volume-colored, volume-spectral, temporal-colored, temporal-spectral, volume-temporal-colored, volume-temporal-spectral, generic (when all the indices are nonzero).

The *pixel data type* may differ between bands. An image whose pixels are of different data types across bands is called a *heterogeneous band image*.

More than in this complex basic context of the image processing domain, in case of multi-volumetric and multi-parametric data and applications, it is useful to generalize the working space to n-dimensions. So, the source and destination image arrays will be expressed as

$$\text{SRC}(x_1, x_2, x_3,..., x_n,b) \text{ and } \text{DST}(x_1, x_2, x_3,..., x_n,b)$$

and the p-th source/destination image in a set of P images as

$$\text{SRC}_p (x_1, x_2, x_3,..., x_n,b) \text{ and } \text{DST}_p (x_1, x_2, x_3,..., x_n,b).$$

In all our works, the image processing operators are implemented in the most general n-dimensional space, and this is the reason for which the cluster computing approach is the best solution.

Following the standard, our operator model implements three possible transformations of the data objects:

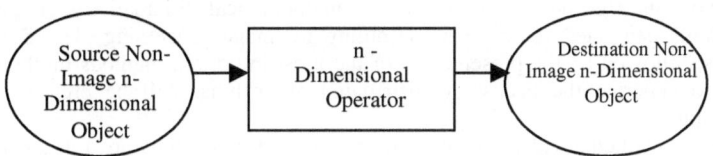

Fig. 2. Non-image to non-image

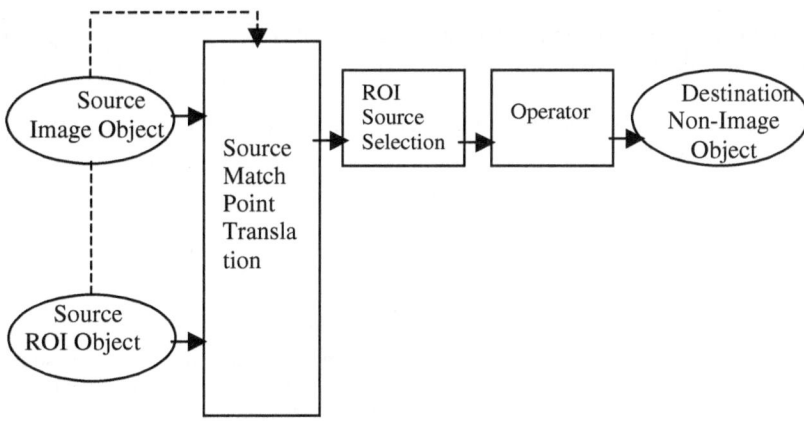

Fig. 3. Image to non-image

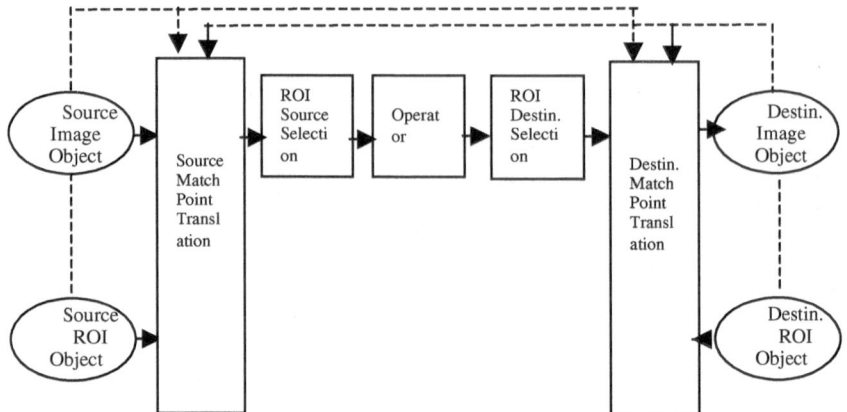

Fig. 4. Image to image

ROI is the abbreviation for Region of Interest, and the role of this structure will be shown in the formal definitions of the operators presented in this paper.

3 Mathematical Background

Our work is rigorously based on the mathematical foundations of distributed algorithms generated for cluster computing in image processing [1]. Some basic notions, followed by the presentation of the most important methods implemented in order to generate the necessary distributed algorithms, will be presented in this paragraph.

From a mathematical point of view, distributed algorithms are formalized in the context of linear spaces. So, let be a linear space denoted by X, X_0 a subset of X, $(Y, //\bullet//)$ a linear space in which it is defined a norm, and an application S of X_0 over Y (i.e. $S: X_0 \to Y$).

The problem of determining an element y, $y \in Y$, so that $//S(x) - y// \le \varepsilon$ (for given positive ε), for all the elements $x \in X_0$, is called as (X_0, S)-*problem* or simply S-*problem*.

The element $x \in X_0$ is called as problem element, S is a solution operator, $s := S(x)$ is named solution element, and

$$\tilde{s} \in Y \quad \text{with the property that}$$

$$\left\| s - \tilde{s} \right\| \le \varepsilon$$

is called as ε-approximation of the solution element s.

In order to obtain an approximation of the element s, they are necessary some information about the problem element x. For this, it is introduced the informational operator, denoted by I, which is an application $I: X \to Z$, where Z is a given set. $I(x)$ is the information about the problem element **x** .

An application $\alpha: I(X_0) \to Y$ is an algorithm $(X_0 \subset X)$.

If S is a given problem, I the informational operator and α the corresponding algorithm, we call (I, α) as method for the S-problem, denoted by μ. So, $\mu = (I, \alpha)$, and $s = \mu(x)$ is the approximation of x given by the method μ.

Generally, there exist many methods in order to solve one given S-problem. If we denote by $M(S)$ (or $M(S,\varepsilon)$) the set of methods which solve the problem S, the error of the method μ is

$$e(S, \mu) = \sup_{x \in x_0} \|S(x) - \mu(x)\|$$

In this acceptance, a method described by a successive set of instructions (operations) executed by only one processor is a *serial method*. But if a method $\mu \in M(S)$ consists of more than one set of operations, which may be executed simultaneously by a corresponding number of processors, this is a *distributed method*. As it is well known, a serial method μ may be converted to a distributed method by dividing the method μ into some independent segments, denoted by $\mu_1, \mu_2, \mu_3, \dots, \mu_r$ $(r > 1)$. In this way, the method μ is achieved by accomplishing simultaneously the segments μ_i, $(i = 1,r)$, and then by assembling the partial results obtained in this way.

In Image Processing, the structure of the image, formed by large sets of pixels, which may be considered as vectors or as matrices, not only enables the distributions of some image processing methods, but strongly requires them, because of the high number of calculations which must be made to process an entire image. As basics of these approach, the serial operations which may be organized as sums of successive independent terms (i.e. $E = T_1 + T_2 + T_3 + \dots T_2^n$), may be transformed in the following manner of organization of the calculus:

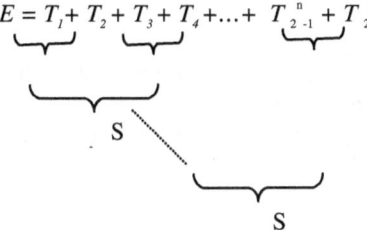

$$E = T_1 + T_2 + T_3 + T_4 + \dots + T_{2^n-1} + T_2^n$$

In this case, we have partially parallel calculation segments, but in the case of image arrays which were defined in the previous paragraph, we must combine the partially parallel methods with integral parallel approaches, by splitting a general problem of operating two source images $SRC_1(x_1, x_2, x_3, \dots, x_n, b)$ and $SRC_2(x_1', x_2', x_3', \dots, x_n', b')$, in appropriates μ_i *integrally parallel segments*.

Another degree of distribution of the calculations is made at the level of threads, which are also distributed to the cluster's stations/processors.

3.1 Complexity Estimations

From mathematical point of view, the notion of *complexity* is defined as follows:

3.1.1. Let be $r \in R$, where R is a set of operations. The time, which is necessary to perform the operation r expressed in given time units (i.e. microseconds), is named complexity of the operation r.

3.1.2. Let be $\mu \in M(S)$, where $M(S)$ is a set of methods in the sense expressed in the first paragraph, and $r_1, r_2,..., r_n \in R$ the operators which are used in the method μ. Let denote

$$cp(\mu, x) = \sum_{i=1}^{n} p_i \, cp(r_i)$$

where p_i is the number of the occurrences of the operation r_i in the method μ. Then $cp(\mu, x)$ is named *complexity of the method* μ concerning the problem element x (*local complexity*).

Let also $x \in X_0$ as it is defined in the first paragraph. Let denote

$$cp(\mu) = \sup_{x \in X_0} cp(\mu, x).$$

Then $cp(\mu)$ is named global complexity of the method μ.

3.1.3. Let be $\mu^P \in M_p(S)$ a parallel method and $\mu_1, \mu_2,..., \mu_r$ the segments of the method μ^P. Let denote

$$cp(\mu^P) = \max_{1 \le i \le r} cp(\mu_i),$$

where $cp(\mu_I)$ is the complexity of the segment I. Then $cp(\mu^P)$ is named *complexity of the parallel method* μ^P.

All our references concerning the complexity are made taking into account the definitions presented above.

4 Implementation Details

The set of Image Processing operators defined in the Image Processing Foundations [2], was implemented on a cluster of computers under GLUNIX.
    The operators are grouped into some distinct categories, such as:

- **Point Operators**: Bit Shift, Complement, Lookup, Monadic Arithmetic, Monadic Logical, Threshold, Unary Integer, Window Level
- **Ensemble Operators**: Alpha Blend, Dyadic Arithmetic, Dyadic Logical, Dyadic Predicate, Split Image

- **Filtering and Morphological Operators**: Convolve Two-dimensional, Morphic Processor
- **Geometric Operators:** Flip, Spin, Transpose, Rescale, Resize, Rotate, Subsemple, Translate, Zoom
- **Presentation Operators:** Diffuse, Dither
- **Colour Operators:** Colour Conversion – Linear, Colour Conversion – Subtractive, Luminance Generation
- **Pixel Modification Operators:** Draw Pixel
- **Analysis Operators**: Accumulator, Extrema, Histogram, Moments

In that follows, we introduce the details over our implementation solution of the last mentioned group, i. e. for the group of Analysis Operators – a class of image to non-image operators that extract numerical information from an image.

4.1. Accumulator Operator: By definition [see 10] it is an unary operation, which accumulates amplitudes of pixels of an image, according to a dimensional cut parameter "m".

Parameter description

Name	Description
in	Source image
roi	ROI object
out	Sum of pixels array object
sum	Sum of all pixels
No	No.of dimensions to cut

Nomenclature:

$SRC(x_1, x_2, \ldots x_n, b)$	$X_1 \times X_2 \times \ldots \times X_n \times B$ operator source image
$R(x_1, x_2, \ldots, x_n)$	$X_1 \times X_2 \times \ldots \times X_n$ operator ROI(Region Of Interest)
$DST(x_1, x_2, \ldots x_{n-m},)$	$X_1 \times X_2 \times \ldots \times X_{n-m}$ operator destination array
m	Number of dimensions to cut $1 \leq m < n$

Formal definition:

Compute the sum of all pixels that respect $R(x_1, x_2, \ldots, x_n) = \text{TRUE}$ condition, according to the m parameter:

$$DST(x_1, x_2, \cdots, x_{n-m}) = \sum_{x_{n-m}}^{X_{n-m}} \cdots \sum_{x_1}^{X_1} \sum_{b}^{B} SRC(x_1, x_2, \cdots, x_n, b)$$

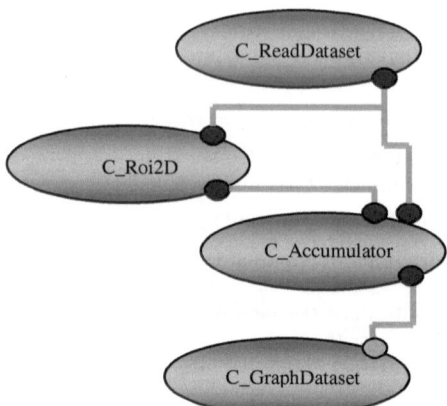

Fig. 5. Network example

The load balancing solution implemented in this case is based on *recursive coordinate bisection* [3]: so, the input domain is split in sub-domains with approximately equal amount of the calculations, by maintaining in same time a minimum amount of communications. It was proved by experiments that, in this case, this is the best solution; moreover, this is true also based on the fact that in the case of *Accumulator* operator, the local communications are of medium complexity.

4.2. Extrema Operator - detects the smallest and largest pixels of an image and records their values in an external array.

Parameter description

Name	Description
in	Source image
roi	ROI object
minima	Minima external array
maxima	Maxima external array
dimensions	No. of dimensions to perform extrema

Nomenclature:

$SRC(x_1, x_2, ..., x_n, b)$ $X_1 \times X_2 \times ... \times X_n \times B$ operator source image

$R(x_1, x_2, ..., x_n)$ $X_1 \times X_2 \times ... \times X_n$ operator roi

m number of dimension extrema is performed on

$(x_{1\,min}, ..., x_{m\,min}, x_{m+1}, ..., x_n)$ - coordinate of the smallest pixel when extrema is performed on m dimensions

$(x_{1\,max}, ..., x_{m\,max}, x_{m+1}, ..., x_n)$ - coordinate of the largest pixel when extrema is performed on m dimensions

Formal definition:

For all x_1, x_2, ..., x_n that respect $R(x_1,x_2,...,x_n)$ = TRUE, the source image is searched for the smallest and largest pixels, and the following maxima and minima arrays are created.

Minima array

$$SRC(x_{1\,min}, ... , x_{m\,min}, 0, \qquad ...,0 \quad)$$
$$\vdots$$
$$SRC(x_{1\,min}, ... , x_{m\,min}, X_{m+1}-1, \quad ...,X_n-1)$$

Maxima array

$$SRC(x_{1\,max}, ... , x_{m\,max}, 0, \qquad ...,0 \quad)$$
$$\vdots$$
$$SRC(x_{1\,max}, ... , x_{m\,max}, X_{m+1}-1,... ,X_n-1)$$

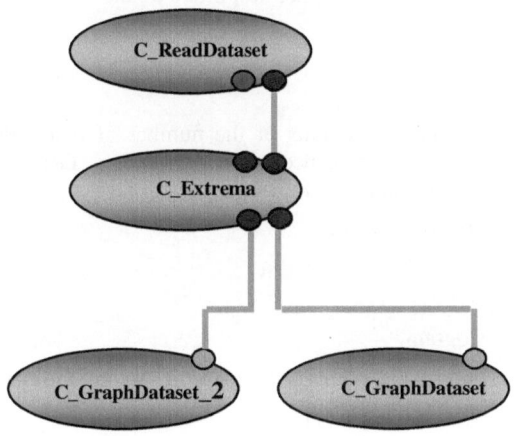

Fig. 6. Network example

The load balancing solution implemented in the case of *Extrema* operator is also based on *recursive coordinate bisection*.

4.3. Histogram, One-dimensional Operator - generates a one-dimensional histogram of an image.

Parameter description

0 Name   Description

in	Source image
roi	ROI object
out	Histogram
bins	Number of histogram amplitude bins
L	Lower amplitude bound
U	Upper amplitude bound
option	Histogram computation option

Nomenclature:

$S(x_1, x_2, ..., x_n, b)$	$X_1 \times X_2 \times ... \times X_n \times B$ source image
$R(x_1, x_2, ..., x_n)$	$X_1 \times X_2 \times ... \times X_n$ operator roi
E	Number of histogram amplitude bins, $E \geq 1$
$H(e)$	Histogram array, $0 \leq e \leq E\text{-}1$
L	Lower amplitude bound
U	Upper amplitude bound

Formal definition:

The histogram array contains the counts of the number of pixels that have certain quantified amplitude values, and respect $R(x_1,x_2,...,x_n) = $ TRUE condition,. The implemented histogram algorithm is as follows:

Step 1. Initialize histogram to zero.

> For $0 \leq e \leq E\text{-}1$
> $H(e) = 0$

Step 2: Compute histogram.

For all $x_1, x_2, ..., x_n$ and for $0 \leq e \leq E\text{-}1$, if a pixel lies within the e-th quantification levels

> $q(e) \leq S(x_1, x_2, ..., x_n) < q(e+1)$

then increment the histogram array by one

> $H(e) = H(e) + 1$

where for *specified histogram amplitude bounds U and L*

$$q(e) = \frac{e[U - L]}{E} + L$$

and for *image extrema amplitude limits*, with

$0 < x_1 < X_1\text{-}1, 0 < x_2 < X_2\text{-}1, ..., 0 < x_n < X_n\text{-}1$

$$q(e) = \frac{e[MAX\{S(x_1, x_2, ..., x_n)\} - MIN\{S(x_1, x_2, ..., x_n)\}]}{E} + MIN\{S(x_1, x_2, ..., x_n)\} \cdot$$

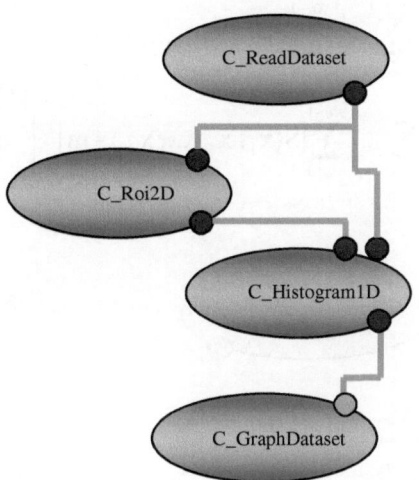

Fig. 7. Network example

By our cluster computing approach, $H(e)$, for $0 \leq e \leq E\text{-}1$ is obtained as totals all $H_i(e)$, $i=1,N$ where N denote the number of the computers of the cluster and i is the identification number of the computer loaded with the "i"-th domain slice. The load balancing solution is also in this case the *recursive coordinate bisection*.

4.4. Moments Operator - computes the mean and standard deviation moments of an image.

Parameter description

1Name	Description
in	Source image
mean	Mean value
deviation	Standard deviation value

Nomenclature:

$S(x_1, x_2, ..., x_n)$	X_1 x X_2 x ... x X_n source image
m	source image mean value
s	source image standard deviation value, $s \geq 0$

Formal definition:

For all $x_1, x_2, ..., x_n$

$$m = \frac{1}{X_1 \, X_2 \, \cdots \, X_n} \sum_{x1=0}^{X1-1} \sum_{x2=0}^{X2-1} \cdots \sum_{xn=0}^{Xn-1} S(x_1, x_2, ..., x_n)$$

$$s = \left[\frac{1}{X_1 \, X_2 \cdots X_n} \sum_{x1=0}^{X1-1} \sum_{x2=0}^{X2-1} \cdots \sum_{xn=0}^{Xn-1} [S(x_1, x_2, ..., x_n) - m]^2 \right]^{1/2}$$

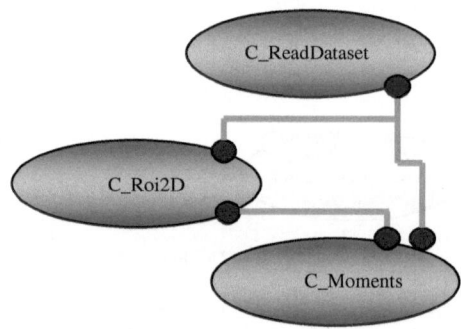

Fig. 8. Network example

The load balancing solution is the *recursive coordinate bisection*. At each step are calculated in an iterative way, on the *N* computers of the cluster, both the mean value and the standard deviation elements corresponding for each domain slice loaded on the computers.

4.5. A different technique of loading the parallel tasks on the computers of the cluster is used in the case of *Fourier Transform* operator, which belongs to the technical profile of our image processing package. This operator is very important due to the major advantages of the *FFT (Fast Fourier Transform)* over other types of frequency analysis, e.g. using filters. This advantage is that retention of phase information makes transformations in either direction possible and in fact relatively simple. It also permits the evaluation of a large number of functions applicable to multi-channel measurements and system analysis, e.g. correlation, coherence etc.

The formal definition of the Fourier transform in 1D case, is the following [see also 3]:

$$X_k = \frac{1}{N} \sum_{j=0}^{N-1} x_j e^{-2\pi i \frac{jk}{N}},$$

where $i = (-1)^{1/2}$. The sequential algorithm is time expensive, being of $O(n^2)$ time complexity. This is the reason for which finding the best solutions to make faster this algorithm was a great challenge for many scientists. Founded in 1965, the solution of Cooley and Tokey is very well known; this solution reduce the complexity of the algorithm to $O(nlogn)$ [11].

Using the notation $\omega = e^{-2\pi i/N}$, we can write the previous formula as:

$$X_k = \frac{1}{N}\sum_{j=0}^{N-1} x_j \omega^{jk}$$

This expression may be written as two sums: one of them for the values of X with odd index, other for the even indexed values. So:

$$X_k = \frac{1}{N}(\sum_{j=0}^{(N/2)-1} x_{2j} \omega^{2jk} + \sum_{j=0}^{(N/2)-1} x_{2j+1} \omega^{(2j+1)k}),$$

A simple rearrangement leads to:

$$X_k = \frac{1}{2}(\frac{1}{N/2}\sum_{j=0}^{(N/2)-1} x_{2j} \omega^{2jk} + \omega^k \frac{1}{N/2}\sum_{j=0}^{(N/2)-1} x_{2j+1} \omega^{2jk})$$

It is obvious that this last formula represents the sum of two Fourier Transforms, each of them being of $N/2$ elements, i.e. :

$$X_k = \frac{1}{2}(X_{even\_indexed} + \omega^k X_{odd\_indexed})$$

for $k = 0, 1, 2,..., N-1$.

Supposing now that **the maximum value of k must be $N/2-1$**, we may split the formula into:

$$X_k = \frac{1}{2}(X_{even\_indexed} + \omega^k X_{odd\_indexed})$$

and

$$X_{k+N/2} = \frac{1}{2}(X_{even\_indexed} + \omega^{k+N/2} X_{odd\_indexed}) = \frac{1}{2}(X_{even\_indexed} - X_{odd\_indexed})$$

where $\omega^{k+N/2} = -\omega^k$, for $0 \leq k < N/2$. X_k and $X_{k+N/2}$ may be calculated separately, as two different Fourier Transforms having each of them N/2 elements. In the same manner, the new sums can be split too, so we may apply the *"divide et impera"* method.

The evolution of the calculation respects so a butterfly topology[3].

So, the immediate parallelization solution is to use a butterfly type network to implement the much faster parallel algorithm, of complexity $O(logN)$. This algorithm is known as "binary-exchange": each processor from the total number of N processors, is allocated to a single sample, producing, finally, one element of the resulting vector. But, because in the usual practice, a general number of p processors are involved, each of them processing N/p data, we implemented this operator for the N_p processors of the cluster, such as N/N_p data are processed on each computer.

Being N steps to do, and Np processors in the cluster, the cost function is of complexity $O(NlogN)$, and the communication operations are of complexity $O(log Np)$. As it is stated in [3], this parallel solution is optimal concerning the costs.

Actually, in our works the single-dimensional approach is generalized to the n-dimensional formula, as follows [see also 12]:

$$DST(x_1, x_2, ...,x_n) = \frac{1}{\sqrt{(J_1, J_2,..., J_n)}} \sum_{j_1'=0}^{J_1-1} ,...., \sum_{j_5'=0}^{J_n-1} C(j_1', j_2',...,j_n') \times$$

$$\times SRC(j_1', j_2',....,j_n')EXP\{2\pi i[x_1 j_1'/J_1 + x_2 j_2'/J_2, +...+x_n j_n'/J_n]\}$$

where

$$C(j_1',j_2',....,j_n') = 1 \qquad \text{for d.c. term at origin}$$
$$C(j_1',j_2',....,j_n') = (-1)^{(j_1' +j_2' +...+j_n')} \qquad \text{for d.c. term at center}$$

And

$j_1',j_2',....,j_n'$ are the bit-reversed values of $x_1, x_2, ...,x_n$.

The N-Dimensional mode, inverse transform is:

$$D(j_1, j_2, ...j_n) = \frac{1}{\sqrt{(J_1, J_2,..., J_n)}} \sum_{j_1'=0}^{J_1-1} ,...., \sum_{j_5'=0}^{J_n-1} S(j_1', j_2',....,j_n')$$

$$\times EXP\{2\pi i[j_1 j_1'/J_1 + j_2 j_2'/J_2, +...+j_n j_n'/J_n]\}$$

In the case of the n-dimensional Fourier Transform, the parallelization is made for each dimension in the manner shown at the 1-dimensional transformation, the successive dimensions being performed one after the other.

5 Particularities of Our Approach

Taking into account the fact that, in the concrete hardware context of various particular users, the number of available processors changes, our system is a parametric one in order to allow to automatically adapting the parallel method to the user's particularities. In such a way, we assure the scalability of the system, obtaining the best (smallest) complexity concerning the parallel method.

As it is stated above, the load balancing solutions are also adapted to the particularities of each operator, in order to obtain the maximum advantages which is possible in the context of the cluster.

Conclusions

As it is illustrated in this paper, the implementation of the distributed version of the Image Processing tools, respects the formal definition given in *ISO IEC 12087 Image Processing Standard*. In the actual Cluster Computing approach, the software package is much more performant, being also very useful in any kind of real time processing applications.

References

1. Coman, Gh.: Analiza Numerica, Cluj-Napoca, 1996.
2. Pratt, W.K.: PIKS Foundations, Greenwich, 1995.
3. Grigoras, D.: Calculul Paralel, Computer Libris Agora, Cluj-Napoca, 2000.
4. Wilkinson, B., Allen, M.: Parallel Programming, Prentice Hall, New Jersey, 1999.
5. http://www.ics.forth.gr/~zicos/publications/02_mie97dipe/mie97dipe.html
6. http://www.joeljeffery.co.uk/Joel/JMRI/welcome.htm
7. http://www.ehere.com/eheretec/djip/wljiphome.html
8. http://www.icg.tu-graz.ac.at/WWW-Softserver/dips/
9. http://www.cs.utk.edu/netsolve/applications/IPARS.html
10. ISO/IEC 12087 –2: (1994)(E) – "Image Processing Standard"
11. Randall, R.B., Techn, B.: Frequency Analysis, Bruel&Kjaer, Sept. 1987.
12. Grigoras, D., Mitrea, P.: Parallelized Image Processing Algorithms for HPC Systems" SGI'(2000), Krakow, Poland, Oct. 2000.

DisMedJava – A Distributed Application for Medical Image Processing

Cristian Buţincu [1] and Dan Grigoras [2]

[1] Technical University "Gh. Asachi" Iasi, Romania,
Computer Science Department
cryb@easynet.ro
[2] University College Cork, Ireland,
Computer Science Department
d.grigoras@cs.ucc.ie

Abstract. This paper presents a scalable distributed application for medical image processing. This application, called DisMedJava, is a scalable client-server multi-slaveServer distributed application. In other words, it is a typical client-server application, where the server monitors the system and manages the database, and several slave servers (workers) are used for image parallel processing tasks. This system can be accessed from both local (intranet) and remote (internet) locations. Image processing techniques are used for manipulating and displaying images. The DisMedJava system provides two main functions: distributed image processing and database support.

1 Introduction

Huge amount of information, especially images, is managed and processed in hospitals. Many digital equipments like CT Scanners produce data related to patients. Medical staff need computer support not only for storing these data but also in analysing and making decisions. Sometimes, medical images need to be digitally enhanced in order to obtain improved images which can be more easily analysed. As medical images are high-resolution they impose a lot of time-consuming processing. Few terminals in hospitals have sufficient computing resources and, as a consequence, dedicated image processing servers should be used to accomplish the image-related processing job.

Fig. 1. Simple diagnostic process chain

D. Grigoras et al. (Eds.): IWCC 2001, LNCS 2326, pp. 308-320, 2002.

Figure 1 presents the common diagnostic chain when interpreting medical images. It is considered that only 5% of information is used and 95% is lost. Computers can raise significantly the first percentage. Allowing doctors to filter certain regions of interest of the image, the analysis can be more effective. The distributed application we designed, called DisMedJava, plays that supporting role.

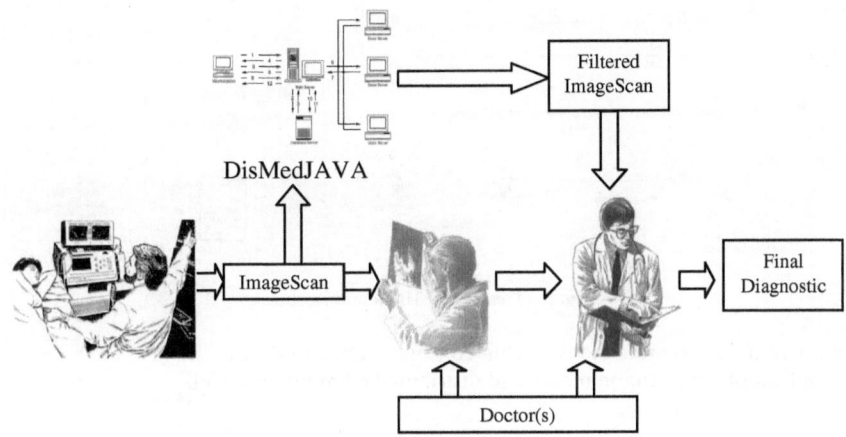

Fig. 2. DisMedJAVA diagnostic process chain

The DisMedJava application consists of a scalable distributed image processing system and storing support. We are using Sun Microsystems JAI (Java Advanced Imaging) Java extension package combined with distributed algorithms, in order to achieve parallel processing of images. The storage is implemented by ORACLE DBMS [1-2].

Section 2 will introduce the application architecture, section 3 presents some preliminary performance data and the paper ends with conclusions.

2 Application Architecture

DisMedJava is a typical client-server application, where the server monitors the system and manages the database, and several slave servers (workers) are used for image parallel processing tasks. The system architecture is illustrated in Figure 3.

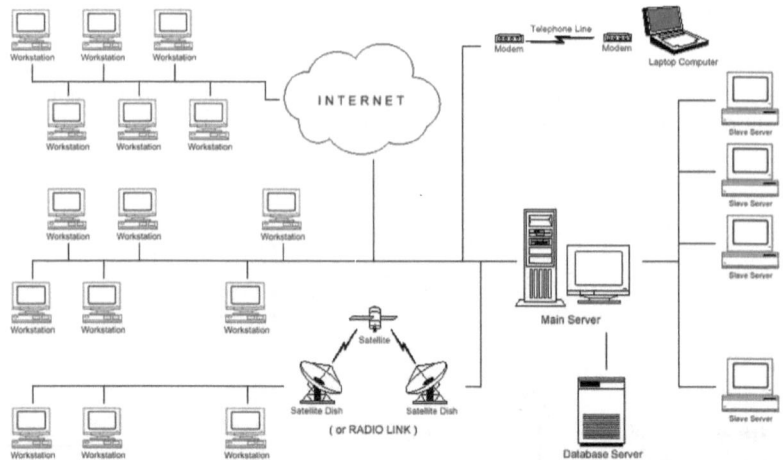

Fig. 3. The DisMedJava architecture

We will try to separate the two main concepts (models) [3] that stand at the base of this application: application model and distributed computing model.

2.1 Application Model

This application's goal is to help doctors in hospitals to achieve more accurate diagnostics in a much less time than before. The main interaction between doctors and the application's system is carried out by the client program.

The client program is the interface between the user and the DisMedJava system, and provides all tools that the user needs to interact with the system. Its GUI [4] reflects the three main function the system provides:

- **user database** - provides all tools the user needs to interact with private databases, maintained on the mainServer side
- **shared database** - provides all tools the user needs to (only) read data from a portion of database of another user, also maintained on mainServer side
- **imageScans workspace** - is the place where the user interacts with image processing techniques in order to filter an image and to obtain an enhanced version of it [5]

The client program provides a wide range of built-in image filters which range from single image ones (image filters that can be applied only to a single image) to dual image filters (image filters that combine two images). A two image synchronization mechanism is provided in order to synchronize images that may be involved into a dual image filter processing in order to obtain correct results. Almost all provided image filters can make use of mainServer participation, except dual image filters that were excluded from distributed processing for performance reasons. The client program gives user the possibility to set the image processing local computer participation (in percents) interactively through a GUI slider. Other features are briefly enumerated here: image previews before opening an image, image compression/quality settings before saving an image locally, undo mechanisms, ergonomic GUI, different GUIs for different platforms (Windows, Motif and Java).

The client program makes use of JPEG compression internally (maximum quality) in order to take up the minimum amount of resources and to minimize the communication to the mainServer. It also implements a cache mechanism in order to reduce disk accesses and communications with the mainServer. The client program provides functions such as drop and free viewport in order to free memory and to take up as minimum resources as possible.

The client program provides a self recovery from crashes mechanism (that is, the mainServer link is broken). It will attempt to reconnect to mainServer every time the user requests a function that implies it.

2.2 Distributed Computing Model

The DisMedJava system provides two main functions: distributed image processing and database support.

The previous section contains a brief overview over the mainServer component of this application. Actually, the mainServer is the core component of the distributed system implemented by this application. As you will see later in this paper, the application has two more components besides the client component: mainServer and slaveServer component. These two components make up the distributed processing mechanism of this application and are described in detail in the next sections.

We used in previous section the syntax "mainServer participation". We mean by that the participation of all distributed computing resources, and that also includes the slaveServers.

2.2.1 The Main Server Component

The mainServer program acts like a bridge between client and both database and slaveServers. All security checks take place at this level. It performs all security checks in order to allow a user to access databases and to benefit from image processing power provided by its subordinated slaveServers. In the case the user requests an image processing, the mainServer splits the received image into several slices accordingly to the number of online slaveServers, forwards each of these slices to its assigned slaveServer along with image filter parameters, collects the results from slaveServers as they finish the jobs, and when all pieces of processed image were retrieved, reassembles and sends the filtered image back to the client. Generally, the slices have different sizes (resolutions) according to the slaveServer weights. That is, if a slaveServer has a weight of 60 and another has a weight of 30, the first one gets a slice twice as big as the second one.

The mainServer implements a powerful built-in security system. It's description and complexity doesn't make the object of this paper.

A slaveServers self tuning weights mechanism is also provided. The slaveServer weights are relative to each other. This mechanism adjusts slaveServers weights after an assigned job was finished in such a way to reflect as close as possible the slaveServers performance relative to each other. The performance factor is measured in pixels/millisecond, and takes into account the processing time and the communication time between mainServer and slaveServer, that is the time elapsed from the moment when the mainServer assigned the job to a slaveServer and the moment when the processed result is available back on the mainServer side. Note that the performance factor includes both the slaveServer performance and the communication network performance. This is the correct way of computing the performance factor.

All image data involved in communications are first encoded to a JPEG format in order to reduce communication times between mainServer and both clients and slaveServers. The mainServer role in the image processing phase is very limited due to performance reasons. All image processing is carried out by the slaveServers that are subordinated to the mainServer.

The mainServer implements a self recovery from crashes mechanism [6]. If a slaveServer crashes during an image processing job due to a malfunction on the communication network or to any other error, the mainServer detects this crash, marks this slaveServer as unavailable and reassigns its job to another online slaveServer. This last slaveServer, is chosen by the mainServer in such a way that it has the maximum weight, that is, it is the slaveServer that has the maximum performance relative to any other online slaveServer.

The mainServer gives administrator the possibility of adjusting slaveServers weights "on fly". The administrator can disable the slaveServers self tuning weights mechanism although this is not recommended. It also gives administrator the possibility to temporarily disable one or many slaveServers in order to exclude them from job scheduling. This option is materialized through a GUI "On Line" checkbox. Another administration tool gives administrator the possibility to dynamically add or remove slaveServers from the list of slaveServers maintained by the mainServer, that is, to alter the image processing power "on fly" without need to restart the mainServer. As a consequence, the mainServer GUI is dynamically altered in order to reflect the new slaveServers list.

The mainServer implements a self generated log mechanism. It maintains two log files: users.log and slaveServers.log. The users.log file records all user interactions with the mainServer and includes information like time of request, user authentication, requested function type, function parameters and so on. The slaveServers.log includes all information about the assigned image processing job such as slaveServer name, slice size (resolution), image filter to use, image filter parameters, start time, end time, performance tips, self calibration log and crashes log. Also, both log files include mainServer startTime and endTime information.

2.2.2 The Slave Server Component
The slaveServer program performs all image processing jobs submitted to it by the mainServer. It receives the image and the image filter parameters from mainServer, performs the image processing job and send the result (processed image) back to the mainServer.

2.2.3 The Distributed Model Trace-Cycle
Figure 4 presents a trace-cycle of the DisMedJAVA system involving image data request, distributed processing and database update.

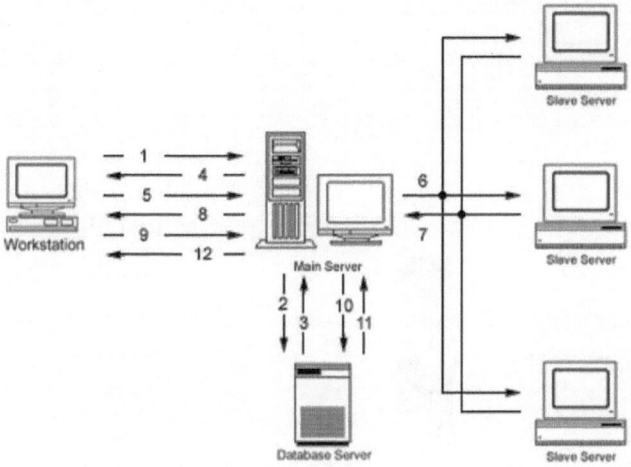

Fig. 4. The DisMedJAVA protocol

1   the client requests an image from the mainServer
2   mainServer performs all security checks and forwards the user request to the database
3   the image is retrieved from database and made available at the mainServer level
4   the mainServer transmits the image to the client (workstation)
5   the client requests a distributed image processing by sending that image along with filter parameters to mainServer
6   the mainServer splits the image and forward the resulting slices to the slaveServers for processing
7   the slaveServers perform filtering and return the results back to the mainServer
8   the mainServer assembles the results into one image and transmits this filtered image back to the client
9   the client requests mainServer that this new image be saved to the database
10   the mainServer forwards this request to the database
11   the database was updated successfully
12   the client is informed that its update request was accomplished

2.3 Application Snapshots

Figure 5 presents a snapshot of the first subGUI of the client program, the user database subGUI.
Figure 6 presents a snapshot of the third subGUI of the client program, the imageScans workspace subGUI.
Figure 7 presents a snapshot of the third subGUI of the mainServer program, the slaveServers configuration subGUI.
Figure 8 presents several images obtained from a single source image by applying some of the image filters available on the DisMedJava system

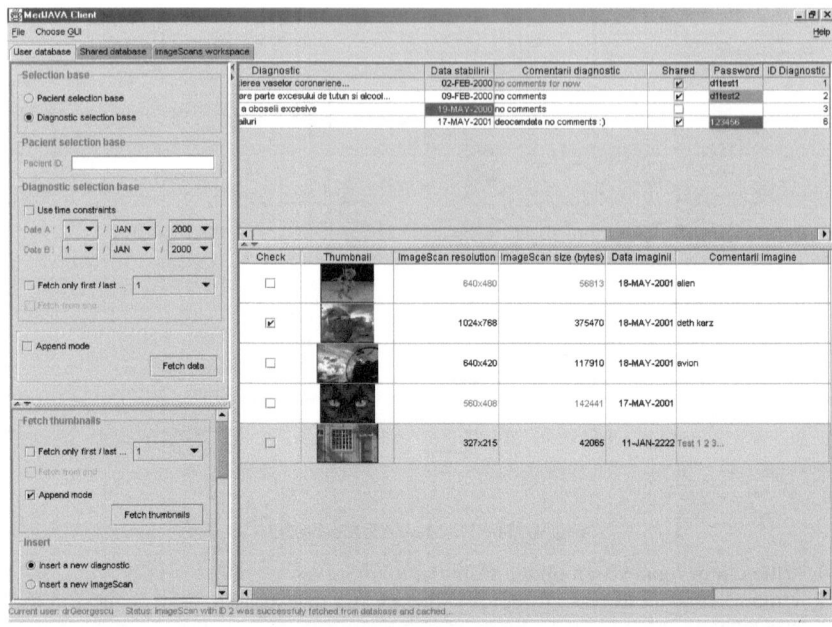

Fig. 5. The client program user database snapshot

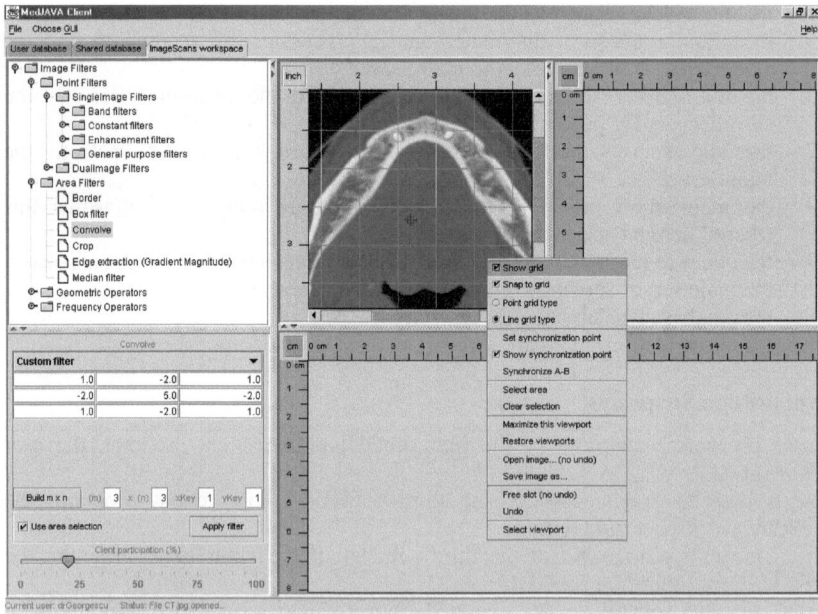

Fig. 6. The client program imageScans workspace snapshot

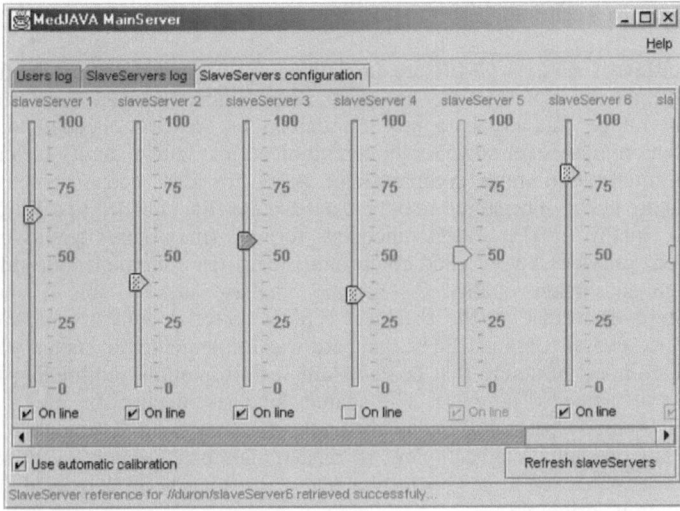

Fig. 7. The mainServer program slaveServers configuration snapshot

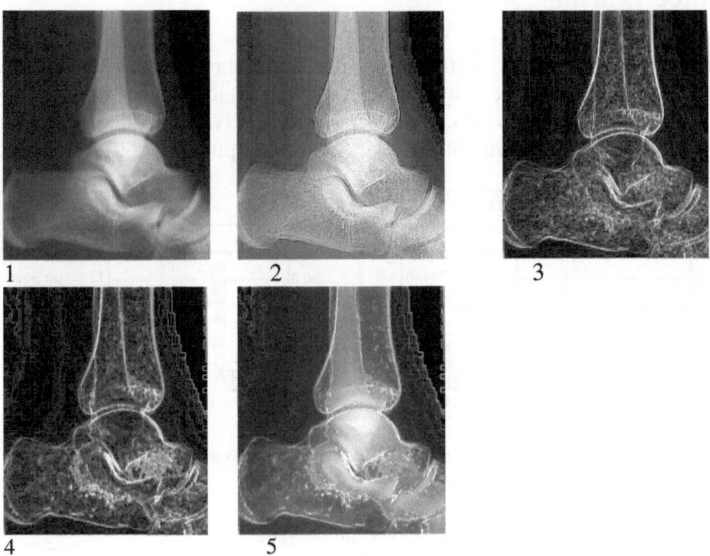

Fig. 8. Image 1 – source image; Images 2, 3, 4 and 5 are obtained from the source image (image 1) by applying some of the image filters available on the DisMedJava system

2.4 DisMedJava Technologies

All DisMedJava functions [7-10] are implemented using background threads. This application makes use of RMI technology as communication layer. For performance reasons, all image data involved in communications are first encoded to a JPEG format (even on mainSever-slaveServer communications) with a quality factor of 1.0F (maximum quality/minimum compression). Also, for disk economy reasons, all images that are about to be stored into the database are first encoded to a JPEG format (maximum quality). The JPEG encoded format (maximum quality/minimum compression) provides a very good compromise between communication times, disk space usage and image quality. As for the database support, this is completely transparent to user, that is, the database can be stored locally to mainServer or distributed to several computers. The database was implemented in such a way that it has a very compact structure that contains ample information, minimizing this way the amount of needed disk space. The shared database mechanism allows users to establish a "shared" password for each diagnostic they own. Using this "shared" password, any one authorized can view the related diagnostic (only relevant parts) and any imageScans attached to it. This mechanism was primarily implemented due to the "second opinion" principle.

3 Performance Tracing

The following charts show some performance measurements of the DisMedJava system. Each job represents a single distributed image processing request assigned by the mainServer to several slaveServers. In this case four slaveServers were online, from which two were launched locally at the mainServer computer (duron).

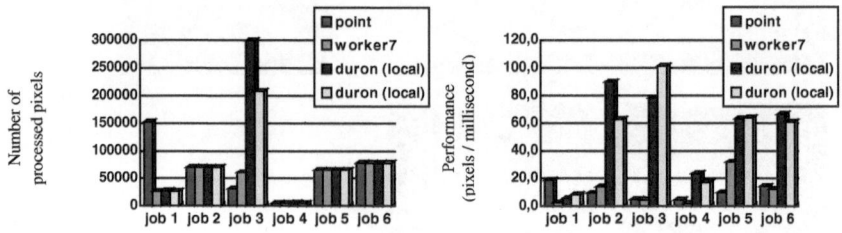

Fig. 9. Performance measurements of the DisMedJava system

Table 1. slaveServer computer types

slaveServer	slaveServer computer type
point	Intel Pentium II 550 MHz, 128MB Ram
worker7	Intel Pentium II 400 MHz, 64MB Ram
duron (local)	AMD Duron 600 MHz, 256MB Ram

Table 2. Job types

job	job type
job 1	gradient magnitude
job 2	gradient magnitude
job 3	gradient magnitude
job 4	invert
job 5	amplitude rescaling
job 6	gradient magnitude

Table 3. Average performances

slaveServer	average performance	slaveServer computer type
point	10.18	Intel Pentium II 550 MHz, 128MB Ram
worker7	11.17	Intel Pentium II 400 MHz, 64MB Ram
duron (local)	53.51	AMD Duron 600 MHz, 256MB Ram

Table 4. Proposed mainServer, slaveServer and client computer configurations and performance predictions

	proposed computer type	performance prediction (low resolutions)	performance prediction (high resolutions)
mainServer	Intel Pentium II 800 MHz, 256MB Ram	-	-
slaveServer	AMD Duron 600 MHz, 128MB Ram	15 – 20	13 - 18
client	Intel 386(486), 32MB Ram (minimum)	3 – 7	1 - 4

All performances are measured into pixels per millisecond and take into account the processing time and the network communication time, except that performances for local and workstation (client) computers that take into account only processing time.

From the average performances chart results that the overall performance of a slaveServer is about 20% from its stand alone performance (processing performance), as a result of network communication.

$$ssOp = ssPp * 20\% \qquad (1)$$

where

      ssOp   - slaveServer overall performance
      ssPp   - slaveServer processing performance

The slaveServer overall performance is the performance perceived at the mainServer level. However, due to DisMedJava parallelism, the overall performance of DisMedJava system at mainServer level is:

$$op_{msL} = \sum_{i=1}^{ssNo} ssOp_i \tag{2}$$

where

    op_{msL} - overall performance at mainServer level
    ssNo   - slaveServers number
    $ssOp_i$ - slaveServer i overall performance

Note that equation (2) is available only when all slaveServers finish their jobs in the relatively same time. This condition can be met by means of a load balancing mechanism.

At the client (workstation) level, because of the network communication times, the perceived performance is about 20% of the performance obtained at the mainServer level. Therefore, based on equation (2), the perceived performance at client (workstation) level is:

$$cPp = op_{msL} * 20\% \tag{3}$$

where

    cPp   - performance perceived at client (workstation) level
    op_{msL} - overall performance at mainServer level

As a result from equations (1), (2) and (3), the perceived performance at client (workstation) level can be increased in many ways as follow:

- ❏ by increasing ssPp (slaveServer processing performance)
  this assumes an upgrade to the slaveServer computers (processors and ram)
- ❏ by increasing ssOp (slaveServer overall performance)
  this assumes an upgrade to the network communications on DisMedJava mainServer-slaveServers system
- ❏ by increasing op_{msL} (overall performance at mainServer level)
  this assumes an increase to the slaveServers number
- ❏ by increasing ccPp (performance perceived at client (workstation) level)
  this assumes an upgrade to the network communications on DisMedJava client-mainServer system

However, the perceived performance at the client (workstation level) cannot be increased infinitely due to the network limitations and to the fact than an image contains a limited number of pixels that can be processed in parallel only by a limited number of slaveServers.

As a result from the proposed configuration systems (last table), the DisMedJava system can deliver up to three times faster performance than single workstations for low resolution images and up to five times (and even more) faster performance than single workstations for high resolution images.

The recommended number of slaveServers is a minimum of 5 computers, this number allowing to maintain a constant performance gain for up to 25 simultaneous connections.

To avoid losing performance for more than 25 simultaneous connections, the solution is increasing the number of slaveServer computers, or upgrading existing ones by faster processors and more main memory.

4 Conclusions

The DisMedJava application is a scalable client-server multi-slaveServer distributed application. The system can be accessed from both local (intranet) and remote (internet) locations. Image processing techniques are used for manipulating and displaying images. Examples of image processing techniques range from simple operations such as contrast enhancement, cropping, and scaling to more complex operations such as advanced geometric warping and frequency domain processing. These are used in a variety of applications including: Astronomy, Medical Imaging, Geospatial Data Processing, Defense and Intelligence, Photography, E-Commerce and Retail.

The Java Advanced Imaging API extends the Java platform for developing image processing applications and applets in Java. It streamlines the process of creating powerful imaging software solutions like the DisMedJava application.

The client program can be used as an independent application with the cost of losing database interaction and distributed image processing. This way, the client program can be used even by an unauthorized user (authorization is required only by the mainServer) or even if the communication link with the mainServer is broken, with the costs mentioned above. In this case, all image processing filters are available but only locally, that is, the client participation slider must be set to 100%.

In other words, the client program can be used as an independent stand-alone image processing application with all image processing capabilities available locally.

Due to its flexible structure, the DisMedJava distributed application can be relatively easy modified for another domain like the ones listed above. The only part that needs to be modified is the part related to the database structure.

References

1. Seth White, Maydene Fisher, Rick Cattell, Graham Hamilton, Mark Hapner: JDBC™ API Tutorial and Reference, Second Edition: Universal Data Access for the Java™ 2 Platform (Java Series), published by Addison Wesley Longman, Inc., (1999)
2. Graham Hamilton, Rick Cattell, Maydene Fisher: JDBC Database Access With Java: A Tutorial and Annotated Reference (Java Series), published by Addison Wesley Longman Inc.
3. Prashant Jain, Seth Widoff and Douglas C. Schmidt: The design and performance of MedJava. Experience of developing performance-sensitive distributed applications with Java, (1998), http://www.cs.wustl.edu/~schmidt/PDF/MedJava.pdf
4. Kathy Walrath, Mary Campione: The JFC Swing Tutorial: A Guide to Constructing GUIs. (1999), http://java.sun.com/docs/books/javatutorial/jfc.html
5. Programming in Java Advanced Imaging, November (1999), http://java.sun.com/products/java-media/jai/forDevelopers/jai1_0_1guide-unc/index.html
6. Yatin Chawathe and Eric A. Brewer: System support for scalable and fault tolerant Internet services, (1999), http://www.cs.berkeley.edu/~brewer/sns-crc.pdf
7. The Java Tutorial – A practical guide for programmers, February (2001), http://java.sun.com/docs/books/tutorial/index.html
8. Mary Campione, Kathy Walrath, Alison Huml: The Java Tutorial Continued: The Rest of the JDK: The Java Series, (1998), http://java.sun.com/docs/books/javatutorial/continued.html

9.   Mary Campione, Kathy Walrath, Alison Huml: The Java Tutorial Third Edition – A Short
      Course on the Basics, published by Addison Wesley (2000),
      http://java.sun.com/docs/books/javatutorial/third-edition.html
10. Bruce Eckel: Thinking in Java, 2nd Edition, (2000), http://www.mindview.net/Books/TIJ/

Author Index

Lecture Notes in Computer Science

For information about Vols. 1–2252
please contact your bookseller or Springer-Verlag